JAPAN IN INTERNATIONAL POLITICS

*Published in association with the
Japan Forum on International Relations*

JAPAN IN INTERNATIONAL POLITICS

The Foreign Policies of an Adaptive State

EDITED BY
Thomas U. Berger
Mike M. Mochizuki
Jitsuo Tsuchiyama

LYNNE
RIENNER
PUBLISHERS

BOULDER
LONDON

Published in the United States of America in 2007 by
Lynne Rienner Publishers, Inc.
1800 30th Street, Boulder, Colorado 80301
www.rienner.com

and in the United Kingdom by
Lynne Rienner Publishers, Inc.
3 Henrietta Street, Covent Garden, London WC2E 8LU

Library of Congress Cataloging-in-Publication Data
Japan in international politics : the foreign policies of an adaptive state /
Thomas U. Berger, Mike M. Mochizuki, Jitsuo Tsuchiyama (co-editors).
    p. cm.
  Includes bibliographical references and index.
  ISBN-13: 978-1-58826-483-1 (hardcover : alk. paper)
  ISBN-13: 978-1-58826-459-6 (pbk. : alk. paper)
1. Japan—Foreign relations—1989– I. Berger, Thomas U. II. Mochizuki, Mike.
III. Tsuchiyama, Jitsuo.
  DS891.2.J386 2007
  327.52—dc22

                                                    2006032419

British Cataloguing in Publication Data
A Cataloguing in Publication record for this book
is available from the British Library.

Printed and bound in the United States of America

The paper used in this publication meets the requirements
of the American National Standard for Permanence of
Paper for Printed Library Materials Z39.48-1992.

5   4   3   2   1

| Contents |

Foreword, Kenichi Itō   vii

1   Japan's Changing International Role
    Mike M. Mochizuki   1

2   The Domestic Foundations of Japan's
    International Contribution
    Masaru Kohno   23

Part 1   Security Policy

3   War Renunciation, Article 9, and Security Policy
    Jitsuo Tsuchiyama   47

4   Participation in UN Peacekeeping Operations
    Go Ito   75

5   A Defense Posture for Multilateral Security
    Michael O'Hanlon   97

Part 2   Economic Relations

6   Adapting to Global Economic Change
    Edward J. Lincoln   115

7   Building Stable International Financial Relations
    Yoshiko Kojo   133

8   Responding to the Asian Financial Crisis
    Juichi Inada   151

Part 3   Regional Diplomacy

9   The Politics of Memory in Japanese Foreign Relations
    Thomas U. Berger   179

10 The Role of Human Rights: The Case of Burma
    Catharin Dalpino   213

11 Dealing with a Rising China
    Mike M. Mochizuki   229

Part 4   Conclusion

12 The Pragmatic Liberalism of an Adaptive State
    Thomas U. Berger   259

List of Acronyms   301
Bibliography   305
The Contributors   331
Index   333
About the Book   349

| Foreword |

The Gulf War of 1990–1991 and the Asian economic crisis of
1997–1998 motivated the Japanese to discuss their country's "international
contribution" (*kokusai kōken*) for the first time in the post–World War II
era. During the 1990s, many foreign observers criticized Japan for not contributing to the maintenance of international peace and prosperity in a manner commensurate with its capabilities and position in the world community. Article 9 of the Japanese constitution, however, prohibited Japan from
providing direct military support for the multilateral coalition to liberate
Kuwait from Iraqi occupation. Nevertheless, since the first Gulf War, Japan
has been doing its best to enhance its contribution to international peace and
stability within the constraints of the constitution and the domestic political
context.

In 1998, the Japan Forum on International Relations (JFIR) launched a
project to examine how Japan's domestic politics and norms have shaped,
for better and worse, Japan's "international contributions." With funding
from the Center for Global Partnership of the Japan Foundation, the JFIR
asked the Brookings Institution to be its partner for this endeavor, and the
JFIR and the Brookings Institution jointly organized a team of Japanese and
US scholars. The Japanese group was chaired by Jitsuo Tsuchiyama and
included Juichi Inada, Tsuyoshi Ito, Yoshiko Kojo, and Masaru Kohno. The
US group was chaired by Mike M. Mochizuki and included Thomas U.
Berger, Catharin Dalpino, Edward Lincoln, and Michael O'Hanlon.

After numerous preparatory meetings in Tokyo and Washington, D.C.,
an international workshop, "Japan's Pursuit of an International Role:
Domestic Sources and Constraints on Japan's International Contributions,"
was convened in Tokyo on June 12, 2000, to discuss the research results.

Based on this discussion, the project members prepared a study report for publication. Just as this report was about to go to press, the September 11, 2001, terrorist attacks occurred. The attacks had such profound consequences for international politics and Japanese foreign policy that the project was reconstituted, and the Japanese and US study team members decided to rewrite their respective pieces to reflect the implications of the 9/11 attack and the subsequent wars against Afghanistan and Iraq.

We are grateful to Lynne Rienner Publishers for agreeing to publish the book that grew out of our collaborative project. On behalf of JFIR, I would also like to thank Jitsuo Tsuchiyama and Mike M. Mochizuki for their special contributions. It goes without saying that without their dedication this book could not have been published.

—Kenichi Itō,
President and CEO,
Japan Forum on International Relations

JAPAN IN INTERNATIONAL POLITICS

| 1 |

Japan's Changing International Role

Mike M. Mochizuki

Japan's foreign policy since World War II has been a stunning success and stands in sharp contrast to what preceded it. After its seizure of Manchuria in 1931, Japan's military expansion into China soon turned into a disastrous quagmire. Political paralysis at home and strategic indecision abroad made it difficult for Japan to extricate itself from its continental adventure. Instead it embraced an overambitious and delusional vision of liberating East Asia through conquest and linked its international hopes to a victorious Nazi Germany in Europe. This course led to international isolation, a devastating war with the United States and its allies, and total defeat. Learning the bitter lessons of this tragedy, Japan then charted a different diplomatic course that served its people well. It is now hard to think of another major country that has pursued a more successful foreign policy—one that brought both prosperity and security for its own citizens with minimal costs.

The Yoshida Doctrine and Its Legacy

Prime Minister Yoshida Shigeru* established the basic parameters of Japan's post–World War II foreign policy and its international role.[1] In

---

*In the text of this volume, Japanese, Chinese, and Korean names are written with the surname preceding the given name, with the exception of cases in which Japanese authors of English-language publications have listed their names with given name first. Long vowels are indicated by macrons, except when referring to authors and works published in English and to the names of commonly used place-names, such as Tokyo.

negotiating the peace settlement with the United States, Yoshida struck a basic strategic bargain. In return for an early end to the US occupation of Japan, he agreed to US access to military bases on Japanese territory and to the signing of a bilateral security pact. He resisted US pressures on Japan to rearm itself and to become a more active US ally in countering Soviet-led communism in Asia, however. Yoshida insisted that Japan must concentrate its efforts on economic reconstruction and development, and he agreed to only a minimal defense policy, preferring to have his country rely ultimately on the United States for national security. He shrewdly recognized that US interest in fighting the Cold War would keep the United States strategically committed to Japan and supportive of its economic revival. Historians and political scientists would later refer to this diplomatic course as the "Yoshida doctrine."

As Japan's economy recovered from its postwar devastation and the country evolved into an industrial and technological powerhouse, the country had to recalibrate the Yoshida doctrine. Under strong pressures from the United States, it took halting steps to open its markets to foreign goods and services. To counter US criticisms that Japan was free riding on the US security guarantee, it gradually engaged in more defense "burden-sharing" by modernizing its defense forces and providing "host-nation support" to US forces stationed in Japan. These adjustments did not amount to a fundamental shift away from the country's neomercantilist foreign economic strategy and a pacifistic security policy, however. Japan continued to rely on an export-oriented growth strategy and engaged in strategic protectionism to cultivate frontier industries and technologies. It limited its defense spending to about 1 percent of its gross national product and adhered to a strictly defensive defense posture. Content with the prosperity and security that a recalibrated Yoshida doctrine brought, Japan refrained from vigorously seeking the international prestige and national security autonomy that would have been more commensurate with its economic capabilities. It seemed happy to live in the shadow of the United States and to reap the benefits of Pax Americana. According to Edward Lincoln, Japan was a nation "that desired nothing more than for the rest of the world to leave it alone."[2]

Japan's foreign policy, however, was not without its critics. Some argued that Japan did not have a foreign policy of its own, but only a US policy. Others dubbed Japan as just a reactive state responding to external pressures or *gaiatsu* (mostly emanating from the United States) rather than trying to shape the international environment. According to Kent Calder, this reactive foreign policy had its roots in domestic politics. Weak executive authority, factionalism in the ruling Liberal Democratic Party, bureaucratic sectionalism, and Japan's unique electoral system all worked to prevent Japan from pursuing a more proactive foreign policy even when it had the capability and incentives to do so.[3] Other scholars, such as Akitoshi Miyashita, attributed Japan's reactive behavior to its asymmetric dependence on the United States for markets and security.[4] Put differently, it was Japan's adherence to the Yoshida doctrine and its subsequent recalibrations that explain Japan as the reactive state.

The Harvard diplomatic historian Akira Iriye made this indictment of Japan's behavior: "Japan has not made sufficiently clear how it proposes to behave in the world, beyond pursuing its own security and economic interests. The nation has not made a notable contribution to the international order. Its foreign affairs have tended to be devoid of a sense of purpose going beyond self-interest."[5] But according to Sakaya Taichi, the prolific Japanese commentator and economic planning minister in the Obuchi government, Japan's underachieving behavior stemmed from modesty and realism based on historical experience. He wrote, "Japanese learned the importance of using the world structure and international order and the danger of trying to change it. To contemporary Japanese, the world order seems to be a natural phenomenon, such as gravity, not something that can be controlled by mere human beings."[6]

Masaru Tamamoto, now of the Japan Institute of International Affairs, echoed this theme:

> Postwar Japan clearly lost the stomach for the harshness of international politics. If *shutaisei* [independence] comes from great power status, Japan's orientation in the world during the past half century has pointed to the explicit denial of such ambition. . . . It harbors no desire for national greatness in international politics. It wishes to enjoy the material benefits of hard work. It wants to be a wealthy and orderly small power, whose per capita gross national product and equitable distribution of wealth mean more than aggregate gross national product as measure of comparative national power.[7]

This Japanese modesty, however, did not mean that Japan felt no compunction to give back to the international order from which it benefited so much.

For many Japanese, official development assistance (ODA) was the most visible way that their country contributed to international society. The ODA program got its start as part of Japan's postwar reparations to Southeast Asian countries.[8] Much of the reparations were initially provided in the form of goods; but by the 1960s, the program had evolved into a full-scale economic assistance program involving concessional loans and technical assistance. Through the early 1970s, ODA tended to focus on the Asia Pacific region and facilitated Japanese trade, investments, and resource acquisition in that part of the world. But the oil shocks of the 1970s as well as US pressures steered Japan to broaden its geographic horizons and its assistance objectives. After becoming the leading bilateral provider of ODA in Asia in 1978, eleven years later Japan became the global leader of bilateral economic assistance.

A major component of this expanded ODA continued to be linked closely to Japan's national interest, such as the security of oil supplies from the Middle East or the expansion of production networks in Asia.[9] But Japan also enhanced its aid to areas where Japan's interests were not so direct, such as humanitarian assistance to sub-Saharan Africa.[10] ODA programs began to be framed in terms of "comprehensive security," a concept developed in the early 1980s to integrate the defense, economic, and social dimensions of public policy for people's security and welfare. This notion projected a broader and perhaps somewhat more enlightened view of Japan's interests. Rather than pursuing commercial interests in a narrow sense, Japan could help to alleviate world poverty by recycling its burgeoning trade surplus through its aid programs. Japan would then contribute to fostering a more peaceful and secure international environment from which Japan would ultimately benefit. But this new economic diplomacy sometimes failed to meet the expectations and needs of the developing world. Developing countries floundering in international debt did not always welcome the big infrastructure projects that Japan sought to fund.[11]

End of the Cold War and Its Domestic Consequences

With the end of the Cold War in 1989, Japan no longer had to worry about being caught in the crossfire of a Soviet-US military conflict. But this structural change in international politics also presented Japan with new concerns and challenges. With the collapse of its Cold War adversary, the United States could revert back to isolationism and dismantle its forward military deployments in the Asia Pacific, leaving Japan exposed to deal with possible security threats on its own. As US-Japanese tensions over trade issues intensified, some US pundits even began to see Japan as the new threat to US strategic interests. Examples of this view were sensational books such as *The Coming War with Japan* and novels such as *Rising Sun*.[12] Bilateral disagreements about how to co-produce Japan's new FSX fighter plane suggested that economic frictions could spill over into security policy and damage the US-Japan alliance itself—the bedrock of Japan's postwar foreign policy.[13] In addition to growing US protectionist sentiments, the Japanese found disconcerting the rise of economic regionalism, such as the formation of a unified European market and the North American Free Trade Agreement (NAFTA), which could hamper Japan's access to lucrative markets in the advanced industrial world.

Perhaps the most acute post–Cold War shock to Japanese foreign policy was the Gulf War of 1990–1991. Because of constitutional constraints, pacifist norms, and weak political leadership, Japan failed to respond quickly. Unable or unwilling to provide even humanitarian or rear-area support for the US-led multinational coalition to liberate Kuwait, Japan resorted to a hefty monetary contribution of $13 billion to the war effort against Iraq.[14] Although this contribution required raising taxes, Japan received little international gratitude or recognition. Forced to wait out in the hallways while permanent members of the UN Security Council debated how to respond to the Iraq-Kuwait crisis, some Japanese diplomats complained that this was "taxation without representation." Never again should Japan's honor be so tarnished. Japan must make a greater "international contribution" (*kokusai kōken*) in a visible manner so as to earn the world community's respect and to gain a voice in shaping global policy. The traditional low-posture foreign policy that had focused primarily on economic objectives and means and had worked so well in the past was no longer sufficient.

This Japanese sentiment about expanding international contributions went beyond the matter of global honor, status, and influence. Japan began to face new uncertainties in its own neighborhood. The 1994 North Korea nuclear crisis, the 1996 large-scale Chinese military exercises (including missile firings) in the Taiwan Strait, and the 1998 launch of the North Korean Taepodong missile over Japan impressed on many Japanese that national security could not be taken for granted. Even in the economic realm, the East Asian financial crisis of 1997 demonstrated how vulnerable the Japanese economy had become in the globalization era. A decade of economic stagnation after the burst of the financial bubble in 1991 certainly diminished Japanese self-confidence in economic and commercial matters, but it also motivated many Japanese to think how Japan could help develop a more stable as well as more prosperous regional economic environment.

In the context of these international developments, Japan's domestic politics and institutions have changed in ways that facilitate a more proactive foreign policy.[15] In Chapter 2, Masaru Kohno emphasizes three such changes: (1) preference change of the Ministry of International Trade and Industry (MITI), (2) shifts in the majority coalition and the Liberal Democratic Party (LDP), and (3) reform of the electoral system and its impact on the socialists.

For much of the postwar period, MITI served as a domestic-oriented pilot agency for Japan's industrial development policies and tended to resist economic liberalization. But as Japan's position in the world economy rose and the national economy was increasingly challenged by and embedded in globalization, this ministry, which was renamed and reorganized as the Ministry of Economy, Trade, and Industry (METI) in 2001, became more outward oriented and committed to multilateral norms and institutions for free trade. The LDP has undergone a similar transformation, moving gradually away from a relatively passive international posture. As the political weight of its traditional domestic-oriented constituencies (many of which involved protectionist producer groups) declined, the LDP sought to mobilize support among the growing number of urban voters. Finally, the endogenous institutional change of electoral reform in 1993–1994 had the profound side effect of destroying the Japan Socialist Party (JSP) as a significant political party. The JSP's demise meant the loss of Japan's most stalwart parliamentary voice on behalf of a pacifist foreign policy, thereby encouraging a more robust security policy.

In addition to the changes mentioned by Kohno, another domestic development has been the enhanced authority of the prime minister and his office in making and implementing foreign policy.[16] While prime minister during the mid-1980s, Nakasone Yasuhiro stressed the need to concentrate more information and advisory channels in the prime minister's office and talked about a "presidential-style prime ministership." To counter the bottom-up decisionmaking style that tended to reinforce bureaucratic conflicts, in 1986 Nakasone and his chief cabinet secretary Gotoda Masaharu established a more robust advisory structure of three policy offices housed in the Cabinet Secretariat. This innovation, however, was insufficient to produce a more proactive foreign policy. Much depended on who served as prime minister. For example, someone like Prime Minister Kaifu Toshiki, who was not that versed in foreign affairs and lacked a strategic vision of his own, did not use the Nakasone changes to respond decisively to the 1990–1991 Gulf War crisis.

A succession of ineffective responses to other crises (e.g., the 1995 Hanshin earthquake, the 1996–1997 hostage crisis in Peru, and the 1997 oil spill in the Sea of Japan) spurred Japanese leaders to strengthen further the prime minister's ability to deal with crises and to address urgent policy issues. In 1998 a new position of director of crisis management was created within the Cabinet Secretariat, and a year later the Cabinet Law was revised to give the Cabinet Secretariat greater authority to direct and coordinate policy.[17] But just as important as these organizational changes was the increasing significance of the prime minister's public image for voter mobilization and thus for his ability to constrain factional politics within the ruling LDP and to rebuff intraparty opposition.[18] As exemplified by Koizumi Junichirō, a high level of public and media popularity can allow the prime minister to be bolder regarding foreign policy.

Japan may now have more will and institutional capacity to pursue a more active and assertive international role, but the substance of this role is still not clear. The Japanese have been engaging in a lively domestic debate about national strategy and diplomacy.[19] Although this debate has addressed numerous concrete policy questions, two frames of reference have shaped the general contours of this discussion. One frame of reference pertains to the tension between internationalism and nationalism; the other concerns the question of autonomy with respect to Japan's alliance with the United States.

Internationalism and Nationalism

Japanese internationalism has both inward-directed and outward-directed elements. The former involves the internationalization (*kokusaika*) of Japan itself.[20] Prime Minister Nakasone first took up the theme of internationalization when he declared in a 1984 National Diet session that Japan must become an "international country" (*kokusai kokka*). This meant that Japan needed to transform itself in ways that would reduce frictions with the rest of international society. In concrete terms, the internationalization agenda has encompassed a broad range of items such as liberalizing domestic markets to foreign goods, services, and investments; increasing the number of foreign students; becoming more receptive to immigrants and foreign workers and more comfortable about ethnic diversity; and improving the English-language ability of its citizens.

More than two decades after Nakasone launched the internationalization campaign, Japan is indeed a much more open society than before. Not only have foreign goods and investments increased, but also the foreign presence in Japan has become much more visible, especially in large urban areas. Even a nativist tradition such as grand sumo or Japanese wrestling now has many foreign wrestlers, including those of European descent, competing in the top ranks—something unimaginable in the 1960s. Nevertheless, as Mayumi Itoh argued, the "secluded nation" (*sakoku*) mentality of Japanese has continued to hamper a full embrace of internationalization.[21] For example, xenophobic reactions to internationalization, especially when foreigners are involved in crimes, are not uncommon. But as Apichai Shipper recently showed, homegrown activists have also mobilized to correct biased information regarding illegal foreigners in Japan and to demonstrate that they tend to be more victims than criminals.[22]

The outward-directed aspect of internationalism concerns the effort to increase Japan's *kokusai kōken*. To some extent, international contribution entails a defensive notion of international cooperation, enabling Japan to avoid the kind of isolation it experienced in the 1930s.[23] But there is an unmistakable proactive feature as well. In the abstract, international contribution implies helping to provide international public goods such as security, open trade, financial stability, and a cleaner environment.

The prime minister's office has been polling Japanese citizens annually to ascertain their views on their preferred roles of Japan in international society. When asked to select two priority issues, 49.7 percent of those surveyed in 1991 chose "contributing to solving worldwide problems such as the global environmental problem." The next most frequently selected item, with 37.5 percent, was "the maintenance of international peace through contribution policies that include human support and mediation of regional conflicts." "Contributions to the wholesome development of the world economy" (34.4 percent) and "cooperation for the development of developing countries" (29.2 percent) came in third and fourth respectively. By 2005, Japanese public priorities appeared to have shifted away from economics to security. In the survey taken that year, the "international peace" contribution was the top item selected, with 51.9 percent. The choice of "global environment" fell to second place (38.4 percent). "Human support for refugees" became the third most selected contribution (25.0 percent). Contributions related to economics dropped in terms of priority. Only 19.9 percent selected the "wholesome development of the world economy" and only 15.0 percent selected "cooperation for the development of developing countries."[24]

Even as Japanese supported contributing more to international society, they debated how best Japan could make this contribution. In general, Japanese found themselves more comfortable about working with existing international institutions such as the United Nations and its network of global organizations. The United Nations provided a convenient way for Japanese officials to frame their more proactive foreign policies, because this world body, unlike the US-Japan alliance, garnered widespread public support that bridged the ideological divisions in Japanese politics.[25]

By 1986, Japan had become the second-highest financial contributor to the United Nations after the United States. And by 1998, Japan provided more funds to the UN than the combined contributions of the permanent members of the UN Security Council excluding the United States (i.e., the UK, France, China, and Russia).[26] The service of Ogata Sadako as UN High Commissioner for Refugees and Akashi Yasushi as the UN Special Representative in Cambodia symbolized the increasingly high-profile role that Japan was beginning to assume. In the late 1990s, Japanese responses to global environmental issues (e.g., biodiversity, global warming, and the depletion of the ozone layer) were usually embedded within the UN framework.[27] Similarly, as Go Ito shows in Chapter 4, Japan's expanding security role has manifested itself most clearly in UN peacekeeping operations.

Akiko Fukushima has argued that the logic of "multilateralism" has been a key characteristic of Japanese internationalism and extends beyond the United Nations. Whereas Japan in the past tended to free ride on existing multilateral institutions to pursue it own national interests, it has now become much more an architect and navigator of new institutions and processes, especially in the Asia Pacific region. Notable examples are the Asia Pacific Economic Cooperation (APEC) forum and the Association of Southeast Asian Nations (ASEAN) Regional Forum.[28]

While Japan was embracing a more active internationalism, a counter-tendency also emerged: a new nationalism. Even during the postwar years of low-posture diplomacy, Japan was in many ways nationalistic. Total defeat in World War II did not wipe away Japan's strong sense of national identity, and wartime economic destruction motivated the Japanese to work hard and to work together to enhance Japan's industrial and technological power. But what is new about post–Cold War nationalism is its outward assertiveness. This new nationalism probably got its start during the period of intense economic frictions between Japan and the United States. Symptomatic of the growing Japanese resentment about US pressures on trade was the book *The Japan That Can Say "No,"* written by novelist turned politician Ishihara Shintarō, who now serves as governor of Tokyo.[29]

After bilateral trade tensions abated because of the economic revitalization of the United States and the stagnation of Japan, confirmation of the abduction of Japanese citizens during the late 1970s and early 1980s by North Korean agents provided new fuel for nationalism. Emotionally charged media portrayals of these abductions galvanized the Japanese public to insist that their diplomats be more energetic in pressing the security and welfare interests of Japan's own citizens. The North Korean missile tests and Chinese military probing near Japanese airspace and territorial waters reinforced this growing public sentiment. When Chinese armed police entered the Japanese Consulate in Shenyang in May 2002 to apprehend North Korean asylum seekers, the Japanese media, public, and politicians responded emotionally, causing Japanese diplomats to be much tougher with their Chinese counterparts than before.[30] Japanese blue-ribbon panels on foreign policy strategies now openly discuss the need for Japan to define more clearly its national interests.[31]

Another aspect of this new nationalism is the effort by political conservatives to reemphasize national symbols. Since the late 1950s, the conservative Education Ministry has tried to persuade teachers to raise the national flag (Hinomaru) and sing the national anthem ("Kimigayo"). Many teachers backed by the leftist Japan Teachers' Union, however, refused to do so. But the political party realignments after 1993 that produced the heretofore unthinkable LDP-JSP governing coalition and the subsequent demise of the JSP as an influential parliamentary force created a favorable environment that in 1999 resulted in legislation officially recognizing the Hinomaru as the national flag and "Kimigayo" as the national anthem. Leftists had opposed the use of these national symbols because they had been so closely associated with Japan's prewar imperial system and militaristic nationalism. Conservatives had sought to revive these symbols precisely to inculcate greater popular pride in Japan as a country and even to weaken postwar pacifism, thereby facilitating a more expansive Japanese security role.[32]

The new nationalism also has a generational dimension. The Japanese youth of today not only have no memory of World War II and the postwar

years of reconstruction but also have not experienced the student disturbances of the 1960s and 1970s that opposed conservative rule in Japan and
the US-Japan security relationship. In other words, the younger generation
is not burdened by feelings of guilt about their country's militarist past and
is less influenced by leftist or progressive political ideas. Instead, many in
this generation are captivated by nationalistic comic books written by
Kobayashi Yoshinori, who advocates the virtues of being arrogant.[33] So
when Chinese boo and ridicule the Japanese team in a soccer match,
Japanese youth respond angrily by saying that Japanese should not be made
fools of any longer.

As significant as this new nationalism is in Japanese discourse about
foreign policy, it is also important to emphasize what this nationalism is *not*.
This new nationalism is not the nationalism of Meiji Japan that mobilized
human resources to expand national power. It is not an irredentist nationalism, either. Japan has certainly become more energetic about protecting its
control over the disputed Senkaku Islands (the Diaoyu Islands for the
Chinese) and pressing its claims regarding maritime exclusive economic
zones (EEZs) under the UN Convention on the Law of the Sea. But at the
same time, there is no serious discussion in Japan about using force or coercive diplomacy to take back the Takeshima/Dokdo Islands from South
Korea or the "northern territories" from Russia.

The new nationalism is more about being irritated about foreign med-
dling than about pursuing an ambitious revisionist international agenda.
Most Japanese nationalists simply want Japan to be a "normal country"—
whatever that might mean—rather than a great power. Much more in line
with Japanese mainstream thinking is Soeya Yoshihide's notion of Japan as
a "middle power."[34] When Japan failed in its efforts to become a permanent
member of the UN Security Council, a nationalistic backlash from the
Japanese public was virtually nonexistent.

Alliance and Autonomy

In the tension between internationalism and nationalism in Japanese foreign
policy, the US factor looms large. Both internationalists and nationalists
often refer to the United States in defining their respective foreign policy
agendas. Should Japanese internationalism be pursued primarily in cooperation with the United States, or should it be pursued autonomously from the
world's sole superpower? Is it better to harness US pressure and expectations on behalf of Japanese nationalism, or is it better to define a nationalism that stands more independent of or even opposed to the United States?

Since the end of the Cold War, Japan's relations with the United States
have taken a remarkable turn. At the beginning of the 1990s, it looked as if

Japan-US relations were falling apart because of basic disagreements about both economic and security policy and the disappearance of the geopolitical glue of a common adversary.[35] By 2004, however, Japan's ambassador to the United States, Katō Ryōzō, could argue with a straight face that bilateral relations had never been better.[36]

During the 1990s, with the regional and global uncertainties of the post–Cold War era, Japanese leaders decided that it was far better and less risky to reaffirm the US-Japan alliance and tighten it further to prevent Tokyo's abandonment by Washington than it would be for Japan to pursue a self-help international strategy. From the perspective of the United States, even with the collapse of the Soviet Union, Japan remained critical for forward military deployments to deal with possible contingencies regarding the Korean peninsula and the Taiwan Strait. The end of the Soviet-US competition did not mean the resolution of East Asian conflicts that emerged in the context of the Cold War. The United States still needed Japan as an ally. From the mid-1990s onward, Tokyo and Washington took incremental, yet meaningful, steps to enhance bilateral defense cooperation.[37]

In the post–September 11 world, Japan under Prime Minister Koizumi Junichirō's leadership took the unprecedented step of providing diplomatic and logistical support for US military operations against both Afghanistan and Iraq.[38] For many Japanese nationalists who want Japan to develop more muscular defense capabilities, US expectations and even pressure are more than welcome. And now that these nationalists see North Korea and China as the primary threats to Japan, they are willing to stand with the United States as long as the United States shares these perceptions. Many Japanese internationalists also support a more robust US-Japan alliance because this alliance still provides the best way to maintain regional security through deterrence and because the United Nations remains ineffective in providing the public good of international security.

As the United States and Japan became stronger defense allies, major contentious economic issues practically disappeared from the bilateral agenda. Part of this had to do with the fact that an economically revived United States felt less threatened by a Japan suffering from stagnation. But in addition, Japan was compelled to adopt some sweeping market-oriented reforms in order to make its economy more efficient. So rather than the Japanese model of technological development serving as a good example for the United States to emulate, Japan was now importing—at least partially—US business practices. The clash of different capitalist systems that some scholars and pundits had warned about did not happen.

Despite all the benefits that Japan has reaped from its close ties with the United States, the theme of foreign policy autonomy (*jiritsu*) persists in Japan. In fact, many Japanese pundits have criticized Koizumi for just following the US lead even though much of the Japanese public was skeptical of, if not opposed to, the US war against Iraq. But the reality is that even while keeping the United States the bedrock of its foreign policy, Japan has practiced more autonomy than is generally recognized. During the early Cold War years, Japan expressed its autonomy by being a reluctant ally of the United States, one that repeatedly sought to transgress the Cold War political divide in East Asia in order to pursue its economic interests. In contrast to the US emphasis on bilateralism in Asia, Japan was an early proponent of Asian regional integration and institution building.[39] During the Cambodian peace process of the early 1990s, Japan overrode US opposition to pursue its own diplomatic initiative.[40]

As early as the late 1950s, Japanese conservative leaders realized that it would be better to work with the United States rather than against the United States in order to enhance Japan's voice and maneuverability in international affairs. This paradoxical logic has indeed operated in Koizumi's foreign policy. For example, by supporting the Bush administration on Afghanistan and Iraq, Koizumi was able to get US support for pressing North Korea to come clean about its abductions of Japanese citizens. He also gained the freedom to make two visits (the first in September 2002 and the second in May 2004) to Pyongyang in an effort to push forward Japan–North Korea normalization while President George W. Bush continued to call North Korea a member of the "axis of evil" and refused to engage in bilateral talks with Pyongyang. The close personal rapport between Koizumi and Bush enabled Japan to exercise autonomy on Iran policy as well. Despite Washington's displeasure, in 2004 Japan signed an agreement with Iran to develop the Azadegan oil field for an estimated $2.8 billion.[41]

Takashi Inoguchi and Purnendra Jain invoked the metaphor of karaoke (literally translated as "empty orchestra") to characterize Japanese foreign policy.[42] Just as the karaoke singer sings to the musical accompaniment offered by the karaoke machine, Japan basically pursues a foreign policy from the set menu of choices offered by the United States. Tokyo may have a certain degree of autonomy, but that autonomy is circumscribed by the basic parameters established by Washington. But as Inoguchi and Jain themselves suggested, Japan may be moving beyond karaoke diplomacy, at least in some areas. By acting like a loyal ally of the United States, Japan can expand the areas of US tolerance in pursuing policies that might contradict US policies. It can also find geographic and issue pockets—places where the United States does not pay much attention or is not that involved—in which to pursue autonomous diplomatic initiatives. In other words, the US karaoke machine does not determine all of the tunes Japan may choose to sing.

There has been a lot of Japanese grumbling about US unilateralism and hubris. Most Japanese were appalled by how the Bush administration reneged on US commitments to the Kyoto Protocol to deal with global warming. A 2002 report drafted by an advisory panel to the Ministry of Foreign Affairs declared that the United States had evolved from a "superpower" to a "hyper-power" that was becoming less tolerant of opposing views and different value systems.[43] As a consequence, the United States may be losing its moral authority in international affairs. And this negative assessment was articulated *before* the US political and military debacle in Iraq. Both Japanese nationalistic and internationalistic pundits have sharply criticized Bush's United States. But for now, anti-Americanism has been held in check. Rather than openly confronting or challenging US leadership, Japanese leaders still believe that it is more prudent to pursue diplomatic autonomy while maintaining a solid alliance with the United States. And the Japanese public appears to go along with this because the costs of backing the United States have not been that great and the net benefits of this diplomatic posture are still apparent.

The degree to which Japan has become more proactive and the limits of this activism can best be explored by examining in more detail concrete issue areas of Japanese foreign policy. Such an examination will also illustrate the relative weight of internationalist and nationalist tendencies and show how Japan has balanced between the alliance and the quest for autonomy.

Security Policy

Perhaps the most visible signs of Japan's changing international role have been in security policy. Two decades ago, it would have been hard to imagine that Japan would be refueling US warships in the Indian Ocean and be deploying ground forces in Iraq. But these steps and others demonstrate how far Japan has expanded its security horizons. After Prime Minister Hashimoto Ryūtarō and President Bill Clinton issued their joint security declaration reaffirming the bilateral alliance in the spring of 1996, Japan and the United States crafted a new set of defense cooperation guidelines that mandated, among other things, Japan's willingness to provide rear-area support for US forces not only for the defense of Japan but also during contingencies in areas surrounding Japan. Japan agreed to develop with the United States a more advanced ballistic missile defense system. In the 2004 National Defense Program Guidelines, Japan added a new Self-Defense Forces (SDF) mission of international cooperation beyond Japan's territory to prevent the emergence of security threats, and the Defense Agency was elevated to a full-fledged ministry in January 2007.[44]

But how does this incremental "normalization" of Japan as a security actor relate to Japan's constitutional constraints? In Chapter 3, Jitsuo

Tsuchiyama traces how the "war renunciation" norm articulated in Japan's postwar constitution emerged and has evolved over time. He shows how the Japanese government has adapted this constitutional norm in order to alter defense policies in the face of changes in the international environment but points out that the constitution now appears to be stretched to its doctrinal limits. Tsuchiyama examines the current debate about constitutional revision (or reinterpretation) and concludes that there has not been much concrete progress toward formal revision of Article 9. Nevertheless, he believes that Japan can still contribute meaningfully to international security even within existing constitutional constraints.

In Chapter 4, Go Ito takes a closer look at Japan's participation in international security activities, particularly those under the umbrella of UN peacekeeping operations. After discussing the historical roots of Japan's so-called UN-centered diplomacy, Ito argues that the 1990–1991 Gulf War marked a major turning point by shaking Japan's policy immobilism. Thereafter, Japan took the historic step of passing legislation that enabled the dispatch of the SDF overseas for UN-mandated peacekeeping operations—albeit initially with tight restrictions. After several years of positive experience in such operations, it then relaxed these restrictions. But as Chapter 4 shows, Japan also recognized the need to buttress its alliance with the United States through greater bilateral defense cooperation. This two-track approach to international security (one centered on the United Nations and the other centered on the US-Japan alliance) provided the groundwork for Japan's unprecedented support of the US-led operations in Afghanistan and Iraq.

As diplomatically significant as these contributions may be, in Chapter 5 Michael O'Hanlon articulates another vision for how Japan could contribute more to international security. For O'Hanlon, given the large size of its defense budget, Japan could be doing much more in a meaningful way. In the spirit of liberal internationalism, he advocates altering Japan's defense posture for the purpose of multilateral security missions throughout the world, ranging from humanitarian relief all the way to peace enforcement. Through this reorientation, Japan might be able to reduce the risks of "Japan's being seen as dangerously nationalistic by its neighbors."

But even as Japan has become more receptive to participating in overseas security missions, it is most concerned about threats to its own homeland, just as any other nation is. Actual and potential threats close to home have indeed been as much a driver of Japan's security "normalization" as the perceived necessity to contribute more to global security. Under current policy, Japan has tight restrictions about when Japan can exercise its right of individual self-defense and how it can use force. Three conditions must be met: "(1) there is an imminent and illegitimate act of aggression against Japan, (2) there is no appropriate means to deal with this aggression other than the resort to the right of self-defense, and (3) the use of armed strength is confined to the minimum necessary level."[45] The third condition has proscribed the acquisition of offensive weaponry such as intercontinental ballistic missiles (ICBMs), long-range bombers, or offensive aircraft carriers.

If Japan feels acutely threatened by neighboring states such as North Korea or China, however, it could inflate its "individual self-defense" inner tube and redefine what is "the minimum necessary," and such a redefinition could still be technically within the existing parameters of official constitutional interpretation. For example, Japan could deploy the SDF or even the Coast Guard more assertively to defend its broader maritime economic interests and territorial claims. It could even opt for retaliatory capabilities (e.g., cruise missiles) to beef up deterrence. The risk of such moves is that they could rub up against competing interests and conflicting claims by China and South Korea. In short, even a Japan under the "peace constitution" could help trigger a regional arms spiral and produce a more unstable region.

Economic Relations

One of the common criticisms of Japanese foreign policy has been that Japan is doing much less in the international arena than it is capable of, given its enormous economic power. Ironically, soon after Japan finally began to embrace the notion of "international contribution," its economy fell into a decade-long slump. In Chapter 6, Edward Lincoln analyzes how Japan's changing economic circumstances have affected both domestic demands on foreign policy and international expectations for Japan's contributions to global public goods. Although economic capabilities remain important for Japanese involvement and influence in international affairs, he also highlights the factor of Japan's human capacity, which has expanded independently of national economic fortunes. Lincoln shows how Japan has gradually shifted from its traditional insularity to greater openness and how its view of national economic interests has broadened. The loss of national confidence resulting from weak economic performance has constrained Japan's international activism, however. As a result, Japan's proactive economic diplomacy has tended to be focused in the Asia Pacific region more than at the global level.

In Chapter 7 on international financial relations, Yoshiko Kojo provides a good look at how Japan's attitude toward global cooperation changed as its economic performance declined. During the 1980s, when the national economy was still growing and Japan was becoming a global financial powerhouse, Tokyo played a constructive role in forging the 1988 Basle Accord for regulating the international banking industry. At the time, according to

Kojo, the agreement was hailed as "one of the most significant steps to date toward standardization of international regulation." But this case study also illustrates the limits of Japan as a world leader. Although Japan had become the leading creditor country by the 1980s, its government tended to defer to the United States and the United Kingdom regarding the substance of this new regulatory regime. When Japan's economy stagnated, its bankers began to blame the Basle Accord for its financial woes. But echoing Lincoln, Kojo notes that despite its domestic economic troubles, Japan became more active in the Asia Pacific region to promote financial stability after the 1997–1998 regional economic crisis.

In Chapter 8, Juichi Inada analyzes how Japan responded to this Asian financial crisis. Inada disagrees with both the view that sees Japan challenging US-led global institutions such as the International Monetary Fund and the World Bank to create an East Asian economic bloc and the view that emphasizes the ineffectiveness of Japan's response and the "bankruptcy" of Asian regionalism. He instead takes a middle view by arguing that Japan has been fostering regional arrangements designed to complement rather than supplant the existing global financial management regime. In short, his case study provides a good example of how Japan asserts its autonomy from the United States in an internationalist way by filling in some of the gaps in the US-led order rather than openly confronting that order. In her analysis of this same crisis, Saori Katada referred to Japan's behavior as a "counterweight strategy."[46]

There are also limits to Japanese regional leadership in economic affairs. After Japan's economic bubble burst in 1991, the "flying-geese" model of a Japan-led regional economic order also crashed.[47] The 1997–1998 regional financial crisis disrupted Japanese-led production networks, and China burst forward as an economic challenger. The much heralded APEC process, of which Japan was a chief architect, lost its dynamism after the failure of the Early Voluntary Sectoral Liberalization (EVSL) initiative and after the forum expanded to include too many economies.[48] Rather than region-wide efforts, the salient modality for economic liberalization became the negotiation of bilateral free trade agreements (FTAs). Although Japan and South Korea first triggered this move toward bilateral FTAs, other countries soon followed suit, creating an FTA bandwagon.[49] Even China actively joined in this bandwagon, creating the impression that China was taking the regional initiative away from Japan.

In the meantime, Japan now appears to be pursuing a multilayered approach to international economic affairs that involves a mix of bilateralism, regionalism, and multilateralism. Although Japan is both unwilling and unable to help lead the way in furthering the process of global economic liberalization, in part because of persistent domestic agricultural protectionism, it is quite willing to use global multilateral economic regimes such as the World Trade Organization (WTO) to embed bilateral trade disputes. For example, Japan has vigorously used the WTO to challenge US antidumping policies, providing another illustration of how Japanese multilateralism can work against US policy preferences.[50]

Regional Diplomacy

As vital as the alliance with the United States has been and will continue to be for Japanese foreign policy, the end of the Cold War made Japan realize that this alliance was no longer sufficient. Japanese leaders came to recognize that it must do more to cultivate in Asia an environment more hospitable for their country's long-term security and commercial interests. For example, business leader Kobayashi Yōtarō in 1991 urged Japan to "re-Asianize" and to learn from the German example.[51] While maintaining strong ties with the United States, Germany built a congenial home in Europe as well. Japan must try to do the same in Asia. Senior diplomat Ogura Kazuo called for an Asian restoration whereby Japan and other East Asian countries could contribute more actively to world civilization, rather than just borrowing from the West.[52] This new focus on Asia did not mean, however, that Japan had to choose between the United States and the West on the one hand and East Asia on the other.

Japan's economic interests were now global in scope, not just regional. Despite the dynamism of the East Asian economies, the United States would remain an important market and source of technology for Japanese businesses. Although East Asia had become peaceful compared to what the region had experienced during much of the twentieth century, too many military uncertainties lingered on even after the end of Soviet-US competition. Historical memories continued to make Asians wary about Japanese power, and East Asia was too diverse and unwieldy to present a viable strategic alternative to the alliance with the United States. So rather than the option of an East Asian community, most Japanese concluded in the early 1990s that Japan should promote an Asia Pacific community with the United States and other Western countries inside. It would go against Japan's interest to draw a line down the Pacific. Instead, Japan should promote an "Asia Pacific fusion" and pursue an Asia policy without "Asianism."[53] Or as one business executive put it, Japan's optimal orientation would be Shin-Bei, Nyū-A (close to America and entering Asia).[54]

In Chapter 9, on the politics of memory, Thomas Berger shows how Japan's so-called history problem continues to burden its Asia diplomacy and could have a corrosive impact on regional affairs. Contrary to popular perceptions, he argues that Japan has not suffered from "historical amnesia." Debates about the past have figured prominently in Japan's public life and have affected the country's domestic politics and foreign relations. Berger therefore traces how Japan's collective memory has been shaped and reshaped across different periods in its post–World War II political development. He shows that during the 1990s, domestic and international conditions made Japan much more responsive to demands from neighboring countries to address the history issue more forthrightly. Unfortunately, Koizumi's persistent pilgrimages to the controversial Yasukuni Shrine after he became prime minister in 2001 helped to undo much of this progress. It remains to be seen whether a confluence of political will and national interest will compel Koizumi's successor, Abe Shinzō, to promote historical reconciliation between Japan and East Asia.

If the issue of history has weakened Japan's "soft power" in Asia, Japan has attempted to recover some of its moral authority in the region by trumpeting its commitment to democratic principles and institutions. For example, Prime Minister Koizumi joined President Bush in June 2006 in defining the US-Japan alliance as one based on "universal values" as well as "common interests": "The United States and Japan stand together not only against mutual threats but also for the advancement of core universal values such as freedom, human dignity and human rights, democracy, market economy, and rule of law. These values are deeply rooted in the long historic traditions of both countries."[55] This commitment to democracy is difficult to operationalize as foreign policy, however. In contrast to the doctrinaire approach of the United States, Japan's policies about promoting democracy abroad have been more pragmatic and ad hoc, with a clear preference for persuasion over coercion.

As Catharin Dalpino argues in Chapter 10, however, the Japanese approach has been less effective in advancing political reconciliation and democratization in Burma than in Cambodia. The legacy of World War II fostered a "special relationship" between Japan and Burma that then steered Japan's diplomatic machinery and business community to support economic incentives in hopes of encouraging the Burmese military junta, which seized power in 1988, to relax its repressive practices. Japan therefore tended to side with other Asian countries rather than with the West in backing positive engagement with the notorious Rangoon regime. But as Dalpino shows, neither the persuasive approach of Japan nor the coercive approach of the West has had much effect in compelling Burma to adopt democratic reforms. The continuing Burmese political stalemate, however, has spawned the emergence of Japanese nongovernmental organizations (NGOs) and quasi-NGOs that have become active not only in nudging Japan's Burma policy in a somewhat tougher direction but also in serving as a tool for staying engaged in Burma and for providing humanitarian assistance.

The rise of China has emerged as perhaps the biggest factor for shaping Japan's Asia diplomacy. As Mike Mochizuki shows in Chapter 11, Japan has gradually shifted from a relatively conciliatory approach toward China to one based on frankness and the pursuit of national interests. After the 1989 Tiananmen massacre, Japanese public attitudes toward China became more negative, and this downward trend has continued in response to what many Japanese perceive as Chinese hostility and arrogance. Domestic political changes have also reinforced Japan's tougher diplomatic stance toward its giant neighbor. But Mochizuki argues that even though Japan has come to put more emphasis on a policy of balancing against and constraining a rising China, it also continues to pursue a policy of engaging and integrating China into the regional order. China's stunning economic growth provides attractive commercial opportunities for Japanese business interests. Moreover, the potential negative side effects of China's rapid industrial development pose concerns for Japan about environmental degradation and potential social instability in China that could spill over to Japan. Tokyo therefore has strong incentives to promote cooperation with Beijing while managing the competitive elements of bilateral relations.

In the wake of the 1997 Asian financial crisis and the floundering of the APEC process, Japan began to downplay the notion of "Asia Pacific fusion" and to embrace a regional dialogue consisting of the ten countries in ASEAN plus Japan, China, and South Korea (ASEAN Plus Three; APT). First launched informally in 1997, APT has evolved into an annual summit meeting of the countries and has promoted the objective of East Asian community building. Although community building will ultimately hinge on the will and ability of countries to forge cooperation in a variety of functional areas, much of the initial attention has focused on the scope of membership. Like the controversial Malaysian proposal for an East Asian Economic Caucus (EAEC) back in the early 1990s, this APT dialogue excludes the United States.

Although many Japanese find the opportunity for East Asians to talk among themselves without a US presence to be quite attractive, they are nevertheless ambivalent because of relative power calculations. Japan would be facing an increasingly powerful and influential China in a regional context without the counterbalancing effects of the United States. Japan has therefore opted to insist on a two-tiered approach to regional community building.[56] On the one hand, it has backed the APT countries as the core group for an East Asian community. On the other hand, Tokyo has insisted on an enlarged regional forum, the East Asia Summit, which includes Australia, New Zealand, and India in addition to the APT. By having these three additional countries present, Japan hopes that China's weight would be offset somewhat and that the community-building process would be more consonant with democratic values.

In Chapter 12, Thomas Berger reviews the scholarly literature on Japanese foreign policy and distinguishes between two models: one that sees Japan primarily as a "reactive state" and a second that views Japan as more of a "strategic state." Berger argues that Japan's foreign policy after the end of the Cold War and much of the scholarly analysis of this period (including the chapters in this book) suggest another model: Japan as an "adaptive state." Although Japan's adaptation to international change has manifested itself in many ways, he concludes that Japan has tended to pursue a policy of pragmatic liberalism.

Notes

1. Pyle, *The Japanese Question: Power and Purpose,* 20–41.
2. Lincoln, *Japan's New Global Role,* 2.
3. Calder, "Japanese Foreign Economic Policy Formation: Explaining the 'Reactive State,'" 517–541.
4. Miyashita, "Gaiatsu and Japan's Foreign Aid: Rethinking the Reactive-Proactive Debate," and *Limits to Power: Asymmetric Dependence and Japanese Foreign Aid Policy.*
5. Iriye, *Japan and the Wider World: From the Mid-Nineteenth Century to the Present,* 188.
6. Sakaya, *What Is Japan? Contradictions and Transformations,* 26.
7. Tamamoto, "Ambiguous Japan: Japanese National Identity at Century's End," 206.
8. Robert M. Orr Jr., *The Emergence of Japan's Foreign Aid Power,* 52–102.
9. Robert M. Orr Jr., "Japanese Foreign Aid: Over a Barrel in the Middle East," 289–304; Arase, *Buying Power,* 93–146.
10. Inukai, "Why Aid and Why Not? Japan and Sub-Saharan Africa," 252–274.
11. Fukushima, "Official Development Assistance (ODA) as a Japanese Foreign Policy Tool," 162–163.
12. Friedman and LeBard, *The Coming War with Japan;* Crichton, *Rising Sun: A Novel.*
13. Lorell, *Troubled Partnership: A History of U.S.-Japan Collaboration on the FS-X Fighter.*
14. Unger, "Japan and the Gulf War: Making the World Safe for Japan-U.S. Relations," 137–163.
15. Mochizuki, *Japan: Domestic Change and Foreign Policy.*
16. Shinoda, *Kantei gaikō,* 127–165.
17. Shinoda, "Koizumi's Top-Down Leadership in the Anti-Terrorism Legislation: The Impact of Political Institutional Changes," 25–28.
18. Krauss and Nyblade, "'Presidentialization' in Japan? The Prime Minister, Media, and Elections in Japan," 357–368.
19. For an excellent examination of this recent debate, see Samuels, "Japan's Goldilocks Strategy."
20. Hook and Weiner, *The Internationalization of Japan.*
21. Itoh, *Globalization of Japan.*
22. Shipper, "Criminals or Victims? The Politics of Illegal and Foreigners in Japan," 299–327.
23. Okawara, *To Avoid Isolation: An Ambassador's View of U.S.A.-Japanese Relations.*

24. Naikaku-fu Seifu Kōhō Shitsu, *Seron chōsa gaikō,* October 1991 and October 2005.

25. Immerman, "Japan in the United Nations," 181–192; Dore, *Japan: Internationalism and the UN;* Fukushima, *Japanese Foreign Policy: The Emerging Logic of Multilateralism,* 54–106.

26. Drifte, "Japan's Quest for a Permanent Security Council Seat," 99–102.

27. Yu-Jose, "Global Environmental Issues: Responses from Japan," 23–47.

28. Fukushima, *Japanese Foreign Policy: The Emerging Logic of Multilateralism,* 130–178.

29. Ishihara, *The Japan That Can Say "No."*

30. Wan, *Sino-Japanese Relations: Interaction, Logic, and Transformation,* 287–303.

31. Mochizuki, "Strategic Thinking Under Bush and Koizumi: Implications for the U.S.-Japan Alliance," 90–91.

32. Itoh, *Japan's Neo-Nationalism: The Role of the Hinomaru and Kimigayo Legislation.*

33. Clifford, *Cleansing History, Cleansing Japan: Kobayashi Yoshinori's Analects of War and Japan's Revisionist Revival.*

34. Soeya, "The Misconstrued Shift in Japan's Foreign Policy" and *Nihon no "Midoru Pawā" Gaikō.*

35. LaFeber, *The Clash: U.S.-Japanese Relations Throughout History,* 381–405.

36. "Ambassador Katō and Baker Converse on a Relationship That Has Never Been Stronger," *Japan Now* 1 (2004).

37. Mochizuki, "A New Bargain for a Stronger Alliance"; Hughes and Fukushima, "U.S.-Japan Security Relations—Toward Bilateralism Plus?"

38. Kliman, *Japan's Security Strategy in the Post-9/11 World: Embracing a New Realpolitik,* 67–92.

39. Mochizuki, "U.S.-Japan Relations in the Asia-Pacific Region," 13–32.

40. Kohno, "In Search of Proactive Diplomacy: Increasing Japan's International Role in the 1990s."

41. Mochizuki, "Japan: Between Alliance and Autonomy," 114–120.

42. Inoguchi and Jain, "Beyond Karaoke Diplomacy?" xv–xviii.

43. Mochizuki, "Strategic Thinking Under Bush and Koizumi: Implications for the US-Japan Alliance," 91.

44. For a fuller discussion of the recent evolution of Japan's defense policy, see Hughes, "Japanese Military Modernization: In Search of a 'Normal' Security Role."

45. Japan Defense Agency, *Defense of Japan, 2006,* 93–94.

46. Katada, "Japan's Counterweight Strategy: U.S.-Japan Cooperation and Competition in International Finance," 176–197.

47. MacIntyre and Naughton, "The Decline of a Japan-Led Model of the East Asian Economy."

48. Krauss, "The United States and Japan in APEC's EVSL Negotiations: Regional Multilateralism and Trade."

49. Munakata, "Has Politics Caught Up with Markets? In Search of East Asian Economic Regionalism."

50. Pekkanen, "Bilateralism, Multilateralism, or Regionalism? Japan's Trade Forum Choices."

51. Kobayashi, "'Sai Ajiaka' no susume."

52. Ogura, "'Ajia no fukken' no tame ni."

53. Funabashi, *Asia Pacific Fusion;* Ikeda, "'Ajia shugi' de wa nai Ajia gaikō."

54. Terashima, "'Shin Bei Nyū A' no sōgō senryaku o motomete."

55. Japan-US Summit Meeting, "The Japan-U.S. Alliance of the New Century, June 29, 2006." Available at http://www.mofa.go.jp/region/n-america/us/summit0606.html (accessed July 10, 2006).

56. Hitoshi Tanaka, "The ASEAN+3 and East Asia Summit: A Two-Tiered Approach to Community Building."

| 2 |

The Domestic Foundations of Japan's International Contribution

Masaru Kohno

Since the late 1980s, the notion of *kokusai kōken* (international contribution) has become popular among the observers and practitioners of Japan's foreign policy. Especially during and after the Gulf War, the term *international contribution* began to appear frequently in various works, including governmental publications, the mass media, and the writings of leading politicians and intellectuals in Japan. Substantive policy issues raised in its context are extremely broad. Most often, the theme of international contribution has been addressed in association with two prominent issues, namely, Japan's economic assistance to developing countries and Japan's participation in the United Nations peacekeeping operation activities. Yet, it has also been raised in discussing Japan's participation (and/or representation) in almost all sorts of international organizations as well as Japan's adherence to the rules and norms of these organizations, ranging from world trade and international financing to human rights and environment, counterterrorist and AIDS-combating measures, and technological and business standards.

Perhaps precisely because of its ubiquity, however, the usage of the term *international contribution* has been inconsistent, confusing, and, in some cases, even misguided by false assumptions about Japan's foreign policy. Many arguments made either for or against Japan's increased contribution have been based on the erroneous premise that Japan in the past did not play a sufficient role in contributing to the stability and development of the international community. It is most problematic that in the existing literature there is a pervasive tendency to view Japan's increased international role and commitments largely as a response to new pressures originating from the external environment, be it the formidable force of economic/technological globalization, the ending of the Cold War, or the resultant emergence of a unipolar international system led by an assertive and increasingly unilateral hegemon, the United States.

In this chapter, I challenge such a conventional characterization that Japan is simply reacting to these international pressures in an idiosyncratic way. Instead, through the presentation of three case studies, I seek to highlight the domestic foundations of Japan's international behavior, such as the changing preferences of key political actors and the endogenous evolution of institutional contexts under which these actors interact. It is true that Japan had to face an enormous challenge from the rapidly changing international environment in the 1980s and 1990s, but the external pressure interacted with Japan's domestic dynamics in a complex manner, triggering significant changes in the preference and strategies of various actors and resulting in some major reforms of important institutions. Japan's decisions to increase its commitments in the regional and global communities were not simply a reactive behavior but were firmly anchored in the domestic context of Japan's political economy.[1]

Discourse and Confusion About Japan's "International Contribution"

Since the late 1980s, the Japanese public has been bombarded with discussions of international contribution, a phrase that has frequently been used by both the practitioners and critics of Japan's foreign policy in regard to such important issues as Japan's economic assistance to developing countries and Japan's participation in UN peacekeeping operations. The theme of international contribution has been raised in other contexts as well, generally referring to Japan's role in the international community and Japan's commitments to the established norms and standards of international institutions.

Around the time of the Gulf War, the public awareness of the importance of international contribution was raised dramatically. As documented elsewhere,[2] Japan during this international conflict was heavily criticized for the "too little, too late" mode of its contribution made on behalf of the multilateral alliance's operations led by the United States against Saddam Hussein of Iraq. The Japanese public is said to have been awakened by the "Iraqi shock," and some evidence supports such a claim. Figure 2.1 presents the number of times the phrase *kokusai kōken* appeared annually in *Asahi Shimbun,* one of Japan's leading newspapers, from 1987 to 1999.[3] As is clear from the figure, it was in 1991, the year in which the Gulf War occurred, that the frequency jumped dramatically from the preceding year.[4]

The view that the increase in the public's awareness toward Japan's

Figure 2.1 Frequency of *Kokusai Kōken* in *Asahi Shimbun*

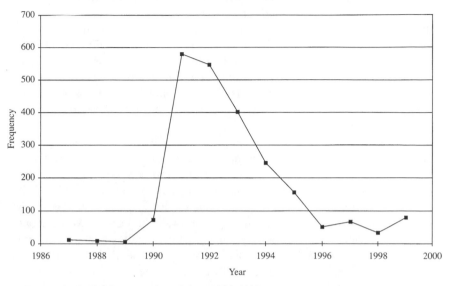

Source: Asahi Shimbun, morning editions, 1986–1999.

international role originated in the Gulf War and its aftermath is too myopic, however. The concept, if not the phrase, of international contribution gained prominence in Japan much earlier than the 1990s. A survey of governmental publications (which are excellent vehicles to elucidate the long-term trend because they are published regularly) reveals that the beginning of domestic discussion of international contribution predated the Gulf War. In the case of Japan's Diplomatic Bluebook (Gaikō Seisho), such notions as Japan's responsibility (*sekinin*) and role (*yakuwari*) in the international community had been used consistently since the early 1980s.[5] In the case of the annual white paper on the ODA, also edited by the Ministry of Foreign Affairs,[6] the notion of international contribution has been recognized far more explicitly, and the exact wording *kokusai kōken* has been used consistently. This governmental document series positioned the ODA, as early as the mid-1980s, as one of the most central policy tools for "Japan's contribution toward the international community." Ever since, the idea of international contribution has been closely linked with Japan's ODA program.

Although the idea of international contribution has become accepted as an important pillar of Japan's contemporary foreign policy, there has been a great deal of ambiguity and inconsistency associated with this term. The ambiguity and inconsistency, in turn, make it difficult to evaluate various arguments made about the nature and appropriate scope of Japan's international contribution. Take, for example, a famous controversy that took place between two prominent politicians, Ozawa Ichirō and Takemura Masayoshi, in the early 1990s.[7] This debate represented the basic cleavage in the evolving discourse on this topic, focusing on whether or not to include the military-security aspects of activities in Japan's policy of international contribution. Ozawa, on the one hand, argued that Japan's contribution must include a military-security dimension, stressing the need for Japan to become a normal state.[8] Takemura, on the other hand, noted that what the world expected from Japan was largely nonmilitary activities, especially under the United Nations framework.[9]

This debate was confusing because neither side clearly defined the fundamental objective of Japan's international contribution or "to what" Japan should be contributing. International contribution was treated, not as the means with which to achieve certain policy goals but as the end itself of Japan's foreign policy. Instead of specifying the underlying objectives, both Ozawa and Takemura invoked the expectation of the outside world about Japan's behavior in order to justify their respective claims about the nature and appropriate scope of international contribution. The difference between their positions thus hinged upon the difference in their assessment of what that outside expectation was, not about Japan's foreign policy objectives.

This confusion (between the ends and means), to a certain extent, reflects grammatical characteristics of the Japanese language.[10] In English, the word *contribution* or the verb *to contribute* requires one to specify "to X," either explicitly or implicitly, to complete the sentence. In Japanese, there is no such grammatical rule, and the users of this term do not necessarily have to specify "to what" Japan should be contributing. Thus, especially when the word *kōken* is used as a noun (with an adjective *kokusai*), the term becomes vague, and its meaning becomes open to a wide range of interpretations.[11] Theoretically Japan can be engaged in international contribution for various foreign policy objectives, ranging from a pursuit of narrowly defined national interests to a more altruistic motivation of providing international collective goods.

Beyond linguistic ambiguities, however, the confusion about international contribution also embodies deeper conceptual problems associated with some misleading perspectives on Japan's foreign policy. First, some arguments, especially those that call for expanding Japan's contribution, are premised on the assessment that Japan, in the past, did not play a sufficient role internationally. Such an assessment is often linked with the assertion that Japan should expand its international contribution to "pay back its debt" to the world. This view cannot be justified no matter how one defines the scope of international contribution. It is true that during the earlier decades of the post–World War II period, Japan benefited enormously from the international public goods, such as collective security and international economic order, underwritten by the United States, but the benefit was by no means in one direction. Throughout the period of the Cold War, the US naval and air bases in Japan were vital to the US containment strategy and to US military operations in East Asia. It is hard to deny that the US-Japan bilateral security treaty played a crucial role in maintaining the regional and global balance of power. On the economic front, Japan, together with the United States, provided markets, capital investments, and industrial technologies to the East Asian countries. There is no doubt that Japan's efforts contributed to the successful economic developments of these countries during the final quarter of the twentieth century.[12]

Second, it is often taken for granted that the recent expansion of Japan's international contribution has largely been a response to external pressures or *gaiatsu*, not based on Japan's own independent decision. This view is promoted most often by the "Iraqi shock" hypothesis discussed earlier, which suggests that a shocking external event, such as the Gulf War, was a necessary precondition for the public awareness to mature and the policy to change in Japan. But, more broadly, Japan is frequently seen as simply reacting to various strains imposed by the changes in the international environment, such as the ending of the Cold War and economic/technological globalization. Indeed, the notion of Japan as a "reactive state" is advocated by many students of Japan's foreign policy, almost as a conventional wisdom in depicting the pattern of Japan's diplomacy dating back to the era of Perry's "black ships" and the Meiji Restoration.[13]

It would be absurd, of course, to deny the impact of the changing international environment on foreign policy of any modern state. As the recent literature of the so-called second image *reversed* perspective in international relations theory suggests, however, foreign pressure in the international system interacts with domestic political actors and institutions in a complex manner. The Japanese case is not an exception, and a more sophisticated analysis of Japan's international behavior must take into account the political process in which these external forces affect the incentives of domestic actors, the power balance among them, and the foundations of existing political institutions.

Domestic Sources of Japan's International Contribution: A Framework

In the existing literature of international relations theories, two perspectives are used to analyze the interaction between domestic politics and the international environment. On the one hand, the "second image" perspective, to borrow Kenneth Waltz's classic typology,[14] sees wars, trade, and various other patterns of interstate conflict and cooperation as the outcomes of states' characteristics.[15] The "second image *reversed*" perspective, on the other hand, focuses on domestic consequences of international phenomena.[16] In what follows, I build upon a framework developed by Geoffrey Garrett and Peter Lange in the latter tradition to analyze how the external pressure formed the domestic foundations for the evolution of Japan's international behavior.[17] Although their original framework concerns mostly the impact of economic aspects of globalization, its insights are applicable generally for analyzing foreign-domestic interactive process.

The force of external pressure inflicts an impact on the domestic political economy of a modern state at various stages. Most immediately, such a pressure affects the preference of relevant domestic actors within the state. Under the strain of globalization, for example, those engaged in traditional industrial sectors may be forced to increase their productive varieties and embark upon structural reforms of their operations and organizations. Consumers and internationally competitive firms, in contrast, are likely to welcome the new development and reinforce their preference for open trade and freer access to international capital markets. At minimum, the external pressure thus heightens the cleavage, which otherwise might have been latent and inconsequential, between different sets of domestic actors.

Next, the external pressure affects the preference of some key political actors in a more indirect way, by changing the power balance among domestic socioeconomic actors. Under globalization, internationally competitive sectors are likely to increase their profits and business opportunities and thus their potential political resources, compared to the traditional noncompetitive sectors that demand governmental protection in order to absorb the shock of global competition. The change in the power balance between sectors may reach the point at which it threatens the majority status of the socioeconomic coalition upon which the power of governing political elites rests. In such a case, these elites may opt for the formation of an alternative majority coalition, shifting the support base away from the traditional to the more competitive sectors.

Further, the shift in the underlying power balance may eventually lead to the situation in which the existing political institutions must be altered. This development, or what Garrett and Lange call "endogenous institutional change," might occur because the existence of any political or administrative institution is premised on the support of a particular majority coalition. The change in the makeup of this coalition may thus result in an institutional reform. If this occurs, the strategies of some important actors are likely to be affected. That is, even if the preference of actors remains unchanged, the shift in the institutional environment may alter the strategic calculations of options available to them and the way they further their underlying interests.

To summarize, the external pressure fosters the transformation of the domestic political economy through at least three conceptually separable, though practically interlinked, processes: (1) the stimulation on the actors' preference, (2) the shift of the majority coalition, and (3) the change in the actors' optimizing strategy under the altered institutional setup. During the 1980s and 1990s Japan experienced all of these, and the change in Japan's international behavior was thus firmly anchored in the evolving domestic context. The following three cases illustrate each pattern of these changes in turn and discuss their respective implication for Japan's international role in the contemporary era.

Case 1: MITI's Preference Change

It might be surprising to consider a governmental agency as an example with which to depict an actor's preference change, because public bureaucracy is usually thought to be among the slowest to adapt to a changing environment. It might be particularly surprising to think of a bureaucratic organization in Japan in this category, given that hierarchy, formal rules, and traditions are respected persistently within the Japanese culture. In fact, when critics attack Japan for the paucity of its international contribution, the Japanese bureaucracy has often been the target of their blame, for its (claimed) organizational rigidity and overwhelmingly inward-looking policy orientation.

Perhaps as an exception to this generalization, an observation of MITI reveals that this governmental organization underwent a fundamental transformation in its mission and character to adapt to a new international environment.[18] Some aspects of the change that MITI experienced are directly relevant to the question of Japan's international role and commitments. To be more specific, since the late 1980s MITI has played a major role in contributing to the development of the Asian regional economy and in leading Japan to uphold established rules and standards of important multilateral institutions.[19]

In the earlier decades of the post–World War II period, MITI was regarded as the regulatory powerhouse whose policy objective was to protect domestic industries and to promote Japan's own economic growth. Chalmers Johnson's classic treatment on the subject described MITI as the central organ of the "developmental state," which, largely insulated from societal forces, pursued Japan's long-term, national interest.[20] In trade and other economic negotiations between the United States and Japan, MITI was frequently criticized as the source of Japan's deviation from established international norms and practices.[21] According to this line of characterization, it would be difficult to consider MITI's putting any priority on promoting Japan's international contribution.

It is no longer accurate, however, to view this bureaucratic agency simply as an organ of Japan's developmental state. Nor is it appropriate to define its goal in terms solely of the success of the Japanese economy and industries. MITI began extending the reach of its industrial policy beyond the national border, especially toward East Asia, after the regional economic crises in 1998.

Some very concrete examples of MITI's innovative, microlevel initiatives, reminiscent of its earlier policy in the domestic context, illustrate this change. In the summer of 1998, MITI announced that it would send a group of specialists to Indonesia for a two-year period so that the Indonesian manufacturers of furniture and consumer electronic products could learn sophisticated design technologies. Indonesian products are competitive in price, but their exports to Japan were not expanding owing to their poor design qualities. Behind this initiative was MITI's recognition that an increase in exports to Japan would be an important ingredient for Indonesia's economic recovery. Also in the summer of 1998, MITI decided to provide direct subsidies to Japanese companies operating in ASEAN, in order to decrease the number of layoffs of locally hired workers. According to one estimate, this initiative was to prevent approximately 10,000 workers in the region from becoming unemployed.[22] Further, MITI utilized a scheme of export-import insurance administered by its Trade Bureau for the recovery and expansion of Asian regional economy. This insurance had traditionally been used for the Japanese government to take over the risk of Japanese firms' trade and direct investment overseas. MITI expanded this framework so as to take over the risk of Japanese financing to Asian countries. In either of these cases, it is difficult to view MITI's behavior as reflecting the narrowly defined national interest of Japan.

These examples should not be taken to constitute another version of the conventional "Japan as a reactive state" story, in which an exogenous shock, the Asian economic crisis, triggered MITI to deal with its consequences. The changing behavior of this ministry reflected a more long-term, structural transformation of its vision and preference. MITI's obvious emphasis on East Asia in its various policy packages reflected its recognition of the growing interdependence between Japan and that particular region. Even more fundamental perhaps was MITI's vision of Japan's changed position in the world economy. The previous inward-looking, if not protectionist, orientation in MITI's policy was the product of the latecomer status of Japan's industrialization in the earlier decades. By the mid-1970s, however, major Japanese manufacturing firms became larger in size and their products internationally competitive,[23] and the Japanese economy as a whole became the second largest in the world. As Japan's relative position shifted, the cleavage between competitive sectors and less competitive sectors grew. MITI, at this point, redefined its ministerial mission and shifted the policy emphasis away from protecting the latter to promoting the former.

MITI's new orientation was evident not only in the extension of its industrial policy beyond the national border toward East Asia but in its overall trade policy as well. MITI's preference shifted in support of international regimes that promoted open trade, recognizing that the liberal international environment benefited, rather than hindered, the overall Japanese economy. Thus, throughout the 1970s and 1980s, MITI took the lead in lowering Japan's tariff rates both unilaterally and through various rounds of negotiations under the General Agreement on Tariffs and Trade (GATT). In the late 1980s, MITI began a vigorous campaign for the importation of industrial goods, in its attempt to stimulate competition in manufacturing sectors where Japanese industries were said to be lacking efficiency. To my knowledge, Japan is the only country among the advanced industrialized nations that has ever implemented an explicit and systematic policy of importation.

Further, MITI significantly increased its commitment toward multilateral norms and rules embodied in the GATT/WTO regime. In the past, Japan had been only a reluctant participant in this international trade regime. When the United States and other countries threatened to use sanctions against Japanese predatory trade practices, MITI's traditional way of settling disputes had been to negotiate voluntary export restraints bilaterally, deviating from the established procedure of the GATT. Starting in the late 1980s, however, MITI stopped relying on this convention and began turning to multilateral dispute settlement.

> Previously, Japan had appeared in GATT dispute panels many times as the target of complaint, usually settling the case before a panel was established or a decision was reached. . . . The 1988 case against the EC [European Community] marked a turning point. The case involved EC regulations which imposed a surcharge on goods produced in "screwdriver assembly" plants. Japan pursued the case through the panel procedure and won its claim, although the EC refused to comply with the ruling. With the establishment of the WTO, Japan began pursuing more cases in the dispute settlement procedures. Japan filed one of the first cases in the WTO, against the U.S. for retaliatory tariffs in the 1995 automobile dispute. . . . In the dispute with the U.S. over photographic film and paper, Japan insisted that the case be brought to the WTO, refusing to even negotiate the case bilaterally except in Geneva, under the auspices of the WTO.[24]

The year 1998 was another turning point, as MITI began promoting bilateral trade and investment agreements with selected countries. Ever since, especially with the disappointing development of APEC as an effective regional institution, Japan has seemed quite eager in seeking bilateral economic agreements. In my view, however, this does not represent the ministry's retreat from its commitment toward the WTO and multilateralism. In light of the emerging economic regionalism in North America and

Europe, officials at what is now METI clearly recognize the benefits of forming these bilateral agreements in increasing Japan's bargaining position in the WTO negotiations.[25] Moreover, it should be stressed that Japan's engagement in these selective negotiations started only after so many other countries had begun forming similar agreements, and bilateralism thus had become accepted as a norm that supplements the WTO framework. Hence, the shift of emphasis by MITI and METI first on multilateralism and then on a limited usage of bilateral strategy shows nothing more than Japan's adherence to established rules and institutionalized norms in the international community.

In sum, the extension of its industrial policy to Asia and the acceptance of prevailing international rules and norms are illustrative of the change in MITI's fundamental preference under the new international environment. Japan's METI now plays an important role in contributing to the regional economy and to the development of the liberal open-trade regime.

Case 2: Shifting Majority Coalition and the LDP

The governing political elites face a fundamental dilemma when they experience an event, phenomenon, or trend that threatens the majority status of the socioeconomic coalition upon which their power rests. Japan's ruling conservative party, the LDP, confronted such a dilemma when the strains imposed by the changing international environment affected the power balance among the domestic socioeconomic actors. Viewed from a long-term perspective, however, the shift in the nature of Japan's majority coalition was also affected by various internal trends originating in the gradual and underlying societal realignment. The important point to analyze, then, is how the external pressures interacted with the domestic evolutionary process. Such an interaction had a critical impact on the changing pattern of Japan's international behavior.

It is hard to deny that the governing LDP itself stood, for decades, as one of the major obstacles for Japan to increase its international role and commitments. One reason for this stemmed from the nature of party competition shaped by the underlying societal cleavage in Japan. The Japanese party system, often called "1955 system," was formed in the early postwar period at a time when the Japanese public was harshly divided into two opposing camps over the highly ideological issues of postwar settlement, US-Japan security arrangements, and Japan's rearmament.[26] Hence, the LDP feared that the endorsement of foreign policy opting for Japan's more aggressive international posture might electorally benefit the JSP, the LDP's main rival, which had been appealing to the pacifist and isolationist sentiments shared by many voters. It was not until the early 1990s that the LDP was able to escape from this latent fear. I will return to analyze this development more fully in the next section,

Another, more direct reason why the LDP stood against Japan's positive engagement in international matters also had to do with its own electoral concern. At some risk of simplification, it is fair to claim that the core political support for the LDP came from socioeconomic groups that did not necessarily favor the idea or policy of Japan's international contribution. Japanese farmers, for example, vehemently opposed Japan's importation of agricultural products, although they recognized that the price of their own products was highly inflated from the international standards, annoying both the rival overseas producers and domestic consumers. Likewise, small and medium-size business owners continued to ask the LDP government for protective measures in order to maintain the exclusive competitiveness of their products, often invoking harsh criticisms from the United States and other countries. Special interest groups, such as the association of physicians, local post office headmasters, construction industries, and pharmaceutical firms, also pressured the LDP to uphold the existing regulatory regimes related to their respective professions, asserting the uniqueness of their own products and services and that of market needs in Japan. In short, the majority coalition on which the LDP's power was based originally consisted of socioeconomic groups whose interests were protected by the inward-looking, predatory policy implemented by the LDP government itself.

Gradually, however, the nature of the LDP's governance has changed, and it would now be inaccurate to regard the LDP support base simply as a reluctant or impeding social force against Japan's international contribution. Nothing was more symbolic of this change than the selection of Junichirō Koizumi, who vigorously campaigned for the "destruction" of LDP's old mold, as its leader. In the past, the LDP's remarkable ability to win plurality in election after election emanated from the distribution of political favors to the societal groups listed earlier through the provision of fiscal subsidies and preferential tax treatments. Koizumi knew that those happy days were over. His persistent endorsement of "structural reforms" was aimed at delinking the LDP from its traditional ties with these groups and was in turn meant to appeal to the much wider electorate.

Of course, Koizumi did not appear suddenly. The LDP's metamorphosis indeed was a long and complex process. It was in the mid-1970s that the LDP first showed some difficulty in maintaining its majority in parliament by relying solely on its traditional conservative coalition. As Japan's economic growth and modernization continued, the LDP's inward-looking policies had marginalized many voters, especially in urban electoral districts. As the immigration of population from rural areas into big cities progressed, the number of urban middle-class voters increased. Those voters, being predominantly consumers, as opposed to producers, of Japanese agricultural or manufacturing goods, did not directly benefit from the LDP's distributive policy package. The transformation of Japan's industrial structure also eroded the LDP's traditional support base. As the industrial emphasis shifted away from agricultural and manufacturing to service sectors, the conventional provision of political favors became less and less effective in mobilizing votes, enhancing the political salience of the urban middle-class voters.

In addition to the domestic dynamics, the strains imposed by the international trends surrounding Japan also contributed to many voters' disappointment with the LDP's conventional mode of governance. Since the first oil shocks in the early 1970s, the LDP government had begun to accumulate significant budget deficits, highlighting the daunting prospect that the continuation of its traditional protective policies might eventually lead to a fiscal crisis. Furthermore, the increasing pressure of economic and technological globalization only accelerated the pace with which Japan's industrial structure was transforming, further eroding the LDP's electoral stronghold. The development of the East Asian economies, together with the yen's dramatic appreciation after the 1985 Plaza Accord, threatened Japanese manufacturing industries, many of which had no choice but to relocate their production to overseas.

Voters' sense of marginalization was reflected as a steady trend of their dealignment from the established parties. Figure 2.2, based on the monthly survey results conducted by Jiji Tsūshinsha, shows the change over time in the percentage of survey respondents who identified themselves as "independents" or those who did not support any particular political party. As indicated by this figure, independents grew consistently under the LDP's rule.

Figure 2.2 also shows that the LDP's popular support did not decline as sharply and thus did not necessarily correspond to the increase of self-identified independents. Nevertheless, the growth of independents was still a considerable concern for the LDP because if some exogenous shock had triggered a sudden electoral mobilization of these unattached voters, they might have posed an enormous potential threat to the conservative incumbents.

It was precisely for this reason that the LDP explored a number of ways to attract these marginalized voters.[27] Since the late 1970s, for example, the LDP had made a series of attempts to introduce an indirect tax. Although it took about a decade (and thus several administrations), the LDP was finally successful in April 1989 in introducing a nationwide consumption tax. Originally at least, this major reform of the revenue policy was intended to reduce tax privileges thus far given to limited professionals and business owners and to appeal instead to the middle-class, urban dwellers.[28] During the 1980s, the LDP also took some measures to liberalize Japan's agriculture policy. The LDP allowed the importation of beef and oranges, promot-

**Figure 2.2 Support for the LDP and Independents,
Selected Months, 1960–1994**

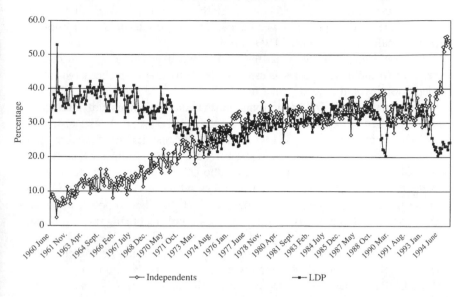

Source: Jiji Seron Chōsa Tokuhō [Jiji Public Opinion Survey Special Reports], various years.

ed an extreme rationalization plan of agricultural lands, and even hinted at the possibility of opening the rice market. Further, the LDP endorsed the revision of the Large-Scale Retail Stores Regulation Law, which had long protected small "mom-and-pop" stores in local economies; the law was notorious for having fostered an inefficient distribution system and thus having disadvantaged domestic consumers. Beginning in the late 1980s, a series of revisions was made to this law, and it was later abandoned entirely.

Some observers may raise reservations and stress that these new policy initiatives were the direct result of Japan's integration into the globalized economy and particularly of *gaiatsu* applied by the United States. It is true that the United States, especially after the early 1980s, stepped up its pressure, urging that Japan adjust various aspects of its domestic political economy to established international standards. It is also true that the LDP sometimes used the US pressure in setting the agenda and legitimating its changed policy stance. As described above, however, it was ultimately the LDP's own electoral concerns that determined the course and scope of the reforms in the 1980s. As documented in Leonard Schoppa's careful case study on US-Japan Structural Impediment Initiatives negotiations, US pressure was effective in bringing changes in Japan's behavior only in the areas where US negotiators were able to ally with Japan's domestic socioeconomic groups that together pressured the LDP government for policy changes.[29] The LDP removed some of the long-standing barriers against Japan's international commitments, not because of the outside pressure but rather because the change in the power balance among domestic socioeconomic groups finally motivated the LDP to do so.

I must emphasize that what the LDP faced then was a difficult dilemma. On the one hand, there was much uncertainty as to whether new policy orientations would indeed attract unattached voters to support the LDP. On the other hand, the LDP knew, for sure, that the abandoning of traditional political clients was bound to incur some political cost. In the past, the LDP's distributive politics had worked well because its benefits were specific and concentrated in certain organized interest groups, whose votes therefore were easier to count on. Now, the LDP had a much harder task of going after the urban middle-class voters who were not organized and whose interests were relatively dispersed. As Ōtake Hideo noted, the LDP leader who most vigorously "sought to spark a political realignment through a multi-faceted strategy of 'expanding the LDP to the left'" was Nakasone Yasuhiro, but "even Nakasone was not prepared to abandon completely the agricultural sector and retail shop owners, staunch LDP supporters; the rest of the LDP Diet members were even less willing. As long as 'expanding the LDP to the left' stopped short of offending farmers and retail shop owners, Nakasone's attempt to reach the urban new middle class remained at best halfhearted."[30]

The LDP's decision not to depart entirely from the old socioeconomic coalition at this point was reasonable and an expected one. Figure 2.3, combined with Figure 2.2, shows the growth of independents was closely (negatively) correlated with the level of LDP support, but it had less to do with the trend of the JSP support, indicating that this largest opposition party was failing to appeal to these independents as a credible alternative to the LDP. While the LDP was struggling to shift its socioeconomic support basis, the JSP had its own problem of not being able to reverse the long-term decline in popularity because of its persistent leftist ideology and idealistic policy platform.[31]

In essence, then, the peculiar political situation gave the LDP a temporal moratorium. That is, as long as the JSP (or any other party for that matter) was failing to appeal to the growing number of independents, the LDP could afford to let go of urban middle-class votes but still maintain its plurality status based on the traditional conservative coalition. Because of this temporary standoff, Japan's commitment toward liberalization remained halfhearted during the 1980s. The very fact that it remained halfhearted highlights the importance of the domestic context of Japan's international behavior.

The political stalemate was finally broken by two events in the late 1980s. The first was the stunning development in the international environment, namely the ending of the Cold War. The second was the JSP's major

Figure 2.3 Support for the JSP, Selected Months, 1960–1994

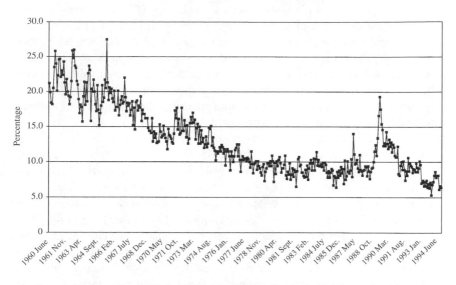

Source: Jiji Seron Chōsa Tokuhō [Jiji Public Opinion Survey Special Reports], various years.

victory in the upper house election in 1989. The interaction between these two political events, one international and the other domestic, forced the LDP to reconsider its strategy entirely and led to an important institutional change, the process and consequence of which I elaborate in the third case study.

In sum, the evolution of LDP's policy orientation was affected not only by external factors but also by long-term, domestic trends. In the earlier years, the LDP's inward-looking predatory policy package had worked well for its electoral success, but in the long run this package proved to be self-defeating in the sense that it marginalized the growing number of urban voters and thus threatened the LDP's own majority status. This governing party, then, faced a fundamental political dilemma. The way the LDP struggled with this dilemma affected the scope and pace at which Japan expanded its international role and commitments.

Case 3: Endogenous Institutional Change and Japanese Socialists

The shift of power balance among socioeconomic actors often leads to a major reform of important domestic institutions that constrain the range of options available to each political actor. If such an "endogenous institutional change" occurs, the strategy with which each political actor furthers his or her own interest is likely to change as well. The reform of Japan's electoral system that took place from 1993 to 1994 was a typical example of such an endogenous institutional change. Although this reform had enormous implications for the subsequent development of Japan's domestic politics, it also brought about a nontrivial consequence for Japan's international behavior: the Japan Socialist Party's abandonment of its "unarmed neutrality" policy and its implication for Japan's increased engagement in matters related to the regional security and world peace.

As discussed in the preceding section, Japanese domestic politics entered into a kind of stalemate in the 1980s. The LDP, on the one hand, could not depart completely from its traditional style of governance even though it was clearly disappointing urban middle-class voters. The LDP's main rival, the JSP, on the other hand, also failed to attract these voters because the JSP was hardly recognized as a credible alternative to the LDP for its increasingly archaic ideology and policy platform. The JSP did discard many aspects of its Marxist doctrine in 1986, but even then it clung to the idealistic unarmed neutralism and still regarded both Japan's alliance with the United States and Japan's Self-Defense Force as unconstitutional and unwarranted for the claimed danger of Japan's involvement in a global conflict.

The stunning development in the international environment, namely the ending of the Cold War, introduced a new rhythm. This exogenous shock provided a realistic potential, for the first time since the end of World War II, to transform the underlying cleavage that had divided Japanese society between two opposing camps, conservative and progressive, upon which the competition between the LDP and JSP had been based. For the governing LDP the most worrisome possibility was that the JSP might recognize more positive roles of the US-Japan alliance and Japan's Self-Defense Force and attract unattached voters by outgrowing its old mold. Indeed, just as the East-West tension was easing in a dramatic way in the international arena, the JSP recorded a surprising electoral victory in the 1989 upper house election. The LDP lost the majority in the upper chamber of the bicameral parliament for the first time since 1955 and was thus forced to form a de facto coalition with other parties for legislative purposes. This electoral upset might have been caused by idiosyncratic factors, including a series of political scandals, but for the LDP it was a powerful reminder that urban middle-class voters, if mobilized, could bring about a major change in the electoral results.

The upper house election in 1989, combined with the exogenous shock of the ending of the Cold War, led the LDP to explore a fundamental solution to the tradeoff between the prospect of losing traditional support and that of attracting urban voters. Although the LDP did manage to maintain its majority in the next lower house election in 1990, some LDP leaders, such as Ozawa Ichirō, the party secretary, decided to attempt an electoral reform by introducing a first-past-the-ballot system to elect the members of the lower house. Ozawa argued that such an Anglo-American type of electoral system, believed to promote a competition between two major parties, would lead competing candidates to run their electoral campaign on salient policy issues and thus force them to aggregate a diverse set of special interests into a simple majority-seeking platform. If successful, such an institutional reform would pressure the LDP to outgrow its traditional mode of governance and to transform itself into a party based on a new coalition of socioeconomic groups. Ironically, Ozawa and his group had to make a political sacrifice of leaving the LDP, but the electoral reform actually took place from 1993 to 1994 under the non-LDP multiparty coalition government pieced together by Ozawa.

This reform has brought about a number of salient consequences for Japan's domestic politics,[32] an important one being the JSP's abandonment of its unarmed neutrality policy. Under the previous electoral system, whereby typically three to five members were elected to the House of Representatives from the same district, it was possible for the JSP to run a campaign targeted exclusively to its hard-core supporters, most typically the leftist labor unions. A consolidation of their support was sufficient for a JSP candidate to clinch at least one of the multiple seats in that district, and many incumbent candidates of the JSP, some of whom themselves were former union members, thought that such a strategy was the safest bet. The introduction of the new electoral system, however, changed the strategic calculation of the JSP, just as it was supposed to change that of the LDP as Ozawa had originally planned. That is, the JSP recognized the futility of holding on to such an idealistic foreign policy platform if the party was serious about seeking a majority of votes in order to win any seat under the single-member district competition. JSP leader Murayama Tomiichi, when he was offered the post of prime minister in a coalition with the LDP in June 1994, thus announced that the US-Japan security treaty and Japan's Self-Defense Force were constitutional.[33]

The JSP's shift in its foreign policy orientation was both a symbolic and substantively critical development because its unarmed neutralism had long stood as a major impediment for Japan to increase its international role and commitments. In the earlier decades, the JSP's unarmed neutralism had appealed to the pacifist sentiments widely shared among the Japanese public beyond the party's hard-core supporters. Having to face the JSP as the largest opposition party throughout the 1960s, 1970s, and 1980s, the governing LDP had thus been pressured not to deviate from foreign policies that limited Japan's role in the bilateral defense with the United States and restrained Japan from taking assertive diplomatic initiatives. Moreover, the LDP had often used the domestic opposition, represented by the JSP, as a convenient shield in evading the US demand for increasing Japan's contribution in regional security matters.[34] The reversal of the JSP's position, then, meant that substantial psychological and political obstacles were finally removed from Japan's domestic context in order for Japan to pursue more positive roles and commitments in the international community. With the banner of unarmed neutralism gone from the main political scene, it certainly has become easier for a domestic consensus to form regarding the issues of Japan's defense, its contribution to the regional stability, and global peace.

When the peacekeeping operation bills were being debated in parliament in the aftermath of the Gulf War, the JSP fiercely opposed the bills, only to be unsuccessful. That turned out to be the last incident in which the JSP's unarmed neutralism had any memorable effect on Japan's legislative discourse. In accordance with the shift in the electoral institution, Japan's party system subsequently underwent a major realignment. A large part of the original JSP has since been absorbed into the newly created Democratic Party, a more moderate political force that includes elements of former centrist parties as well as former LDP members. As the JSP's political influence diminished, Japan's participation in the activities under the United Nations framework for peacekeeping purposes gained legitimacy and support among the general public in Japan.

The reform of the electoral system described above, of course, was not the only consequential "endogenous institutional change" that has occurred in Japan. Just as Japan's party system had to go through a major transformation as a result of the electoral reform, Japan's bureaucracy and administrative institutions experienced manifold changes, including the complete restructuring of bureaucratic organizations, the strengthening of executive power, and the reform of administrative procedures for increased transparency and accountability, all of which have affected Japan's domestic capabilities to conduct foreign policy. Clearly, Japan today is far better equipped institutionally than before to gather information, make swift decisions, and execute coordinated actions under the increasingly competitive and complex international environment.

Nonetheless, in my view, the political disappearance of the JSP, the party that had long opposed Japan's involvement in world affairs, cannot be matched in its significance. Under democracy, what ultimately determines national policy is the nature of party competition and the voice heard in electoral campaign and legislative debates. That the moderate Democratic Party has since replaced the JSP as the largest opposition party is therefore likely to have a pervasive, structural, and long-term effect on Japan's international role.

Conclusion

The central problem with the often-cited "Japan as a reactive state" hypothesis is its failure to recognize the importance of Japan's domestic political process. Japan (or any modern state for that matter) should not be treated as a unified entity or a "black box" that conducts foreign policy independent of its own internal political dynamics. In the modern world, external pressures exist, and these pressures often impose an enormous impact beyond the states' control. The external pressures always interact with the domestic political context, however, to determine the ultimate course of foreign policy. The recent expansion of Japan's international role and commitments must also be analyzed and understood in such complex foreign-domestic interactions.

In the three case studies, I focused on three key actors in Japan's political economy: MITI, the LDP, and the JSP. The changes that these three actors experienced, as I have tried to show, have been consequential for Japan's foreign policy. Some skeptics may object, arguing that my cases are limited and that there are other significant actors that I should have examined in addition to or instead of these three. Why not, for example, the Ministry of Foreign Affairs or Japan's Defense Agency, both of which are obviously important bureaucratic branches relevant to Japan's international behavior? Or why not economic organizations such as Keidanren or certain citizens' groups that often exercise a major influence in affecting Japan's foreign policy? The point of selecting these three actors is that in the past they all stood as either a reluctant or impeding force against Japan's positive engagement in international matters, for respective reasons. MITI's underlying inward-looking orientation prevented Japan from endorsing established norms and standards of international institutions. The LDP's original political support came from a coalition of socioeconomic forces whose interests lay in the continuation of Japan's traditional regulatory regimes. The JSP's policy of unarmed neutralism represented a banner of postwar progressiveness and functioned as an anchor that limited Japan's behavior in the regional and international security. But they all changed, and it is precisely the mechanism of these changes that this chapter has attempted to explore. Taken together, the three case studies show that, although the external pressures provide the initial stimulus, it is ultimately the shift in the nature of the domestic political economy that forms the foundations of Japan's international contribution.

Some critics might, even at this point, argue that the degree to which Japan's international behavior has changed has been minimal and that Japan still has a long way to go in fulfilling the role and responsibility commensurate with its relative power and status in the international system. Maybe so, maybe not. The judgment as to whether Japan's contribution meets international standards simply begs the question about what those standards are. The aim of the present chapter is not to prove the sufficiency of Japan's international contribution but rather to demonstrate that Japan's changing international behavior has been firmly grounded in its own domestic dynamics. Japan does not react to external pressures. If Japan appears to react to external pressures, there is always a reason and logic behind such a reaction.

If my assessment above is correct, one important conclusion can be drawn. That is, one should be able to predict that the expansion of Japan's role and commitments in the international community is likely to continue for the foreseeable future. Japan's international behavior is not an idiosyncratic reaction but rather is structurally anchored in the domestic political-economy context. For that reason, it is unlikely that Japan's foreign policy will reverse its course for some time.

Notes

1. During the 1990s, as a reaction to the predominance of the Waltzian systemic analysis of international relations of the previous decades, several theoretical strands blossomed to focus on the interaction between the domestic political process and foreign policy making. The analysis of the present chapter corresponds to these intellectual trends.

2. See Blaker, "Evaluating Japan's Diplomatic Performance"; Purrington, "Tokyo's Policy Responses."

3. Online database search was used. For consistency I used morning editions of *Asahi Shimbun* printed in Tokyo, excluding local pages.

4. The discussion of international contribution also took place in other forms of publications, including books written by influential Japanese politicians during the early 1990s. Although they differed in their view of the appropriate scope and exact details of international contribution, these books generally reflected upon the post–Gulf War legislative debate during the 1991 extraordinary and 1992 ordinary Diet sessions, during which the so-called peacekeeping operations (PKO) bills finally passed authorizing the Japanese Self-Defense Force participation in the UN peacekeeping operations. See Ozawa, *Nihon Kaizō Keikaku;* Takemura, *Chiisaku tomo Kirari to Hikaru Kuni Nippon;* Gotoda, *Sei to Kan;* and Hashimoto, *Vision of Japan.*

5. To be sure, the earlier usage of these terms was largely in the context of emphasizing Japan as "a member of the West(ern alliance)" or "a member of the liberal-democratic world." This emphasis faded away with the ending of the Cold War.

6. The Ministry of Foreign Affairs began publishing an annual report, *Waga Kuni no Seifu Kaihatsu Enjo,* in 1984, but it was not until 1994 that this report was renamed as the white paper (*Hakusho*). For the sake of simplicity, I use the term *white paper* consistently.

7. These two politicians played a critical role in ending the Liberal Democratic Party's one-party dominance in 1993, although they parted ways in later years.

8. As Ozawa wrote: "How can Japan, which so depends on world peace and

stability, seek to exclude a security role from its international contributions? For many people, the thought of Japan playing any sort of role in the security arena conjures up images of a rearmed, militarist Japan. But this is, quite simply, not an issue of militarization or aspirations to military superpower status. It is a question of Japan's responsible behavior in the international community. We need to think rationally about this and develop a system in which Japan can assume appropriate responsibility" (Ozawa, *Nihon Kaizō Keikaku*, 95).

9. See Takemura, *Chiisaku tomo Kirari to Hikaru Kuni Nippon*.

10. My comment on this point was inspired by discussion with Mike Mochizuki.

11. In some instances (as in the case of government publications), the term *contribution* is used following the phrase "to the international community" (*Kokusai Shakai e no*). This modification alone, however, is not helpful without further clarifying for what aspects or what kind of activities of the international community such a contribution is intended.

12. For a similar view from the realists' standpoint, see Kōsaka, "Reisen-go no Shin-Sekai Chitsujo to Nippon no 'Koken.'"

13. For the classic statement of this view, see Calder, "Japanese Foreign Economic Policy Formation." See also Lincoln, *Japan's New Global Role;* and Blaker, "Evaluating Japan's Diplomatic Performance." For dissenting or more nuanced evaluations, see Yasutomo, *The New Multilateralism in Japan's Foreign Policy;* Hirata, "Japan as a Reactive State?"; and Miyashita, "Gaiatsu and Japan's Foreign Aid."

14. Waltz, *Man, the State, and War;* Waltz, *Theory of International Politics.*

15. According to classic works in this tradition, such as Kant and Lenin, as well as more recent studies centered on "democratic peace" (e.g., Doyle, "Kant, Liberal Legacies, and Foreign Affairs"; Doyle, *Ways of War and Peace;* Russett, *Grasping the Democratic Peace;* Schultz, "Domestic Opposition and Signaling in International Crises"; Schultz, "Do Democratic Institutions Constrain or Inform?"), the domestic regime characteristics matter in determining the state's foreign policy behavior and thus ultimately the level of stability in the international system. For the problems of states' commitments and international cooperation, see Cowhey, "Domestic Institutions and the Credibility of International Commitments"; Milner, *Interests, Institutions, and Information;* and Martin, *Democratic Commitments.*

16. See the classic work of Rogowski, *Commerce and Coalitions,* which argued that the changing power distribution in the international system affected the domestic coalition patterns and thus states' preferences and strategies in their foreign economic policies. See also Keohane and Milner, *Internationalization and Domestic Politics.*

17. Garrett and Lange, "Internationalization, Institutions, and Political Change."

18. As a result of the bureaucratic reorganization in January 2001, the familiar name Tsūsan Shō (shortened from Tsūshō Sangyō Shō) disappeared, and the ministry was renamed Keizai Sangyō Shō, or the Ministry of Economy, Trade, and Industry. Because my discussion is concerned primarily with the activities and changes of this ministry prior to this reorganization, I use the acronym MITI throughout this chapter.

19. The evidence and argument below draw from a more general analysis of MITI's change in Kohno, "A Changing Ministry of International Trade and Industry (MITI)."

20. Johnson, *MITI and Japanese Miracle.*

21. See Prestowitz, *Trading Places;* and Johnson, "Trade, Revisionism, and the Future of Japanese-American Relations."

22. *Nihon Keizai Shimbun,* August 9, 1998; *Nihon Keizai Shimbun,* August 15, 1998.

23. Callon, *Divided Sun.*

24. Searight, "MITI and Multilateralism," 5–6.

25. *Asahi Shimbun,* December 13, 1998.

26. Ōtake, *Adenauā to Yoshida Shigeru;* Ōtake, *Saigunbi to Nashonarizumu.*

27. Cf. Murakami, "The Age of New Middle Mass Politics."

28. Ōtake, *Nihon Seiji no Tairitsu-Jiku,* 25.

29. Schoppa, *Bargaining with Japan.*

30. Ōtake, "Political Realignment and Policy Conflict," 136.

31. Kohno, "Electoral Origins of Japanese Socialists' Stagnation."

32. See Kohno, *Japan's Postwar Party Politics,* esp. chap. 8, for the transfer of power from the LDP to non-LDP coalition government in 1993, during which the reform took place. For the institutional details of the reform itself and its consequences, see Christensen, "Electoral Reform in Japan"; and Kohno, "Nihon ni okeru Heiritsu-sei Dōnyū no Kōzai."

33. The existing literature that discusses the JSP's reversal of foreign policy orientation, including Murayama's own memoir (Murayama, *Sōja-no*), usually describes it as a sudden decision made personally by Murayama himself. The conventional interpretation also emphasizes that Murayama only reluctantly accepted the constitutionality of the US-Japan alliance and Self-Defense Force when he was about to form a government. As is clear from the main text, I disagree with these interpretations to the extent that I believe that the JSP's decision was motivated by its electoral concerns under the newly adopted single-member competition. The JSP's abandonment of unarmed neutralism thus reflected a positive, forward-looking choice based on the interests of the party as a whole and was not simply a product of Murayama's personal decision.

34. Kohno, "Japanese Defense Policy Making."

| Part 1 |
Security Policy

| 3 |

War Renunciation, Article 9, and Security Policy

Jitsuo Tsuchiyama

The debate on whether Japan should revise Article 9 of the constitution, the renunciation of war clause, has come back once again. The September 11, 2001, terrorist attacks on the World Trade Center towers and the Pentagon destroyed the sense of security that had existed in post–Cold War Japanese society. Responding to this crisis, the Diet of Japan passed the Anti-Terrorism Special Measures Law (ATSML), the so-called antiterrorism bill, in October 2001. The new law allows the SDF to operate in noncombat areas, provide fuel and supplies to US forces and those of other countries, transport weapons and ammunition by sea, provide medical care to wounded soldiers, and help refugees.

The debate on that legislation attracted attention to the limitations that Article 9 presented. The progressives, including the Social Democratic Party of Japan (SDPJ) and the Japan Communist Party (JCP), pointed out that the antiterrorism law violated the constitutional ban on the exercise of Japan's right to collective self-defense, since SDF troops would be working with US military forces. The conservatives said that the government was avoiding a review (and revision) of its constitutional interpretation that would allow Japan to exercise the collective self-defense.

As the administration of Koizumi Junichirō submitted the so-called emergency legislation bills to the Diet in April 2002 and the Bush administration's move to launch a "preemptive defense" attack on Iraq became an immediate concern for Japanese policymakers, the debate on Article 9 received further attention in the fall of 2002. In 2003 the Japanese government took further steps—two controversial laws were put into force. The military emergency law set out procedural guidelines for a response to a military attack against Japan. The other law, the Law Concerning Special

Measures on Humanitarian and Reconstruction Assistance (LCSMHRA), authorized the dispatch of SDF troops to Iraq. Even though the Democratic Party of Japan (DPJ) supported the military emergency law, it opposed the dispatch of SDF to Iraq on constitutional grounds. At the same time, the increasing levels of anxiety caused by such crises as the Gulf War and North Korea's Taepodong missile launch strengthened the voices in favor of constitutional revision.

The debates over constitutional revision have been a controversial issue in Japanese politics, and they have many aspects: nationalists support revision because they consider the 1947 constitution as a symbol of US-dominated occupation, so that they suggest reinstating the emperor as a head of state; liberalists oppose revising the constitution because they expect the constitution to promote Japan's democratization. Not surprisingly, Article 9 has been the most controversial issue since its inception. For almost six decades, conservatives have regarded Article 9 as a heavy constraint in conducting an active foreign policy,[1] whereas progressives have regarded it as the principal foreign policy guideline. Yet the great irony has been that since the conservatives (LDP) were in power, they had to conduct foreign policy based on Article 9 even though their party platform called for constitutional revision. They also shrewdly used Article 9 as an excuse to water down Japan's involvement in international crises during the 1960s and 1970s.

Opposition parties, on the other hand, have used Article 9 to attack the government's foreign policy. In retrospect, their pacifism functioned as an ideology and norm of nonintervention principles in world affairs. As a result, most of Japan's key foreign policy principles were negative in nature: no dispatch of the SDF overseas, nonnuclear principles, no export of weapons, no offensive military doctrine and arms, and so on. There was no serious debate in Japan on what Japan should do for international security prior to the Gulf War (1990–1991). Partly as a result of Japan's geopolitical, cultural, and historical situation, Japanese have almost not succeeded in conceptualizing Japan's national interest in terms of international security compared with the foreign policies of other advanced countries.

With the end of the Cold War and the outbreak of the Gulf War, however, the Japanese public came to realize that the renunciation of war alone could not bring international peace. From the early 1990s onward, Japanese began to think about their role in international security. The crises and negotiations that followed the Gulf War—including the North Korean nuclear crisis, China's missile crisis vis-à-vis Taiwan, the US-Japan negotiation for the new Guidelines for the US-Japan Defense Cooperation, the "Taepodong shock" of August 1998, and the September 11 attack—provided Japan further chances to shift its foreign policy from a low-profile and exclusively defensive-oriented defense policy known as the Yoshida doctrine to a more active security policy with closer ties to the United States. Perhaps no developed democratic country has debated "international contribution" as much as Japan has. During the processes of Japan's policy shifts in the mid-1990s and in its debates on international contribution, revision of Article 9 became one of the central issues for Japanese politics.

As we try to deal with Japan's security policy, we cannot understand it without referring to its domestic norms, especially Article 9 of the constitution. In fact, Article 9 has been the most significant norm of postwar Japan's security politics, whether one likes it or not. Either in spite of or because of this, it is probably true that no other country has experienced such a wide gap between norm and reality in security policymaking as has postwar Japan.

This chapter addresses the questions of (1) why and how Japan came to adopt Article 9, (2) what sort of normative problem Japan had when the new reality known as the Cold War emerged immediately after the new constitution had gone into effect and when the US-Japan Security Treaty was concluded in 1951, (3) how the Japanese government adjusted to these realities without amending Article 9, (4) what Japan's future options are to resolve its Article 9 problem, and (5) what Japan should do with this matter in the new era emerging since the post–Cold War era, a new era in which we are fighting a war against international terrorism.

After analyzing all those points, this chapter suggests that Japan is now facing a political situation that makes a constitutional revision more likely than ever before and that the growing support for constitutional revision does not necessarily mean there is yet a strong national as well as international consensus to revise Article 9. The chapter also looks at whether Japan's increasing international contribution to regional as well as global security requires Article 9 revision.

Norm of War Renunciation

Methodologically, this chapter takes an approach that is now called constructivism in a very broad sense, focusing on the roles of norms both in international and domestic politics. Generally, norms are defined as "shared expectations about appropriate behavior" held by the members of a society.[2] Norms have action-guiding functions: (1) to provide policy guidance, (2) to impose constraints on or rule out or prescribe the policies that may contradict norms, and (3) to justify as well as legitimize actions that abide by norms. Norms do not always take the form of rule, but all rules are norms. A constitution is the very basic norm that governs the state's behavior.

The idea of renouncing war is an old norm that has been discussed since the early 1700s. To borrow from Martha Finnemore and Kathryn

Sikkink, Saint-Pierre (1658–1743) and Immanuel Kant (1724–1804) are "norm entrepreneurs" in this case.[3] In his "Perpetual Peace," Kant wrote that "standing arms shall be entirely abolished in the course of time."[4] Reflecting this liberal philosophy, in September 1791, just after the French Revolution, France adopted an article in its constitution that renounced war.[5] Despite these earlier efforts, the norm of war renunciation did not gain larger support until the twentieth century, because wars had generally been accepted as a national policy to gain power and security.

Before and during World War I, some states adopted a war renunciation clause in their constitutions, including Brazil in 1911 (Article 34), Portugal in 1911 (Article 26), and Uruguay in 1917 (Article 79). In the international arena, one of the most significant steps to internationalize the norm of war renunciation was taken in the Kellogg-Briand Pact (General Treaty for Renunciation of War as an Instrument of National Policy) of 1928. Adopting a phrase from the Kellogg-Briand Pact, several countries renounced war in their constitutions afterward: Spain in 1931 (Article 6), the Philippines in 1935 (Paragraph 3 of Article 2), Burma in 1947 (Article 211), and Italy in 1947. Thus, in that sense, the Japanese constitution can be viewed as another one in that trend.

Construction of the New Constitution

Soon after World War II ended in the Pacific, Japan was occupied by the Allies, led by General Douglas MacArthur, the supreme commander for allied powers (SCAP). On October 4, 1945, the MacArthur-Konoe meeting was held, during which MacArthur suggested that Prince Konoe Fumimaro, vice premier in the Higashikuni Naruhiko cabinet, take the initiative in revising the Meiji constitution. Konoe, who had probably in fact gone to MacArthur's office to find out if he had been listed as a war criminal, was relieved to hear what MacArthur told him. A few days later, Konoe asked Professor Sasaki Sōichi of the University of Kyoto to draft the new constitution, and on October 11 Konoe himself was appointed by the Office of the Lord Privy Seal to be an "unattached Court official" (*goyōgakari*) to draft the new constitution. Yet, the US media became critical of the idea that people like Konoe were working on constitutional revision, owing to their alleged war guilt. For example, an editorial in the *New York Times* (October 26, 1945) stated that if Konoe could draft the new constitution, even a person like Hermann Göring could become a US president. Japanese newspapers carried those critical articles. Under these circumstances, SCAP issued a press release on November 1 denying any connection with Konoe. It stated that "SCAP has only conveyed the message to Konoe who acted on behalf of Premier Higashikuni." It also said, "however, since the Higashikuni government resigned en masse on the next day (October 5), the relations between prince and SCAP relating to this matter ended." On December 16, the day of his planned arrest as a war criminal, Konoe committed suicide.

In parallel with Konoe's efforts authorized by the Office of the Lord Privy Seal, another group was working for the revision of the constitution in the Shidehara Kijūrō government under a special cabinet minister, Matsumoto Jōji. Again, the Matsumoto Committee's efforts were practically forced to end, owing to the scoop that appeared in the *Mainichi Shimbun* of February 1, 1946, leaking one of the drafts prepared by the Matsumoto Committee. That draft was criticized by Japanese newspapers as being too "conservative" in nature, in part because it left the status of the emperor essentially unchanged. Since it was perfect timing for SCAP to take over the role of constitutional revision, there have been speculations as to whether the scoop was pure "accident."[6] Then, on February 3, MacArthur decided that the Government Section (GS) of SCAP would draft a new constitution, and MacArthur handed a memorandum (now called the "MacArthur Notes") to the chief of the Government Section, Brigadier General Courtney Whitney. Among the three points mentioned in the memo, point two stated:

> War as a sovereign right of the nation is abolished. Japan renounces it as an instrumentality for settling its disputes and even for preserving its security. It relies upon the higher ideals which are now stirring the world for its defense and its protection.
>
> No Japanese Army, Navy, or Air Force will ever be authorized and no rights of belligerency will ever be conferred upon any Japanese force.[7]

Starting on February 4, twenty-seven members of GS committed to drafting a new constitution by February 10. Although the steering committee headed by Charles Kades was composed of three lawyers, no specialist of constitutional law was among them. On February 13, SCAP officials, headed by Whitney, handed the draft prepared by GS to Japanese government representatives, including Foreign Minister Yoshida Shigeru, Minister of the State Matsumoto, and a deputy chief of the Central Liaison Office, Shirasu Jirō, a protégé of Yoshida. The Japanese side was shocked not only by the war renunciation clause in the draft but also by Whitney's comment that general headquarters could not answer for whatever might happen to *"the person of the Emperor"* if the draft were not accepted (emphasis added).[8] Thus, the safety of the emperor and the Japanese government's acceptance of the draft presented by SCAP were tacitly but tightly linked.

As noted earlier, the draft was written within a week. Ideas and phrases were drawn from many sources. The US Constitution, Abraham Lincoln's Gettysburg Address, the Tehran Conference declaration, the US Declaration of Independence, and the UN Charter were used in writing the preamble; the US Constitution was used for Chapter 3 covering civil and human rights; the phrase describing the emperor as "the symbol of the state and of the unity of the people" (Chapter 1) was drawn from the Westminster Charter of 1931; and the Kellogg-Briand Pact and the UN Charter were the basis for Chapter 2, Article 9 (war renunciation), a most important point. The new constitution was also drawn from the English translation of the Meiji constitution; Itō Miyoji, the translator, had been involved in drafting the Meiji constitution.[9]

Though minor changes were accepted, the basic form of the draft of February 13 was never changed. The Shidehara government published the draft of the new constitution as its own proposal on March 6, and then MacArthur issued a statement of "approval" of the draft. In June, the Yoshida government presented the Constitution Revision Bill to the Diet, and the emperor promulgated the new constitution on November 3. The Japanese public's reactions to the new constitution were mostly favorable, even if we take into consideration the fact that all publications were subject to the strict censorship of SCAP. Thus a new norm began in postwar Japan, and it was accepted by the majority of people. To use the words of Richard Finn, who was in Tokyo in the capacity of a foreign service officer as part of MacArthur's staff, "MacArthur and GS acted forcefully to win acceptance of their draft constitution," and they succeeded.[10]

The Philippine Analogy for the War Renunciation Clause

The final version of Article 9 of the new Japanese constitution reads:

> Aspiring sincerely to an international peace based on justice and order, the Japanese people have forever renounced war as a sovereign right of the nation and the threat or use of force as means of settling international dispute.
>   In order to accomplish the aim of the preceding paragraph, land, sea, and air forces, as well as other war potential, will never be maintained. The right of belligerency of the state will not be recognized.

Here, the following two points are of great interest. First, Article 9 does not include the phrase that was in the MacArthur's Notes of February 3, which prohibited a war "even for preserving its own security." This phrase was excluded in the February 13 draft by GS and was never restored. This is one of the reasons that people believed that Japan's right of self-defense was preserved. Charles Kades, who wrote the draft of Chapter 2, Article 9, often stated afterward that he intentionally excluded that phrase to make clear that the constitution did not deprive Japan of its right of self-defense.[11]

Second, the first phrase of Article 9 was notably a replica of the first article of the Kellogg-Briand Pact; it also borrowed words from paragraph 4 of Article 2 of the UN Charter. The Kellogg-Briand Pact connection has two implications here. For one thing, if a Kellogg-Briand Pact analogy were justified, it is reasonable to assume that the right of self-defense had been preserved even when the draft was written. Another thing is that there was a similar case in which a constitution adopted the phrase from the Kellogg-Briand Pact prior to the Japanese case—that was the Philippine constitution of 1935.

When the Philippines became a US commonwealth as a transition to independence, it adopted a war renunciation clause in its constitution, making the US president's approval necessary in order for the Philippines to go to war. Tacit understanding of that clause is that the Philippines' right to fight a war with foreign states, the United States in particular, would never be authorized. At that time, MacArthur was there as military adviser to the commonwealth government of the Philippines, and Whitney was practicing law in Manila (1927–1939) before he became a member of MacArthur's staff in 1940. Considering their backgrounds, it is quite reasonable to suppose that both MacArthur and Whitney had the "Philippine analogy" in mind when they included the war renunciation clause in the draft of Japan's new constitution.[12] Thus, the norm of seventeenth-century Europe became internationalized in the twentieth century and then became a domestic norm in some non-European countries, such as the Philippines and Japan, through US will and hands.

Controversies

Whose Initiative?

Two of the controversies on the drafting processes of Article 9 need to be examined. As has been suggested in the preceding section, this chapter is based on the assumption that the effort to include Article 9 originated with MacArthur (and, quite possibly, Whitney), not with Premier Shidehara Kijūrō, to whom MacArthur later gave credit. Shidehara, who signed the Kellogg-Briand Pact as a foreign minister, had a critical view of the military. According to MacArthur's memoirs, Shidehara told MacArthur on January 24, 1946, that he was planning to introduce a war renunciation clause in the revised constitution.[13] This is not convincing, however, because it would have been practically impossible for Shidehara to talk about war renunciation at that particular point. The Matsumoto Committee was still busy drafting the new constitution at that time, and Shidehara had never discussed war renunciation in the committee's meetings.

There are at least two reasons why MacArthur may have wanted the American people to believe that Shidehara took the initiative. First, the Japanese should be the ones who drafted the Japanese constitution. If SCAP drafted it, that action would be a violation of Article 43 of the Hague Treaty of 1907. Second, the timing when MacArthur started to suggest that Shidehara took the initiative appears to be very crucial. MacArthur first made such a statement during the US Senate hearings on his dismissal, held May 3–7, 1951. There, MacArthur stated as follows: Responding to Shidehara, who expressed his desire to introduce a war renunciation clause in a new constitution at the January 24, 1946, meeting, MacArthur told Shidehara that people might not accept war renunciation, and it was more likely to be subjected to ridicule. Probably, MacArthur had to say it in 1951, because he had been accused of policy failures caused by the unexpected war going on on the Korean peninsula.

As we will see later, MacArthur did more than Washington expected in 1946. The US disarmament and demilitarization policy of Japan in September 1945 was to apply during the occupation period.[14] In this sense, MacArthur's decision to include a no-war clause for an indefinite period without having communicated with Washington was "an arrogant act."[15] Looking back at the process of drafting the constitution, Justin Williams (chief of the Parliamentary and Political Division, GS, 1946–1952) stated that if he "had participated in the drafting process, [he] might have been against [the no-war clause]."[16] Article 9 was a curious mixture of MacArthur's military realism and his idealism: the intention of disarming Japan was realistic, but at the same time the article also reflected, in the opinion of Charles Kades, MacArthur's peculiarly antimilitaristic idealism.[17]

A War for Self-Defense Permitted?

Another controversy is related to the question of self-defense. Responding to a question from Nosaka Sanzō, leader of the Communist Party, as to whether Japan should renounce even a war for self-defense, Prime Minister Yoshida stated before the Diet on June 29, 1946, that "the new Constitution would prohibit all war including a war for self-defense, because most wars in the past have been waged in the name of self-defense."[18]

Whether or not Japan is able to fight a war for self-defense has been a central concern in dealing with the so-called Ashida amendment. On July 29, 1946, Ashida Hitoshi, the chairman of the lower house subcommittee to review the draft constitution, proposed to add a few words at the beginning of the second phrase that would read "*For the above purpose*, land, sea and air forces, as well as other war potential, will never be maintained. The right of belligerency of the state will not be recognized" (emphasis added).[19]

Conventionally, it has been explained that the added words "for the above purpose" in the second paragraph made possible an interpretation that it did not prohibit all sorts of war as a means of settling international disputes; that is, armament for self-defense could be permissible. Ashida himself, in his book published in November 1946, said that was the intention of his amendment.[20] This story was repeatedly heard afterward. Neither the document in the Diet nor Ashida's diary indicated such thinking, however, at least as of July 29. Analyzing the records of the participants in that amendment, recent studies have revealed that the story may not be exactly true.[21] It is most probable that Ashida offered the amendment without realizing that it could make such an interpretation possible at that particular point. For example, Kades stated in 1981: "Neither in his meeting with me when I said there was no objection to his amendment nor when he presented them to the House of Representatives do I recall Ashida's mentioning either the right of self-defense or a defensive war."[22]

Nevertheless, at least three Japanese bureaucrats—Kanamori Tokujirō, Iriye Toshirō, and Satō Tatsuo, all of them in the Cabinet Legislation Bureau (CLB)—realized that the Ashida amendment left room for interpretation.[23] Ashida may have come to realize the implication of his amendment for the first time when Satō told Ashida on August 20 that the amendment could invite SCAP's misunderstanding that Japan was conspiring to rearm Japan.

Two other persons who also became aware of this implication at the early stage were the Chinese representative to the Far Eastern Commission and Kades. To avoid such a "misunderstanding," for instance, Kades changed the English translation of the phrase at the top of the second paragraph from "for the above purpose" to "in order to accomplish the aim of the preceding paragraph."[24] These facts suggest that only a few people understood the possibility of interpreting the Ashida amendment as reserving the right of self-defense. With the exception of Ashida, these individuals did not publicly speak of their interpretations for the next few years.

The tacit interpretation of the Ashida amendment was made public after the war broke out in Korea. Then a story or myth was gradually formulated, retroactive to July 1946, by the Japanese government officials and the former SCAP officials, to wit: on July 29, 1946, Ashida had purposefully worded the amendment to establish a loophole for self-defense, and it had been tacitly understood among key policymakers, including SCAP, that armament for self-defense was still permissible.

Contradictions

The Changes in 1947

Though Article 9 is sometimes called a child of the Cold War, I do not take this view, simply because the Cold War had not really emerged yet during the first half of 1946. Rather, Article 9 is a mixed product of the "power vacuum" that existed in East Asia and a legacy of Franklin Delano Roosevelt's Wilsonian idealism.

By the time the new constitution went into force in May 1947, however, the international scene had been shifted to a world that was distant from the ideal international society described in the preamble of the new constitution. Japan was still suffering from heavy damage caused by the war, especially the loss of the lives of 3 million of its citizens. In China, the Kuomintang was at the last stage of power. All of the European powers, including the Soviet Union, were busy rebuilding their political and economic systems. The US-Soviet alliance faded out with the end of World War II, and their relationships had become fragile since then. Overall, only the United States had maintained a substantial margin of strength.

The GS officers who drafted the new constitution might have believed the logic that said that the shifts in norms would change domestic regimes and that if norms expanded internationally, the structure of international politics could eventually be transformed. In fact, Article 9 did have a significant impact, at least on Japanese politics in general and security policy in particular.

In contrast to the logic on which the constitution was drafted, the international politics in 1947–1948 were being transformed by a different logic—geopolitical thinking based on the balance of power. One of the first advocates who saw Japan's role in the possible US-Soviet rivalry was Nicholas John Spykman of Yale University, who believed that "there is no real security in being just as strong as a potential enemy; there is security only in being a little stronger," and wrote in 1942 that "if the balance of power in the Far East is to be preserved in the future as in the present, the United States will have to adopt a similar protective policy toward Japan."[25] This is the basic approach on which US containment policy was constructed. George F. Kennan, the architect of this policy, and his people, for example, wrote in Policy Planning Staff (PPS) 13 (November 6, 1947) that "all in all, our policy must be directed toward restoring a balance of power in Europe and Asia."[26]

In the summer of 1947, Japan took a diplomatic initiative that is worthy of mention here. Recognizing the potential rivalry between the United States and the Soviet Union, Ashida, now a foreign minister of the Katayama Tetsu Socialist Party–led coalition government, handed a memorandum to US officials in Tokyo on three occasions in the summer of 1947. The last memo, submitted in September, stated that Japan would allow the United States to retain its military bases in Japan after the peace treaty was concluded. Nothing came of these memos, however. After he returned to power, Yoshida followed this line of foreign policy introduced by Ashida.

Usually, Ashida's diplomatic move is considered as a balance-of-power calculation. But it also reflected the logic of the norm—Article 9. Once Japanese public opinion had accepted Article 9, the main forces that guaranteed Japan's safety became the US military forces stationed in Japan. On the one hand, Japan had a war renunciation clause; on the other hand, it had US forces. That political environment in 1947 became the prototype of postwar Japan's security policy. The Ashida memo, mentioned above, tried to seek the possibility of extending that prototype following Japan's independence. It was not only a strategically calculated move but also a normatively appropriate option. Despite the fact that the US officials did not accept the Ashida memo in 1947, both Japan and the United States found mutual interests in pursuing the policy prescribed in that memo three years later.

US-Japanese Security Treaty of 1951

The influence of GS on the SCAP began to decline in the summer of 1948, whereas the G-2 (Intelligence Section) headed by Charles Willoughby gained influence on SCAP. Guided by Shirasu, the second Yoshida administration gradually formed a "coalition" with G-2, which shaped the US-Japan alliance.

In the spring of 1950, a couple of months before the outbreak of war in Korea, Yoshida sent a message similar to the Ashida memorandum to Washington through the hands of another of his protégés, Finance Minister Ikeda Hayato. Ikeda expressed the desire for a peace treaty as soon as possible and told Joseph M. Dodge, fiscal adviser to SCAP in Washington, that the Japanese government would offer the US government permission for its military presence once the peace treaty was concluded. Japan's strategy was clear: Japan would allow the United States to use its military bases; in return, Japan would expect to get a US security guarantee. A month later, the Korean War broke out.

The outbreak of war in Korea proved that the US military bases in Japan were crucial for conducting the war in Korea and that Japan should be rearmed because occupation forces in Japan should be transferred to Korea. On July 8, 1950, MacArthur issued a de facto order to the Japanese government to create the National Police Reserve (NPR) of 75,000 men. It was ironic that MacArthur, who had disarmed Japan, now had to rearm it. Neither MacArthur nor the Japanese government tried to amend Article 9, however. Because MacArthur had made the amendment procedure in the constitution (Article 96) very tight in order to be sure that the new constitution could not easily be amended once the occupation ended, it might have been difficult if not impossible to amend it, even for such strong leaders as MacArthur and Yoshida, had they wanted to do so. The NPR was reorganized as the National Safety Force (NSF) about two years later and became the SDF in 1954.

As suggested earlier, there was a wide gap between the world that drafters of the constitution had assumed immediately after World War II and the actual world that drifted into the Cold War. As a consequence, Japan's security policy has suffered from the contradiction between the existence of Article 9 and the SDF. For example, constitutionally Japan does not have any war potential. In reality, however, it is obvious in everybody's eyes that it does have such potential. The Yoshida administration had publicized the fact that Japan did not have any war potential because war potential meant the capacity to fight a "modern war," and in those terms neither the NPR nor the NSF possessed war potential. The Hatoyama Ichirō administration stated a different view from that of its predecessors. It took the position that the SDF was not unconstitutional, because the possession of a "minimum level" of the military forces for self-defense was not unconstitutional. Subsequently, the Kishi Nabusuke administration took the position that Article 9 prohibited such military forces as were offensive in nature (e.g., ICBMs), so that the SDF was not unconstitutional as long as it did not have offensive weapons and doctrine.

Overall, Article 9 has been a constraint on the remilitarization of Japanese society. Japan has been reluctant to use force even for self-defense, to exercise the right of collective defense, to go nuclear, and to make large expenditures for defense. Because of Japan's constitutional restrictions, Japan's alliance policies have been constrained, preventing it from undertaking what an ally is usually expected to do. The US-Japan Security Treaty of September 1951 reflected Japan's unique situation. The Security Treaty stated in its preamble:

> On the coming into force of that Treaty [of Peace] Japan will not have the effective means to exercise its inherent right of self-defense because it has been disarmed.
> In exercise of these rights [of individual and collective self-defense], Japan desires, as a provisional arrangement for its defense, that the United States of America should maintain armed forces of its own in and about Japan so as to deter armed attack upon Japan.

And Article 1 of the treaty reads: "Japan grants, and the United States of America accepts, the right, upon the coming into force of the Treaty of Peace and this Treaty, to dispose United States land, air and sea forces in and about Japan." The treaty did not say anything about collective military action between the two. Considering the basic structure and content of the treaty, one may consider that it was not an alliance in the correct sense. In the words of Nishimura Kumao, head of the Treaty Bureau of the Ministry of Foreign Affairs at the time, it was more like an interim base-lending agreement. In fact, the treaty was expected to hold good for only fifteen years during the negotiations. Contrary to their expectation, the basic form of arrangement made in 1951 has remained intact for more than fifty years, though there have been some changes.

The Process of Deconstruction

As we have seen, Article 9 and the US-Japan Security Treaty have been the two central pillars of Japan's security policy, which is sometimes called the Article 9–Security Treaty regime. This policy orientation is also called the Yoshida doctrine, named after Premier Yoshida. Yet, it has been clear that contradictions existed between the two ideologies, whose "cultures" are almost diametrically opposed to each other. In short, Article 9 discourages Japan's use of force for conflict resolution, whereas the treaty encourages Japan to use it under certain conditions.

The differences in these two reasonings were quite clear, and Japan's domestic forces were also clearly divided by the line drawn between them; the conservatives were for the security treaty, and the opposition parties were for Article 9. Between these reasonings, the Japanese public has suffered from what can be described as a cognitive dissonance problem: the public generally supports the SDF, yet they feel that the SDF is unconstitutional when they read Article 9 literally.

To cope with this problem, the Japanese government has skillfully sought a way to reconcile Article 9 with reality by encroaching on the perimeter of Article 9 step by step, starting with the Ashida amendment, which made it possible to read Article 9 as reserving Japan's right of self-defense. By then, the forces for self-defense had twice come to be viewed as not being "war potential": once in 1950 (the time the NPR was created) and again in 1954 (the time the NPR became the SDF). The security treaty of 1951 also recognized Japan's right to collective self-defense, though the Japanese government since 1956 has officially maintained the position that Japan cannot exercise collective self-defense because of constitutional restrictions. One of the reasons why the government adopted such a position probably was the fact that the exercise of collective self-defense would likely require the dispatch of troops abroad, which was considered historically and politically unacceptable. Therefore, when the House of Councilors passed the Self-Defense Law in June 1954, they also passed a resolution that stated that the SDF could not be sent abroad because of constitutional restrictions. Ever since, this has been the most painful issue in postwar Japan, dividing Japanese foreign policy elites and the public into two camps: the "constitution school" and the "security school." The Japanese government has had to maintain a delicate balance between those two norms.

During the first two decades after the war, the constitution school had the stronger influence on Japan's foreign policymaking, in part because of Japanese "fear of entrapment" in US conflicts in Asia. As a result, most of Japan's key foreign policy principles put heavy constraints on its security policy: no dispatch of the SDF overseas, no offensive military doctrines and armaments, no export of weapons, and no nuclear principles. Hence Japan's security policy had been severely restricted by Article 9.

In the early 1970s, however, the security school began to gain influence, since, to put it simply, the alliance dilemma had begun to shift from the "fear of entrapment" to the "fear of abandonment." This shift occurred because a series of events that took place during the first half of the 1970s changed Japanese perception of US commitment to Asian security.[27]

Those events and moves stimulated "the fear of abandonment" among the Japanese foreign policy establishment. As a result, the Japanese government took several security policy initiatives, two of which became the National Defense Program Outline (NDPO) of 1976 and the Guidelines for the US-Japan Defense Cooperation of 1978. Japan's host nation's support, the so-called sympathy budget that made it possible for Japan to expand financial support for the US military presence in Japan, also started in 1978. In this context, the debates on the exercise of collective defense quietly emerged.

The second wave of the debates on collective self-defense took place in the early 1980s, during the new Cold War period. For example, the Suzuki Zenkō administration committed to protect sea lines of communication (SLOC) to 1,000 miles from Japan. The Nakasone Yasuhiro administration accelerated Japan's military buildup, including a program known as the Mid-Term Defense Estimates (MTDF) for 1986–1990 under the name of "burden sharing." Nakasone's decision to remove the Diet's resolution limiting Japan's defense expenditures to 1 percent of gross national product (GNP) also served as a symbolic gesture toward taking on a larger burden.

The third wave started after the Gulf crisis erupted in an abrupt manner in August 1990 and escalated into a war in January 1991. At the end of the same year, the Soviet Union suddenly collapsed, meaning that the United States and Japan lost the key rationale of their alliance. Both the United States and Japan faced difficulties adjusting to those changes. Partly because of the loss of the common threat of the Soviet Union, the fact that Japan's bubble economy (and mercantilist policies) reached its zenith at the same time came to be regarded as a new threat to the West and to the US economy in particular. All of those events led to US frustration with Japanese free riding. Under those circumstances, the Japanese response to the Gulf War was most severely criticized by the United States as "too little and too late." Thus, Japanese fear of abandonment reached a critical point.

As the Cold War ended, the domestic confrontation between the Right and the Left gradually began to evaporate. In response to US criticism, Japan sent minesweepers to the Gulf in April 1991, passed the International Peace Cooperation Law in June 1992, and then sent the SDF to Cambodia to participate in the UN peacekeeping activities immediately after that. All of those acts were unprecedented. Thus, the new norms of international cooperation began to prevail over Article 9, which had long prevented Japan from having an active security policy.

For the Japanese, the Gulf crisis was not only an international crisis but also a domestic crisis, because security debates that arose from the crisis destroyed the right (LDP)–left (SDPJ) division over the constitution. Within this context, the revision of Article 9 came to be discussed by the group headed by Ozawa Ichirō, who split the Takeshita faction into two groups and left the LDP to form a coalition government in 1993. In doing so, Ozawa advocated that Japan be a "normal" state, suggesting (1) rewriting Article 9 so as to regain Japan's right to have war potential for self-defense and to exercise the right of collective self-defense, (2) sending the SDF to participate in UN PKO, and (3) gaining a seat as a permanent member of the UN Security Council. In this way the amendment of the constitution and Japan's "international contribution" came to be linked to each other and discussed openly within that context. The Hosokawa Morihiro coalition government, whose principal designer, Ozawa Ichirō, had ended the LDP's thirty-eight-year rule, carried those foreign policy debates over.

The fourth wave of the debate on the exercise of collective self-defense began when the US and Japanese governments started the revision of the Guidelines for the US-Japan Defense Cooperation. The new guidelines revised in 1997 enabled the SDF to extend its rear-area support and search-and-rescue operations to US forces in "situations in areas surrounding Japan," which probably would go beyond the stipulation of Article 6 of the security treaty. The Japanese government was saying that though Article 9 did not permit Japan to send the SDF to foreign land, sea, and airspace, the new guidelines made it possible to dispatch SDF overseas in order to cope with the situation in areas surrounding Japan. The government explained that the SDF was not permitted to use force in those situations. Public opinion indicated a positive response to those policy changes: these developments were understood as a de facto redefinition of the security treaty, and the public reluctantly accepted that the reality Japan faced went beyond the stipulation of Article 9.

The fifth wave of the debate has occurred in the aftermath of the September 11, 2001, attacks on New York and Washington. The ATSML has been in force since October 2001; it provides rear-echelon support measures in noncombat zones for the US military as well as other nations as they fight the "war on terrorism." Behind the push to pass that legislation was the bitter memory of the Gulf War, when Japan's contribution of $13 billion went largely unappreciated.

Less than a month after the attacks, the Japanese government sent SDF C-130 transport airplanes to Pakistan to provide relief support for Afghan refugees by using an existing law concerning cooperation with UN peace-keeping operations and later sent several Maritime Self-Defense Force vessels to the Indian Ocean to conduct "investigation and research" activities at first, then to provide fuel. Thus, the new law cleared the way for the dispatch overseas of Japanese forces to engage in nonmilitary activities in non-combat areas for the first time since the end of World War II. In this sense, it was a watershed in Japan's postwar security policy.

It was still difficult, however, for the Koizumi administration to lift the government's constitutional interpretation ban in order to exercise the right of collective self-defense, despite orchestrated efforts of proconstitutional revision forces such as the *Yomiuri Shimbun*. The government did not move further because it saw that no solid national consensus existed regarding whether the September 11 terrorist attacks on the United States in fact constituted a case in which the government could exercise the right to collective self-defense. There is no doubt that the September 11 attacks have had a significant impact on Japan's debates on security and international contribution. It provided Japan a good opportunity to take a further step toward becoming a more active player. Yet, a significant departure from the current security policy stance based on Article 9 appears to be unlikely; changes are still cautious, gradual, and incremental.

As mentioned earlier, the Koizumi administration proposed the "emergency legislation bill" (the Law Concerning Measures to Ensure National Independence and Security in a Situation of Armed Attack) to the Diet in 2002. The studies on emergency legislation relating to the SDF activities had started in 1977 with Prime Minister Fukuda Takeo's approval. The subject of the studies has been divided into three categories: category 1 (laws under the jurisdiction of the Japan Defense Agency [JDA]), category 2 (laws under the jurisdiction of other ministries), and category 3 (laws not falling clearly under the jurisdiction of any particular ministries). The JDA has emphasized that those studies are being conducted within a framework of the constitution. Hence, it says that martial law and conscription are out of the question. Therefore, the current emergency legislation bill should be carried out within the framework of Article 9 of the constitution, as JDA has said.[28]

Shortly after he became a prime minister, Koizumi said before the Diet: "I believe that it is the duty of the political leadership to consider what kind of structure can be created in the event that the state or the people are exposed to crises and I intend to move forward with consideration on emergency legislation, bearing fully in mind the views expressed by the ruling parties last year."[29] Prime Minister Koizumi repeated these remarks in the Diet in September 2001 by saying, "Be prepared and have no regrets." Though the Diet did not pass the emergency legislation package in 2002, it passed the bills in the following year. In the past, the debates on emergency legislation had been closely tied to constitutional revision. This time around, however, the discussions did not relate directly to concerns about constitutional revision.

To Amend or Not to Amend

The Japanese have ambivalent attitudes vis-à-vis relations between the constitution and security: they now generally accept the constitutionality of the SDF, yet at the same time they want to retain Article 9 as it is. There appear to be at least five groups involved in this contradiction of Japanese constitutional politics. The first two groups are basically against constitutional amendment. The leaders of the first group, who advocate "protecting" Article 9, used to be the SDPJ and the JCP. The SDPJ lost its consistency and credibility, however, once it formed a coalition government with the LDP in 1994 and made compromises on constitutional interpretation matters in order to be in power. In retrospect, it was a tragedy for the SDPJ that the party changed its security policy principles without obtaining agreement with longtime supporters. Later, their voice became even more insignificant, and their foreign policy doctrine, known as "unarmed neutrality," lost its political meaning. As Glenn D. Hook and Gavan McCormack correctly observed, the Socialists feared entrapment, whereas the LDP was inclined to fear abandonment. The appeal of the entrapment argument lost its persuasiveness as a way to oppose the US-Japan alliance with the end of the Cold War and a sudden collapse of the USSR.[30]

The second group includes the moderates in the LDP and many in other political groups, such as the DPJ. They also have supported retaining Article 9 unrevised, and they believe that Japan can conduct meaningful foreign policy without amending Article 9. This is the view often expressed by the *Asahi Shimbun* and by former prime minister Miyazawa Kiichi, who objects to exercising the right to collective self-defense. Responding to the *Yomiuri Shimbun*'s proposal to amend the constitution (to be explained later), the *Asahi Shimbun*'s editorial in May 1995 made a counterproposal for international contribution, composed of six components, including the establishments of International Cooperation Law as well as a Peace Support Force and a reform of the SDF. It emphasized that Article 9 should be retained as it is.[31] Miyazawa shared the basic ideas contained in the *Asahi Shimbun*'s editorial. Though Miyazawa said neither that Japan could not exercise the right to collective self-defense nor that Japan could do it, he said that Japan could not use its military forces outside Japan even under UN auspices.[32] In an interview with the *Asahi*, Miyazawa said, "The new anti-terrorist legislation has nothing to do with Article 9 or the Japan-U.S. Security Treaty, or Japan's right to participate in collective self-defense," since he believed that the September 11 attack itself was not a war, but a criminal, act.[33]

The next three groups generally support constitutional revision, but with different logics. The third group supports the constitutional revision in order to take a larger role in international security and safety fields such as UN peacekeeping activities and antiterrorist operations. According to this group, Japan should be able to use military forces for international conflict resolution, with the constitutional amendment or reinterpretation of Article 9.

A champion of this group was Ozawa Ichirō, the head of the Liberal Party in 1998 and the leader of the DPJ now, who initiated the debate on constitutional revisions in the early 1990s. He proposed adding a third paragraph to Article 9: "The preceding second paragraph does not prevent Japan from exercising its right of self-defense and from maintaining armed forces to exercise that right." Furthermore, Ozawa added a new chapter titled "International Peace," which would have followed Article 9: "The Japanese people should actively contribute to international peace through participating in international peace [-building] activities, for maintaining and restoring the peace and security of international society . . . and through taking every possible means including military."[34]

And yet, the Ozawa proposal had a big presupposition: the creation of a standing UN force. For the constitutional revision alone, his proposal sounded realistic. Considering the feasibility of a standing UN force, however, his prerequisite was too idealistic in the short run. In this connection, some LDP members advocated that Japan should examine Article 9 if Japan wanted a permanent seat on the United Nations Security Council. This logic may also reflect the hope shared by the key figures of the George W. Bush administration, who insisted that a nation wishing to sit permanently on the council must be ready to deploy its military force in the interest of the international society.

The fourth group advocates a constitutional amendment or reinterpretation of Article 9 to make it possible for Japan to exercise the right to collective self-defense, which is expected to enhance the Japanese military as well as diplomatic capability, and to tighten security and diplomatic relations with the United States. This is the position supported by the majority of the LDP, the SDF, and the JDA. They generally view the September 11 attack itself as an act of war, so they believe Japan could exercise the right to collective self-defense just as North Atlantic Treaty Organization (NATO) countries have done.

A leading advocate of this group is former prime minister Nakasone.

His most recent proposal for constitutional revisions was to rewrite the second paragraph of Article 9 to mean that Japan could maintain a minimum level of military forces for self-defense. He also advocated revising Article 9 to stipulate that Japan should be able to exercise its right to collective self-defense, since the alliance relationship would presuppose the exercise of this right to conduct collective defense actions in a crisis. To exercise the right to collective self-defense, he said, the National Security Law could also permit Japan to do so in the case that the constitutional revisions were too difficult.[35]

Nonetheless, we should not take what Nakasone said at his word. What Nakasone was actually saying was much more moderate than his proposal suggested. Nakasone has insisted that Japan can exercise the right to collective self-defense even without revising Article 9. The National Security Law he proposed should be enacted within the framework of Article 9, he said. For Nakasone, constitutional revisions are not an absolute necessity, since the SDF is legitimate and the right of self-defense (collective self-defense included) is retained. Legally, they have never been unconstitutional. Still, however, constitutional revision is desirable, since it has been a source of controversy since its inception.[36]

The most straightforward proposal was made in October 1999 by Hatoyama Yukio, then chairman of the DPJ, perhaps responding to Ozawa's proposal made a month earlier. Hatoyama proposed to rewrite Article 9 to mean that "Japan shall maintain land, sea, and air forces, as well as the war potentials. Japan shall neither use these forces for acts of aggression nor shall Japan employ conscription."[37] As can be seen, Hatoyama's proposal made clear what the Japanese government has intended to explain. This is somewhat similar to the *Yomiuri Shimbun*'s proposal made in November 1994. A major difference between the two was that the *Yomiuri* proposal retained the first paragraph of Article 9 (a commitment to "renounce war as a sovereign right of the nation and the threat or use of force as means of settling international disputes"), whereas the Hatoyama proposal said it in a different way in his second sentence. Unlike Hatoyama, the *Yomiuri* also added a new chapter on international cooperation, committing Japan to send its armed forces for the maintenance and promotion of peace and or humanitarian support activities.

In May 1995, the *Yomiuri* further elaborated its view on constitutional revision, calling for the establishment of a Comprehensive Security Council that would quickly respond to an emergency in the areas of defense, terrorism (such as the Tokyo subway sarin attack of March 1995), and natural disaster (such as the Hanshin-Awaji earthquake of February 1995).[38]

The fifth group supports the constitutional amendment out of nationalism. They want to revise the constitution for the same reason that they supported the National Anthem and Flag Law. Ishihara Shintarō, governor of

Tokyo, is a typical example. What this group is saying is clear and straightforward: Japan should behave as all other sovereign states do. They want constitutional revision per se, simply because of the fact that the current constitution was written by SCAP. Obviously, they do not share the understanding of Shigeru Yoshida, who wrote that the drafting process of the constitution was more like a treaty negotiation with foreign countries.

If the last two groups gain more influence among the public and take an initiative to revise the constitution, there would be a good chance to give rise to a controversy. On the contrary, if the third group took the initiative to form a coalition with the fourth and a part of the second group and attempted to carry out the constitutional revision based on a higher and broader perspective, Japan might be able to succeed in amending Article 9 without creating serious domestic and international frictions. One of the key factors that will decide the creation of coalitions depends on the domestic politics in the years to come, especially the course of action that the LDP and the DPJ are going to take. In particular, it is crucially important if the DPJ can speak with one voice on this matter.

Pros and Cons of Constitutional Revision

Japan's security policy has been constrained by the controversies over the constitutionality of the SDF and its activities, especially before the late 1980s. Yet, the basic problems have remained unresolved in spite of the fact that significant improvements were introduced into Japan's foreign policy during the 1990s. For the people who believe that Japan has been trapped by Article 9, only constitutional revision can remove the obstacle to more active diplomacy. They generally anticipate four benefits of constitutional revision.[39]

First, revising Article 9 would remove Japanese excuses that have prevented Japan from participating in the activities of UN peacekeeping forces (PKF) activities. The revision could show that Japan could become a "common" member of the UN community whose involvement in UN PKO would not be limited only to logistical operations. Second, in a similar vein, the constitutional revision would make it possible for Japan to become a more reliable allied partner of the United States in a crisis. As already mentioned, Japan's military contribution to the US-Japan alliance in the "situations in areas surrounding Japan" is limited to logistical supports. The constitutional revision could get over the legalistic barriers in conducting those operations. Third, as a result, the Japanese might be able to gain more confidence in managing Japan's international security policies by revising the constitution, which would decrease Japan's dependence on a US security guarantee. Fourth, it could relieve Japanese "occupational mentality" (Japanese psychological dependence on the United States and the inferiority complex of the Japanese people), which still exists deep in the society.

The problem is that we do not know how much political cost the Japanese would have to pay for the revision. It might not be too difficult, not only because the majority is in favor of revising the constitution but also because emotional opposition to the constitutional revision has faded out during the past several years. And yet, it would not be easy to obtain the support of a two-thirds majority in both houses in the Diet in order to revise Article 9. The failure in this venture would be devastating.

Considering pros and cons of constitutional revisions, many Japanese people still believe that the revision of Article 9 is not a prerequisite for Japan to conduct active diplomacy as long as Japan can do all that the international society expects Japan to do in security fields without amending Article 9.

Future Options

From the mid-1990s onward, opinion polls taken by the *Yomiuri Shimbun* and other newspapers have indicated that the majority of the public is in favor of amending the constitution. Even among the supporters of the SDPJ and the Kōmei Party, a majority prefers constitutional revision. The Japanese entered a new stage of the debate when the Constitutional Research Commissions were set up in the Diet for the first time and started their deliberations in January 2000. After five years of discussions, the commissions formulated a recommendation in April 2005. Yet, according to the Constitutional Research Commissions' reports, the commissions, especially in the upper house, have not formed a consensus to revise Article 9. Similarly, the LDP New Constitution Drafting Committee made public a proposal for constitutional revision in the spring of 2005 to revise the second paragraph in Article 9 and to revise the constitutional amendment procedure from the current one in Article 96. Instead of the current requirement of a two-thirds supermajority in both houses of the Diet and a simple majority in a national referendum, the proposed amendment procedure would require a simple majority in the Diet. The Kōmei Party, which is in power, does not support amending Article 9. Despite ongoing debates over constitutional revision, there appear to be some obstacles to reaching a consensus on changes to Article 9.

On the future options for constitutional revision, the following courses of actions are considered. The first option would be no change in Article 9, with or without revision in constitutional amendment procedure, to lower the requirements for revision. If the revisionist movements stop gaining wider support, this may be the choice. The second option is revision of

Article 9 to make clear that Japan can have the right of self-defense and war potential and that it can use these rights for its own self-defense. This is the option proposed by opposition party leader Hatoyama Yukio of the DPJ, though he also suggested that Japan should pledge "it will never conduct a war of aggression."[40] The third option would be an elimination of the second paragraph in Article 9 in case there is no national consensus formed to revise Article 9. A number of LDP leaders, including Yamasaki Taku, LDP secretary general during the 2001–2003 period, advocate this choice.[41] The fourth option would be revision of Article 9 to permit Japan to exercise a collective self-defense right. The fifth choice would be revision of Article 9 to permit Japan's participation in UN or other international security activities such as antiterrorist operations. Finally, if there are difficulties in undertaking the first five options, the government could use two types of alternative approaches that would require either a new law such as the National Security Law or reinterpretation of Article 9 to gain the objectives in the first five options without having to formally revise Article 9. Those are options supported by people such as Nakasone.

Which is the best option for Japan? Let me quickly examine what is necessary to make it possible for Japan to conduct more constructive policy in the area of international security. First, do we need to spell out that a war for self-defense is permitted in Article 9? As has already been explained, since Article 9 is a replica of the Kellogg-Briand Pact, it is widely believed that the right of self-defense is preserved even without mentioning it. This is why many leaders, including Nakasone, support retaining the first paragraph. Therefore, it may be redundant to write in Article 9 that Japan has the right of self-defense, as it can be argued that it already possesses it, even though one may believe it would be clearer if said outright.

Second, the second paragraph of Article 9 is interpreted to mean that land, sea, and air forces, as well as other war potential for a war of aggression, will never be maintained. It also reads that the "right of belligerency of the state will not be recognized." Usually, this has been interpreted to mean that Japan does not have the right of belligerency to fight a war of aggression. In fact, when the MacArthur Notes said that "no rights of belligerency will ever be conferred upon any Japanese force," it perhaps meant that the right to conduct a war of aggression was not allowed, because "the right of belligerency" was used instead of "the right of belligerencies," which is commonly used in international law. Taking this and other factors into consideration, it is possible to read the second paragraph to mean that Japan is able to maintain force and to use it for self-defense, as the Defense Agency has taken the position that "it is recognized as a matter of course that Japan can make use of minimum force for self-defense."[42] Even though it might become clearer if the constitution were to spell out that Japan has such a right, it appears not to be a crucial necessity.

Third, the CLB has maintained its 1981 interpretation of the relationship between Article 9 and a collective self-defense right: "The government believes that exercise of the right of collective self-defense exceeds that limit [the minimum necessary level for the defense of the country] and not, therefore, permissible under the Constitution."[43] The Japanese government also maintains the position that Japan has been forbidden to send the SDF abroad since 1956, and this may have been an unavoidable course of action in order to obtain public support for securing the right of self-defense in the nation from the 1950s through the 1980s. Nevertheless, a careful scrutiny suggests no clear connection between Article 9 and the CLB's interpretation of the right of collective self-defense. Once again we might not need to amend Article 9 if the Japanese reached a national consensus (in the Diet, for example) that Japan could exercise collective self-defense, though the CLB would be required at least to change its interpretation in such a direction.

Fourth, should Japan revise the constitution if it wants to send the SDF equipped with arms to participate in UN PKO? After the Gulf War, quite a few commentators advocated constitutional revision to enable Japan to take part in UN PKO, but such a revision may not be necessary. As Professor Takano Yuichi, a specialist of international law at the University of Tokyo, wrote in 1965, Japan could send the SDF for UN peacekeeping activities without revising the constitution; according to him, to use force for the international peace is not prohibited by the constitution but rather is encouraged by it.[44] If Takano's position were accepted by the government, Japan could send the SDF with arms to participate in UN PKO as well as UN PKF without necessitating constitutional revision.

Considering all those factors, it appears to be that the first option (do nothing) is unlikely because the momentum is moving toward constitutional revision. Yet options 2, 3, 4, and 5, requiring constitutional revisions, may prove politically costly both inside and outside of Japan, and Japan does not have a strong leadership to mobilize the public in that direction. Therefore, the most feasible and likely option is number 6, in which reinterpretation of Article 9 or the formation of a new law would be taken as the first step. If carried out well, these options would clarify what Japan should do in the US-Japan alliance and in the UN system.

Conclusion

As mentioned at the beginning, Japan has been undertaking larger security roles through the adoption of new security concepts and frameworks such as "situations in areas surrounding Japan," which appeared in the 1997 Guidelines for the US-Japan Defense Cooperation, and the strategies based on ATSML or LCSMHRA that took place after the September 11, 2001, attack. Japan's shifts in its international security policy have significant implications not only for Japanese foreign policy but also for international politics in general. Despite its constitutional constraints on the exercise of collective self-defense, the Japanese government has sent Japanese SDF vessels and troops to the Indian Ocean and Iraq, carefully avoiding constitutional restrictions. Japan is already adopting a military role that is larger than that designed by the 1997 defense guidelines. In reaching agreement in May 2006 on the realignment of US forces in Japan, the Japanese and US governments succeeded in making a blueprint for a new alliance centered on close cooperation between the Japanese SDF and the US military. Therefore, Christopher Hughes wrote that "Japan is now seen to have reached the point of no return in moving towards acting as a 'normal' military power, a partner for international security cooperation and more committed US ally."[45]

In this context, the debates on constitutional revision of Article 9 have become a central concern for policymakers and the Japanese public.[46] Contrary to media reports, there appears to be no significant progress on constitutional revision. In this sense, Japan's security policy in the post–September 11 period has still continued to follow what Hughes called "the path-dependence approach of the Yoshida Doctrine."[47] Japan is carefully tightening its security cooperation with the United States while at the same time circumventing excessively close strategic integration. In Iraq, for example, Japanese SDF troops sent there have been permitted to operate only in noncombat areas. And despite the speculation often reported by the foreign media, Japan is very unlikely to go nuclear. Because of Japan's increased cooperation with the US military, Japan is likely to face a security dilemma problem vis-à-vis China in the case of a Taiwan crisis. China may not be tolerant of the broader and stronger US-Japan alliance.[48] Thus, Japan is carefully maintaining the balance between a newly developed closer security cooperation policy with the United States and the traditional Japanese foreign policy principle known as the Yoshida doctrine. It is inevitable that those changes in Japan's security policy and its international environment have had impacts on constitutional revision debates on the one hand, whereas constitutional revision itself would have an impact on maintaining the balance described just above, on the other hand. In this context, constitutional revision, and particularly revision of Article 9, requires a delicate sense in observing and calculating participants' desire and power.

Japan can contribute to international security through various activities. It can do many things in the field of international security even if Article 9 remains unchanged. Though Japan's constitution is certainly a key factor to be taken into consideration when determining Japan's contributions to international security, a satisfactory solution of constitutional revision may not be drawn when we assess the policy options only through the lens of constitutional concerns. Rather, what must be discussed is Japan's concrete international policies instead of ideological debates on how Article 9 has been interpreted. Even if the Japanese cannot reach a national consensus as to what they want to do over constitution revision, it is not difficult to make a meaningful contribution to the international peace and stability.

We should keep in mind that one's international "contribution" in international security could become a disservice to the other parties. After all, security means an effort to protect acquired values from perceived threats. To the extent that the Japanese can share the values to be protected with other members of international society, Japan should extend the support to protect the shared value with them. To do so, Article 9 is not a barrier, and it should not be used as one.

Notes

1. For example, conservative critic Etō Jun wrote that he felt sadness and anger because Japan's sovereignty was constrained after the war (Etō, *1946 Kempō—sono kōsoku*, 203–205).
2. Finnemore, *National Interests in International Society*, 22.
3. Finnemore and Sikkink, "International Norm Dynamics and Political Change," 255.
4. Kant, "Perpetual Peace: A Philosophical Essay," 202.
5. It said, "La Nation Française renonce à entreprendre aucune guerre dans la vue faire des conquêtes, et n'emploira jamais ses forces contre la liberté d'aucun peuple" (The French nation renounces the undertaking of any war with a view of making conquests, and it will never use its forces against the liberty of any people).
6. Suzuki Akinori, *Nihonkoku Kenpo o Unda Misshitsu no Kokonokakan*, 335.
7. McNelly, *The Origins of Japan's Democratic Constitution*, 5.
8. Yoshida, *Yoshida Memoirs*, 133.
9. For example, Article 4 of the Meiji constitution reads, "The Emperor . . . exercises them [the rights of sovereignty], according to the provision of the present Constitution," and MacArthur's note says "his duties and power will be exercised in accordance with the Constitution." Apparently, the latter only replaced "them" with "his duties and power." Since Ito's English translation of *Tōchiken* was "the rights of sovereignty," when MacArthur's note said "war as sovereign right of nation is abolished" it might have meant that the declaration of war and the conclusion of peace as the emperor's right of sovereignty should be abolished. On this point, see Sasaki, "Sengokaikaku ni okeru Makkāsā Note no yakuwari," 6, 12–13. See also his *Sensō Hōkijōkō no Seiritsukeii*.
10. Finn, *Winners in Peace*, 104.
11. Iokibe, "Nihon no Anzenhoshōkan wa Ikani Suii Shitaka," 74–75.
12. See, for example, Nakagawa, "Nippi Ryo Kenpō ni miru Ruien."
13. MacArthur, *Makkāsā Kaisōki*, 163–164.
14. Finn, *Winners in Peace*, 102–103.
15. Ibid., 103.

16. Suzuki, *Nihonkoku Kenpō o Unda Misshitsu no Kokonokakan*, 335.
17. Kades, "Discussion of Professor Theodore McNelly's Paper 'General Douglas MacArthur and the Constitutional Disarmament of Japan,'" 37.
18. Tanaka Akihiko, *Anzen Hoshō*, 28.
19. Satō, *Nihonkoku Kenpō Tanjōki*, 140–141.
20. Ashida, *Shin Kempō Kaishaku.*
21. See, for example, Koseki, *Shin Kenpō no Tanjō*, chap. 9.
22. Kades, "Discussion of Professor Theodore McNelly's Paper, 'General Douglas MacArthur and the Constitutional Disarmament of Japan,'" 40. See also McNelly, *The Origins of Japan's Democratic Constitution.*
23. Koseki, *Shin Kenpō no Tanjō*, chap 9. Yokota Kisaburo, an international law specialist at the University of Tokyo who later became the chief justice of the Supreme Court, also had a view that the right of self-defense was reserved even in the first paragraph of Article 9. See Yokota, *Sensō no Hōki*, 22–23.
24. Satō, *Nihonkoku Kenpō Tanjōki*, 140.
25. Spykman, *America's Strategy in World Politics*, 21, 470.
26. Cited in Etzold and Gaddis, *Containment: Documents on American Policy and Strategy*, 27. Kennan laid great stress on industrial bases as the most significant element in the balance of power. Therefore, he considered Japan to be the cornerstone of the Pacific security system, not China, for maintaining the balance vis-à-vis the Soviet Union. He visited Japan in February–March 1948, representing the view of the State Department. His visit coincided with the visit of William H. Draper, who brought the Army Department's view. Those two visitors met with MacArthur on March 21. There, in response to Draper's suggestion that Japan might have to be rearmed in order to save US defense expenditures, MacArthur was consistently opposed. By then, however, it was clear that Japan's Article 9 was no longer viewed as a realistic approach to cope with the emerging new international environment in the eyes of the officials in Washington. In retrospect, their visit became a turning point of US occupation policy of Japan, namely from demilitarization and democratization to industrialization.
27. A series of events in the early 1970s began with the return of Okinawa, which increased Japan's commitment to East Asian security. In the Satō-Nixon joint communiqué of November 1969, for example, Japan committed to the Korean and Taiwanese security for the first time by stating that "the security of Republic of Korea is essential to Japan's own security, . . . [and] the maintenance of peace and security in Taiwan area is also a most important factor for the security of Japan." See Hosoya Chihiro et al., *Nichibel Kankei Shiryōshu*, 790.
Furthermore, later events changed the Japanese perception of US commitment to Japan's security: two "Nixon shocks" in 1971 (announcement of Nixon's planned visit to China, and a new international economic policy), the Sino-US rapprochement of 1972 and the conclusion of the US–North Vietnamese peace treaty of 1973, the Watergate scandal and the War Power Act, OPEC's oil embargo in 1973–1974, the collapse of the Saigon regime in 1974, and the US plan to withdraw the US ground forces from South Korea that was announced in 1976. See Tsuchiyama, "Why Japan Is Allied? Politics of the US-Japan Alliance," 71–85.
28. Japan Defense Agency, *Defense of Japan 2001*, 129.
29. Ibid., 129–130. For details of the emergency legislation bills, see Japan Defense Agency, *Defense of Japan 2002*, 146–159.
30. Hook and McCormack, *Japan's Contested Constitution*, 30–31. See also Ishibashi, *Zōho Hibusō Churitsuron.*
31. *Asahi Shimbun*, editorial, May 3, 1995.

32. Miyazawa and Nakasone, *Tairon Kaiken Goken,* 109.

33. *International Herald Tribune/Asahi Shimbun,* November 7, 2001, 25.

34. Ozawa, "Nihonkoku Kenpōkaisei Shian," 98. This English translation is from Itoh, "Japanese Constitutional Revision: A Neo-liberal Proposal for Article 9 in Comprehensive Perspective," 315.

35. Nakasone, "Waga kaiken ron," 60–61.

36. Miyazawa and Nakasone, *Tairon Kaiken Goken,* 111–113.

37. Hatoyama, "Jieitai o Guntai to mitomeyo," 262–273.

38. *Yomiuri Shimbun, Minna no Kenpō 3.*

39. Itoh, "Japanese Constitutional Revision," 325–327.

40. Hatoyama, "Jieitai o Guntai to mitomeyo," 263.

41. Yamasaki, *Kenpō kaisei.*

42. Japan Defense Agency, *Defense of Japan, 1999.*

43. Sase, *Shūdanteki Jieiken,* 125.

44. Takano, *Shūdan Anpō to Jieiken,* 318. See also Yokota, *Sensō no Hōki,* in which the author suggested for the first time that Japan under the new constitution could have the right of self-defense with armament (22–23) and also mentioned Japan's future admission to the United Nations.

45. Hughes, *Japan's Re-emergence as a "Normal" Military Power,* 133.

46. For the policy implications of constitutional revision, see Boyd and Samuels, *Nine Lives? The Politics of Constitutional Reform in Japan,* 48–64.

47. Hughes, *Japan's Re-emergence as a "Normal" Military Power,* 140.

48. Christensen, "China, the U.S.-Japan Alliance, and the Security Dilemma in East Asia"; and Tsuchiyama, "From Balancing to Networking: Models of Regional Security in Asia."

| 4 |

Participation in
UN Peacekeeping Operations

Go Ito

On September 11, 2001, New York and Washington, D.C., were attacked. Following the attack, President George W. Bush announced that terrorism would be a new kind of war in the twenty-first century. Three weeks later, on October 7, the Global Coalition Against Terror began retaliatory operations in Afghanistan. The initial force consisted of the US and British governments, together with units from Canada, Italy, France, Australia, and Germany, with Japanese logistic, intelligence, and humanitarian support.

This chapter looks back over the recent years and argues that Japan's response has been part of a larger process of redefining its security role in the Asia Pacific region. The Gulf War in 1990–1991 was a turning point in Japan's foreign policy. According to the Foreign Ministry's 1991 *Bluebook*, then prime minister Kaifu Toshiki said that "this crisis is a major time of testing for Japan as a nation of peace and the most severe trial we have faced since the end of the war."[1]

Since the Gulf War, the "UN-centered diplomacy," which Japan had adopted since its entry into the United Nations in the middle of the 1950s, has been compelled to go beyond mere rhetoric. Although Japan contributed $13 billion to the activities of the UN coalition forces in the Gulf, the Japanese government was unable to find "Japan" in the "Thank You List" made by Kuwait. Then Japan began to adopt a more activist stance of human contributions, mindful of the world's expectations that it should play a more global role commensurate with its economic power. International contributions through UN-centrism emerged as the most significant debate for Japanese foreign policy for the first time, not in words but in deeds.

Since the experience in the 1990–1991 Gulf War, the Japanese govern-

75

ment's statements have been replete with the need for "positive contributions" toward international peace and stability. The key element for the contributions has been Japan's multilateral engagement through SDF participation in peacekeeping missions. For the assertive pacifist Japan that had desired to contribute substantially to world affairs through nonmilitary means, the UN provided an ideal forum in which to carry out its global responsibility and to enhance its status and prestige.[2]

Since the International Peace Cooperation Law (the Peacekeeping Law) passed in the Diet in 1992, the Japanese government has been eager to increase the number of SDF officers who can be sent to the conflict areas. Despite the announcements, however, only 45 SDF members are in operation in the Golan Heights, and a great deal of domestic regulations and principles have prevented Japan's effective conduct of peacekeeping activities. Compared with forces from other Group of Seven (G7) countries, such as 700–800 Americans and more than 100 Italians, Japan's outcome has been seen as insufficient to be called an "international contribution."

Given the shortage of Japan's international contributions in the peacekeeping arena for the 1990s, this chapter examines what has been at stake in the overall discussions of Japan's dispatch of peacekeeping operations, documents recent cases of Japan's peacekeepers, and articulates the regulations and principles of the Japanese activities. The discussion will shed light on the issues and agendas that have been discussed as Japan's international contributions for the 1990s. The chapter also traces the history of Japan's PKO activities since Japan reentered the UN in 1956 and articulates the principles of Japan's dispatching of peacekeeping operations.

Ideas and Agendas of the International Contributions

Since the Japanese government was criticized for failing to make military contributions to the Gulf War, the Japanese government has created several ways it can be regarded as a positive actor for international peace and security. As far as the field of international development is concerned, Japan had already been ranked as the first donor of official development aid. Facing the international criticisms, however, Japanese politicians and bureaucrats recognized that the traditional economic diplomacy could not be substituted for the maintenance of a security agenda. Foreign Ministry officials remember that Japan's experience during the Gulf War was traumatic, because it was excluded from the Security Council's deliberations on the UN action. Ambassador Hatano Yoshiro went as far as to mention that Japan could have put together a package of proposals for action if it had had a seat on the Security Council.[3]

The term *international contributions* started to emerge as the way to reform Japan's immobilism in foreign policy. From 1990 through the passage of the Peacekeeping Law in June 1992, the international contributions were focused especially on three agendas.

First, human contributions have been valued more than the financial contributions. Although during the Gulf War the Japanese government's financial contributions compensated for almost one-third of the coalition forces' military operations, those contributions were condemned as "too little, too late." Given that it took only a year and a half for the passage of the Peacekeeping Law, it was clear that the Japanese government rushed to indicate its readiness to conduct troop contributions that could avoid the other countries' criticisms, a reaction called "checkbook diplomacy."

Second, within the human contributions, dispatching SDF personnel has been discussed as the central factor. For the Japanese government, the UN has been accepted as the major institution in which Japan can play an international role, whereas the fears of East Asian countries that a unilateral contribution would correspond to Japan's militarization have depressed Japan's dispatch of SDF units abroad.[4] Main discussions and struggles for the passage of the Peacekeeping Law in the Diet focused on whether and to what extent the Japanese government would be able to dispatch its SDF units abroad while maintaining the traditional "pacifist" stance with Article 9 of the constitution.

Thus, along with the passage of the Peacekeeping Law, there was a serious constraint imposed when SDF personnel were sent to conflict areas. In the Peacekeeping Law, the Diet distinguished substantial, military-related operations (i.e., PKF) from less military, rear-area, support-oriented peacekeeping operations and said that the former should "not be implemented until the date to be set forth by a separate law." The Japanese peacekeepers can conduct election monitoring, provide bureaucratic advice and guidance (e.g., police administration, medical care, transportation, construction), and conduct humanitarian relief operations (e.g., rescue and repatriation of war refugees); "rear-area support" does not include monitoring a cease-fire, patrolling buffer zones, or inspecting weapons.

Third, issues of Japan's peacekeeping operations have opened a more general debate on whether the Japanese government, with its military operations restrained by Article 9 of the constitution, can be changed into a "normal state" that can conduct military operations when necessary. The discussions of Japan's PKO contributions related to the establishment of diplomatic norms that would create a more positive Japan whose role in international security could transcend the traditional "pacifist" stance.[5]

During the 1990s, in fact, Japan's international role in security expanded toward not only conducting UN-centered peacekeeping operations but also multiplying functions of the allied relationship with the United States. Such issues as collective self-defense rights and US-Japan security guidelines emerged as the basis of an updated US-Japan security relationship. In this sense, discussions of the international contributions have sought to attain something more positive than conducting normal contributions to the UN activities.

The great breakthrough of Japan's international contributions that it was compelled to make after the Gulf War related to the drastic changes in the above three policy agendas. The next section looks into the history and decisionmaking process of Japan's peacekeeping operations.

History and Decisionmaking Process of Japan's International Contributions

Initial Stage After Japan's Reentry into the UN

Debates concerning Japan's participation in UN peacekeeping operations can be traced back to the late 1950s and the early 1960s. Since its reentry into the UN, the Japanese government has repeatedly emphasized the importance of the institution for international peace and stability. The "UN-centered diplomacy" was announced in 1957 by former prime minister Kishi Nobusuke as one of three pillars of postwar Japanese foreign policy: (1) use of the UN as the major area in which Japan should pursue its national goals, (2) close cooperation with "free, democratic states," and (3) identification with Asia.[6]

The announcement attracted a wide range of popular support and consolidated into a national consensus. It was hoped at that time that Japan could eventually rely on the UN to maintain its security and world peace. As Robert Immerman once wrote, "the only major tenet of postwar Japanese foreign policy that has received the support of all segments of the domestic political spectrum—from the conservatives . . . to the Socialist and Communist parties constituting the left opposition—has been the nation's commitment to an otherwise undefined 'UN-centered diplomacy.'"[7]

With that said, there has been no consensus on the definition of "UN-centered diplomacy." From today's perspective, the intention was not to make the UN the central focus or arena of Japanese foreign policy but only to have Japan's diplomacy in line with the purposes and principles of the United Nations charter. Moreover, for Premier Kishi, whose foreign policy priority at that time was to modify the US-Japan Security Treaty, the emphasis on the UN provided a good excuse to attract civilian support between the idealistic "identification with Asia" and the more realistic "cooperation with free, democratic states."[8] In the Japanese government, there were no specific or realistic policy options impinging on how international peace has been maintained within the collective security system.

Soon after Japan's entry into the United Nations in 1956, there were at least two occasions when the UN sought to solicit the contributions of Japanese SDF officers and other personnel. In 1958, UN Secretary-General Dag Hammarskjöld requested that the Japanese government send SDF officers to Lebanon in order to monitor weapons. In the Diet debate, Foreign Minister Fujiyama Aiichirō rejected the dispatch of SDF units, since the SDF Law had no statement of sending the units abroad. A few years later, Japan's UN ambassador, Matsudaira Koto, criticized the government's immobility, saying that "it is not logical that the Japanese government emphasizes the importance of the UN, while at the same time it avoids participating in the UN Forces."[9]

The second case happened two years later when Congo, a newly independent country, requested UN intervention after Belgium unilaterally sent forces to its former colony. Although there was no formal mandate from the UN regarding Japan's involvement, rumor held that the UN inquired of the Japanese government about the possibility of Japan's dispatch. In reality, rising tensions between the conflicting parties made it impossible even for the normal UN missions to monitor the buffer zone, and the Japanese government judged it too dangerous for the SDF members to conduct the mandate within Japan's constitutional framework.[10]

Japan as a Rising Economic Power

After the initial period of Japan's UN-centered diplomacy, the UN increasingly came to be seen as a place for Third World or nonaligned states, whereas more powerful countries, frustrated with the situation, had established some other forums where only advanced countries could discuss their own policy issues.[11]

From the 1970s until the middle of the 1980s, there was no atmosphere that could compel the Japanese government to take initiatives on UN activities. The UN as an international organization had changed into one that would reflect the interests of the Third World countries, and the US-Japan relationship was also in crisis owing to the Nixon administration's abrupt announcements of an opening to China and a new economic policy. In the UN General Assembly, the Japanese government sought to play a role as a mediator between the North and the South, mindful of its traditional national interest of sustaining natural resources.[12]

A major breakthrough stemmed from Takeshita Noboru's inauguration as prime minister in November 1987. Eager to expand Japan's involvement in international issues, he announced the International Cooperation Initiative in 1988. It included stepped-up contributions to the UN activities for the prevention and resolution of conflicts. In Takeshita's ideas, Japan, which had achieved global economic prominence, should pursue its own global theme. He took the initiative several times, playing a substantial agenda-setting role on humanitarian issues and UN reform. Dispatching Japanese peacekeepers for international peace and stability was also an issue for urgency. The Foreign Ministry stepped ahead toward sending an official to Afghanistan and Pakistan (United Nations Good Offices Mission in Afghanistan and Pakistan; UNGOMAP) and also another official to the border between Iran and Iraq (United Nations Iran-Iraq Military Observer Group; UNIIMOG). In 1989, thirty-one Japanese personnel were sent to Namibia (United Nations Transition Assistance Group; UNTAG) for the election monitoring, and similar assignments were also conducted in Nicaragua (United Nations Observation Mission for the Verification of Elections in Nicaragua; ONUVEN) and Haiti (United Nations Observer Group for the Verification of the Elections in Haiti; ONUVEH).[13]

Despite the policy change in the Takeshita cabinet, the dispatch of Japanese peacekeepers to the UN was strictly limited to "civilians." The government still maintained the 1950s stance of the SDF Law that had no clear statement of sending Japan's SDF officers. The Foreign Affairs Establishment Law that was enacted after the US occupation was still active with respect to Japan's involvement. It was not until the Diet considered the passage of the Peacekeeping Law that SDF officers could be sent to conflict areas.

The Gulf War and Japan's Turning Point

The Gulf War changed Japan's immobilism. The US criticisms of the Japanese government for "checkbook diplomacy" moved the government toward changing the established "nondispatch" principle. The passage of the Peacekeeping Law (Law Concerning Cooperation for United Nations Peacekeeping Operations and Other Operations) in the 1992 Diet enabled the Japanese government to send its Self-Defense Forces to conflict areas. The Foreign Ministry's long-standing hope of dispatching SDF abroad was finally realized at this time.

The decisionmaking process of the passage of the Peacekeeping Law can be divided into two stages. The first was Premier Kaifu's October 1990 submission of the Peacekeeping Law to the Diet without enough consensus with opposition parties (e.g., the Kōmei Party and the Democratic Socialist Party). It stated that Japanese peacekeepers would conduct cease-fire and election monitoring, administrative assistance, transportation, and humanitarian relief operations. The peacekeepers would be able to carry small arms with them, although its use could not go beyond the "use or threat of force."

The central point of the opposition parties' questioning of the validity of the Peacekeeping Law was whether the dispatch of SDF officers would

violate the principles of Article 9. The government's responses to the opposing Diet members were also circumscribed by its own statement in 1980
that the SDF's participation in the UN-led forces would be against Article 9,
provided that the purpose and missions of the UN forces, in which Japanese
peacekeepers participated, would include the use of weapons.[14] The government sought to distinguish "participation" from "cooperation" and argued
that Japan's involvement would not go beyond "cooperation," but the lack
of popular support finally prevented the passage of the legislation.

The second stage started when the LDP began to converge its policy
stance with that of the opposition (more centrist than left-wing) parties.
When the initial submission of the Peacekeeping Law was turned down, the
LDP established an agreement with the Kōmei Party and the Socialist
Democratic Party with respect to the future creation of a separate unit that
could conduct international relief operations. Also, the LDP made several
concessions when submitting the new version of the Peacekeeping Law.
The SDF's participation should not be limited to PKF activities and to logistical and rear-area support. If the SDF should be sent to conflict areas with
small arms, it would need the Diet's approval. The opposition parties also
demanded that if SDF officers were exposed to dangerous conditions in
conflict, they could withdraw from the assignment.[15] With these conditions
imposed, the bill was finally passed in June 1992.

Several cases of Japan's dispatch of peacekeeping operations should be
documented (see Table 4.1). The first test case was the United Nations
Transitional Authority in Cambodia (UNTAC). Right after the passage of
the Peacekeeping Law, 8 SDF soldiers, 41 civilians (for election monitoring), 75 civilian policemen, and about 600 SDF engineers were sent to
Cambodia. Although much of their assignment went smoothly, the SDF soldiers were asked to fulfill more duties than those indicated in the original
Implementation Plan. For the Japanese government, which restricted the
substantive activities of peacekeeping forces, the most critical issue was to
keep the balance between the international contributions satisfactory for the
international community and the safety of the members being engaged in
the operations. The rigid implementation of the Peacekeeping Law in the
operating field, however, sometimes frustrated the UN personnel and the
Cambodians in need of the assistance. Given the dilemma, the Japanese
members had hesitations about conducting effective operations at the borders.[16]

Unlike the fabulous image of the UNTAC, the participation in the
United Nations Operation in Mozambique (ONUMOZ) attracted less atten-
tion. In 1993, UN Secretary-General Boutros Boutros-Ghali proposed that
Japan would send SDF units to Mozambique. The Foreign Ministry and the
International Peace Cooperation Headquarters (IPCHQ) had already investi-
gated the safety in the region and urged the dispatch. The Miyazawa cabinet

Table 4.1   Japan's Major Participation in International Peacekeeping

Dispatches Based on International Peace Cooperation Law	Dispatches Based on Other Ministry of Foreign Affairs–Related Laws
Cambodia, September 1992–September 1998[a] SDF soldiers 8 Civilians 41 Civilian police 75 SDF engineers 600	Yugoslavia, March 1994–December 1995[a] MOFA 1 Organization for Security Cooperation in Europe (Bosnia-Herzegovina), September 1996[b] Civilians 36
Mozambique, May 1993–January 1995[a] SDF soldiers 5 SDF members for transportation 48 Civilians 15	Organization for Security and Cooperation in Europe, September 1997[b] Civilians 29
Rwanda, September–December 1994[b] SDF for transportation 118 SDF for medical care 283	Iraq, March–July 2003[b] SDF officers 100
Golan Heights, February 1996–[a] SDF officers 2 SDF for transportation 43	
East Timor, January 2002–June 2005[a] SDF officers 2,300	

Notes: a. UN peacekeeping operations.
b. Other activities.

sent fifty-three SDF officers for liaison offices and transportation and fifteen civilians for election monitoring to the conflict area. The operation was rather safe, and the participation lasted for eight months, but the Japanese public was ignorant of the area, which they felt had little relevance for Japan.

The above two cases were UN peacekeeping operations, but Premier Murayama Tomiichi's decision to send missions to Rwanda was a humanitarian relief operation. In that area, thousands of refugees, who had already fled to neighboring countries, were suffering from the lack of nutrition, water, and sanitation. At the suggestion of Ogata Sadako, the director of the United Nations High Commissioner for Refugees (UNHCR), the Murayama cabinet, the first coalition between the LDP and the Socialist Party, sent almost 400 SDF officers and ministry officials for transportation and administrative liaison offices.[17]

Finally, Japan's dispatch of forces that are still in operation is in the Golan Heights (the United Nations Disengagement Observer Force; UNDOF). In this case, the Diet's debate focused on two issues: whether or not SDF officers' transporting of ammunition and foreign combat troops would violate the Peacekeeping Law and whether the UN mandate of asking Japanese officers to be assigned for two years would be possible. After more than a year's debate, forty-five SDF officers were sent to the area, two of whom have been engaged in administrative liaison offices.

Other than the above cases, Japanese peacekeepers have been sent to monitor elections in Angola, El Salvador, South Africa, Palestine, Romania, and Bosnia and Herzegovina, although the government failed to do so in Somalia, Yugoslavia, and East Timor. Compared with the initial period of Japan's nominal UN-centered diplomacy, the passage of the Peacekeeping Law enabled the government to send SDF units abroad. Given that the law resulted from a compromise among the three political parties, Japan's dispatch of peacekeeping operations has had unique principles. Next we look at the details of how the international contribution policies in Japan have been implemented.

Japan's "Human Contributions" and Allied Relationship with the United States

Another step toward changing Japan's security role presented itself in the making of US-Japan security guidelines during the mid-1990s. After the end of the Cold War, the decline of a global threat, combined with an existing regional threat of strife in East Asia, was given as one of the reasons for the formulation of the new guidelines. The parties to the deliberations on the future of US-Japan alliance were concerned with the lingering potential for strife in the region while at the same time trying to develop a structure well suited to the less hostile post–Cold War global environment.

With the April 1996 US-Japan Joint Declaration on Security, both governments started to seek new roles for the alliance. The new US-Japan security guidelines, announced in September 1997, tried to apply the joint declaration to post–Cold War East Asia in two ways. First, the "Various Types of Security Cooperation" item noted that the "bilateral [Japan-US] cooperation to promote regional and global activities in the field of security contributes to the creation of a more stable international security environment."[18] In other words, it was the new global role of the alliance and its complex functions within the region that were being given a particular importance. These functions include UN peacekeeping, international humanitarian relief operations, and emergency relief activities in major disasters. They also include encouraging security dialogue, defense exchange, and regional confidence building as well as arms control and reduction—alternatives to focusing on the containment of an adversary.

Second, the US-Japan security guidelines expanded the geographical breadth and reach of the alliance. The guidelines sought to incorporate neighboring areas under US-Japan political and economic cooperative relationships. Under Article 6 of the Japan-US Security Treaty, US forces were granted the use of facilities and areas in Japan for the purpose of contributing not only to Japan's security but also to that of the Far East region. Given the article, the guidelines sought to announce a need for US-Japan joint cooperation for the areas surrounding the Japanese territory. For the Japanese government, this implied the enlargement of the areas in which Japanese SDF members should conduct military operations with US personnel. That is, if a military conflict happens in the areas surrounding Japan, it is lawful for the Japanese government to dispatch SDF personnel for joint military actions led by the US military, although Japan's support should be limited to support-oriented logistics.

The gradual changes in the US-Japan security relationship came to be tested in 2001. In response to the September 11 terror, the Japanese government expressed shock and sympathy for those killed and injured in the incident. Japan became more galvanized when US deputy secretary of state Richard Armitage reportedly asked Yanai Shunji, Japanese ambassador to the United States, on September 15 that Japan "show the flag" in the upcoming US operations in Afghanistan.[19] Although the US operations in Afghanistan were prepared under the code name Infinite Justice, the Japanese government prepared its own "cooperation" plan, which crystallized into Prime Minister Koizumi Junichirō's Seven Point Plan on September 19.[20] In accordance with the Seven Point Plan, on September 21, the Japanese Maritime SDF was mobilized to escort a US aircraft carrier scheduled to sail from Yokosuka to the war zone.

The legislation to incorporate Prime Minister Koizumi's design for active engagement in Afghanistan was drafted by the Foreign Ministry and passed both houses of the Diet in October 2001. In the process, the Japanese government found it difficult to dispatch SDF units under the established legal framework. Since Secretary-General Kofi Annan made no further statements than the right of "self-defense" regarding US bombing, it was difficult for the Japanese government to dispatch its SDF personnel under UN peacekeeping operations. Moreover, with regard to applying US-Japan guidelines to the Enduring Freedom operations, it was questionable whether Afghanistan and the Indian Ocean could be included within the "areas surrounding Japan." Given these insufficiencies within the established legal framework, the Koizumi cabinet decided to enact a new law to send SDF personnel to the conflict areas.

Moreover, Japan's dispatch of Self-Defense Forces to Iraq was implemented as a postconflict rehabilitation activity. Three hours after President George W. Bush's final announcement on the US intention of attaching Iraq, Koizumi announced Japan's readiness for "total cooperation." For the first month, until the United States announced the regime change of the Hussein government, Article 9 prevented Japan from sending SDF. Then about 400

Ground SDF officers, along with military units consisting of the "Coalition of the Willing," were sent to conduct such activities as counterterrorism, refugee assistance, medical treatment, and other logistical support.[21]

Eventually, along with the passage of the Anti-Terrorism Special Measures Law, two other laws on Japan's international peacekeeping activities and Coast Guard were also modified, in order to enable the Japanese government to dispatch SDF personnel for "substantial activities" of peacekeeping and also to authorize the Japanese Coast Guard to use weapons against suspicious vessels in the Japanese territories. There seem to be drastic changes in Japan's security policy after the September 11 events, but the movement of redefining its security role in the context of US-Japan relations has been continuing.

Foreign Policies of the International Contributions

Five PKO Principles

When the Japanese Diet approved the Peacekeeping Law in June 1992, it was stipulated that Japan's participation in UN missions must meet five requirements.[22] The first three of the principles are actually preconditions for general PKO participation, whereas the other two are applied solely to Japan's involvement. In order for the Japanese government to engage in actual operations, all of these preconditions should be satisfied so that Japan's SDF participation in UN operations will not violate the Japanese constitution.

The first three principles relate to Article III of the Peacekeeping Law. First of all, the article requires that the parties to a conflict agree to, and maintain, a cease-fire. Only then can Japan participate. This requirement is intended to reduce the chances that Japanese personnel would need to use weapons.

Second, the parties in the conflict must consent to the deployment of a peacekeeping unit and to Japan's involvement. According to the Peacekeeping Law, Japan can dispatch its personnel only with the consent of both the host state and other parties to the conflict. They must consent not only to the UN operations themselves but also to Japanese participation in the operations. In terms of the dispatching process, the UN Security Council seeks to obtain the consent and sends a letter to Japan informing it that the parties have consented to Japanese participation. Then, the Japanese government considers it as the authoritative evidence for the required consent.

Third, any peacekeeping operations in which Japan is involved must maintain strict impartiality and neutrality. The impartial nature of peacekeeping operations stemmed from the original principle of UN Emergency Forces for the Suez Crisis in 1956. Article III stipulates that Japan's involvement in peacekeeping operations must be impartial so that Japan's participation would not cause unintended attacks from any of the conflicting parties.[23]

Although the above principles are preconditions, it is not clear to what extent they have been observed in the actual SDF's operations. In Cambodia, for instance, domestic stability deteriorated as one of the parties to the Paris Peace Agreement began to negate UN authority (UNTAC). By chance, the situation grew worse after the SDF officers were dispatched in October 1992. In reality, there were a number of cease-fire violations and some direct attacks on UN personnel. In May 1993, when a Japanese civil policeman was killed and several others injured, some Diet members claimed that the cease-fire agreement had collapsed and that Japanese personnel should be withdrawn. The government refused to do this, pointing out that the defiant party was still committed to the cease-fire.[24]

Also, with respect to the second principle of acquiring the consent of conflicting parties, the Peacekeeping Law allows Japanese participation in "preventive" deployments (which literally means the UN operations are designed to prevent conflicts before they occur). In this circumstance, consent for such operations will be required only from the host country. In theory, preventive deployments are undertaken prior to the outbreak of a conflict, so there is no need for either a cease-fire or impartiality toward conflicting parties. In reality, however, the areas of preventive deployments are usually on the verge of open conflict. For instance, in Macedonia, despite a great deal of preventive efforts by peacekeeping operations, there remained potentials for armed conflict, and whether both conflicting parties consented to the UN involvement in the region was questionable.

Furthermore, the "neutrality" principle is also in question. Although all UN peacekeeping operations meet this requirement in theory, whether or not they do so in practice is not clear. Since the condition of impartiality may be subjective, the question of who determines whether or not an operation is impartial becomes important. It is not clear whether the Japanese government will determine whether or not this condition has been met or will respect a determination made by the United Nations.[25]

With these points up in the air, the Japanese government maintains the following fourth and fifth principles that are, in some sense, unique only for Japan's participation.

The first of them is the possibility of Japan's withdrawing from the contingent peacekeeping activities, if any of the prior three requirements (cease-fire agreement, consent of the conflicting parties, and impartiality of the operation) fails or ceases to be satisfied. Besides, the Japanese government argued that, if UN peacekeeping forces engage in the use of force, it would be possible that Japanese contingents might also do so. Even if they do not actually use force, Japanese contingents may be considered an integral part of the action involving the brutal activity. The suspension and termination requirement thus ensures that corps and SDF personnel will never be part of operations using force and that Japanese participation in UN operations will comply with Article 9 of the constitution.

In terms of the decisionmaking process of dispatching SDF personnel, the rights of suspending or terminating Japanese participation in UN operations are important for the Japanese government, since the decision can be made without consideration for the commands of the UN Secretary-General. The Japanese prime minister can decide the matters, and his decision does not need to conform to the commands of the Secretary-General.

As far as the standard UN practices are concerned, every state participating in UN peacekeeping operations has the right to terminate its participation. The participating countries may withdraw their troops for any reason, including domestic requirements, as long as they give reasonable notice. That is, theoretically, this principle is not applicable only to the Japanese government, although the clarification of this principle may jeopardize the total functions and efficiency of peacekeepers at work.

The second point of Japan's unique participation relates to the probability of using weapons. The Peacekeeping Law provides that corps personnel and SDF units participating in peacekeeping operations may use weapons at the minimum level. It implies (Article 24) that the use of weapons should be within the limits considered necessary to protect themselves or other SDF or corps personnel "present with them on the same spot." In this circumstance, Japanese peacekeepers cannot directly protect non-Japanese UN personnel, nor can they be dispatched to other areas to protect Japanese or non-Japanese UN personnel. They can protect only Japanese personnel "present on the same spot" in self-defense. Moreover, Japanese peacekeepers cannot be ordered to use arms. The judgment of when and to what extent weapons are to be used depends on the judgment of the individual in operation rather than on the individual's superior officers.[26]

In relation to Article 9 and its constitutional interpretations, since the use of weapons is for self-defense of the individual, the government does not consider this to be an unconstitutional use of force. Also, since weapons may be used only to protect Japanese corps personnel or SDF members, the government avoids any claim that they are engaged in collective self-defense.[27]

By incorporating these five principles within the Peacekeeping Law, the government has sought to ensure that Japanese contributions to UN peacekeeping operations are within constitutional strictures. As seen above, however, these principles do not differ greatly from the original three principles of UN peacekeeping operations. It is logically possible (although unlikely to happen in reality owing to the lack of mention of sending SDF officers abroad in the SDF Law) that if Japanese peacekeepers could be dispatched to conflict areas without having enough weapons, the Japanese government would be able to send more uniformed personnel for international peacekeeping. In effect, Japan's principles have led to conflicts with the spirit and practice of UN peacekeeping operations. Worse, they may even call into question the effectiveness and propriety of Japanese participation in such operations.[28]

The Diet's Control over Participation in UN Peacekeeping Operations

The Diet's involvement since 1992 has made differences in Japan's dispatch of international peacekeepers, since it enabled SDF officers to be sent abroad. Civilians could be dispatched to conflict areas even before the passage of the Peacekeeping Law in June 1992, but the lack of statements in the SDF Law with respect to dispatch abroad prevented the SDF from contributing to the peacekeeping in conflict areas.[29]

In the actual decisionmaking, the Diet not only discusses plans for SDF participation in UN peace operations (Article 7 of the Peacekeeping Law) but also rejects the dispatch of SDF units intended to carry out certain military tasks. The Diet considers the five PKO principles, judging whether the issues being debated can be applied to the principles. It has complete discretion regarding SDF participation, and the same applies when the cabinet plans to extend SDF participation beyond two years.[30]

That is, the Diet's control restricts the activities of Japan's peacekeepers, especially those with small arms. If the tensions in the conflict areas stay at a level requiring that peacekeepers should retain small arms, Diet members judge the safety of the operations. The Diet also seeks to restrain the possible use or threat of weapons by Japanese peacekeepers, if Japan's dispatch of SDF officers has the possibility of violating Article 9 of the constitution.

Japan's Tradition of Nonintervention and UN Peace-Enforcement Operations and Peacekeeping Forces

Along with the need to gain the Diet's approval, the principle of gaining consent among the parties in conflict has been almost perfectly observed by the Japanese government. Although peacekeeping operations have been conducted in conflict areas where a cease-fire was not fully agreed upon (e.g., Somalia and East Timor), the Japanese government still maintains the principles of separating politics from economy as well as nonintervention. Japan is able to engage in the areas where there is no legitimate government, as seen in Cambodia in the early 1990s, but has been reluctant to jeopardize diplomatic relations with established political regimes (e.g., East Timor).

According to UN practice, consent, especially from conflicting parties other than the host country, is a matter of degree. In cases in which the government of a country has disintegrated, the United Nations has no way to obtain consent for the deployment of a UN peacekeeping operation. In a multiparty conflict, however, some parties' consent can be hard to maintain. Some factions within the host country, including armed elements, may object to that presence, and in the worst case, peacekeepers may need to use force as a last resort to defend themselves or restore order to a deteriorating field situation.[31]

In the multiparty situation, the Japanese government has been reluctant to intervene in domestic issues. It paid consideration to the Indonesian government in the case of East Timor, there were harsh multiparty conflicts in Yugoslavia, and conflicting parties attacked UN peacekeepers in Somalia, all of which made the Japanese government hesitate to go beyond the traditional "neutral" peacekeeping operations.[32]

Moreover, although not explicitly stated in the Peacekeeping Law, the Japanese government has been unlikely to dispatch its SDF personnel when a resolution of the Security Council refers to Chapter 7 of the UN Charter. As seen in the cases of Somalia, Yugoslavia, and East Timor, the unintended expansion of UN missions and roles in conflict areas would endanger the Japanese unit that seeks to maintain the fivefold principles.

Under the government's interpretation of the constitution, Japan is prohibited from participating in any UN peace-enforcement operations that involve the use or threat of force. The term *use of force* is not clearly defined, however.

Judging from the Diet's debate on the Peacekeeping Law, Japanese peacekeepers cannot participate in operations that are outside of the UN command but authorized by the Security Council under Chapter 7 of the Charter to use "all necessary means." Examples of UN-authorized enforcement operations are numerous: the multinational coalition force during the Gulf War, the United Task Force (UNITAF) in Somalia, the French-led force in the Rwandan civil war, the US-led force in the Haiti situation, and a multinational Implementation Force (IFOR) in Bosnia-Herzegovina.[33]

Japan is also unlikely to participate in an operation under the command of the United Nations with a mandate to conduct enforcement actions. The UN operation in Somalia is a typical example, and the Rapid Reaction Force in Bosnia-Herzegovina as a part of the UN Protection Force was also authorized to use force. Peace-enforcement actions were virtually unknown when the Peacekeeping Law was under discussion in 1991 and 1992. Based on this statement and the government's interpretation of the constitution, the Japanese government has been hesitant to conduct this kind of more forceful peacekeeping operation.

It can be seen from the above discussions that Japan's dispatch of peacekeepers has been circumscribed by the safety and danger in conflict areas. The original purpose of Article 9 of the constitution was to limit Japan's threatening of other countries. In peacekeeping operations, however, if SDF officers do not hold arms, they are in danger. The result then has been that Japanese peacekeepers should be sent to areas of traditional peacekeeping operations with no peace enforcement relating to Chapter 7 of the UN Charter. Lack of consent among conflicting parties may also endanger the Japanese peacekeepers, so Japan's dispatch should maintain the "nonintervention" principle. The limitation of having weapons, which originally sought to circumscribe Japan's threatening of others, has been altered to the hesitation of dispatching Japanese peacekeepers for their safety. In the argument, Article 9 has been used as a means to restrain Japan's involvement in UN operations.

When any one of the above factors presents itself in the decisionmaking process, Japan will be unlikely to send SDF units abroad, although individual civilians and civil servants may be dispatched based on the Ministry of Foreign Affairs (MOFA) Establishment Law. It provides that, by observing these factors, Japan has to look for less dangerous conflict appropriate for its action. Japan's dispatch of peacekeeping operations is then determined by these exogenous factors, and from that perspective, it will be difficult to consider policy options in terms of Japan's interest. In order for Japan to project its endogenous identity for international peace, there should be less dangerous conflicts to which Japan never dispatches its SDF as well as somewhat conflicted areas where Japan is able to engage in substantial peacekeeping operations.

Toward a New US-Japan Alliance: The Defense Program Outline

Looking back on the recent "human contributions" after Premier Koizumi took office, the year 2004 stands out as important for decisive changes. The prime minister started a new council on Japan's security defense capabilities in April 2004, and the council issued a report on their future vision.

Integrated security strategy is the key element in this vision and has two goals. The first is to prevent a direct threat from reaching Japan, in order to minimize the damage; the second focuses more on creating a stable international environment, emphasizing the importance of "reduc[ing] the chances of threats arising in various parts of the world . . . affecting the interests of Japanese expatriates and corporations overseas."[34] The goals of the strategy can be attained by three efforts: Japan's own efforts, cooperation with an alliance partner, and cooperation with the international community. The two goals and three efforts implied the "integration" of Japan's security strategy, and the report argued a need for the government to apply the "integrated decision-making mechanism." It also emphasized the roles of the Security Council, which is supposed to mix the constituents of the strategy.

Along with the overall plan, the report also identified the role of defense forces to support the new security strategy, calling for a "multi-functional flexible defense force."[35] The pivotal requirement of a flexible defense force is the ability to collect and analyze information. Broadening Japan's defense roles to include (1) responding to emergency situations, (2) strengthening intelligence capabilities, (3) reforming the defense industrial and technological base, and (4) emphasizing its international peacekeeping roles, the report envisioned Japan's more "global" roles in international security issues.[36]

In response to this council, the Japan Defense Agency issued a new outline of the defense program looking ahead to the upcoming decade. It assumed that the primary goal in seeking to create a stable international environment was to address "new threats" such as international terrorism or weapons of mass destruction. Given that, it paid more attention to the international dispatch of Japan's Self-Defense Forces along with the increase in its transportation capabilities. Compared with the 1970s conception of the "basic defense force" that stemmed from the international environment of growing détente, the new outline indicated Japan's readiness to prepare for more positive roles in international security. The outline also touched upon Japan's concern about North Korea's development of nuclear weapons and China's rise in military capabilities, the clear indication of which had appeared for the first time after the Japanese government issued the defense program outline in 1976.

The outline assumed Japan's more global role, reaching from East Asia toward the Middle East. That is, the role of the SDF is not limited to domestic defense issues within the Japanese territory but rather is focused on its international aspect. The internationalized role corresponds to the collaborative work with the US military, and the outline emphasized the importance of Japan's alliance with the US government while at the same time seeking to enlarge both allies' security tasks, reaching a wider geographic area.

Although the budgetary amount of the new program seems to be restrained under the banner of the "administrative reform," the substantial functions and transportation capabilities of the SDF should be advanced more. The Defense Agency outlined a plan of reducing the number of SDF officials, although the current shortage of personnel will result in the maintenance of the number of uniformed people in the near future.

The outline also indicated a need to reexamine the principle of banning the export of arms, at least to the United States. In the current joint technological research on ballistic missile defense by Japan and the United States, it assumes it is necessary to uphold the philosophy of the ban and instead to pursue the enhancement of procurement and research and development in the defense capabilities.

Conclusion

In the aftermath of the September 11 terrorism in New York and Washington, those who watch Japanese politics were surprised to see the decisiveness with which Prime Minister Koizumi acted to lend Japanese support to the US war on terrorism. Although Japan's response to the 1991 Gulf War had been condemned as "too little, too late," the Bush administration in 2001 praised Japan's swift cooperation, including the dispatch of SDF personnel. In the process, the long debate regarding "the threat and use of force," which is prohibited by Article 9 of the constitution, was interrupted over the shock of the terrorist attack, and about 600 SDF personnel came to be dispatched toward the oversea war zones.

What has distinguished the PKO debate from previous foreign policy controversies is precisely that it takes place in the midst of an international systemic change. The end of the Cold War and the US victory in the Gulf War challenged established global relationships and opened a new range of options for the Japanese government. Japan's pursuit of a more assertive role has been expected in relationship to Japan's formidable economic and technological capabilities. The international circumstances provide Japanese advocates for change with a chance to pursue their policy agenda with their conservative parties in power.[37]

Since the Gulf War, Japan's international role with respect to security has expanded to include not only the conducting of UN peacekeeping operations but also closer work with its chief ally, the United States. Collective self-defense rights and US-Japan security guidelines have emerged as key issues in the updated Japanese security roles. In the process, the conception of "Asia" has been widened for Japanese foreign policy. For five decades, Japan saw only China, Taiwan, the two Koreas, and Southeast Asian countries—all of which had profoundly negative memories of Japanese war crimes—as its neighbors. The legacies of imperialism and colonialism have prevented its relationships with other Asian countries from developing and maturing. Although Japanese war crimes are unforgivable historical facts, it is also true that there has been an excessive emphasis on the issue for other political purposes by Japan and its neighbors alike.

The long-term success in this regard required changing the existing domestic political institutions. For instance, dispatching SDF officers to conflict areas has been mainly discussed within the Foreign Ministry, not the Self-Defense Agency or National Police Agency. Under the circumstances, the SDF officers and civilian policemen are conducting more than what they were assigned when they entered the Self-Defense Forces. Other ministries, not directly related to peace and security in the world, are usually (also intentionally) indifferent to the issues. Although peacekeeping operations require a great deal of expertise, such as education, medical care, construction, water supply, and so forth, the Foreign Ministry in charge of the peacekeeping operations has dispatched quite a small number of officials to the conflict areas.[38] It would take some time to change Japan's domestic constraints toward the new international environment in the post–Cold War era. Today's interdependent world and Japan's position have pressed the Japanese government, however, to consider more contributions for international peace and security.[39]

Notes

1. Foreign Ministry, *Diplomatic Bluebook 1991,* 360.
2. Iwanaga, "The UN in Japan's Foreign Policy: An Emerging Assertive UN Centrism," 43.
3. Suzuki Yoshikatsu, "Anpōri Kamei: Gaimushō no Shosō."
4. Hook et al., *Japan's International Relations: Politics,* 323.
5. Shinyo, *Kokusai Heiwa Kyoryoku Nyumon,* chap. 2.
6. Ministry of Foreign Affairs, *Diplomatic Yearbook, 1957.*
7. Immerman, "Japan in the United Nations," 185.
8. Kawabe, *Kokuren to Nihon.*
9. Kozai, *Kokuren no Heiwa-iji Katsudo,* 485–486.
10. Heinrich, Shibata, and Soeya, *United Nations Peace-keeping Operations: A Guide to Japanese Policies,* 10–11.
11. The holding of economic summits starting in the mid-1970s is a typical example. In the face of the increasing influence of Third World countries on the UN General Assembly, the G5 established a small club that could discuss macroeconomic issues. Kawabe, *Kokuren to Nihon.*
12. Saito, "The Evolution of Japan's United Nations Policy," 1–2. Given the situation, although Foreign Ministry officials started a new effort in the late 1970s to study the UN peacekeeping operations and considered the possibility of Japan's participation, the report did not attract wide attention. Heinrich, Shibata, and Soeya, *United Nations Peace-keeping Operations,* 16–17.
13. Iwanaga, "The UN in Japan's Foreign Policy: An Emerging Assertive UN Centrism," 39–40.
14. Tanaka Akihiko, "Kokuren Heiwa-katsudō to Nihon," 141.
15. Ibid., 145–147.
16. Heinrich, Shibata, and Soeya, *United Nations Peace-keeping Operations,* 24–27.
17. The data are taken from the following IPCHQ Web site: http://www.pko.go.jp/PKO_E/rwanda_e.html.
18. Ministry of Foreign Affairs, "The Guidelines for Japan-U.S. Defense Cooperation." Available at http://www.mofa.go.jp/region/n-america/us/security/guideline2.html (accessed April 5, 2006).
19. "Backing of U.S. Revives Debate on SDF," *Japan Times,* September 28, 2001.

20. Infinite Justice was later changed to Enduring Freedom to mollify the anger of Muslims around the world.

21. Sakurada and Ito, *Hikaku Gaiko Seisaku: Iraq Senso heno Taio Gaiko.*

22. Information from IPCHQ Web site: http://www.pko.go.jp/PKO_E/pref_e.html#5rules.

23. Durch, *The Evolution of UN Peacekeeping: Case Studies and Comparative Analysis,* chap. 1.

24. Kohno, *Wahei Kōsaku: Tai Cambodia Gaikō no Shōgen,* chap. 4. He was, as a Foreign Ministry official, in charge of Japan's dispatch to the UNTAC. See also Drifte, *Japan's Quest for a Permanent Security Council Seat: A Matter of Pride or Justice?* 70–72; Drifte, "Japan's Quest for a Permanent Seat on the Security Council."

25. Heinrich, Shibata, and Soeya, *United Nations Peace-keeping Operations,* 63.

26. Ibid., 64.

27. That is, the limitations imposed on Japan's participation are much stricter than the UN policy on self-defense, which allows UN personnel to use force to protect their own lives and the lives of other UN personnel as well as UN posts, vehicles, and other facilities and to counteract attempts to prevent them from performing their UN duties.

28. Shinyō, *Kokusai Heiwa Kyōryoku Nyūmon,* chap. 4.

29. The Foreign Ministry can dispatch civil servants and other civilians to participate in UN peacekeeping and election monitoring without invoking the Peacekeeping Law. The legal basis is the Ministry of Foreign Affairs Establishment Law and other related laws, which allow the ministry to send national and local public servants to international organizations. Since the passage of the Peacekeeping Law, the dispatch of civilians is also examined by the Diet. Although the dispatch of SDF officers should be judged by the Diet, it is not that clear in which case civilians' participation is examined.

30. During the debate over the Peacekeeping Law, some politicians were concerned that the complicated process of dispatching Japanese peacekeepers would delay approval for participation in peace operations. As a result, the final draft of the bill included a provision that each house of the Diet would endeavor to make a decision within seven working days.

31. Durch, *The Evolution of UN Peacekeeping,* 5.

32. An example of a potentially delicate situation is that of how the Japanese government will respond if there is a crisis between mainland China and Taiwan. The recent trend of Japan's attitude has been to establish emergent cooperation with the US government (e.g., Guidelines for the US-Japan Defense Cooperation), not to resort to the UN for peacekeeping (or peace enforcement) activities toward the cross-strait issues. It implies that whether the Japanese government will break the sovereign principle in international society depends not on Japan itself but on the other country's decision.

33. This part of the Peacekeeping Law was modified in June 1998. Reflecting the lessons and experiences of previously dispatched operations, the law now enables Japan to contribute to international election monitoring activities implemented *outside* the framework of UN peacekeeping operations in areas of conflicts. Second, the law enables Japan to take part in international humanitarian relief operations *without cease-fire agreements having been reached,* if they are conducted by certain international organizations. Third, the law stipulates that the use of weapons should be conducted under the orders of a senior officer in order to ensure more

appropriate use of weapons. Also in June 1998, Japan's International Peace Cooperation Headquarters established a registration system for International Peace Cooperation Corps candidates. The registration started with the area of international humanitarian relief operations. It seeks to register a pool of a wide range of individuals with expertise and desire to become members of the corps and to prepare them for dispatch with necessary training. See Prime Minister's Office, *Paths to International Peace: Japan's Contributions to World Peace* (emphasis added). See also Ministry of Foreign Affairs, *Japan and the United Nations,* 2.

34. Council on Security and Defense Capabilities, *Japan's Vision for Future Security and Defense Capabilities,* 5.

35. Ibid., 11–13.

36. The report also touched upon the need to reexamine Japan's constitution in the future. It mentioned a need to discuss the exercise of the right of collective self-defense with an eye to clarifying what Japan should and could do for the international roles outlined in the report.

37. Doyle, Johnstone, and Orr, *Keeping the Peace: Multidimensional UN Operations in Cambodia and El Salvador,* chap. 1.

38. Interview with a Foreign Ministry official, New York, August 1999.

39. Doyle, Johnson, and Orr, *Keeping the Peace,* chap. 1.

| 5 |

A Defense Posture for Multilateral Security

Michael O'Hanlon

Japan presently spends the equivalent of more than $40 billion annually on its military. That means that, in rough terms, Japan, France, the United Kingdom, China, and Russia are effectively tied for second place in world military spending. Although that spending level is quite modest compared to a US total of more than $400 billion (not even counting the costs of war), it is still quite significant.[1] Yet despite Japan's recent decision to send several hundred troops to Iraq, it contributes little to regional or global security with that budget; it arguably does much more simply by hosting US military forces and supporting them to some extent financially. Its military does a good job of providing defense for Japanese territory, but the need for such a defense has greatly diminished since the end of the Cold War and does not warrant $40 billion in yearly defense outlays.

More than sixty years after World War II and nearly two decades after the fall of the Berlin wall, it is time for Japan to do more in the international security sphere. It need not mimic the United States or otherwise develop unilateral power projection capabilities that would unsettle some neighbors and displease many Japanese. Nor need it necessarily increase defense spending. (Whether or not it would be wise to make security-related constitutional changes is debatable, and not a subject I address here.) But what Japan does need to do is reexamine the basic way in which it structures and equips its military and plans for its possible use.

Yet Japan must also be careful. It has shown some signs of expanding its global security role of late, including contributions to the possible defense of Taiwan, in its recent National Defense Program Guidelines and other official declarations. These decisions, welcome as they often are in Washington, can hurt Japan's image, especially when they are coupled with perceptions in China and Korea of the Japanese public's increasing nationalism. They are among the reasons that Japan is having difficulty gaining support for its bid to become a permanent member of the UN Security Council. They also run the risk of worsening crises over disputed islands and seabed resources, and more generally of worsening overall relations, with China and South Korea. Controversial decisions are not necessarily wrong, of course. But Japan has a particular need—and a particular national interest—to reassure its neighbors even as it broadens its global security role.

This chapter offers one notional way of doing so: a reorientation of the Japanese armed forces within approximately ten years, accomplished in a way that should minimize the dangers of Japan's being seen as dangerously nationalistic by its neighbors. The main objective is to make Japan much more capable of deploying and supporting modest numbers of infantry troops overseas for purposes ranging from humanitarian relief to peacekeeping to peace enforcement to limited counterterrorism operations should circumstances so dictate. An additional goal is to make Japan capable of helping transport and supply other countries' militaries involved in such missions, since Japan has the resources to purchase the relatively expensive equipment needed for such purposes (and most other countries do not).

This approach to restructuring the Japanese military does not require a complete abandonment of existing Japanese defense priorities. Japan could still pursue naval and aerospace excellence, acquire technologies designed to promote what some argue is an incipient revolution in military affairs, and ensure the defensibility of its home islands. But under the approach suggested here, unless it wanted to increase national defense spending by at least $5 billion a year, it would have to scale back these efforts or undertake them in more selective, and inexpensive, ways.

The Japanese Self-Defense Forces in 2006

Japan's armed forces today are composed of approximately 240,000 active-duty uniformed personnel. About 148,000 are in the army, 45,000 in the navy (including naval aviation), and 46,000 in the air force. Another 40,000 individuals are in the reserves, almost all in the army (that is, the Ground Self-Defense Forces).[2] These numbers have changed little in recent years.

The army's forces are predominantly organized into nine infantry divisions. Japan also has an armored division, an airborne brigade, several other independent brigades, and numerous other, generally smaller units focused on missions such as air defense, engineering, and antitank warfare by helicopter. Naval forces feature 16 attack submarines, 53 surface combatants, 31 mine countermeasures ships, 5 amphibious vessels with a combined troop carrying capacity of roughly 1,200, and 80 P-3 aircraft for maritime surveillance as well as certain combat missions. Finally, the air forces include about 130 ground-attack planes, 150 fighter aircraft, 20 reconnaissance planes, 14 airborne warning and control aircraft, and a modest air transport fleet with approximately 30 mid-size, medium-range transport aircraft, a few 747s (principally for carrying important personnel), and several dozen transport helicopters.[3]

Stepping away from all the detail, this is a military that places most of its people in ground units but spends most of its weapons dollars on air and naval systems. Japan's military is larger than Britain's and Italy's in size and comparable to those of France and Germany. Japan has much smaller reserves than most of the above-mentioned European countries with comparable defense budgets and active-duty troop strengths.

As is well-known, Japan's military missions revolve primarily around providing defense for the nation's territory and for helping to defend sea lanes and airspace extending out as far as approximately 1,000 miles from Tokyo. That latter mission became important during the later decades of the Cold War and continues today despite the lack of a serious threat. Likewise, Japan's Ground Self-Defense Forces retain most of their characteristics from the Cold War, despite the absence of a plausible threat to Japan's territory from any power. In fact, it is remarkable how little Japan's armed forces have been adapted to the post–Cold War era. The United States has reduced its military strength by one-third since 1990, and European NATO countries have cut their forces by almost as much on average. Japan's military, by contrast, remains only a few percent smaller than a decade ago.

A Liberal Internationalist Vision for Japan's Security Policy

In my judgment, Japan should adopt a military that cannot only defend the home islands and neighboring regions but also contribute to certain types of multilateral security operations abroad. In other Asian countries, many would oppose such a Japanese security policy out of fear of latent Japanese militarism. Within Japan, that worry exists too. So does a pacifist-leaning belief that countries should no longer build armed forces to employ on each other's territories, be that country Japan or anyone else.

But Japan has many options besides becoming a "normal" power or remaining a civilian, largely pacifist power. A number of Japanese politicians, notably Ozawa Ichirō, have suggested how this might happen in the Japanese context.[4] The basic idea of a military middle ground for Japan would expand the country's physical capacities for operations abroad but keep legal, diplomatic, and military checks on these new capacities so as to reassure Japan's neighbors and the Japanese people about the nature of the effort. The goal would expressly not be that Japan become an independent, global military power.

Under this proposed framework, Japan would consider projecting power only in the context of multilateral security missions. According to Ozawa Ichirō, a UN Security Council resolution would be needed to authorize such an operation (unless Japan's security were at direct risk). Such UN approval would be preferred, but Tokyo would retain the option of acting in a collaborative operation with the United States and other countries even in its absence. An additional restraint would arise from the nature of Japanese democracy today. Elements of latent Japanese militarism indeed do still exist within Japanese society today, just as similar forms of nationalism and militarism exist in many if not most other countries. But the political strength of such ideas is generally rather weak, and the prospects for their increased strength rather limited. That is hardly surprising; modern industrial societies, whatever their other flaws, do not generally appear to relish overseas military operations, largely because such operations tend to offer little economic or political gain, cause casualties, and run great risks of escalation. Thus the Japan of 2007 is not the Japan of the 1930s and 1940s and has little chance of becoming like the latter in the future. This is not a judgment shared by all, particularly not by many in China and Korea. But upon further reflection, some may change their minds—if not immediately, then eventually, once Japan has demonstrated the purposes for which it has acquired the new military capabilities and shown that it has no intention of truly remilitarizing.

As an additional argument for those who doubt this conclusion, it is worth invoking the parallel situation in Germany, which recently dropped bombs on a former World War II victim in NATO's 1999 Operation Allied Force against Serbia. If Germany can go so far without still being hamstrung by the past, why not Japan? Granted, multilateral security structures for Asia comparable to NATO do not now exist, and Germany would not have acted as it did outside a NATO context. So the pace of change may wind up being slower in the case of Japan. And the challenges are different. But that does not invalidate the basic idea that change should be possible.

Those who still worry about the latent Japanese national character can take solace in a more concrete fact. Under my proposal, Japan would acquire only very limited capabilities for power projection. The capabilities would be significant for humanitarian and peace operations, particularly in light of the presumed multilateral context, but far from adequate to pose a threat to any country of moderate to large size in Asia or elsewhere. The alternative force structure outlined below would involve no more than a couple tens of thousands of mobile ground combat troops, far too few to threaten a country like China, Korea, or even the Philippines or Vietnam. Yet those numbers would be quite substantial when measured against the demands of global humanitarian, peacekeeping, and peace enforcement missions, which have tended to require 50,000 to 100,000 troops from all countries combined, worldwide, over the last decade.

Granted, once Japan had a modest overseas military capability, it could in theory expand it. But there is little reason to think that the Japan of today would move in such a direction, as argued before. Moreover, in light of the transparent, public nature of Japanese military planning today, there would be numerous signs of any such policy long before it could be implemented.

The basic logic of my proposed security policy actually shares many of the philosophical and moral concerns of Japanese pacifists, even if it goes about addressing them in a much different way than those who eschew the development and use of Japanese military power. It is premised on the idea that countries left to their own devices, and acting unilaterally, are more likely to become aggressive and dangerous. Far better to continue strengthening global security structures that bind countries together in alliances and that try to use UN procedures to guide any international uses of military force.

It is better, by this cooperative security logic, for Japan to broaden its cooperation with its ally, the United States, and with other countries to the extent possible than to consider a more unilateralist approach to security. It is also better for it to do so than to simply sustain the status quo, which risks a backlash in the United States from Americans who may someday become frustrated that they must bear higher economic, and perhaps blood, costs to protect mutual US and Japanese interests in Asia. The status quo also leaves Washington with most of the influence in the alliance—something Japanese pacifists should presumably oppose, unless they believe that the United States is incapable of making major mistakes in its security policy (an assumption that few Americans would themselves share). Checks and balances on the use of military force can be a desirable product of alliances characterized by genuine burden sharing. The US-Japan alliance does not fit that description today, however.

Finally, the logic for this type of security vision is that the world continues to have serious security problems. Be they genocides in Cambodia, Rwanda, and Bosnia; threats from international networks of terrorists; threats to citizens of countries such as Japan living or traveling abroad; or simple criminal acts by pirates in the South China Sea and elsewhere, there will continue to be a need for projecting military power if one is to safeguard lives and promote international stability. Thus, the same liberal and moral values that influence many pacifists can lead to a strong argument in favor of Japan's doing its fair share to help with global security problems that are likely to remain prevalent and to put many innocent lives at risk in the future.

Ideas and Models for Japan's Military from Other Countries

With a military budget that, although large, is hardly enormous and with its need to provide a certain capability for defense of nearby airspace and waters, how could Japan find the resources to develop more capable power projection forces?

There are reasons to think that this should be possible. A number of examples from other countries' experiences and militaries may point the way. Great Britain, another island nation, which maintains not only substantial naval and air forces but also a nuclear deterrent, nevertheless has the ability to move tens of thousands of troops overseas for combat or peace-keeping purposes—as it did in Desert Storm and the Iraq War, and as it was reportedly ready to do if NATO had conducted an invasion of Kosovo in 1999. (Alas, Japan is hardly alone among major US allies lacking significant power projection capability; most other European militaries remain quite limited in these areas.[5])

Throughout much of the post–Cold War era, the United States Marine Corps has had a budget of some $20 billion a year. (Admittedly, it gets assistance from other US military services for shipping, reconnaissance, research and development, and certain other defense costs, but it must nonetheless provide its own combat forces, airpower, and logistics support.) Even with such a limited budget, it also has the ability to quickly move tens of thousands of troops overseas and sustain them there.

If Japan chooses to move toward the proposed alternative national security policy and force posture, it will probably do so out of the recognition that its home islands are now much more secure against possible invasion than was the case during the Cold War—meaning that active-duty ground forces may not be needed in the numbers currently maintained. If so, in addition to considering the examples of Britain and of the United States Marine Corps, it is natural to examine the cases of Switzerland and the Scandinavian countries—small nations with some geographic defensive advantages that have traditionally used those advantages well to resist much larger potential aggressors nearby.

Switzerland represents an extreme example of how to defend a territory enjoying natural defensive advantages with an inexpensive military. Switzerland has a population of just 7.5 million, less than 10 percent of that of neighboring Germany, and a defense budget of only $4 billion or so. It makes maximum use of that limited budget by maintaining a force that is almost entirely constituted by reserves. Specifically, its active-duty forces number only 4,300, but its reserves exceed 200,000 (almost all in the army, with about 30,000 in the air force). Its army forces are primarily infantry units, though it does own more than 200 tanks and comparable numbers of armored personnel carriers, armored infantry fighting vehicles, towed artillery, and self-propelled artillery (as well as much larger numbers of mortars and antitank weapons).[6]

One might argue that at this point in history Switzerland may face less of a possible threat from abroad than Japan. It strains credulity, however, to think that even a hostile and embittered China would really try to invade and subjugate Japanese territory. Moreover, Switzerland has used this type of defense strategy for decades, if not centuries, and demonstrated its relative efficacy even in more difficult geostrategic times.

The Scandinavian countries, facing a Soviet threat more directly than Switzerland ever has for most of the last half century (and thus sharing a number of defense challenges with Japan), have not gone to quite the extreme of Switzerland in their reliance on the reserves. But they nonetheless have adopted some of the same ideas. Neutral Sweden, with a population of 9 million and a defense budget of about $6 billion, has an active-duty military of about 30,000 and reserves of 260,000. Its army is easily its largest military service, but its navy and air force together have about half as many active-duty personnel and one-sixth as many reservists. Finland has a population of 5 million, a defense budget of less than $3 billion, active forces numbering about 30,000, and reservists numbering about 240,000. Its army is its largest force, constituting an even higher percentage of total military strength than is the case in Sweden. Finally, NATO member Norway, with a population of 4.5 million and defense budget of about $5 billion, has 25,000 active-duty uniformed military personnel and 210,000 reservists. Its active-duty air force and navy are together half as large as its army; its reservists are primarily ground forces.[7]

Of course, all of these countries have much different histories, security positions, national self-identities, and regional diplomatic contexts than Japan. The last four are also all much smaller than Japan. But together, their ways of providing for defense—something that all are considered to do rather well, judging not only by their effort but also by their results—hold out an intriguing potential lesson for Japan. If the self-defense forces restructured their ground component, relying much more on reserves for territorial defense and restructuring the active-duty units into a smaller, more mobile army, Japan could develop the capacity to contribute meaningfully to multilateral security operations abroad without having to increase its defense budget—and without giving fair-minded neighbors any real reason to worry that Japan was remilitarizing.

An Alternative Japanese Defense Posture

Taking the above ideas and combining them into a different Japanese defense posture, designed to remain affordable at the current $40 billion annual level of defense expenditure (based on existing exchange rates), leads to this set of ideas:

• A Japanese air force generally similar to today's, though with less emphasis on northern Japanese islands, given the rapid and essentially irreversible decline of Russian military strength.

• Greater capacity for long-range airlift in the air forces to move not only Japanese troops but those of other countries who may be participating in peace operations or humanitarian relief missions—necessitating the purchase of modest numbers of intercontinental transport aircraft and some refueling aircraft as well.

• A Japanese navy similar to today's but with somewhat less focus on the antisubmarine warfare mission (though still substantial capability). The navy would also gain freedom to operate more than 1,000 miles from Tokyo and to participate if necessary in risky operations such as minesweeping during hostilities and actual enforcement (rather than just monitoring) of maritime embargoes.

• Increases in dedicated military sealift capable of operating in undeveloped ports and of rapidly loading and unloading equipment and available for immediate use by the JSDF or, should Tokyo so decide, the forces of other countries in the event of crisis.

• A drastically reduced active-duty army for territorial defense.

• A substantial increase in the strength and capabilities of reserve units in the Ground Self-Defense Forces.

• Creation of an expeditionary ground capability, numbering perhaps 20,000 to 50,000 individuals (so as to permit sustained deployment of at least two brigades and ideally of at least a full division as well as numerous other capabilities such as military police and translators). Soldiers would be equipped logistically for sustained operations abroad and trained for a full spectrum of missions, ranging from humanitarian relief to armed forcible intervention to stop genocides and other civil conflicts, to hostage rescue and counterterrorism.

About how much would this agenda cost? Is it really true that it could be afforded at present defense spending levels? And how great might some of the specific capabilities be—for example, how much airlift and sealift might be acquired?

The Maritime Self-Defense Forces

Consider each of Japan's military services in turn. The navy would need to add only a modest amount of dedicated, roll-on/roll-off sealift. It might, for example, purchase enough to transport roughly one heavy division of ground forces—that is, their equipment and supplies for several weeks of operations. The United States has two categories of ships used most prominently for this purpose, SL-7s and large medium-speed roll-on/roll-off vessels (LMSRs), and presently owns about 24 in all (with a goal of 27).[8] It takes about 6 to 10 of these vessels to move a division and its supplies, depending on the precise nature of the division and the amount of support equipment and supplies transported. Thus, Japan might buy 10. Alternatively, it could purchase smaller roll-on/roll-off ships, each with a capacity about one-third as great as the larger ships, that are more useful in small and shallow harbors and that have the added benefit of being less expensive (perhaps $40 to $50 million versus $250 to $300 million in costs per ship).

To gain the benefits of each type of ship, I would advocate a mix of perhaps four LMSR ships with a dozen smaller vessels. Total acquisition costs might be $1.5 billion to $2 billion and might be spread over approximately a ten-year time horizon (as fast as can be imagined, in political terms, even given the spirit of this rather ambitious proposal). Modest annual operating costs of $50 million to $75 million would result thereafter, and of course the capital investment would in theory eventually have to be replaced, though not for several decades.[9]

How would the maritime Self-Defense Forces pay for these increased expenditures of roughly $150 to $200 million a year in the near term and up to $75 million annually thereafter? Most logically, by reducing the size of the surface combatant fleet. I am incapable of developing a complete force structure alternative here. But it is notable that two of Japan's five major naval bases, specifically those in Ominato on northern Honshu and Maizuru on western Honshu on the Sea of Japan, appear far less important than those located or facing more southward (at Yokosuka, Kure, and Sasebo). The drastic decline in Russian capabilities, the unlikelihood that Japan would need to or wish to play a major maritime role in any future war between the Koreas, and the undesirability of contemplating any long-range naval competition with South Korea tend to argue against maintaining large naval forces at those bases.

In any case, one need not adopt a radically new maritime concept to implement this plan. Needed cuts in forces are modest—probably fewer than ten ships—and would hardly require complete disengagement from the Sea of Japan or other northern waters.

Alternatively, of course, Japan could also increase its defense budget modestly to fund this or any other initiative considered here. It could also consider reducing host-nation support payments for US forces on the grounds that, if it does more in wielding force itself, it need not do quite as much in supporting the US military. Throughout the rest of this discussion, however, I will assume a fixed defense budget and constant host-nation support payments.

Once the sealift was purchased, Japan might also consider a modest expansion in its amphibious fleet, budgets and domestic and regional politics permitting. But that is a less essential matter to consider at present.

Japan's Air Forces

Japan's air forces would have to make somewhat greater investments, in budget terms, to provide the capabilities I advocate. They too are modest in scale, however, and would be quite small once an initial five-year transition period had been completed.

Again, the needed funds might be found, without any increase in overall spending, by making modest cuts in Japanese defense efforts in northern parts of the country. Japan might also consider scaling back purchases of advanced aircraft in the future, to fund airlift and refueling planes. For example, it might decide to make do without aircraft such as the F-22 and joint strike fighter that the United States is now developing for its own future forces (and hoping to sell abroad). Upgraded F-15s and F-16s, equipped with more advanced sensors, munitions, computers, and communications systems, would be quite adequate for regional defense given the limited strides being made by China in these types of high-technology areas and the steep decline in the Russian combat aircraft industry. Or Japan could buy modest numbers of next-generation planes and larger numbers of existing types.

What sort of airlift and refueling aircraft armada would make sense for Japan? The United States is purchasing close to 200 C-17 aircraft, and it has 125 of the supersized C-5s, for a total of more than 300 dedicated long-range transport planes.[10] Under the above proposal for sealift, Japan would acquire roughly one-third of US modern roll-on/roll-off capability and 10 to 20 percent of total US military sealift by tonnage. Were it to seek a comparable amount of airlift, that would imply purchase of 30 to 60 C-17s.

Alternatively, Tokyo might consider a mix of C-17 aircraft, capable of carrying tanks, helicopters, artillery, and trucks, together with adapted civilian aircraft for carrying bulk supplies. Such a mix would be cheaper, though the 747s or DC-10s or other large commercial planes would be more constrained in their use of various runways around the world. For its refueling needs, Japan might purchase ten to twenty DC-10-like aircraft. It could also do what the United States does and purchase some planes usable for either refueling or transport (these are variants of the DC-10 known as KC-10s). All in all, I will assume here that Japan might purchase twenty C-17 lift aircraft and thirty KC-10 lift/refueling dual-purpose aircraft under this initiative.

How many troops, tanks, and other supplies might these airplanes carry? A large military transport aircraft might hold 40 to 50 tons of equipment, meaning that Japan might be able to transport up to 2,000 tons per sortie using its entire fleet. A single heavy division in the US military weighs about 100,000 tons, and even light and airborne or air mobile divisions weigh 20,000 to 30,000 tons. In rough terms, those 2,000 tons of supplies that Japan could transport would not be enough to equip more than 1,000 soldiers. This is a very modest capability. It could be significant for peace operations, particularly assuming secure airfields that permit rapid reinforcements with additional planeloads of supplies and people. It could not be significant against a hostile foe with a sizable military, meaning that it should not, in and of itself, incite legitimate concern among Japan's neighbors.

The cost of this initiative might be $250 to $300 million per C-17 and about half that much per plane for the civilian aircraft. Total investment costs could approach $10 billion, with operating costs of $300 million to $500 million thereafter. Assuming a ten-year acquisition period, that translates to $1 billion a year in investment and would cost one-third to one-half as much thereafter. This would amount to less than 10 percent of the annual cost of the Japanese air forces.

Japan now has about 280 combat aircraft.[11] The average annual cost of having an air force of that size is roughly $3 billion to $5 billion a year (though costs fluctuate substantially, depending on how many aircraft are being purchased at a given time, of course). Cuts of about 25 percent in these fighter and ground-attack aircraft could thus fund the airlift/refueling initiative. Alternatively, smaller cuts, together with reductions in other types of air force assets, could fund the proposed program.

The Ground Self-Defense Forces

Rather than have an army with 148,000 soldiers and 35,000 reservists, virtually all of whom are focused exclusively on home-island defense, Japan could radically restructure its ground-combat capabilities. It might wind up with a nucleus of 50,000 active-duty soldiers for territorial self-protection in the extremely unlikely event of an attempted invasion by a foreign power in the twenty-first century, around which 100,000 or even more reservists might mobilize to form a larger home defense capability. It could then develop another arm of the ground-defense forces, or a new military service entirely, with up to 50,000 active-duty troops for overseas efforts.

Since reservists in the ground forces typically cost only one-fourth to one-third as much, per person, as active-duty troops (counting training and equipment), it would actually save money to adopt this option. An increase in reserve units of 50,000 to 75,000 individuals would cost less than the savings generated by cutting active-duty forces by 45,000. Net savings might not materialize for several years, however, since the overseas units would need mobile equipment and support capabilities that they do not currently possess.

What would these new support capabilities cost? The capabilities would consist of what a modern military force separated from its home economy typically needs in order to support its troops and their weapons. Notable on the list of required assets are mobile equipment repair depots and hospitals, transport trucks, mobile bridging and other engineering equipment, water purification and distribution systems, mobile fuel storage containers and dispensing equipment, and more mundane requirements such as food distribution and preparation facilities for troops. In some types of peace operations, a number of these capabilities will not be needed, since host nations will be cooperative and ample time will be available to contract for indigenous logistics support. But in more urgent, more hostile, or more rudimentary and undeveloped environments, one cannot assume that such capabilities will be present.

Indeed, as much as its high-technology capabilities, it is the US military's simple ability to transport and then sustain itself far from home that makes it a global military power. Japan hardly needs to approach US capabilities in scale, but it can create what would be in effect a miniaturized version of the United States Marine Corps—or perhaps, as a better analogy, a capability like that of the rapid-reaction forces now being created by the European Union, designed to rapidly deploy and support up to 60,000 troops outside of NATO territory for extended periods.

About $5 billion might be needed for this hardware acquisition, averaging out to $500 million a year over a decade-long period.[12]

Japan and the Iraq Deployment

Before concluding, a word is in order about the most salient military issue of the day in Japan. After much difficult deliberation and debate, the Koizumi Junichirō government deployed 600 Japanese troops to the US-led stabilization operation in Iraq for several years. They worked alongside approximately another 25,000 foreign troops, including just over 10,000 British and 3,000 South Koreans as well as more than 100,000 US soldiers. They departed Iraq in July 2006.

Japanese leaders and the Japanese people are to be commended and thanked for their willingness to send even a modest force to Iraq. The United States is greatly in need of help in this mission. The operation is proving extremely demanding on its all-volunteer military. It is also giving rise to an unfortunate perception among the Iraqi people and much of the world that the United States desires to dominate their country and region through largely unilateral uses of military force.

Japan's assistance has thus been quite important. And the Japanese government's willingness to take political risks, both domestically and in regard to other countries in the Asia Pacific region that have mixed feelings about its decision to send even small forces abroad, is courageous.

Those of us who would like to see Japan do a good deal more in the international security arena, and particularly in peace operations, must also ask, however, if Iraq was the optimal place for Japan to take its next big steps. But the broader issue of what Japan should do next with its capable Self-Defense Forces remains relevant regardless.

There is a serious case that Japan should send forces to other critical multilateral peace and stabilization missions—in the Balkans, Sierra Leone, or Congo, for example—rather than missions such as Iraq or even Afghanistan. These operations in other parts of the world are also all very important. And for most of them there are not sufficient numbers of available skilled forces.

In Congo, for example, a force of about 15,000 UN peacekeepers is attempting to shore up a peace in a country more than ten times the size and population of Bosnia or Kosovo (and twice that of Iraq). Yet missions in these other countries have generally been endowed with several times as many peacekeepers.

Japan is a very casualty-averse country and a rather pacifist one as well. These facts have their advantages and disadvantages, but the point is that they are facts, and ones that policymakers would do well to remember. They derive from Japan's entire national experience and political psyche of the last sixty years.

Given the Japanese public's well-known reluctance to tolerate casualties to its own troops, as evidenced in the Cambodia mission a decade ago, it is not clear that Japan should dive into missions such as Iraq headfirst. One must walk before one can run.

This is not to say that operations in places such as Congo would be safe or easy; indeed, Japan's excellent military capabilities would be greatly beneficial in these places. But in Congo, the greatest risks are likely to be the country's huge size and the possibility of accidents or the occasional random gunfight—not the concerted terrorist actions of a hardened group of angry, hateful guerrillas bent on defeating the United States and its allies at any cost.

Focusing on missions such as Operation Iraqi Freedom may be the best way to please Japan's only ally, but it also may be the riskiest next step for the Japanese polity to take in its gradual, noble, and necessary efforts to do more in global peace operations. A catastrophe in Iraq could cause a major setback in Japan's gradually increasing willingness to use its military as a force for good in the international system. And that outcome would outweigh any benefit it could provide to the United States in the interim.

Conclusion

Japan is a secure country today. It is also a nation with strong democratic institutions and no more latent tendencies toward aggressiveness or militarism than most of the world's major powers. The first fact means that Japan can now afford to spend some of its more than $40 billion equivalent annual defense budget on needs other than its own territorial self-defense and protection of nearby seas and airways. The latter fact means, in this US observer's judgment at least, that it should have far fewer qualms about developing limited capacities for overseas military deployments than many of its neighbors, and indeed many of its own citizens, would prefer emotionally and viscerally.

That latter fact is especially true given that it is possible to sketch out an agenda for Japanese power projection that would provide useful capacities for humanitarian missions, peace operations, and other limited military activities without approaching the levels that would hypothetically be needed for an aggressive power.

In addition, although there are admittedly international political risks if Japan tries to do too much in the security sphere, there are also risks if it and other countries around the world do too little. Civil violence continues to claim nearly half a million lives a year globally; many of those lives could be saved by more muscular peace operations that would be possible to contemplate if the world's capacity for carrying them out increased. International terrorist networks continue to exist, with some apparently willing to target Japanese citizens abroad, at least in the recent past. And the Asia Pacific region remains vulnerable to destabilization from conflicts of the type that can be addressed through a combination of wise diplomacy and capable multilateral military forces. The world should be thankful that Australia provided most of the necessary capabilities in East Timor earlier in this decade, doing Japan and other regional countries (and the United States) an enormous favor in the process. Tokyo should not continue to count on such help or in good conscience expect it from others without contributing itself.

Notes

1. International Institute for Strategic Studies, *The Military Balance 2007*, 354–357.
2. Ibid.
3. Ibid.
4. Ozawa, *Nihon Kaizō Keikaku*, 106–121.
5. O'Hanlon, *Expanding Global Military Capacity*, 56.
6. International Institute for Strategic Studies, *The Military Balance 2007*.
7. Ibid.
8. Ibid.
9. Congressional Budget Office, *Moving U.S. Forces*.
10. Ibid.
11. Ibid.
12. O'Hanlon, "Transforming NATO: The Role of European Forces."

| Part 2 |
Economic Relations

6

Adapting to Global Economic Change

Edward J. Lincoln

Changes in Japan's domestic and international economic environment have had a profound impact on constraining, propelling, and shaping the nature of the nation's broader international engagement. New or changing economic circumstances over the past three decades have led to a shifting set of domestic demands on foreign policy and rising international demands for greater Japanese involvement in providing global public goods. At the same time, economic developments have affected the supply side as well, expanding the capacity of the state to engage in multilateral policy formation.

The past half-century divides into three phases. The first, from 1945 to 1973, was one of great insularity. Although Japan developed a reputation as a successful export nation, actual economic engagement with the outside world was minimal—firms remained at home, outward capital flows were low, and a variety of official barriers largely kept out both manufactured imports and foreign capital. The nation concentrated on domestic economic development and regarded international economic developments and policy issues at the multilateral institutions as being largely beyond the scope of proactive policy possibilities.

The second phase ran from 1974 through 1990. A variety of changes— the large size of the economy in international comparison, the sudden disruption of crude oil supplies and the accompanying price increase, macroeconomic changes producing a large net outflow of capital, and the sudden appreciation of the yen in 1985—all drove the nation into a much broader economic engagement with the rest of the world. Taking on a more active role in regional and global affairs was hindered, however, by continuing serious asymmetries on trade and investment. Even though Japanese firms and investors advanced rapidly into the outside world, access to the Japanese economy remained more difficult than was the case in other industrialized economies, leading to skepticism about Japanese leadership and to intense pressure to make markets more open.

The third and current phase, from the beginning of the 1990s to the present, has been somewhat mixed. Some of the trends that began in the 1980s—such as rising outward foreign direct investment, larger amounts of foreign aid, and increased financial flows—either flattened out or declined. Poor domestic economic performance from 1992 through 2002 damaged the confidence of the Japanese government and diminished the willingness of other nations to consider seriously Japanese international policy initiatives. Human capacity building, on the other hand, has continued. Furthermore, some of the trade and investment asymmetries have diminished. With greater human capacity and an economic revival that began in 2002, the government has continued to play a more active role in regional and global affairs.

Economic factors certainly do not determine the nature of Japan's foreign policy, but they provide an important ingredient in shaping the issues to which the government must respond and the capacity to be actively engaged. In many respects the government continues a modest role in multilateral policy discussions, but the economic incentive to be more active is certainly strong, and the government's role is far more proactive than it had been in earlier years.

1945–1973: Insularity

The key issue for the economy during this time period was domestic economic development. Recovery from the devastation of the war and completion of the century-long goal of catching up with the leading industrial nations of the world drove government policy and private-sector activity. With this domestic orientation, international economic developments were simply exogenous facts to which the private sector and government had to adjust. The government joined the principal multilateral institutions but played virtually no proactive role in shaping their agenda or policies.

Exports were critical to economic success (to pay for imported raw materials, capital goods, and technology), but exports involved little active engagement in the outside world. Either foreign businesses sent their representatives to Japan to make the purchases, or a small number of human "gatekeepers"—either from the manufacturing firms or, more commonly, from the large general trading companies—worked abroad, transmitting the necessary information to domestic manufacturers. On imports, the government maintained high barriers—both quotas and high tariffs—to limit the penetration of foreign goods while domestic industry was growing and absorbing foreign technology. The US government tolerated these import barriers until the early 1960s, but foreign pressure led to eliminating most quotas in the several years following 1963.

Meanwhile, strict capital controls kept both the inflow and outflow of capital at low levels. One of the long-term goals of the state had been to build a nation owned and operated by Japanese nationals, and that goal was reaffirmed in the severe postwar controls on inward direct investment and other forms of capital flow, reinforcing the impact of high import barriers. Desiring domestic firms to remain focused on domestic development, the government also imposed severe controls on the outflow of direct investment and other investment flows. Few companies other than the general trading companies had major foreign operations, and few banks had offices abroad or could make foreign loans.

The domestic focus of economic activity and financial flows was consistent with broader economic conditions. The combination of foreign technology and domestic labor was unusually profitable, implying that Japanese manufacturers had little incentive to invest abroad. Therefore, rather than preventing a flow of investment from Japan to the rest of the world, the capital controls appear to have been more important in preventing outside investment or severely limiting it from coming into Japan.

Given the heavily domestic economic orientation, individuals had little incentive to develop the kind of international language skills or experience that would underwrite a broader or more active participation in global affairs. With attention on absorbing technical information, foreign language instruction focused on deciphering written language with little emphasis on spoken language. Few individuals sought a foreign education, and corporations did not attach any value to foreign degrees. The lack of foreign direct investment by Japanese firms implied that few individuals (other than those of the general trading companies) lived abroad—and those who did often went without their families, so their children were not exposed to an international experience. In short, the inward focus of the economy resulted in a paucity of individuals with the kinds of personal skills that would enable them to play an effective role in international government policy formation.

The government became a formal member of the principal multilateral institutions—the United Nations, GATT, the International Monetary Fund (IMF), the World Bank, and the Organization for Economic Cooperation and Development (OECD). But membership in these organizations did not lead to any strong sense of participation. Pronouncements by these organizations were treated as an additional set of exogenous demands to which the nation must respond. The sense of national responsibility in meeting the rules or commitments expected was strong. Government was extremely committed to the fixed ¥360-per-dollar exchange rate commitment under the Bretton Woods system, for example, and the government's resistance to any change in that exchange rate was one of the factors leading to US abandonment of the regime in August 1971.[1]

1974–1990: Increasing International Orientation

The initial phase of insularity of the economy came to an end by 1974. A series of economic factors contributed to a stronger external orientation in the rest of the 1970s and early 1980s. These were then powerfully reinforced in the mid-1980s by exchange rate movements.

The Oil Shock of 1973

When crude oil supplies were temporarily disrupted and the price tripled in the wake of the 1973 Yom Kippur war, the Japanese government was confronted with a new vulnerability. The government faced the need to take actions on the international stage to reduce vulnerability and uncertainty in energy supply (and imported raw materials more broadly) and began to recognize its need and ability to shape the external environment facing the economy.

The initial response to the oil shock was to break with US foreign policy by accepting the Arab boycott of Israel, showering foreign aid money on Middle East and other oil suppliers, promoting direct investment by Japanese companies in oil-producing countries, promoting government policies to shift sources of oil supply away from the Middle East, and developing direct purchasing links between oil-producing countries and Japanese-owned refineries (distancing Japan from dependence on the major international oil companies).[2] In 1977, the share of Japanese bilateral foreign aid destined to the Middle East soared to 24.5 percent (up from 0.8 percent in 1972) before subsiding to an 8 to 10 percent level in the 1980s.[3] Consider also the Japanese government's treatment of Indonesia—a nation that sits along a major choke point on the crude-oil transportation route from the Middle East to Japan and is itself a supplier of oil and gas to Japan. The government treated Indonesia lavishly—making it the largest or second largest (after China or, more recently, India) recipient of bilateral foreign aid in most years since the 1970s.

The 1973 oil crisis was actually only one aspect of the early 1970s global inflation in raw material prices, and the Japanese government reacted to this more general sense of raw material vulnerability. Following the temporary embargo on soybean exports by the United States in 1973, the Japanese government pursued a policy initiative (ultimately ill fated) to make Brazil a major supplier of soybeans, other foodstuffs, and raw materials. Into the early 1980s, the Japanese government and private-sector groups spoke of financing a second canal in Central America to facilitate a flow of raw materials and foodstuffs from Brazil and other South American sources to Japan. Although neither the Brazilian projects nor the canal came to fruition, they were part of the change of attitude in the government in a more activist direction.

Economic Size

Japan was no longer a small, poor nation by the mid-1970s. Having become the second-largest economy in the world by that time, and one of the most affluent, Japan was no longer insignificant. This change had two important implications. First, foreign nations reacted quite quickly to the fact that Japan was a large, affluent nation with new expectations for Japanese participation in global affairs. The administration of Jimmy Carter, for example, put pressure on Japan to increase its foreign aid and defense spending to bear a greater part of the "burden" of global peace and development. The government responded to these pressures. On foreign aid, for example, net foreign aid quadrupled from 1975 to 1989.[4] And later, US pressure led the government to make a $14 billion financial contribution to the Gulf War of 1991.

Second, the Japanese began to recognize that their large economic size implied they had a nontrivial impact on global developments. One of the most important lessons of the 1973 and 1979 oil shocks, for example, was that Japan had strong bargaining power with supplier nations because of its large share of global oil purchases.

Rising Current Account Surplus

During the 1950s and 1960s, Japan's current account balance was close to zero—with small chronic deficits in the early postwar years and small but rising surpluses after 1964. Once the economy had finished the "catch up" period by the mid-1970s, however, domestic growth decelerated, creating a chronic excess of domestic savings over the domestic demand for investment. The result has been a sizable current-account surplus.[5] Appreciation of the yen after August 1971, plus the two oil shocks of 1973 and 1979, masked the tendency for surplus during the rest of the 1970s, as shown in Figure 6.1. Once the temporary effect of the second oil shock was over, the surplus became larger and more permanent. Since 1983, as indicated in Figure 6.1, the surplus has fluctuated in most years between roughly 2 and 3 percent of gross domestic product (GDP).

In economic accounting terms, any surplus or deficit on the current account (which consists of merchandise trade, services trade, repatriated

Figure 6.1 Japan's Current Account Balance as a Share of GDP

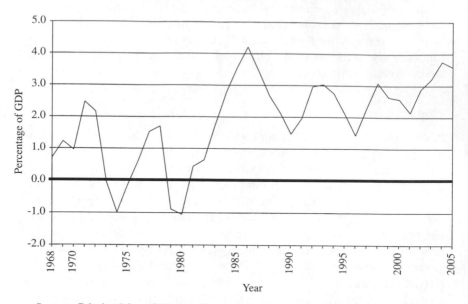

Year

Sources: Calculated from GDP data, Economic Social Research Institute, Cabinet Office, available online at http://www.esri.cao.go.jp/jp/sna/qe054-2/gaku-mcy0542.csv (accessed March 17, 2004); Current-account data from Bank of Japan, *Balance of Payments Monthly,* various issues; Statistics Bureau, Ministry of Internal Affairs and Communications, *Japan Monthly Statistics,* available online at http:// www.stat.go.jp/english/data/getujidb/index.htm (accessed April 25, 2006).

profits on foreign assets, and foreign aid flows) must be offset by an equal net flow of capital out of or into the nation. Therefore, emergence of a long-term large current-account surplus implied that Japan also developed a long-term net outflow of capital. Firms and individuals became owners of a rapidly rising amount of foreign assets. The new current-account surplus also meant that international capital controls needed to be dismantled—a process that continued from the early 1970s through the mid-1980s, at which point most controls were gone. This change enabled the recycling of the current surplus as well as much larger gross flows of financial capital into and out of Japan. Table 6.1 indicates the impact of the chronic current-account surplus and capital control deregulation on the cumulative international gross and net asset position of Japan. From less than $10 billion in 1976, net assets rose to $328 billion by 1990, and gross assets rose from $68 billion to $1.9 trillion.[6]

Ownership of foreign assets gave the Japanese government new foreign policy concerns. Fluctuations in exchange rates, economic growth or recession in foreign countries, revolution, and expropriation of foreign assets—

Table 6.1 Japan's External Assets and Liabilities (billions of US dollars, end of each calendar year)

Year	Direct Investment Assets	Liabilities	Loans Assets	Liabilities	Portfolio Securities Assets	Liabilities	Total Assets	Liabilities	Net
1976	11	2	5	2	4	11	68	58	10
1977	12	2	4	2	6	12	80	58	22
1978	14	3	9	2	12	18	119	83	36
1979	17	3	15	2	19	22	135	107	29
1980	20	3	15	2	21	30	160	148	12
1981	25	4	19	2	32	44	209	198	11
1982	29	4	23	1	40	47	228	203	25
1983	32	4	29	1	56	70	272	235	37
1984	38	5	41	1	88	77	341	267	74
1985	44	5	47	1	146	85	438	308	130
1986	57	7	69	1	258	144	727	547	180
1987	77	9	98	1	340	166	1,072	831	241
1988	111	10	124	1	427	255	1,469	1,178	292
1989	154	9	137	19	534	374	1,171	1,478	293
1990	201	10	130	58	564	335	1,858	1,530	328
1991	232	12	141	100	632	444	2,007	1,623	383
1992	248	16	143	120	656	431	2,035	1,522	514
1993	260	17	152	136	696	457	2,181	1,570	611
1994	276	19	158	139	754	532	2,424	1,735	689
1995	261	37	1,036	1,039	938	599	2,877	1,984	893
1996	276	32	860	885	1,022	607	2,778	1,828	950
1997	292	29	927	883	1,007	636	2,864	1,834	1,030
1998	238	23	829	718	976	583	2,573	1,555	1,018
1999	223	41	700	677	1,156	1,039	2,666	1,922	744
2000	297	54	692	707	1,392	943	3,165	1,931	1,234
2001	326	55	670	655	1,399	722	3,126	1,650	1,475
2002	291	75	649	668	1,334	584	2,920	1,521	1,399
2003	310	83	607	722	1,591	801	3,326	1,835	1,491
2004	357	94	669	840	1,938	1,112	4,009	2,297	1,712

Sources: Edward J. Lincoln, *Japan's New Global Role* (Washington, DC: Brookings Institution, 1990), 60; Bank of Japan, *Balance of Payments Monthly* (April 1995): 87–88, (April 1999): 159–160; for 1996–2002, Bank of Japan, available at http://www.boj.or.jp/en/stat/stat_f.htm (accessed March 8, 2004).

Notes: These data were reported in dollars prior to 1995 and in yen thereafter. For consistency, all data are converted to dollars in this table at average annual exchange rates for each year from 1995 to 2002.

Items included in "loans" shifted when the government switched to yen-based accounting in 1995 (adding government loans that had previously been treated separately but also substantially increasing measurement of bank loans). Therefore, data for this item are not entirely comparable before and after 1995.

all became important issues for the government, issues that had been virtually absent in the earlier period. Being a substantial owner of foreign assets involves an economy and its government much more intimately and in different ways with the outside world than does a simple export relationship.

Recognizing that it had expanded international interests, the government began to demand a higher-profile role in multilateral organizations. In the late 1980s, for example, the government sought and obtained larger voting rights at both the World Bank and the IMF and lobbied successfully to have Japanese elected as the heads of the World Health Organization (WHO) and the Office of the UNHCR.

Yen Appreciation

From the spring of 1985, the yen doubled in value against the US dollar within two years, from ¥260 per dollar to a temporary peak of ¥130. The sharp appreciation of the yen in 1985 and the continuation of a relatively strong yen since that time have had a powerful impact on foreign direct investment. Even with rising wages and earlier yen appreciation in the 1970s, most manufacturing industries other than textiles chose to remain at home. The 1985 appreciation went well beyond the ability of many firms to adjust their cost structures at home and remain competitive internationally.

Figure 6.2 shows annual foreign direct investment flows since 1980

Figure 6.2 Japan's Direct Investment Flows

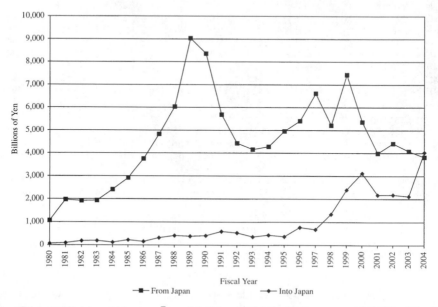

Sources: Ministry of Finance, *Ōkurashō Kokusai Kinyūkyoku Nenpō,* no. 16 (1992): 479, 503 and no. 12 (1988): 518; Ministry of Finance, "Foreign Direct Investment," available online at http://www.mof.go.jp/english/e1c008.htm (accessed April 26, 2006).

(based on data collected by the Ministry of Finance on a notification basis from firms, yielding numbers slightly different from the balance-of-payments data in Table 6.1). After averaging around ¥2 trillion per year in the first half of the 1980s, the flow of new investment shot up to a peak of ¥9 trillion in 1989. This sudden explosion in investment activity meant that many firms were engaged in acquiring, owning, and managing real assets (such as factories, shopping centers, golf courses, or buildings) abroad for the first time.

A firm exporting a product needs to know only relatively simple aspects of other countries—do they want big cars or little cars, red cars or white cars? A firm running a factory abroad needs to know about political stability, labor law, tax rules, capital controls, and cultural aspects of managing local workers. The government needed to worry about political stability and faced new pressures from domestic business to assist developing countries with the necessary supporting infrastructure for Japanese-owned factories (such as utilities and transportation).

Japanese foreign policy responded to these new concerns. For example, a number of bilateral foreign aid projects in Asia were explicitly designed to provide the infrastructure to support industrial parks for Japanese firms.[7] Interest in creating a better environment for regional trade and direct investment also caused the government to play a leadership role (with Australia) in creating the APEC forum in the late 1980s.

Confidence in the Economic System

One of the ingredients of US or European involvement in global affairs over the past 400 years has been the effort to proselytize other countries—be the issue Christianity or anticommunism. Japan appeared to have no concepts to offer the world in the earlier postwar period; its prewar colonial model was thoroughly discredited, and the private sector was too busy earning a profit at home to recognize that it had ideas of interest to others. By the 1980s, however, confidence was building in the validity of the Japanese economic model as a superior alternative to either US or European capitalism. Reinforcing belief in this model was the unusual burst in economic growth during the bubble years from 1987 to 1991—a five-year period during which average annual real economic growth was 5 percent. This acceleration of growth suggested that the underlying economic model was superior to that of other industrial nations.[8] If this were true, then Japan had important concepts to export to the rest of the world—to both developed and developing nations alike.

This new economic self-confidence found expression in pressure on (and financing for) the World Bank to consider the causes of East Asian growth. The Japanese government wanted the World Bank to find that other East Asian nations had followed a Japanese model, causing them to be unusually successful in generating high growth and industrialization. Despite the Japanese funding, the resulting study was not a clear endorsement of Japan, to the chagrin of the government.[9] Undaunted, the Japanese government funded its own analytic reports intended to educate the outside world about the advantages of Japanese-style capitalism and industrial policy.

Rising Human Capacity

Participation in global policy affairs is not simply a matter of voting rights. Effective participation or leadership implies having government personnel who can operate comfortably and successfully in an international deliberative setting. Shifting economic conditions—rising affluence, yen appreciation, and rising direct investment abroad—helped to produce more people with foreign language skills and experience abroad.

In 1975, only 143,000 Japanese were living abroad temporarily, but by 1990 this number had increased two-and-a-half times to 374,000. This group of temporary residents abroad included only 16,000 school-age children (grades one through twelve) enrolled in schools abroad back in 1975, but this number had tripled to 49,000 by 1990.[10] Meanwhile, with low incomes and capital controls, few Japanese traveled abroad in the 1950s and 1960s. In 1975, only 3.3 million Japanese nationals traveled abroad, and even as recently as 1985 the number was just under 5 million (including tourists, business travelers, and all other categories). With yen appreciation, that number more than doubled to 11 million by 1990. Meanwhile, college and graduate education abroad also expanded—breaking the tradition of the earlier period that downgraded the value of foreign degrees. US data indicate that only 12,000 Japanese students were enrolled in US universities in the 1979–1980 academic year, but this number had tripled to 36,000 by the 1989–1990 academic year.[11]

These increases in personal travel and educational or other living experience abroad do not necessarily translate into greater government engagement in international policy issues, but they did increase the opportunity for the government and private sector to make use of the skills of this pool of people if so desired. Thus, this change increased the potential capacity of the government to participate in global affairs.

Asymmetry

All the previous factors increased the demands on the government to be engaged in international affairs and increased the human capacity for being so engaged. Asymmetry in trade and investment ties to the world acted as a constraint, however, by creating an unfavorable image abroad and sparking difficult trade negotiations. As an industrializing nation in the earlier period, protectionism that severely limited the ability of foreign firms to participate in the Japanese market was unremarkable. But as the nation became a successful, affluent, industrialized nation moving onto the global stage as a major international investor itself, exclusion or difficulty of access to markets in Japan rankled businesses and governments of other nations.

A variety of statistics indicated a disparity between the role of manufactured goods imports in Japan and other industrial nations. Manufactured imports as a share of domestic consumption of manufactures, for example, remained much lower in Japan than in other nations through the 1980s. Nations also have had a strong tendency to engage in both exports and imports within narrow industry categories, owing to product differentiation and other factors, a pattern called intra-industry trade. For Japan, the extent of such trade was low and rose little from the 1970s through the 1980s.[12] On foreign direct investment, the government dismantled virtually all formal barriers to inward direct investment by the beginning of the 1980s, but inward investment remained very low, as indicated in Figure 6.2. Although Japanese investment abroad exploded to ¥9 trillion by 1989, inward investment was only ¥500 billion.

The result was US pressure from the late 1970s through the early 1990s to open up the domestic market more fully to imports and investment. Often these negotiations were difficult, prolonged, tense, and highlighted in the media. On the US side, they created skepticism about the nature of Japan's engagement in broader international policy formation. Other governments did not have the clout of the US government but were critical of the conditions of access to Japan as well. This prolonged period of antagonistic negotiations hindered the evolution of Japan's broader international role. US officials, for example, viewed Japan's broader international policy positions as very narrowly self-interested and were disinclined, therefore, to pay much attention to them.

1991 to the Present: Plateau

The 1990s were a disappointing decade for the Japanese economy, marked by the collapse of the stock and real estate bubbles and very low economic growth from 1992 through 2002. These developments had a negative effect on both the demand and supply sides of economic factors affecting international engagement. Japan did not return to the insularity of the 1950s and 1960s, but a number of the upward trends leveled off or were reversed. On the other hand, some of the asymmetries of the 1980s began to diminish, and capacity building continued.

Confidence

The confidence in the "Japanese economic model" as a basis for participating in international policy was shaken by the problems of the 1990s. Indeed, rather than touting the superiority of the Japanese system, much of the domestic debate turned to reform, casting doubt on the superiority of the past system. These developments undercut a principal input to Japanese participation in global affairs. If the Japanese themselves were no longer confident about the superiority of their system, they lost a concept to sell to the world. Losing faith in the superiority of the Japanese approach, developing nations were less inclined to adopt features of the Japanese system for use at home. Industrial nations displayed a distinct disinterest or disdain for Japanese input in a multilateral setting, fueled by continuing economic stagnation and their astonishment at the record of very poor economic policy decisions by the Japanese government over the course of the 1990s.

As a partial result, some of the initiatives begun in the late 1980s faded. The effort to influence the World Bank ceased after the mid-1990s. At the IMF, the government did little to participate actively in the decisionmaking or reform debates of the late 1990s, other than indirectly highlighting the need for reform with its short-lived independent proposal for an Asian Monetary Fund in 1997. At UNHCR and WHO, no effort was made to nominate a new round of Japanese to head the organizations.

Investment Abroad

Table 6.1 indicates that the general increase in net and gross assets abroad continued during the 1990s. Total assets held abroad rose another $2.2 trillion, from $1.9 trillion in 1990 to $4.0 trillion at the end of 2004. Certain aspects of investment faltered; the data in the table indicate that international bank loans by Japanese banks declined by 36 percent from 1995 through 2003 before finally turning up a bit in 2004. Detailed data from the Bank for International Settlements (BIS) show that much of this drop was concentrated in developing countries. From a peak of $145 billion in June 1997, the value of outstanding Japanese loans to developing countries fell 60 percent by June 2003. For loans to Asian countries, the decline was an even higher 68 percent.[13] A similar decline occurred in Japanese foreign aid. From a peak of ¥1.2 trillion in fiscal year 1997, the government's foreign aid budget declined 25 percent to slightly less than ¥800 billion in the fiscal 2006 budget.[14]

The drop in lending and foreign aid complicated Japanese engagement in regional and global affairs. At 40 percent of all outstanding commercial loans to East Asia in 1995, the Japanese had a reputation as a major source of financing in the rest of East Asia. The withdrawal of Japanese loans, however, helped precipitate the 1997 Asian financial crisis.[15] By 2003, Japan's relative importance as a source of financing, both commercial and foreign aid, had dwindled substantially. From the perspective of Asian countries, Japan appeared far less important to them economically than at the end of the 1980s.

Foreign direct investment by Japanese firms also declined from the peak of the bubble years. As Figure 6.2 indicates, direct investment out-flows declined sharply from ¥9 trillion billion in fiscal 1989 to a ¥4–6 trillion range, and were actually only ¥3.8 trillion in fiscal year 2004. The 1990s slowdown did not reverse the move of Japanese companies abroad, but with the flows of new investment down, Japan's position relative to other international investors declined. Around Asia, Japanese firms were a relatively less important share of inflows of direct investment than they were in the decade of the 1980s. In South Korea, for example, Japanese firms had been the source of 48 percent of direct investment inflows in the 1980s, but that share dwindled to 12 percent in the 1990s.[16]

From the Japanese standpoint, involvement in overseas economic and political issues continues to have heightened salience because of the $2.9 trillion in assets that Japanese corporations and individuals own overseas. But the perception by the rest of the world of Japanese firms as formidable investors, or as players in corporate acquisitions, has diminished considerably. As vague as this factor may be, it is of considerable importance. "Japan" was a topic of interest, concern, and discussion in Washington a decade ago; today the silence is deafening. The disappointing economic performance of Japan has led the internationally informed policy community in Washington to refocus its attention to other global players.

Capacity

The number of Japanese nationals traveling abroad continued to grow in the 1990s, though somewhat less rapidly; it reached 16.8 million in 2004—50 percent higher than in 1990.[17] The number of people living abroad temporarily also continued to rise—doubling from 1990 to 2001 (to 835,000). The number of school-age children being educated abroad remained relatively flat at around 50,000 after 1990, however—and rose only slightly to 54,000 by 2004.[18] At the university level, the number of Japanese students in the United States also grew more slowly (and declined slightly after 2000) to 42,000 by the academic year of 2004–2005.[19]

These data indicate that overall, more people were gaining some exposure to the outside world. Although the number of students—primary, secondary, and university levels—stopped growing, the number remained far above what it had been at the beginning of the 1980s. More important, with the passage of time, more people who had lived and been educated abroad for at least part of their education were now in the labor force and working their way up organizational structures, both in the government and the private sector.

Asymmetries

The long period of strong pressure from the United States and other governments to make the Japanese market more accessible continued through 1995. Since that time the pressure has lessened, and some indicators of access have improved.

On trade, the ratio of imports to domestic consumption of manufactures doubled from the early 1990s to 2000, from 10 percent to 20 percent. The indicators of intra-industry trade also rose over time. For both overall penetration of manufactured imports and intra-industry trade, however, indicators for other nations also rose in the 1990s, so that Japan continued to lag behind. Nevertheless, the increased access was sufficient to quell the long period of highly visible, contentious trade negotiations.[20]

On direct investment, Figure 6.2 shows the sharp rise in the inflow of direct investment that occurred after 1995. For the first time ever, some Japanese firms were available for purchase by foreigners—a form of direct investment common in other industrialized countries but uncommon in Japan. It is important to point out, however, that even with a sharp increase, the ratio of direct investment to total domestic capital formation remained much lower than in other countries. In the peak year of 1999, for example, this ratio was only 1.1 percent in Japan whereas the corresponding ratio in the United States was 18 percent and for the world as a whole, 16 percent.[21]

Access can have a human side as well. First, nations endeavoring to play a regional or global policy leadership role may be aided by the existence of policy elites in other countries who have some familiarity or experience with the country. Prime Minister Nakasone Yasuhiro announced in the 1980s an intent to increase the number of foreign students in Japan to 100,000. That goal was achieved in 2004, mostly on the basis of a surge after 1999 (when the number had been only 41,000).[22] Some doubts about the accuracy of these numbers exist (since some Chinese "students" appeared to be in Japan mainly to work, using student visas as a means of entry). By way of comparison, 565,000 foreign students were enrolled in US universities in the 2004–2005 academic year (and the number was 135,000 even as far back as the 1969–1970 academic year).[23] Nevertheless, at least the number of legitimate foreign students in Japan is higher than in the past.

Second, perceptions of nations as international leaders depend in part on the openness of the nation to a broader range of refugees, foreign workers, and immigrants. On this front, little change has occurred in Japan. The total number of foreigners resident in Japan is only about one million (excluding those Chinese and Koreans born in Japan but without formal citizenship). This means foreigners are just under 1 percent of the total population. Comparable data for the United States show that the share of foreign-born individuals in the population was 10 percent by 2000; it was 6 percent in France, 9 percent in Germany, 4 percent in Britain, and 2.4 percent in Italy.[24] A similar story concerns refugees. The United Nations reported 452,548 refugees resident in the United States in 2004, but only 1,967 in Japan.[25] On the human front, therefore, the Japanese government's efforts to portray itself as a caring, progressive global leader contrast with the image of a nation that remains relatively closed to outsiders even though some modest change is under way.

Overall, the government maintained or expanded its international policy activity during this period. Some initiatives, such as the Asian Monetary Fund proposal in 1997, failed. But the continued or expanded economic interests that Japanese firms have abroad led the government to continue or expand its proactive role. This was more evident at a regional level. The government participated actively in the Chiang Mai Initiative (the expanded foreign exchange swap arrangements with central banks in Asia that were created by the initiative were intended to enable developing countries to more easily defend their currencies from speculative attack) as well as in the Asian bond market initiative that was evolving among the APT governments by 2005. More important, the government moved dramatically after 2000 to negotiate bilateral free-trade agreements, mainly with Asian neighbors. By early 2006, Japan had signed agreements with Singapore, Mexico, Thailand, and Malaysia and was pursuing negotiations with Korea, the Philippines, Indonesia, and ASEAN as a whole.[26]

Conclusion

The years from the mid-1970s to the early 1990s marked a fundamental shift for Japan. Economic changes pushed the nation into a broader and more intimate economic embrace of the outside world. No longer could the government accept events in the rest of the world as faraway developments that were either irrelevant to Japan or uncontrollable facts to which the nation would have to adjust. Nor were other governments as willing to let Japan sit on the sidelines of major international economic and security issues. Although some of the economic trends flattened or declined in the 1990s, there is no return to insularity, and likely future economic trends suggest that large flows of direct and financial investments to the rest of the world will continue.

Early efforts of the government to play a more active role in regional and global affairs reflected inexperience and a narrow view of the nation's interests, such as showering foreign aid on countries supplying raw materials to Japan or using foreign aid to build local infrastructure useful to Japanese firms wishing to build factories in developing countries. A more serious problem was the resistance of other nations to Japan's emergence on the global scene, due to the relatively closed nature of the Japanese economy and society.

Since the mid-1990s, much of the tension due to difficult trade negotiations has disappeared, removing one constraint to a more successful participation by the Japanese in broader regional and global affairs. At the same time, the loss of confidence due to domestic economic difficulties appears to have caused the government to return to playing a very low-key role in multilateral institutions. Nevertheless, the third of the periods sketched out in this chapter witnessed continued proactive policy initiatives, particularly at the East Asian regional level.

This third period in the interaction between economic developments and international policy engagement may be coming to an end. Economic growth increased after 2002, and many of the domestic economic problems of the previous decade—huge amounts of nonperforming loans in the banking sector, shrinking employment, and deflation among them—were largely resolved. As a result, by 2005 the corporate sector and the public at large were much more confident once again about the state of the domestic economy. Even the banking sector was approaching a point at which it could once again expand its international lending. The trend of negotiating free-trade agreements (or economic partnership agreements, as the government prefers to call them since they include elements other than merchandise trade) appeared likely to continue. By 2006 there was no doubt that the government was playing a more proactive role in the region, but this left the question of whether it would also pursue a stronger voice at a global level.

Notes

1. For an excellent study of the Japanese government's resistance to yen appreciation, see Angel, *Explaining Economic Policy Failure.*
2. For a review of Japanese policy toward the Middle East during these years, see Lincoln, *Japan and the Middle East.*
3. For a review of the foreign aid response to the oil crisis, see Robert M. Orr Jr., "Balancing Act: Japanese Foreign Aid Policy in the Middle East," in ibid., 29–39; statistical data are from p. 35.
4. Toru Yanagihara and Anne Emig, "An Overview of Japan's Foreign Aid," in Shafiqul Islam, ed., *Yen for Development* (New York: Council for Foreign Relations, 1991), 43.
5. For analysis of the process by which the deceleration of economic growth

after the mid-1970s led to changes in macroeconomic balances to produce a chronic current-account surplus, see Lincoln, *Japan Facing Economic Maturity,* 14–129.

6. Until 1995 these data were reported in the balance-of-payments reports in dollars; thereafter they were reported in yen. Table 6.1 used the dollar figures on the grounds that for assets held overseas by Japanese, the dollar figure is more meaningful, since it largely avoids fluctuations due to exchange rate movements (since a large share of assets held abroad are denominated in dollars).

7. Lincoln, *Japan's New Global Role,* 111–133, 181–183.

8. Principal among such advocates has been Sakakibara, *Beyond Capitalism: The Japanese Model of Market Economics.*

9. World Bank, *The East Asian Miracle: Economic Growth and Public Policy.*

10. Lincoln, *Japan's New Global Role,* 100.

11. Ministry for Internal Affairs and Communications, *Japan Statistical Yearbook,* 1980 edition, 48, and *Japan Statistical Yearbook,* 1995 edition, 70. Note that the number of trips does not correspond exactly to the number of individual people traveling abroad since an individual might make multiple trips, each of which is counted separately. On Japanese students in the United States, see Institute for International Education, *Open Doors: 1980–1981,* 11, and *Open Doors 1990–1991,* 74.

12. See Balassa and Noland, *Japan in the World Economy,* esp. 49–76; Lincoln, *Japan's Unequal Trade,* 12–60; or Lincoln, *Troubled Times,* 17–115.

13. Bank for International Settlements, *Consolidated Banking Statistics for the Second Quarter of 2003,* 32–35, and previous issues of the same publication. Until 1999, BIS data did not include lending among the major reporting countries, so it is not possible to trace back the size and share of Japanese lending to the United States and the major European countries.

14. Ministry of Foreign Affairs, "ODA Yosan." Available at http://www.mofa.go.jp/mofaj/gaiko/oda/index/shiryo/yosan.html (accessed April 25, 2006).

15. See Baily, Farrell, and Lund, "The Color of Hot Money."

16. Lincoln, *East Asian Economic Regionalism,* 103.

17. Ministry for Internal Affairs and Communications, *Japan Statistical Yearbook,* 2006 edition, Table 2-33, "Persons Who Entered or Departed Japan by Nationality." Available at http://www.stat.go.jp/english/data/nenkan/1431-02.htm (accessed April 25, 2006).

18. Ministry for Internal Affairs and communications, *Japan Statistical Yearbook,* 2000 and 2006 editions, Table 22-33, "Education for Japanese Children Abroad and Children Returned from Abroad (1985–98)." Available at http://www.stat.go.jp/english/data/nenkan/1431-22.htm (accessed April 25, 2006).

19. Institute for International Education, *Open Doors.* Available at http://opendoors.iienetowork.org (accessed April 25, 2006).

20. Data on import penetration of manufactures are from World Bank, *World Bank Development Indicators CD-ROM 03.*

21. United Nations, United Nations Conference on Trade and Development, *World Investment Report 2003: Promoting Linkages, Annex B: Statistical Annex,* 267–268.

22. Ministry for Internal Affairs and Communications, *Japan Statistical Yearbook,* 2006 edition, Table 22-32, "Foreign Students Enrolled in Universities in Japan." Available at http://www.stat.go.jp/english/data/nenkan/1431-22.htm (accessed April 25, 2006).

23. Institute for International Education, *Open Doors 2006.* Available at http://opendoors.iienetwork.org (accessed April 25, 2006).

24. World Bank, *World Development Indicators CD-ROM 03*.

25. Office of the United Nations High Commissioner for Refugees, *2004 Global Refugee Trends*, Table 2 (unpaginated).

26. Ministry of Foreign Affairs, "Free Trade Agreement (FTA) and Economic Partnership Agreement (EPA)." Available at http://mofa.go.jp/policy/economy/fta/index.html (accessed April 5, 2006).

| 7 |

Building Stable International Financial Relations

Yoshiko Kojo

Financial stability has been one of the most crucial of the many issues facing the international community since the 1970s. Deregulation and financial globalization have resulted in an increase in international financial transactions. This has led to a number of serious problems destabilizing the international economic system, such as the Mexican financial crisis and Asian financial crisis. The easy spread of the financial crisis of one country to other countries is one of the most serious phenomena in contemporary international economy, because financial crises in the era of financial globalization usually severely deteriorate a state's domestic financial system via capital movement in a short period of time. In these financial crises, international banks have played a crucial role owing to their large overseas lending. For example, the debt crisis in Mexico in 1982 revealed how many big banks in industrial countries had loaned large amounts of money to the Mexican government and how difficult it was not only for the host country but also for the home country of the banks to prevent the damage to the domestic financial system likely caused by the failure of big banks. Faced with a series of banking crises in 1970s and 1980s, the governments of industrial countries, in particular the United States and United Kingdom where big international banks were located, began to act to avoid banking crisis. On the domestic side, they put new regulatory rules on banks, and on the international side, they turned to global financial institutions, such as the Group of Five (G5), the G7, and the IMF. Most multilateral negotiations ended up taking ad hoc agreements, however, and it was difficult for countries to make persistent international rules that would constrain domestic economic policies and institutions.

Among these efforts, the Basle Accord on banking of 1988, which was agreed upon at the BIS, is a successful case that has helped establish an international regulatory regime among industrial countries. The Basle Accord was the first international agreement regarding the supervision of the international banking industry and was considered "one of the most significant steps to date toward standardization of international regulation."[1] Most studies refer to the accord as a rare success in the ongoing attempt to regulate an increasingly global financial market.[2] In September 1992, the Basle Committee on Banking Supervision (the Basle Committee) announced that "the capital agreement has now been fully incorporated within the supervisory framework of all member countries."[3] Since 1988, the accord has been introduced not only in member countries but also in virtually all other countries with internationally active banks.[4] The accord has been amended in order to regulate developing international banking more effectively. In January 1996, the Basle Committee proposed a supplement to the accord of 1988, which was intended to apply capital charges to market risks incurred by banks, and in 1997 this amendment for market risks was introduced.[5] In 1999, the committee issued another proposal that aimed to define capital more precisely; the revised accord, known as Basle II, was agreed upon in 2004.[6]

The Japanese government played a crucial role in shaping the accord in the late 1980s, when Japanese banks expanded their overseas activities rapidly. By analyzing Japan's participation in the Basle Accord, this chapter examines why and how the Japanese government participated in establishing a rare success case of a multilateral framework in an issue of international economy in the late 1980s and 1990s. This chapter deals with two questions. First, what role did Japan play in the accord's development? The Group of 10 (G-10) countries and Luxembourg created the pact after holding negotiations at the BIS.[7] The accord itself was initially proposed by the United States and the United Kingdom, however, and other countries, including Japan, had to decide how to respond to the proposal by the United States and the UK.

The Basle Accord imposed uniform risk-based capital requirements on commercial banks in G-10 countries plus Luxembourg and required them to fulfill the standards by the end of 1992. Among Japanese commercial banks, the average capital-to-asset ratio during the 1980s undercut that of US and UK banks. For Japanese banks, the regulation of the accord imposed a burden on them to increase their own capitals. How did Japan's financial regulatory body, that is, the Ministry of Finance (MOF), and Japanese commercial banks respond to the regulatory framework that the Basle Accord would impose? Examining Japan's attitude toward the Basle Accord will clarify how the country viewed international cooperation in terms of financial dealings.

The second question is how changes in Japan's domestic economy affected its attitude toward an international regulatory framework. When the Basle

Accord went into effect in 1988, the Japanese economy was still booming. The country's commercial banks had rapidly gained international market share. By 1991, it became clear, however, that the boom, or the so-called bubble economy, was over. The drastic turnaround, which was commonly referred to as the collapse of the bubble economy, hit Japanese commercial banks hard owing to sharp declines in stock and land prices. Considering the circumstance, how did Japanese banks view international regulations of capital adequacy? How did the MOF perceive the Basle Accord after the economic bubble burst? Did the drastic change in the Japanese economy color the country's attitude toward international cooperation?

International Financial Crisis and the Basle Accord

Since the 1970s, the international banking system has been faced with a series of financial crises caused by banking crises that have threatened a number of countries either directly or indirectly. As early as 1975, the G-10 countries agreed to establish the Basle Committee to discuss regulation and surveillance on banks. It consists of central bank and supervisory authorities of the G-10 countries. The committee's initial goals were to develop general principles regarding bank supervision and to improve communication among bank supervisors. The committee meets three or four times a year at the BIS in Basle. At the end of the 1970s, the committee members began to pay attention to capital adequacy standards as an effective tool for supervising international banking.

Since the early 1980s, there have been efforts to establish a regulatory framework for international banking. In 1984, the G-10 "charged the Basle Committee with recommending a framework for assessing the comparability of different measures of capital adequacy used by member countries and with developing minimum international bank capital standards."[8] It was difficult for the G-10 to agree on setting a common standard of regulation, however, owing to the difficulty of defining the content of capital and the appropriate amount of capital.

In the 1980s, it was generally proclaimed in international society that an international regulatory framework was needed to prevent financial market failures, such as the debt crisis mainly caused by the overborrowed situation of big commercial banks. Regulating banks was considered necessary for ensuring stable financial dealings at the international level.

Although the G-10 countries agreed that banking regulations were needed, they could not agree on what kinds of regulations were appropriate, owing to their different domestic banking systems. A capital adequacy requirement was always on the agenda of the committee as a measure of regulation, but the committee never reached an agreement on it. There are two reasons. First, the G-10 countries had different definitions of bank capital and different measures of calculating capital ratio.[9] They had to make an agreement regarding the basis of discussion. Second, as a result of calculation, capital ratio was likely to decrease in most countries and varied among countries: about 6 percent in the United States and the UK, about 5 percent in Japan, about 3 percent in Germany, and about 2 percent in France.[10] For the countries whose banks had a lower capital ratio, it was difficult to accept a higher capital ratio because their banks were reluctant to increase their capital. They were afraid that the higher capital ratio standard might erode their competitiveness.

In January 1987, the United States and the United Kingdom, which were frustrated by the committee's slow progress with international negotiations, jointly proposed a regulatory framework with minimum capital requirements. This bilateral proposal pressed the Basle Committee to expedite its negotiations. In December 1987, the committee proposed standard supervisory regulations governing the capital adequacy of international banks. After about six months of negotiations among the G-10, the committee reached an agreement in July 1988 to adopt minimum capital requirements for international banks by the end of 1992.

The newly formed Basle Accord reflected the uneasy state of the global economy that had existed since the early 1980s owing to crises involving large-scale lending institutions. To this end, the accord had two primary objectives. First, the new framework was established to help "strengthen the soundness and stability of the international banking system" by encouraging international banking organizations to boost their capital positions. Second, a standard approach applied to international banks in different countries would help to diminish "an existing source of competitive inequality among international banks."[11]

The agreement of 1988 clarified three important elements. First, the committee defined the content of capital, saying that it would consist of two tiers. The first, core capital, would include "equity capital and published reserves from post-tax retained earnings."[12] The committee stated that "this key element of capital is the only element common to all countries' banking systems."[13] The second tier, supplementary capital, would contain various kinds of capital elements, "each of which may be included or not included by national authorities at their discretion in the light of their national accounting and supervisory regulations."[14] Core capital should comprise at least 50 percent of a bank's capital base.

The second element of the 1988 agreement established a set of five risk-weighted categories. Various types of assets and off–balance sheet items were categorized into five risk weights: 0, 10, 20, 50, and 100 percent. For example, cash and claims on central government are in the 0 percent category. Claims on multilateral development banks, such as the

International Bank for Reconstruction and Development (IBRD) and the Asian Development Bank (ADB), are in the 20 percent category; claims on the private sector and claims on central governments outside the OECD are in the 100 percent category.

The third element is that a target standard ratio of capital to risk-weighted assets was set at 8 percent, of which the core capital element would be at least 4 percent. International banks in member countries were expected to meet this standard by the end of 1992. The accord allowed banks that needed time to fulfill the capital requirement a grace period of about four and a half years. This meant that "banks whose ratios are presently below the eight percent standard will not be required to take immediate or precipitate action."[15]

Negotiation of Standardization of Bank Capital Requirement

Two Important Factors of the Formation of International Agreement

Two important factors underscore the creation of the Basle Accord. The first was a growing recognition on the part of regulators regarding risks that faced the international banking system. Frequent financial crises, such as the Mexican debt crisis and the banking crisis, prompted an international agreement on regulation. Although scholars and public officials could not agree on the best way to stabilize the international financial system, there was little doubt that regulations were needed to head off future international crises.[16] The bank capital adequacy standard became an important topic of discussion at the Basle Committee in 1984, and well before 1984, the Basle Committee was systematically monitoring the capital ratios of banks.[17] This fact alone does not explain why the accord was agreed to in 1988.

The second factor that prompted creation of the accord was the strong support of such financially powerful nations as the United States and the United Kingdom. It was the United States that promoted the idea of a capital adequacy standard. In 1983, following the year of the Mexican crisis, the US Congress enacted the International Lending Act, which placed emphasis on the importance of supervisory measures, including the capital bases of international banks involved in international lending.

Paul Volcker, chairman of the Federal Reserve Board, first raised the issue of convergence of capital standards at a 1984 meeting of the Basle Committee, which was the US government's necessary step required by the International Lending Act for regulating not only US but also foreign banks. After a crisis involving Continental Illinois Bank, the eleventh-largest bank in the United States, the country's banking regulators were pressured by Congress to come up with stricter banking regulations.[18] In order to avoid criticism of a government bailout, the Federal Reserve Board chose to impose a capital adequacy standard as a new regulation.

The Federal Reserve Board, which thought the Basle Committee was moving too slowly, opted to forge a bilateral agreement with the Bank of England first, instead of pushing for multilateral negotiations at the BIS. The Bank of England, which opposed the standardization of banking in the EC, accepted the United States' unilateral proposal. In January 1987, three federal US banking regulators and the Bank of England announced their intent to establish common risk-based capital standards for the institutions they regulated.[19]

After concluding their joint agreement, the United States and the United Kingdom applied a two-track negotiating strategy toward other industrial countries. They pursued bilateral talks with Japan and major Western European countries, such as West Germany and France, and they also continued discussions at the Basle Committee.[20] An agreement was reached with the Japanese government in September 1987. The trilateral agreement put pressure on the Basle Committee, and as a result, in December 1987 the committee finally announced that it had reached a preliminary agreement on the international convergence of capital measurements and capital standards.

Incentives Among Leading Countries for an International Regulatory Framework

There were also domestic factors within powerful countries such as the United States and the United Kingdom that led to promotion of an international regulatory framework for global financial dealings. As for the United States, the country was motivated not only by a concern for international financial stability but also by domestic complaints that US banks were at a competitive disadvantage because their foreign counterparts were subject to fewer regulations.

One objective of the Basle Accord was to level the playing field so that international banks could compete equally. This reflected the US government's concern about the competitiveness of its banks.[21] In this sense, it can be argued that the United States used the international negotiations to change the rules so that it could gain a competitive edge over its main competitor, Japan.[22]

It is hard to say that the US government's main objective for proposing an international regulatory framework for international banks was to reduce the competitiveness of Japanese banks. Actually, an official of the US Federal Reserve Board admitted that a greater burden would probably fall not only on large Japanese banks but also on French banks and certain US banks.[23]

The United Kingdom was one of three countries (the other two countries were Belgium and France) that had already imposed risk-weighted capital adequacy standards on their domestic banks. The move followed the collapse of a series of poorly capitalized financial institutions. Therefore, it was not so difficult for the United Kingdom to accept the US proposal for converging their standards. Besides, the Bank of England wanted to have countermeasures for a planned European Union (EU) financial integration. Such domestic factors prompted the Bank of England to reach a bilateral agreement with the United States.[24]

Japan and the Basle Accord

Japan's Role in International Finance in the Postwar Era

Before examining Japan's response to the US-UK proposal, it is useful to know how the Japanese government committed itself to a multilateral framework in international finance in the post–World War II period. Japanese rejoined the global financial community in 1952 when it joined the IMF. During the 1960s, Japan joined a number of major multilateral financial institutions. It joined the Development Assistance Committee (DAC) of the OECD in 1960, and it obtained Article 8 status within the IMF. Japan also became a full-fledged member of the OECD in 1964.

Prior to 1964, Japan pledged capital in response to an invitation to join the IMF's General Agreements to Borrow (GAB). It became a founding member of the GAB in 1962. At the same time, Japan joined the G-10, the main forum for discussing international monetary issues.[25] In the late 1960s, after repeated requests, Japan also rejoined the BIS. Japan had been a member of the organization prior to World War II.

Even though Japan had become a full member of the club of advanced industrial countries by the mid-1960s, it chose to keep a low profile and played a marginal role in international rule making. Throughout most of the decade, Japan's foreign economic policy consisted of dealing primarily with the United States.[26]

Following President Richard Nixon's announcement of halting convertibility between gold and the dollar, Japan was forced to take a more active interest in international financial issues owing to its increasing economic clout. In the early 1970s, Japan joined the G5 and G7, which addressed a wide range of international monetary and financial issues.[27] In the international multilateral forum, Japan was still a passive participant, however. When macroeconomic policy coordination among major industrial countries was on the G5 discussion table in the late 1970s and 1980s, Japan continued to follow US policies.

In contrast to its passiveness on such matters, there were two areas in which Japan attempted to play a leading role. One was coping with the debt crisis that started in Latin America in the 1980s and posed a threat to the international financial system. US, European, and Japanese banks had major dealings with Latin America. In frequent discussions among industrial countries, the US government proposed programs for coping with the debt crisis. Those programs consisted of the Baker Plan of 1985 and the New Baker Plan of 1987.

The programs proved largely ineffective in providing new money to debtor countries, so in 1988, the Japanese government proposed the so-called New Miyazawa Initiative. The proposed plan, however, was rejected by other G7 countries such as the United States, the United Kingdom, and Germany, despite the Japanese government's best persuasive efforts. In 1989, the United States rolled out a new debt strategy, dubbed the Brady Plan, which turned out to incorporate major elements of the New Miyazawa Initiative.[28] For European countries, the Brady Plan appeared to be the result of US-Japan cooperation.[29]

A second way Japan tried to play a bigger role on the international stage was by increasing its financial support for global financial institutions. Ever since it became a founding member of the GAB, the Japanese government has supported a quota increase of the IMF to construct sound financial bases of the IMF, whereas the United States, the largest shareholder in quota, has been reluctant to adopt such a plan. Japan became the second-largest member in quota in the 1990s. Japan was also the second-largest financial contributor to the World Bank during the decade and the largest to the Asian Development Bank.

Japan's positive stance toward these two issue areas showed that it realized it must play a more active role in world affairs, one that was commensurate with its economic status. Although it still caved in to US political pressure during economic talks with that country, Japan was learning to be more assertive when it came to involvement in multilateral frameworks of a financial nature.

Japan's Response to the US-UK Proposal

How did the Japanese government respond to the risk-based bank capital adequacy proposal from the United States and the UK in the case of the Basle Accord? Did it show its positive attitude toward the accord as well as the above-mentioned issues? In this case, Japan was not an active collaborator. Why? There are two kinds of explanations of why the G-10 countries agreed on the Basel Accord. One emphasizes the power relations among countries. In this explanation, the US government could make other countries agree with its proposal owing to its power. According to this school of thought, Japan was forced to agree by the United States.[30] The other explanation focuses on the interests of countries. It states that since G-10 countries had interest in making an international regulatory framework in the midst of financial crises, they could make the accord.[31] In this explanation, Japan was supposed to have interest in making such a regulatory agreement.

Neither explanation can fully explain the Japanese attitude. The power-focused explanation does not specify what kind of US power worked in this case, and the interest-focused explanation is difficult to account for, given that there were actually some countries that did not see their interest in accepting the US-UK proposal at the beginning, although they recognized that they needed some regulatory measures on banks. The countries whose banks had lower capital ratios, such as France and Japan, were among them. US officials expected to encounter some obstacles when dealing with Japan, whose bank capital structure differed substantially from that of other industrial countries.[32] Their expectation came true. When the US and UK governments proposed a uniform standard of capital adequacy, both the banking industry and the MOF reacted passively.[33] At the negotiation of the Basle Committee, Japan was represented by the Bank of Japan (BOJ) and the MOF, whereas most other countries were represented by their central banks. Although the BOJ and MOF were engaged in international discussions, at home the MOF had much more authority over banks and thus more influence in determining Japan's policy toward the Basle Accord.[34]

The average ratio of capital to risk-weighted assets was lower in Japanese banks than it was in US and UK banks. Indeed, Japanese banks took advantage of this in the international marketplace. The overseas assets of Japanese banks grew by $1.3 trillion in a brief five-year period from 1983 to 1988, nearly doubling their share of international bank assets. The Japanese Bankers Association opposed the US-UK proposal, repeatedly saying it was unrealistic to unify the regulatory frameworks of various countries since each had its own unique banking system.[35] The association also doubted the effectiveness of capital adequacy standards as a tool for supervising international banks and feared that international constraints might be imposed on them.

The MOF was also reluctant to take the initiative to persuade banks to accept the proposal, because it had revised the capital adequacy rule in 1986, just before the US-UK proposal, and felt that it would be difficult to negotiate all over again with banks on the same matter. In the previous year, the BOJ had officially expressed its reluctance toward the rapid standardization of banking at the International Conference of Banking Supervisors.[36] Since 1954, the MOF had enforced a guideline that required banks to hold capital equal to more than 10 percent of their total assets. However, by the mid-1980s, most Japanese banks were holding capital ratios of 3–5 percent on average, which was far removed from the fixed guideline of the MOF.

Faced with the liberalization of Japan's financial market, the MOF recognized the need to revise supervisory measures to reflect the actual activities of its banks. In May 1986, in response to the proposal of the Financial System Research Council in the previous year, the MOF revised the capital adequacy rule. As a result, banks were required to increase capital to 4 percent of assets in the case of domestic banks and 6 percent in the case of international banks. This rule was not a coercive one, however, but merely a guideline. Moreover, the way of calculating capital ratio the MOF had applied was not the asset ratio proposed by the US-UK plan, but a gearing ratio, in which there was no distinction among capital.

The MOF was also confident in the soundness of Japanese banking system thanks to its policies, the so-called convoy system (*gososendan hoshiki*).[37] Actually, Japan had experienced no serious banking crises during the postwar period. Therefore, there was little incentive for the MOF to accept standards that placed an additional burden on Japanese banks.

Another difficult problem encouraged Japan's reluctant attitude toward the US-UK proposal—whether the hidden value of latent revaluation reserves might be included in the categories of capital. Japanese banks had large unreported holding gains on their equity portfolios and real estate assets.[38] The MOF's revised guideline of 1986 allowed banks to include 70 percent of unrealized holding gains on land and equities into capital. In contrast, the United States and the United Kingdom refused to include such reserves in capital because they feared that the hidden value of latent revaluation reserves was exposed to the risk of price fluctuation.

Despite the fact that the MOF and in particular the Japanese banks did not see benefits from accepting the US-UK proposal, why did the Japanese government decide to agree with it? Did Japan give in to the US power? If so, what kind of power? In this case, the United States acted as a "go-it-alone power."[39] A "go-it-alone power" can get rid of other countries' policy options of sticking to the status quo by creating a new institutional arrangement with like-minded countries. Not participating in such a new institutional arrangement would result in less benefit for other countries than sticking to the status quo. We can assume that as the bilateral negotiation continued, the Japanese banks in particular realized that they had to accept the US-UK proposal; otherwise they could get more cost than by opposing the proposal.

There were two types of evidence to support this assumption. First, the Japanese banks did not want to scale back their international activities, which were thriving in the 1980s, particularly in the United States and the United Kingdom. By the same token, they feared being shut out of US and

British financial markets if they did not agree to meet standards imposed by the countries' regulatory authorities.[40] After the bilateral agreement between the United States and the UK, US government officials often implied the possibility that the banks that did not fulfill the US regulatory standard would not be allowed to enter the US market.[41] Japanese banks had a large share in US and UK financial markets, whereas their shares in France and Germany were much smaller.

Second, lowering the rating of Japanese banks by US credit-rating agencies affected the policy preferences of Japanese banks. After the US-UK agreement, US credit-rating agencies such as Moody's lowered the rating of six leading Japanese banks, mainly because they did not meet the US-UK capital adequacy standard.[42] Until then, Japanese banks had always cited the agency's AAA rating on them to show the soundness of Japanese banks, but lowering the rating made Japanese banks worry about their international activities in the future.

As for the Japanese government, despite the MOF's initial reluctant attitude toward the US-UK proposal, officials of the MOF and BOJ reiterated the importance of Japan's maintaining good relations with other countries in light of its growing stature in the international economy.[43] A large current account surplus and the growing presence of Japanese banks in international markets, which sometimes drew criticism from the international community, reflected Japan's burgeoning economic influence. Although they were reluctant, the MOF and the BOJ were not seriously worried about the severity of the constraints the capital adequacy rule would put on the activities of Japanese banks, which up until that point had performed so well.

Once the Japanese Bankers Association changed its policy preferences from sticking to the status quo to agreeing to the US-UK proposal, the Japanese government started to negotiate with the United States and the UK to get better conditions within the framework of the US-UK proposal. Whether or not the hidden value of latent revaluation reserves was to be included in capital was a contentious point. The MOF, backed by the Japanese Bankers Association, asked that 70 percent of the hidden value of latent revaluation reserves be included.[44] The MOF negotiated hard to get concessions on this point of being allowed to include some amount of latent assets.

After nine months of negotiation, the Japanese government reached an agreement with the United States and the United Kingdom in September 1987. In a final agreement hammered out in July 1988, the Basle Committee agreed to include latent revaluation reserves provided that the assets were prudently valued, fully reflecting the possibility of price fluctuations and forced sale. It was also decided that a discount of 55 percent would be applied to the difference between the historic cost book value and the market value.[45] After the Japanese government agreed with the final draft of the accord, the MOF and BOJ expressed their satisfaction with it, saying that Japanese banks were capable of meeting the 8 percent capital ratio standard.[46]

Although the Japanese government had supported an idea of international regulation on banks since the early 1980s, it hardly took a leading role to create such an international framework, despite the increasing presence of its banks in international financial markets. Once the capital adequacy regulation was on the agenda of the Basle Committee by the United States, Japan disagreed with this regulation. Although theoretically Japan had other policy options than just being reluctant followers, they realized, however, how hard it would be to oppose the US-UK proposal for fear of being excluded from those markets, mainly owing to Japanese banks' heavy reliance on the US and UK financial markets. At this point, the Japanese government, reflecting Japanese banks' preferences, was a reluctant follower, but the concession the Japanese government successfully got from the United States and the United Kingdom on inclusion of latent assets in capital showed that due to Japan's inevitable presence in international financial markets, the Japanese government could have some leverage to negotiate with the US and UK governments. For the US and UK governments, without an agreement with Japan, it would have been difficult to put pressure on other G-10 countries to make an agreement at the Basle Committee. In this regard, Japan was more active than a mere reluctant follower in modifying the agreement.

The Effect of the Burst of the Bubble on Japan's Perception

After the conclusion of the Basle Accord, individual countries were given a four-year grace period (until 1992) to comply with its requirements. Although the accord seemed to impose a uniform international regulatory framework on countries, it actually gave individual countries discretion to make domestic regulations that would ensure compliance with the international agreement. Several items were left to the countries' discretion, such as the manner for calculating risk weight, the content of tier-two capital, and the measurement applied during the four-year grace period.

In Japan, the MOF moved aggressively to formulate domestic guidelines for capital requirements. The Japanese Bankers Association put pressure on the MOF to minimize their burden with special treatment during the grace period.[47] As a result of the Basle Accord, the MOF strengthened its supervisory measures toward banks. For example, the MOF could get more detailed information on their capital from the banks.

In comparison with the United States and the United Kingdom, the MOF applied most of the temporary measures that were allowed to be used until 1992. In Japan, banks were allowed to meet an 8 percent capital ratio standard as late as the end of fiscal 1992 (the end of March 1993). On the other hand, most major UK banks were fulfilling the 8 percent capital ratio standard by as early as June 1989. The US government imposed the requirement on all US banks, although the Basle Accord required regulators to apply it only to large international banks.[48]

From 1987 to 1989, Japanese banks achieved 10 trillion yen in equity finance and benefited from rising stock prices. It was not difficult for Japanese banks to comply with the Basle Accord because the stock market boom had provided them with access to a large amount of cheap equity capital as well as capital gains on their stock portfolios. By 1988, the Japanese banks that wanted to conduct international operations had met the 8 percent requirement.

The situation surrounding banks changed drastically, however. The state of the Japanese economy took a sudden turn for the worse when the so-called bubble economy burst in 1991. Banks were particularly hard hit. In early 1990, the Tokyo stock market declined sharply, and as a result, Japanese banks were no longer able to raise new funds. Land prices also started tumbling. Japanese banks had a hard time meeting the 8 percent requirement because they had relied on unrealized holding gains on land and equities.

The burst of the bubble caused a domestic debate over whether Japan should continue to strive to comply with the accord. The heads of several Japanese banks expressed a certain wariness about it.[49] Japanese media fanned the flames of debate by reporting that the accord would harm the Japanese economy even further. An ex-MOF official argued that the Basle Accord would not stabilize international financial relations and that the Japanese government had given in too easily to the pact, without duly considering its negative impact on Japanese banks and industry.[50] This was the prevailing opinion in Japan about the Basle Accord in the early 1990s. The MOF and the BOJ did not change their pro-accord stance. Instead, they continued to participate in international discussions at the Basle Committee.

Japanese banks were severely damaged by the burst of the bubble economy, and as a result, they lost a great deal of their international competitiveness in the late 1990s. This contrasted sharply with the situation a decade earlier. The MOF also suffered from a series of scandals. Moreover, it lost its exclusive power to regulate banks after the problem of bad loans at banks and nonbanking financial institutions worsened. In 1998, the Financial Services Agency was established, and the MOF conceded its supervisory power to it. Under the Basle Accord, Japanese banks chose to liquidate assets and adopt a tight lending policy. This had a seriously adverse affect on small-scale business owing to the credit crunch.

The sharp deterioration of the domestic economy caused not only banks but also the media to turn against the Basle Accord.[51] Several Japanese economists and television commentators went so far as to say that the accord was preventing the recovery of the Japanese economy. Debate raged over whether the Basle Accord could bring stability to the world's financial system.

Conclusion

This chapter, by analyzing Japan's participation in the Basle Accord, has attempted to examine whether Japan's participation in key international issues throughout the late 1980s and 1990s has been changed in the international economy. Despite its initial reluctance toward US and UK positions, Japan finally agreed to go along with the accord, taking part thereafter in good faith in discussions at the Basle Committee.

Underscoring this policy choice was a strong commitment within the MOF and BOJ to cooperate with other nations. Both groups realized that Japan—as a leading economic power—needed to play a bigger role in the effort to create a sound international financial system. In other words, Japan's robust economic performance in the late 1980s stirred a sense of obligation in the Japanese government to cooperate at an international level.

As the case of the Basle Accord shows, the Japanese government's attitude was one of acquiescence toward the United States and United Kingdom in the sense that Japan did not take the initiative in creating the international regulatory regime. Although the Japanese government opposed the rapid introduction of a standardized capital ratio, it could not come up with a better alternative. The only thing the Japanese government could do was to win a concession in terms of the content of capital.

Two factors explain Japan's passiveness with regard to the Basle Accord. The first was the United States' dominant position in the field of international finance. The United States has played a leading role in the field since the end of World War II. Although Japan had become the world's leading creditor nation by the 1980s, the United States held sway in international discussions on international finance, owing to its economic power and expertise. The United States had opened up its financial markets to international competition long before most industrialized countries, so its large financial market in itself was a power resource that made the United States play as a "go-it-alone power" in this case. As a result, there was little room for the Japanese government to initiate its own version of an international regulatory framework reflecting the interests of Japanese banks.

The other factor behind Japan's passive acceptance of the Basle Accord was the Japanese government's confidence in its financial system in the period of booming economy. As for the standardization of the capital adequacy ratio, the MOF and the BOJ were slower than other major industrial states to realize its necessity. This is because they were confident in the Japanese banking system and the country's way of supervising its banks despite their low capitalization ratio. With the domestic economy booming, neither the MOF, BOJ, nor politicians were much interested in initiating a regulatory framework for international finance, despite frequent international financial crises.

By the late 1990s, with the Japanese economy mired in recession, Japanese banks and others began to blame the Basle Accord for the country's problems, saying it was preventing the country from staging an economic recovery. During the mid-1990s, along with other problems, the Basle Accord restricted the activities of Japanese banks far more than the MOF had done during the previous decade. The Basle Accord proved to be burdensome for Japanese banks after the burst of the country's bubble economy. Many people even blamed the credit crunch of the 1990s on the Basle Accord.

Despite these domestic criticisms of the accord, however, by the end of the decade the Japanese government was actively involved in discussions at the Basle Committee to revise the accord. The Basle Committee began to recognize a need for amending the accord so that it could be an effective tool for supervising international banks. Japan's active attitude for amending the accord shows that the burst of the bubble economy forced the Japanese government to consider seriously what kind of regulatory measures would best serve domestic as well as international financial stability.[52]

Apart from an international regulatory framework, by the late 1990s the Japanese government also was trying its best to lead the way in international financial relations. For example, it proposed the Asian Monetary Fund after the Asian financial crisis and also came up with an initiative to reduce world poverty by canceling the debt of heavily indebted poor countries at the Okinawa Summit.

Faced with the Asian monetary crisis, which gravely affected Japan's domestic economy, the Japanese government proposed the Asian Monetary Fund. The fund offered emergency financial assistance to the countries that had been hardest hit by the monetary crisis. Although the proposal was opposed by the United States, the Japanese government is still keen on establishing a regional lender of last resort that can supplement the work of the IMF. In this respect, the Japanese government has tried to play an active role in developing a regional alternative to the global framework promoted by the United States.

On the issue of poverty reduction, the Japanese government regards this as an area where it can and should take the initiative, in contrast to the views of other leading industrialized countries. As stated earlier, Japan made an effort to cope with the debt of developing countries through its proposed New Miyazawa Initiative in the 1980s. The Japanese government placed the issue of poverty reduction high on the list of topics for G8 countries to discuss at the Okinawa Summit in 2000. In this area, Japan is expected to make a positive commitment to the developing world.

By the late 1990s, Japan's way of handling international financial issues differed depending on the particular issue. As for participating in an international regulatory framework, the Japanese government tried to play a more active role in rule making, considering its stagnating domestic economy. At the same time, on other issues such as regional financial funds and debt reduction, Japan also tried to take initiative. As for the ODA, Japan's decision of reducing the ODA owing to the large fiscal deficit in the early 2000s facilitated the Japanese government's serious consideration of the effective way of providing foreign aid for the sake of international security.

The burst of the bubble economy cast Japan into a deep recession. But ironically, this has had a positive effect in the sense that Japanese government and big business have become more sensitive to international economic fluctuations and international rule making. Although Japan's economic might has declined, the present situation has forced the Japanese government to take a hard look at the kinds of economic policies that will best benefit both Japan and others, as well as the precise role Japan should play in the arena of international financial relations under the limited economic capability.

Notes

1. *New York Times,* July 12, 1988, D1.
2. Porter, *States, Markets, and Regimes in Global Finance;* Herring and Litan, *Financial Regulation in the Global Economy;* Kapstein, "Resolving the Regulator's Dilemma: International Coordination of Banking Regulations," 323–347; Kapstein, *Governing the Global Economy: International Finance and the State;* Reinicke, *Banking, Politics, and Global Finance.*
3. Jackson et al., *Capital Requirements and Bank Behavior: The Impact of the Basle Accord,* 1.
4. BIS home page; available at http://www.bis.org/bcbs/history.htm.
5. Market risk was defined as the risk of losses in on– and off–balance sheet positions arising from fluctuations in market prices. Basle Committee, *Overview of the Amendment to the Capital Accord to Incorporate Market Risks.*
6. Basle Committee, *International Convergence of Capital Measurement and Capital Standards: A Revised Framework.*
7. The G-10 is made up of eleven industrial countries (Belgium, Canada, France, Germany, Italy, Japan, the Netherlands, Sweden, Switzerland, the United Kingdom, and the United States).
8. Herring and Litan, *Financial Regulation in the Global Economy,* 108.
9. Italy, Luxembourg, Canada, Japan, and the United States applied the gearing-ratio measure, whereas the other countries adopted the risk-asset measure.

Cooke, "International Convergence of Capital Adequacy Measurement and Standards," 312–315.

10. Ibid. Each country applied different measures of calculating capital ratio in the 1980s, so it is hard to get precise numbers.

11. Basle Committee, *International Convergence of Capital Measurement and Capital Standards*, 1.

12. Ibid., 4.

13. Ibid., 3.

14. Ibid., 4

15. Ibid., 14.

16. Kapstein ("Resolving the Regulator's Dilemma") emphasized the importance of consensual knowledge behind the agreement.

17. Porter, *States, Markets, and Regimes in Global Finance*, 64; Ōta, *Kokusai Kinyū Genba karano Shōgen*, 132–136.

18. There are three bank regulators in the United States: the Federal Reserve Board, the Office of the Comptroller of the Currency, and the Federal Deposit Insurance Corporation.

19. "Agreed Proposal of the United States Federal Banking Supervisory Authorities and the Bank of England on Primary Capital and Capital Adequacy Assessment," in US Congress, House of Representatives, *Hearing Before the Subcommittee on General Oversight and Investigations of the Committee on Banking, Finance, and Urban Affairs* (April 30, 1987), 71–98.

20. Kapstein, *Governing the Global Economy*, 115.

21. Chairman Carroll Hubbard of the Subcommittee on Banking, Finance, and Urban Affairs stated in the congressional hearings that one of the primary goals was "to create a level playing field on which the U.S. banks can compete fairly in the international market." US Congress, *Hearing Before the Subcommittee on General Oversight and Investigations of the Committee on Banking, Finance, and Urban Affairs* (April 21, 1988), 23.

22. Oatley and Nabors claimed that the US proposal was motivated by a need to satisfy competing US banks and voter pressures. Oatley and Nabors, "Redistributive Cooperation," 35–54.

23. Testimony by William Taylor, staff director, Division of Banking Supervision and Regulation, Board of Governors of the Federal Reserve System, in US Congress, *Hearing Before the Subcommittee on General Oversight and Investigations of the Committee on Banking, Finance, and Urban Affairs* (April 21, 1988), 20–21.

24. Cooke, "International Convergence," 325.

25. Volcker and Gyoten, *Changing Fortunes*, 56.

26. Ibid., 57.

27. Japanese finance minister Kiichi Aichi played a crucial role in the founding of the G5 (ibid., 134).

28. Ibid., 223–224.

29. Ōta, *Kokusai Kinyū Genba karano Shōgen*, 130.

30. Many Japanese journalists apply this power relationship explanation. For example, Shiota, *Kinyū-arijigoku;* Higashitani, *BIS kisei no Uso.*

31. Kapstein, *Governing the Global Economy.*

32. Testimony by Paul Volcker, in US Congress, *Hearing Before the Subcommittee on General Oversight and Investigations of the Committee on Banking, Finance, and Urban Affairs* (April 30, 1987), 24.

33. As for the Japanese response to the Basle Accord, see Kurosawa, "*BIS kisei*

no Paradokkusu"; Higashitani, *BIS kisei no Uso;* Shiota, *Kinyū-arijigoku.* For more detailed observations by MOF officials, see Himino, *Kenshō BIS kisei to Nihon.*

34. In the past, the BOJ was a regular participant in the BIS meetings. When the regulation of capital adequacy of banks came to be on the agenda, the MOF insisted on being a major negotiator in international negotiation, and the BOJ gave in to the MOF.

35. *Nikkei Kinyū Shimbun,* February 9, 1988, 1; *Nihon Keizai Shimbun,* March 18, 1987, 3.

36. Ōta, *Kokusai Kinyū Genba karano Shōgen,* 135–136.

37. The convoy system means "a wide set of financial regulations in Japan that discourage competition within the financial sector" and keeps "the laggards falling behind but also discourages the leaders from moving too far ahead." Hoshi, "The Convoy System for Insolvent Banks," 155–180.

38. Japanese banks have been allowed to hold equity portfolio.

39. For "go-it-alone power," see Gruber, *Ruling the World.*

40. Himino, *Kenshō BIS kisei to Nihon.*

41. Testimony by Federal Reserve Board chairman Paul Volcker, "Risk-Based Capital Requirements for Banks and Bank Holding Companies," in US Congress, *Hearing Before the Subcommittee on General Oversight and Investigations of the Committee on Banking, Finance, and Urban Affairs* (April 30, 1987), 13.

42. *Nihon Keizai Shimbun,* May 13, 1980.

43. Finance Minister Miyazawa Kiichi stressed the importance of positive participation in international cooperation (*Nihon Keizai Shimbun,* July 8, 1987, 3).

44. Request to the government by the Japanese Bankers Association, *Nihon Keizai Shimbun,* May 13, 1987.

45. Other European countries, such as West Germany and Italy, also opposed the Japanese proposal about calculating latent assets.

46. *Nihon Keizai Shimbun,* December 8, 1987, 1; December 10, 1987, 3.

47. *Nihon Keizai Shimbun,* December 9, 1987, 3; *Nikkei Kinyu Shimbun,* February 9, 1988, 1.

48. Scott and Iwahara, *In Search of Level Playing.*

49. *Nikkei Kinyū Shimbun,* March 7, 1990, 3.

50. Tokuda, "BIS kisei wa yokai, minaose," 20–22.

51. In the mass media, some attributed the creation of the Basle Accord to the US conspiracy to destroy Japanese banks' competitiveness. Higashitani, *BIS kisei no Uso;* Shiota, *Kinyū-arijigoku.*

52. Interview with ex-BOJ official who engaged in discussion at the Basle Committee, July 18, 2000, Tokyo, Japan.

| 8 |

Responding to the
Asian Financial Crisis

Juichi Inada

The Asian financial crisis of 1997–1998 was a critical event in the development of the East Asian region and has had a major impact on the emergence of regional institutions. It was also a pivotal moment in terms of Japan's relationship to the region and Japan's position in the larger global financial system. The Japanese response to the outbreak of the crisis was unusually proactive, and Japan offered large quantities of aid to help stabilize the region's suddenly precarious economies. At the same time, Japan's diplomatic efforts were marked by an unusual degree of conflict and acrimony, and the initial Japanese initiative, the Asian Monetary Fund (AMF), floundered and ultimately failed as a result of fierce criticism from Washington and parts of Asia. Yet, even after this initial setback, Japan persevered, joining the international bailout of the most troubled Asian economies and later on spearheading the formation of a new regional institutional framework, the APT, dedicated to coping with future monetary crises.

It is possible to interpret these developments in a number of different ways.[1] Some have seen the regional response to the crisis as a sign of the emergence of a new, more independent economic regionalism, a possible precursor to the formation of an East Asian economic bloc.[2] Conversely, others have pointed to the crisis, and Japan's apparent ineffectiveness in dealing with it, as further evidence of the bankruptcy of Asian regionalism and of Japanese regional policy.[3]

I will argue, however, that the truth lies in between these two extremes. A more detailed analysis reveals that Japan is indeed trying to foster the development of regional institutions, and there is little doubt that many in Japan are dissatisfied with the performance of the existing global set of

151

arrangements—centered on the IMF and the World Bank—for coping with financial crises. This dissatisfaction and emphasis on regional institutions mask the basic fact that Japan sees the existing set of arrangements as broadly consonant with its national interests and that it has neither the intellectual nor analytical capacity to offer a coherent alternative. As a result, Japan's efforts at region building have been by and large aimed at complementing, rather than challenging, the existing global financial management regime.

Japan and International Financial Institutions: Conflict or Collaboration?

International Financial Assistance Regime

Japan's response to the Asian financial crisis was critically influenced by the larger global framework within which such interventions occur. As is well known, the IMF and the World Bank are the two institutions that are charged with taking the lead in providing multilateral financial assistance to countries that are faced with a currency crisis. At the same time, these institutions do not freely provide cash to needy recipients on a no-strings-attached basis. In this sense, the popular term *bailout* that is often applied in the media to such operations is a misnomer. The IMF and the World Bank invariably seek to negotiate with recipients extensive (and usually painful) economic reform programs that are intended to attack the root causes of the crisis and prevent their recurrence. Acceptance of these reform programs is made a precondition for granting financial assistance.[4] That "conditionality" of lending has enormous repercussions for the recipients: not only are the multilateral funds from the IMF and the World Bank dependent upon their fulfillment but also bilateral money cannot be offered without the agreement on these requirements.

In principle, a Japanese bilateral yen loan cannot be given until the recipient agrees to undertake the reform measures prescribed by the IMF and the World Bank. The Japanese government has traditionally recognized that IMF conditionality is needed to avoid the "moral hazard" of the recipients, although some Japanese economists have often criticized the contents of the IMF prescriptions. Moral hazard means the tendency of the recipients to borrow money without reforming their economic management, and it is regarded as a main cause of inability of repayment in the future. Japanese financial authorities take almost the same stance as the IMF in this respect.

During the Asian financial crisis, the IMF attached stringent demands with regard to the various measures that were necessary for the structural reform of the Southeast Asian economies. Japan waited for the IMF to negotiate an agreement with the various countries seeking rescue packages before it supported the IMF's bailout programs. The whole process made it clear that the IMF had plenty of expertise when it came to the reform of fiscal, financial, and administrative systems, whereas Japan had only limited experiences in this field.

On the other hand, the United States was determined to use the IMF as the primary agency for managing the Asian economic crisis. The United States used its influence over the IMF to promote significant economic reforms in Thailand, Indonesia, and South Korea. The IMF and the United States, which has great influence on the IMF as the largest donor, were the leaders in formulating international assistance packages to Asia.

Japan's Ambivalent Stance Toward the International Financial Assistance Regime

Despite general Japanese acceptance of the international financial assistance regime, many Japanese, both before and during the crisis, were somewhat skeptical of the way in which the IMF operates in practice. They made the following three arguments: (1) IMF prescriptions are based on so-called neoclassical economics, which is a universal analytical paradigm but often neglects social aspects of economic development and unique characteristics of the specific countries and areas.[5] (2) The IMF conditionality interferes too much in the domestic politics and societies of the recipients. Donors should think much more of the "ownership" (or self-help and efforts) of the recipients.[6] (3) The Bretton Woods institutions (the IMF and the World Bank) are largely controlled by the United States, which is the top donor of both institutions and has effective veto power over their decisions.[7] As a result, there is an inevitable tendency that aid is given on the basis of US economic and political interests rather than on the basis of the interests of Asian countries. Therefore an Asian-centered institution (such as the AMF) should be established to provide assistance to Asian countries.

Despite these reservations, Japan has been coordinating its policy with the international financial assistance regime of the IMF and the World Bank because Japan does not have an alternate universal paradigm that can substitute for the neoclassical economics–based approach of the IMF and the World Bank, nor does Japan have the robust institutional capacity to analyze and give advice about the economic management of the recipients in detail as do the IMF and the World Bank. In fact, the Japanese government realizes that the recipients are in urgent need of reform and supports making those reforms preconditions for the disbursal of funds, but Japan cannot on a bilateral basis insist on such conditionality and therefore prefers to use the Bretton Woods institutions as negotiators to impose hard requirements on the recipients. In other words, although Japan may have some doubts about the ways that the IMF and the World Bank operate in specific instances, it agrees with them on the general principle, and it prefers to rely on them for insisting on policies that might be quite unpopular.

Beyond these general philosophical issues, Japan has also wanted to use its financial power to increase its bilateral influence, and there has been a strong tendency on Japan's part to try to win friendship through the offer of aid through bilateral channels. The New Miyazawa Initiative can be regarded as one such effort.

IMF-centered Assistance Toward the Countries Affected by the Crisis

In reality, the international financial assistance to the countries affected by the Asian financial crisis was offered through the IMF-centered financial rescue packages with its conditionalities. The amount of financial assistance by the international community, Japan, and the United States to each country is summarized in Table 8.1. The Japanese contribution was $4 billion to Thailand, $5 billion to Indonesia, and $10 billion to South Korea in the IMF-centered packages.

The Japanese government was also positive about an Asian-centered monetary framework at the time of the Thai crisis.[8] As the financial crisis spread to other countries and its magnitude expanded, however, Japan began to recognize that the crisis was too large to be dealt with only through Japanese initiative. Within the IMF and other international institutions such as the World Bank and the ADB, the Japanese government (Finance Ministry) closely coordinated its policy with its US counterpart. The US

Table 8.1   International Assistance Packages to Countries Affected by the Asian Financial Crisis

	Recipients		
	Thailand	Indonesia	South Korea
Date of agreement with IMF	August 20, 1997	November 5, 1997	December 4, 1997
Amount of assistance (US$ billions)			
Total	16	36	55
IMF	4	10	21
Japan	4	5	10
United States	0	3	5
Other	8	18	19

Sources: IMF, *Press Release,* No. 97/37 (August 20, 1997); IMF, *News Brief,* No. 97/22 (October 31, 1997); IMF, *News Brief,* No. 97/27 (December 3, 1997).

government (Treasury Department) also came to the same conclusion and agreed about the importance of supporting Asian countries in crisis and of using the IMF as a major apparatus. It was argued that both countries could cooperate to strengthen the capacity of the IMF and improve the IMF prescriptions appropriate to Asian reforming countries.

Japan and the United States: Divergent or Common Interests?

Japanese and US Economic Presence in Asia

As Japan has a particularly close and interdependent economic relationship with Southeast Asia, the repercussions for the Japanese economy have been especially serious. Asia absorbs more than 40 percent of Japan's total exports; much of that is composed of capital and intermediate goods that are used to make final products. Because of the Asian economic crisis, Japan's exports to Asia have sharply declined since the middle of 1997.

There are any number of indicators that show Japan's deep involvement in Asian economies. For instance, Figure 8.1 shows the total cumulative lending from foreign banks to each ASEAN country as of the end of June 1997, based on BIS figures. In Thailand, Japanese private banks loaned $37.7 billion out of a total of $69.4 billion in foreign loans (thus constituting 54.4 percent of total foreign lending); in Indonesia the figures are $23.2 billion out of $58.7 billion (39.4 percent); and in South Korea $23.7 billion out of $103.4 billion (22.9 percent). In contrast, the share of US banks was relatively small: $4.0 billion (5.8 percent) in Thailand, $4.6 billion (7.8 percent) in Indonesia, and $10.0 billion (9.6 percent) in South Korea.

If we look at the cumulative foreign direct investment to each ASEAN country by Japanese and US companies, as shown in Figure 8.2, the Japanese investment was $7.1 billion in Thailand, $17 billion in Indonesia, and $5.3 billion in South Korea, and that of the US was $4.6 billion in Thailand, $6.9 in Indonesia, and $5.2 in South Korea at the end of 1994. The US investment to these three countries was less than that of Japanese companies, but its amount was not small, and the United States was deeply involved in their economies.[9]

In December 1997, the Asian economic crisis reached South Korea. In contrast to the case of Thailand, the United States and the IMF responded to the South Korean crisis and Indonesian crisis with great urgency. In addition to official assistance, on January 28, 1998, a group of foreign private banks agreed with the Korean government to convert $24 billion in short-term debt to long-term debt guaranteed by the government. In this case, it was the US banks who initially formulated this financial package, and the Japanese banks followed that initiative.[10] One reason for the relatively high

Figure 8.1 Foreign Bank Lending to Countries Affected by the Asian Financial Crisis

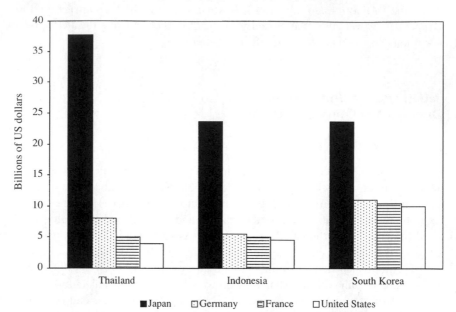

Source: Bank for International Settlements, *The Maturity, Sectoral, and Nationality Distribution of International Lending* (Basel: BIS, 1997).

US concerns about South Korea may be the large US presence in that country. The presence of US companies and banks in South Korea is almost the same as that of the Japanese in terms of private investment and lending. In addition, the United States sent Defense Secretary William S. Cohen to South Korea soon after the crisis developed, suggesting that the United States had a large security stake in the stability of the Korean peninsula.

Multiple Actors in Both Japan and the United States

In formulating the international financial assistance program, Japanese and US interests intermingled deeply. The actual decisionmaking process did not match the image of "Japan vs. the United States," as it has sometimes been portrayed.[11] Rather, a close examination of the history of the crisis shows a complex transnational coalition-building process in which the sudden advent of the crisis led to a number of missteps and generated considerable friction between the two sides, masking an underlying commonality of interests between the two.

To develop a better understanding of the diplomatic side of the crisis, it

Figure 8.2 Direct Investment from Japan and the United States to Asian Countries

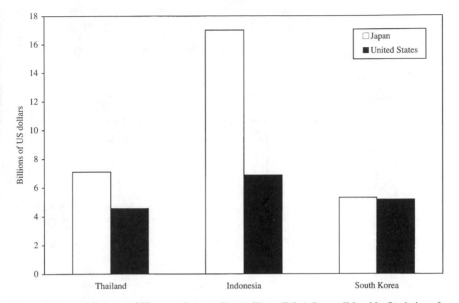

Source: Ministry of Finance (Japan), *Zaisei Kinyū Tōkei Geppō* [Monthly Statistics of Finance], 1995.

is first necessary to get a sense of the chief actors that were involved in the decisionmaking at the time. Figure 8.3 provides an overview of the major actors who formulated the international financial assistance program. In Japan the major actors during the crisis were the Ministry of Finance, the Ministry of Foreign Affairs, and the prime minister. The Japan International Cooperation Agency (JICA), Overseas Economic Cooperation Fund (OECF), and the Export-Import Bank are aid-implementing agencies under these ministries.

Major actors on the US side were the Treasury Department, Defense Department, State Department, Congress, and the president. Core decisionmakers in the Treasury Department were the most influential in policymaking. The US government faced significant domestic constraints, especially Congress's negative stance about increasing US contributions to the IMF. The president and the Treasury Department requested Congress's authorization of $18 billion to the IMF to strengthen the fund's financial basis, but it took almost one year from request to realization.

The Bretton Woods institutions (the IMF and the World Bank) are definitely the key transnational actors in the international financial assistance regime, and the United States has been the dominant player in these institu-

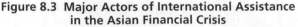

Figure 8.3 Major Actors of International Assistance in the Asian Financial Crisis

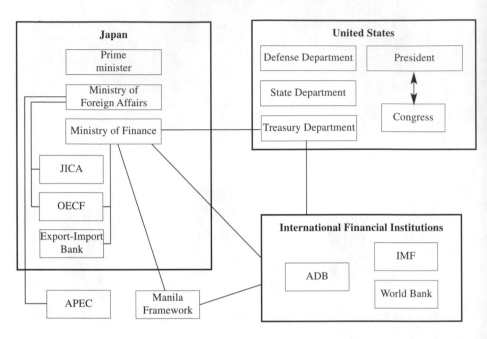

tions. In April 1996, the shares of the US voting power in the IMF, IBRD, and the International Development Association (IDA) were 17.8 percent, 17.4 percent, and 15.1 percent each. All important policy decisions needed more than 11 percent, and this rule gave the United States effective veto power. US policies at the boards of these institutions were basically made by the Treasury Department. Japanese shares of voting power in these organizations in April 1996 were 5.5 percent, 6.2 percent, and 10.8 percent each (second to the United States in all three). The Japanese Ministry of Finance, which is responsible for decisions in these organs, closely coordinated its policies with the US Treasury.

Since the Asian crisis was a financial, balance-of-payment crisis, Japan's bilateral assistance policy centered on bridge loans from the Bank of Japan, Japan Export-Import Bank loans and export credits, and OECF yen loans. It also provided additional ODA beyond the ordinary annual packages. For instance, in addition to its 1997 yen loan of 192.2 billion to Indonesia, Japan announced it would give Indonesia additional aid, including 70 billion yen over two years in yen loans for structural adjustment purposes. It also announced that it would accept approximately 1,000 exchange trainees through JICA, deliver rice and other food assistance at an early date, and provide 3 million yen in medical assistance from the Ministry of Foreign Affairs.

In February 1998, the Japanese government announced an aid policy for Southeast Asia that rested on an emergency loan of approximately 300 billion yen through the Japan Export-Import Bank. Japan's financial contribution to the Asia bailout was estimated at $43 billion in total until the end of 1997 and was certainly not small. On the other hand, the United States used its influence over the IMF to promote significant economic reforms in Indonesia and South Korea. The United States has been determined to use the IMF as the primary agency for managing the Asian economic crisis. In that sense, the IMF and the United States, which has great influence on the IMF, were the leaders in formulating a rescue package for Asia's embattled economies.

Different Perspectives on the Causes of the Crisis

The Asian economic crisis began in Thailand on July 2, 1997, when the Thai government abandoned its policy of pegging the baht to the US dollar. A currency crisis ensued, as the value of the baht plummeted precipitously, followed soon thereafter by a more general regional crisis. The resulting currency crisis spread rapidly to Indonesia, South Korea, and other Asian economies. Speculators overseas were quick to exploit the weaknesses and engaged in massive selling, first of the Thai baht, then of other Asian currencies. Short-term capital also began to rapidly flee from the Asian economies.

Some observers feel that the speculative activities of investors were the major cause of the currency crisis. A long-term perspective suggests, however, that greater attention should be paid to the fragile financial, economic, and political structures that made each country a target for speculative attacks as well as to the fact that their economies were already deeply intertwined with the open global financial market system.

Numerous books have analyzed the causes of Asian financial crisis.[12] The main causes of the Asian economic crisis are summarized in the following discussion.

At the earlier stage of the Asian financial crisis, many focused on the problems of the exchange rate regime, such as overvaluation of currencies under the dollar-peg system, terms of trade deterioration, and the yen-dollar rate deterioration. Later on, many others began to argue that fundamental and structural problems led to the crisis. There were two different views regarding the structural problems.

On the one hand, the IMF and many US commentators argued that financial liberalization and the influx of foreign funds spurred a boom that then turned into a bubble because of inadequate risk management on the part of Asian firms and poor regulation by Asian financial authorities, often because politically powerful actors benefited from the boom. When that bubble popped, the result was an unusually sharp and protracted economic downturn. The IMF pointed out that problems associated with weak financial sectors were the main cause of the crisis, including collapse of the financial boom, loss of confidence in the financial sector, and inadequate financial supervision. Some commentators raised the corrupt links between political authorities and business interests as a major cause of the Asian crisis. All these causal arguments stressed the weakness of the Asian social system and can be called the "crony capitalism" thesis.

On the other hand, many Japanese economists argued that the Asian crisis was not a crisis derived from backwardness of Asian societies but rather a "liquidity crisis" derived from rapidly increased short-term investment capital in a globalized financial market. They argued that large amounts of capital rushed in as Asian economies grew and Asian financial markets liberalized and then rapidly flowed out based on the external account situation. They argued that the real problem was the lack of control over excessive investing capital and rapid capital outflows. This view can be called the "hot money" thesis.

During the early phase of the Asian crisis, these contending arguments caused each side in the debate to blame the other side. Some, especially among Asian and Japanese experts, criticized the international financial community for recklessly lending money and urging liberalization of financial markets without recognizing their emerging fragility. Others, especially some Western experts, blamed the crony capitalists who took advantage of financial liberalization to recklessly borrow and invest money without an adequate understanding of risk management.

Some Japanese economists criticized the IMF prescriptions and conditions for offering financial assistance to recipient countries. But the Japanese government also recognized the necessity to push the recipients to adopt sound economic management and good governance in their assistance programs. Because Japan as a bilateral donor does not have strong negotiating power with Asian recipient countries, it needs the IMF with its strong status as an international institution and its formidable expertise about implementing economic reforms.

In the meantime, although different accounts of the financial crisis gave greater or lesser emphasis to one or the other set of causal factors described above, there was a growing consensus that it was a combination of these factors that brought about the crisis.

Japan's Evolving Initiatives

The Japanese responses and assistance policies to the Asian financial crisis have been evolving since the beginning of the crisis in mid-1997. Do

Japan's active responses indicate that it was becoming more independent of the IMF-centered international framework or becoming more cooperative with this international framework? From 1997 to 1999, there were some important occasions in which Japan and the international community had to engage deeply in the context of the crisis, a process to be analyzed in more detail in this section.

The Search for Asia-Centered Initiatives and the AMF Proposal

After the rapid depreciation of its currency, Thailand turned to the IMF to deal with its economic crisis in August 1997. The government of Thailand, unable to develop an adequate response to the crisis, collapsed and was replaced by a new administration that took a more flexible and positive approach to adopting IMF reform measures.

The total amount of international financial support to Thailand was $16 billion. The Japanese government organized the Tokyo meeting on August 20, 1997, and initiated the formulation of this international assistance program in coordination with the IMF. The offer made on August 11, 1997, included $4 billion apiece from both Japan and the IMF; $1 billion each from Australia, Malaysia, Singapore, Hong Kong, and China; and a half billion dollars each even from South Korea and Indonesia. At that time, the financial crisis had hit only in Thailand and was not expected to spread to other Asian countries. Instead, the Asian regional financial assistance scheme established to address the Thai economic crisis consisted of all major Asian countries in cooperation with the IMF, but without the participation of the United States and European countries. This was regarded as a remarkable new financial support mechanism in Asia.

Japanese initiative was eminent in the case of assistance to Thailand. This was because the Japanese government thought that Japan, as a leading country in Asia, should and could take the initiative to organize an international financial assistance scheme, similar to the role the United States had played at the time of the Mexican financial crisis in 1994,[13] when the IMF and donors led by the United States had provided nearly $40 billion in financial assistance to Mexico. The Japanese government pledged to offer $4 billion to Thailand, which was the largest among the donor countries.

In contrast, the United States refused to participate in this rescue package. The United States seemed to think that Asian economic matters should be dealt with only by Asian countries. Another reason for the lack of US contribution was the opposition from the US Congress. The US government offered a large amount of assistance to the Mexican financial crisis in 1994 without congressional permission, prompting howls of protest from Congress, which then enacted a rule requiring the executive branch to get congressional approval for any foreign assistance program. As a result, the

US government could not respond as quickly to the Thai crisis as it had to earlier crises.

From the outbreak of the Thai crisis in August, competing ideas emerged on how to help countries in financial distress.[14] The alternative to the IMF-led rescue program was the creation of an Asian regional fund. Shortly after the baht crisis, the Thai government called for an Asian fund; Japan responded by proposing the AMF. Presumably, the Thai government was frustrated with the severe conditions the IMF imposed for its assistance (of $4 billion), which turned out to be only a portion of the $17.2 billion rescue package.[15]

In fact, the idea of an Asian regional monetary framework was not totally new; it had been proposed by ASEAN in earlier times. In response to the Thai monetary crisis, Japan and other Asian countries established a support framework for Thailand, and the idea to create an Asia-centered monetary fund emerged more clearly. In September 1997, Japan tried to propose the AMF in the annual meeting of the IMF and the World Bank held in Hong Kong.[16]

Japan and ASEAN proposed this idea based on two reasons. First, the amount of IMF lending to most Asian countries had been limited because of the relatively small share of Asian countries in its fund, so they needed a complementary fund in Asia. Second, it would be better to have a fund in advance to deal with possible financial crises, rather than responding ad hoc to crises after they had occurred.[17]

The United States and the IMF strongly opposed the idea of the AMF. For one thing, they thought it would be better to strengthen the IMF, if the amount of assistance was still small. To create another fund would be a redundant and wasteful investment. In addition, if the new fund (the AMF) offered its own money without regard to IMF assistance, it would undermine negotiations between the IMF and recipients and exacerbate the "moral hazard" problem.[18] In the Hong Kong IMF and World Bank meeting in September 1997, US Deputy Treasury Secretary Lawrence Summers strongly opposed the AMF idea proposed by Japan's vice-minister (for international finance) Eisuke Sakakibara. Not only the United States but also China showed a cautious attitude toward Japan's AMF initiative.[19]

Therefore, the AMF idea could not be realized, but the discussions and efforts for making a regional financial mechanism in Asia remained. In November 1997, a meeting of finance ministers and presidents of central banks in Asia (fourteen countries) was held in Manila, and finance authorities in these countries agreed to establish a mechanism that would monitor the economic and financial situation in Asia and help each other if necessary. This was called the Manila Framework, and this meeting among the heads of finance ministries and central banks in Asia has been held every six months thereafter. The Manila meeting represented the following compromise: emergency relief to the Asian countries would be IMF-led, but the United States would be committed to a second line of support funds for Indonesia and the expansion of the IMF (i.e., a 45 percent increase of IMF capital).

Assistance to Indonesia: Collaboration Among Japan, the United States, and the World Bank and IMF

The next interesting case is the assistance to Indonesia during the 1997–1999 period, which focuses on how the international donor community, especially the IMF and the other two major donors, Japan and the United States, responded to the Indonesian crisis. Detailed analysis of the political process indicates collaborative efforts among these donors.[20] Comparison between the response of Japan and that of the United States (and the IMF and the World Bank) to the Indonesian crisis is very interesting and should be analyzed in detail.

Until the end of the Suharto regime. After the Thai financial crisis in the summer of 1997, the pressure to depreciate the Indonesian rupiah increased, and in October, the Indonesian government requested IMF rescue from its financial difficulty. On October 8, the IMF and the World Bank pledged to support Indonesia. In November, the IMF, the World Bank, and the ADB offered first-line support of $18 billion, and Japan, the United States, and Singapore pledged to offer second-line support of $13 billion to Indonesia. The Japanese offer was $5 billion, the largest among bilateral donors, and the US offer was for $3 billion. In spite of this support program, the Indonesian economic crisis was made worse by the government's failure to sufficiently carry out economic reforms, as expected by the international community.

The fiscal year 1998 budget published on January 7, 1998, increased doubts about the government's ability to institute far-reaching reforms, because its expenditures increased 32 percent over the previous year. The reform measures required by the IMF were delayed owing to fear by Suharto that instituting reforms would undermine the government's control over the nation.

At first, the IMF quickly assembled the second package of support for Indonesia, and serious negotiation began regarding the nature of the reforms. The report that Suharto would introduce a currency board system of monetary management made the IMF harden its stance, and the IMF began threatening to suspend its standby loan to Indonesia. As disappointment spread among foreign investors, the rupiah was sold off on the exchange market, and the Indonesian crisis grew even more serious. The rupiah declined more than 80 percent against the US dollar.

The US government was particularly attentive to the Indonesian case and sent Deputy Treasury Secretary Summers on a mission to Jakarta. Defense Secretary William Cohen also visited Indonesia to meet with President Suharto. The United States believed the Indonesian crisis could not only lead to the collapse of the Suharto regime but also jeopardize the security of the entire Southeast Asia region.[21] President Bill Clinton made a speech saying that Asian economies must be revitalized because they were vital to US economic and security interests. On the other hand, the United States strongly pushed Suharto to implement the reforms proposed by the IMF.

Nevertheless, Suharto remained in power as president. He was reelected in the presidential election on March 10, and he nominated B. J. Habibie as his vice president. At the same time, the donor community began to think that reforms would not be pursued under the Suharto regime.[22]

To prevent the collapse of the Indonesian economy and the Suharto regime, Japanese prime minister Ryutarÿ Hashimoto visited Indonesia and met President Suharto on March 15, 1998, requesting that Suharto carry out the agreement with the IMF.[23] This visit illustrated the Japanese intermediary role between the IMF and the Indonesian government, but it also showed Japanese support for the IMF's conditionality toward Indonesia, despite the claims of some commentators that Japan opposed conditionality.[24] The Japanese Ministry of Finance thought the IMF conditionality was necessary to avoid moral hazard of the recipients, although it did not always have the same stance regarding the IMF prescriptions.[25] Under these pressures, Suharto accepted the IMF requirements on March 21, and the Indonesian situation seemed to ease somewhat at the time.

The domestic political situation, however, grew worse. Antigovernment rioting broke out when state subsidies were withdrawn and far-reaching price hikes were introduced on gasoline and other commodities, as required by the IMF. Anger over the price hikes and the collapse of the economy fed popular dissatisfaction with the lack of political freedom in the country. The movements for independence were also intensified in regions such as Aceh and East Timor.[26] Faced with widespread rioting and international pressures, President Suharto was forced to resign in May 1998, and the Habibie administration began to undertake the reform programs.

From Habibie to Wahid. President Habibie tried to tackle the economic reforms and show a softer stance with respect to political reforms and the East Timor issue, partly to get support from the international community. He also initiated reforms toward decentralization by signing new laws No. 22 and No. 25, which defined the transfer of administrative and budgetary authority from the central government to the provinces.

The IMF and the World Bank offered an additional assistance program for Indonesian economic recovery and structural reforms and reached a loan agreement with the Indonesian government in July 1998. As a result of that agreement, $6 billion in support ($1.3 billion from the IMF, $1 billion from the World Bank, $1 billion from the ADB, and so on) was pledged. In August, the IMF offered additional assistance.

The IMF, the World Bank, and the ADB were basically supportive of Indonesia's new government, but we can find some occasions on which donors suspended their support because of the unstable political situation and the lack of governance. For instance, the IMF suspended its financing in June and July of 1998.[27]

Japan was the country most supportive of Indonesia within the donor community, announcing the New Miyazawa Initiative in October 1998 and offering several kinds of assistance to Indonesia. The Export-Import Bank of Japan offered 210 billion yen in untied loans to Indonesia through the initiative.

Before the general election in June 1999, however, the political situation deteriorated even further. Since April, there had been heated conflicts between the "independence faction" and the "alignment faction" in East Timor. In May, corruption under the Suharto regime was revealed and widespread rioting broke out, with protesters demanding the prosecution of Suharto and his cronies. On May 24, the World Bank announced it would be suspending its financing of $1.1 billion to Indonesia until after the June general election. The IMF made the same decision, and the Japanese government followed these policies.

As a result of the general election held on June 7, the ruling party (Golkar) lost its majority. On June 18, the vice president of the IMF, Stanley Fisher, met with leaders of five opposition parties, confirmed their commitment to furthering reform efforts in Indonesia, and announced the continuation of IMF support to Indonesia. On July 26–27, the Consultative Group in Indonesia (CGI) met in Paris. Donors pledged $5.86 billion in assistance to Indonesia, and Japan offered $1.67 billion, nearly one-third of the total. In August, the Paris Club (a lender countries group) agreed to reschedule $2.6 billion of loans to Indonesia.

This assistance from the international donor community was suspended, however, after the "Bali Bank corruption" was revealed. The IMF and the World Bank temporarily suspended their loans until the investigation over the unclear flows of money was completed and concrete measures to prevent a recurrence of such corruption announced. Once again, the Japanese government took the same stance as the IMF and the World Bank.

Under such pressure and criticism from the international community, the Indonesian government began to investigate corruption under the Suharto regime and also accepted the sending of a PKO from the UN to East Timor. The National Council (the supreme decisionmaking institution in Indonesia) then agreed on October 6 to grant East Timor its independence.[28] This status was officially decided on October 19. In addition, the National Council passed a no-confidence resolution against Habibie and decided to hold an election for a new president.

On October 10, 1999, Adburrahman Wahid became the new president by the election in the National Council, and he nominated Megawati Sukarnoputri as the vice president. Wahid showed a willingness to reveal the corruption under the Suharto regime and to promote political reforms. The international donor community welcomed these political changes and showed a very clear positive stance to support for Indonesian reforms.[29]

Common actions with different approaches. By examining the political process and the relationship between the donor assistance and political situations in Indonesia, we can draw the following conclusions.

The offering of loans by the IMF and the World Bank was highly linked, in reality, with political issues such as the democratization process and East Timor. The periods during which the IMF and the World Bank suspended their loans were (1) the period of turmoil at the last stage of the Suharto administration (from February to April 1998), (2) the period just before the general election under the Habibie administration (from May to June 1999), and (3) the period of turmoil in East Timor and just before the presidential election at the last stage of the Habibie administration (from August to October 1999). Figure 8.4 shows the change of exchange rate of the Indonesian rupiah and the periods of suspension of international financial support.

It can be said that those suspensions of loans were in response to circumstances that made sound economic management impossible, such as political turmoil, corruption, and rent-seeking activities. Those aid suspensions, based on chaotic economic management and the lack of governance, actually questioned the legitimacy of the regime facing those political problems, however.

Economic reforms, worsening economic circumstances, and political instability are in fact interrelated. For instance, in the period from February to March 1998, Suharto resisted the reforms requested by the IMF because he wanted to protect his political power base and the interests of his family's companies. The IMF suspension of loans during that period led to a loss of confidence in the Indonesian economy and worsened the economic situation. Under those circumstances, Suharto lost political support from the public, and in the end he was compelled to resign.

In the period from August to October 1999, the political turmoil in East Timor and criticism against the corruption of the Suharto family led to political instability and a rapid drop in the Indonesian currency. The suspen-

Figure 8.4 Exchange-Rate Change of the Indonesian Rupiah

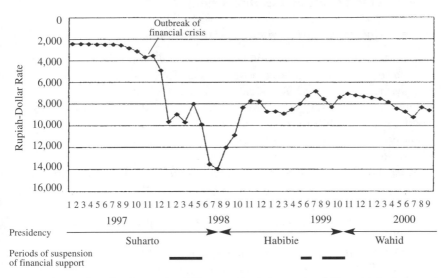

Source: Based on International Monetary Fund, *International Financial Statistics,* various years.

Note: Rupiah-dollar rate, spot rate, monthly data.

sion of loans by the IMF and the World Bank at that time was the final blow to the Habibie administration, and finally Habibie gave up his presidency.

Some have criticized such de facto interference in Indonesian politics by the IMF and the World Bank. On the other hand, if the IMF and the World Bank had continued their assistance in spite of the delay of reforms and domestic political turmoil in Indonesia, the assistance would have been regarded as political support for the regime, which would constitute another kind of de facto interference in domestic politics. Therefore, it can be said that the IMF and the World Bank had no choice but to suspend their assistance.

The Japanese government's stance was almost parallel with the policy of the IMF and the World Bank in a practical sense and was regarded as a passive reaction to political change and bad governance in Indonesia. In contrast to Japan's stance, the US government seemed to think much more of democratic changes and political reforms in its policy toward Indonesia.[30] We can distinguish between the "active support" and the "passive response" to political changes in Indonesia. It can be said that the US policy was active support and the Japanese stance was a passive reaction, although the basic character of assistance policies of both countries for Indonesia's democratic transition was almost the same.

New Japanese Initiatives:
Asia-Centered or Part of a Global Scheme?

The New Miyazawa Initiative and Aid to Vietnam

Japan continued to diligently provide financial and economic assistance to Asian nations after the outbreak of the Asian financial crisis of summer 1997. By the summer of 1998 that aid amounted to $43 billion.

Japan's contribution to the IMF package was $19 billion, which was second to the $35 billion provided by the IMF and almost double the amount provided by the United States. Japan continued its assistance vigorously during 1998. An Emergency Package for Economic Stabilization of Southeast Asia was approved in a cabinet resolution in February 1998. In March, approximately $3 billion was disbursed to the ADB as an Asian Currency Crisis Assistance Fund. In April, an aid package of 700 billion yen for aid to Asia was approved as part of the Comprehensive Economic Action Plan.

In October, the Japanese government announced loan assistance totaling $30 billion under the New Miyazawa Initiative. In November, further assistance to Asian countries under a new Emergency Economic Package was announced, and in December, special yen loans up to 600 billion yen over three years for infrastructure development to help structural economic reforms in Asian nations were announced.

The New Miyazawa Initiative, which was at the center of Japan's assistance policy to Asia, included $15 billion in medium-term yen loans and loans from the Export-Import Bank of Japan and $15 billion to support short-term credit demand such as facilitating trade financing. The beneficiaries of this aid were South Korea, Indonesia, Thailand, the Philippines, and Malaysia, which are the nations where the impact of the economic crisis was particularly great. In May 1999, Vietnam was added to the list. This is the most interesting case, because the Japanese government offered its assistance before the agreement had been reached on loan conditionality between the IMF and World Bank and the Vietnamese government. Why did Japan offer the yen loan before the agreement with the IMF and the World Bank? And what are the implications of this Japanese policy for the international financial assistance regime of the IMF and the World Bank?

A $20 billion economic reform assistance loan was provided by Japan to Vietnam in May 1999, not as a standard yen loan but as part of the New Miyazawa Initiative. There were new characteristics to this loan. First, even though the IMF and the World Bank were still negotiating with Vietnam on loan conditions, Japan went ahead and provided a loan on its own initiative. Second, the three "requirements" attached to the loan covered (1) nurturing the private sector, (2) auditing large state-owned enterprises, and (3) promoting free trade. This made the loan the first "Japanese-style" structural adjustment loan to Vietnam. According to explanations of the Japan Bank for International Cooperation (JBIC), these "requirements" were different from the "conditionality" of the IMF because the Japanese loan would not be suspended even if these "requirements" were not met. They were designed to encourage Vietnamese efforts for improvements regarding these three issues.[31]

According to Japanese newspapers, these requirements implied a Japanese stance independent from the policy of the IMF and the World Bank, but the reality was different. The Japanese government tried to cofinance with the IMF and the World Bank, but the negotiations between them and Vietnam were protracted, and Japan decided to offer its loan without waiting for a final agreement.[32] The three requirements of the Japanese loan were the three items that were already agreed to in the IMF and the World Bank proposals. The World Bank itself said that the Japanese offer of its yen loan did not have any negative impact on the negotiation between the IMF and the World Bank and the Vietnamese government.[33]

Nevertheless, it was a new policy for Japan to offer a loan package before the IMF agreement with the recipient. In fact, the Japanese government had been maintaining close cooperation with the Vietnamese government in connection with the latter's economic reforms. Since 1995, it had brought together experts from academic and other fields to carry out surveys on aid for moving to a market economy in Vietnam, based on joint Japanese and Vietnamese research sponsored by JICA. The final report of the second stage was issued in the spring of 1998.[34] Amid criticism that the IMF prescriptions for structural reforms did not fit the actual circumstances of countries in Asia, Japan attempted to make its own policy advice by offering yen loans and attaching Japan's own lending conditions.

The Chiang Mai Initiative:
Independent Way or Compromise with the IMF?

In November 1999, the leaders of APT agreed at the meeting in Manila to strengthen the mechanism for assistance and self-help in the areas of finance and currency in East Asia. After that, in May 2000, the finance ministers' meeting among APT was held in Chiang Mai, Thailand. In this meeting, they agreed to extend bilateral swap agreements (for instance, between Japan and Malaysia, Japan and South Korea) among Asian countries and to make a regional financial assistance scheme in Asia.[35] Called the Chiang Mai Initiative, this scheme was not set up with a common fund or a common secretariat, but it inaugurated a substantive monetary cooperation framework in Asia. It should be noted that China changed from its previous cautious stance to a more positive one regarding the regional monetary framework initiated by Japan and APT.

APT agreed in the Chiang Mai Initiative to conclude currency swap agreements, but it should be noted that the group was seeking to bring policy implementation in individual countries under international regulation by imposing conditionality similar to that of the IMF and the World Bank. If a member of the group wants to borrow more than 10 percent of the agreed amount, the country must accept the IMF bailout program with its conditionality. Therefore, regionalism can be regarded as part of the system for promoting the enforcement of international rules at the regional level.

By March 2005, this swap agreement among APT countries had been expanded substantially in terms of amount of money and the number of bilateral agreements among those countries. Figure 8.5 shows the outline of the recent swap agreement among APT countries.

Ideas of Closer Asian Monetary Cooperation: What Form Will It Take?

Movement toward closer regional monetary cooperation has been progressing since the Chiang Mai Initiative in May 2000. In January 2001, finance ministers at the Asia-Europe Meeting (ASEM) held in Kobe, Japan, agreed to promote research concerning Asian currency stabilization and the idea of a regional monetary framework. Some economists have pointed out that the yen-dollar rate has paralleled the economic growth rate of Asian economies.[36] Therefore, they have argued that Asian economies need stabilization of the yen-dollar rate or a new mechanism such as an Asian curren-

Figure 8.5 SWAP Agreement Among the APT After the Chiang Mai Initiative (as of March 2005)

Source: East Asia Community Council, *Seisaku Hōkokusho: Higashi Azia Kyōdōtai Kōsō Genjō Haikei to Nippon no Kokka Senryaku* [Policy Report: Situations and Background of East Asia Community Idea and Japan's National Strategy] (August 2005), 27.

cy basket system in which the weight of the Japanese yen increases to about 50 percent from about 10 percent in the past. This is the main reason why the Japanese government and some economists still promote internationalization of the Japanese yen and the idea of an Asian currency unit (ACU) in the Asia Pacific region.[37]

The idea of promoting Asian monetary cooperation still persists in various forums to coordinate monetary policies among Asian countries, such as the Manila Framework (a meeting of fourteen countries' finance ministers and central banks), the finance ministers' meeting of APT, and also a meeting of economic ministers of APEC. Some of these ideas have progressed in recent years. For instance, the Thai government proposed the Asian Bond Fund in April 2004, which was realized as a fund of US$1 billion provided by eleven central banks in East Asia and the Pacific region. In May 2006, the finance ministers of APT agreed to examine the possibility of establishing a regional currency unit in Asia, which would be similar to the Asian currency unit that the ADB had already proposed.

Japan has been proactive in recognizing these ideas as effective mechanisms for financial cooperation in Asia. The relationship between these newly emerging Asian monetary cooperation frameworks and the international financial architecture led by the IMF, plus the Japanese stance toward them, are important issues to be examined in the future.

Conclusion

Japan has extensive economic interests in Asia through trade and investment and has provided large amounts of financial assistance to Asian countries. The Ministry of Finance was the key decisionmaker in shaping Japan's assistance program and initiated both the New Miyazawa Initiative and the idea of an Asian-centered monetary cooperation framework. In contrast, the United States did not get involved in the Thai assistance program, but it was energetic in efforts to contain the economic crises in Indonesia and South Korea. Despite claims to the contrary by some observers, including participants in Japanese decisionmaking at the time, in reality there was close coordination among Japan, the United States, and the IMF and the World Bank in all three cases.

Japan often criticized some parts of the IMF and the World Bank's structural adjustment prescriptions to Asian countries, and Japan tried to increase its own contribution through its own bilateral assistance scheme. For instance, (1) it offered a large amount of bilateral assistance to Thailand, Indonesia, Malaysia, the Philippines, and Vietnam as part of the New Miyazawa Initiative; (2) it offered a "policy support loan" to Vietnam with Japan's own policy requirements; and (3) it sponsored efforts to establish Asia-centered financial cooperation frameworks, such as the AMF, the Manila Framework, and the Chiang Mai Initiative.

Japanese policy and its initiatives were not contradictory to the IMF- and World Bank–centered international financial assistance regime, however. All these Japanese initiatives can be regarded as supplemental to the role of the IMF and the World Bank. Japanese bilateral loans to Asian countries, including aid to Vietnam, were offered basically in parallel with the agreement between the recipient government and the IMF and the World Bank. Monetary cooperation among Asian countries has been deepening and is still in the process of strengthening, but so far that is still complementary to the IMF- and World Bank–centered scheme.

Some have argued that by offering a large amount of yen loans to Asia, Japan was seeking to carve out its sphere of influence based on its own separate interests and on its own conception of how development works that differs from the neoclassical development model.[38] By looking at the Japanese responses to the Asian financial crisis in detail, we can see that this thesis is not true. The reality is that Japan has been cooperating closely with the IMF and the World Bank and with the United States in making financial assistance packages to countries affected by the Asian crisis that are based on market-economic principles and support of democratization.

It is true that Japan remains the largest bilateral aid donor in Asia, reflecting its continued interest in using ODA as an instrument for pursuing its own diplomatic and economic goals in the region.[39] Moreover, even though Japan had adopted a relatively detached stance toward the multilateral aid coordination in the past, in recent years it has become increasingly involved in donor coordination meetings and the economic reform process in developing countries initiated by the IMF and the World Bank. Aid, loan, and policy reforms loom large in the international community's common agenda, and the many donor countries must cooperate in a multilateral framework. Japan has been expected to take a leading role in international donor coordination and in developing a better multilateral framework in Asia, and Japan has been trying to do so in recent years.

Japan's ability to do so, however, remains constrained by the limited "capacity" of its aid policymaking establishment, especially in terms of its ability to articulate a clear and consistent rationale for Japanese policy and to offer independent analyses of the region's economic needs and advice regarding necessary reforms for Asian economies. In addition, Japan is highly sensitive and respectful about the traditional "norm" of noninterference in the domestic politics of recipient countries.

Nonetheless, as the foregoing analysis has demonstrated, Japan is increasingly moving in the direction of becoming a fully integrated member of the global financial assistance regime. Japanese responses to the Asian financial crisis show that Japan has been an adaptive state, one that is changing in a proactive way in response to its international environment. This adaptation has been in a liberal direction by embracing greater international cooperation and a preference for the creation of multilateral institutions as instruments for pursuing cooperatively its national goals. But at the same time, there is a certain Japanese ambivalence about how existing multilateral institutions work and what kind of multilateral institutions work best in the Asian context.

Notes

1. For instance, Pempel, *The Politics of the Asian Economic Crisis;* Haggard, *The Political Economy of the Asian Financial Crisis.*
2. Most of those taking this view came from the mass media in both Japan and the United States. Among experts, Saori Katada argued modestly that Japan's policies in the Asian financial crisis represent Japan's counterweight strategy, which involves a mixture of bargaining plus institution- and coalition-building efforts designed to increase regional and international support for Japan's position. Katada, "Japan's Counterweight Strategy"; see also Krauss and Pempel, *Beyond Bilateralism,* chap. 8.
3. Most of them came from mass media in both Japan and the United States. Among experts, some are skeptical regarding the prospects for East Asian regionalism; see Lincoln, *East Asian Economic Regionalism;* and Stubbs, "ASEAN Plus Three: Emerging East Asian Regionalism?"
4. Regarding the IMF conditionality, see Guitian, *Conditionality;* and Polak, *The Changing Nature of IMF Conditionality.*
5. This is the view, for instance, of Kenichi Ōno (National Graduate Institute for Policy Studies) and Itō Takatoshi (Tokyo University). See *Nihon Keizai Shimbun,* January 12, 1998, February 3, 1998. Some typical examples of deeper Japanese skepticism regarding neoliberal economics are Murakami, *Han-koten no Seiji-keizaigaku;* and Motoyama, *Urareru Ajia.*
6. This view is held, for instance, by Ishikawa, *Kaihatsu Enjo Kenkyū.*
7. An example of this view is found, for instance, in Bhagwati, "The Capital Myth," 7–12.
8. See Bergsten, *Reviving the Asian Monetary Fund,* and Economic Planning Agency, *Tsūka Kinyū Kiki no Kokufuku to 21 Seiki no Keizai Anteika ni Mukete.*
9. In regard to the US interests in the Asian economic crisis, see Harrison and Prestowitz, *Asia After the Miracle.*
10. *Nihon Keizai Shimbun,* January 30, 1998.
11. Vice Minister of Finance Sakakibara Eisuke sometimes portrayed the Japanese perspective and that of the United States regarding the IMF policies toward the Asian financial crisis as a clash between the two, but his successor Kuroda Haruhiko did not emphasize the difference between the two countries.
12. For instance, Goldstein, *The Asian Financial Crisis;* Jackson, *Asian Contagion;* Noble and Ravenhill, *The Asian Financial Crisis and the Architecture of Global Finance;* Rosenberger, "Southeast Asia's Currency Crisis"; Kawai, "Tsūka Kiki Hakyū no Mekanizumu to Kyōkun," 24–31; and Kunimune, *Ajia Tsūka Kiki.*
13. Interview with an official of the Japanese executive director's office of the World Bank, March 27, 1998, Washington, DC.

14. The Manila conference of financial officials from fourteen countries and regions was held in November 1997, immediately after the financial crisis had spread to Indonesia but just before it spread to South Korea.

15. In exchange for the IMF assistance, the Thai government would be required to enact disinflation policies, balance the budget by cutting expenditures and increasing the value added tax, and reform the financial system. See Timothy Lane and Marianne Schulze-Ghattas, "Program Financing and Market Reactions," in Lane et al., *IMF-Supported Programs in Indonesia, Korea, and Thailand,* 20–26. Part of the problem was caused by the relatively small IMF quotas of the Asian countries, compared to the size of their economies, which constrained the size of support they could obtain from the IMF.

16. See Sakakibara, *Kokusai Kinyū no Genba.*

17. Itō, "Ajia Tsūka Kiki to America no Taiō."

18. Ibid.

19. Ōhashi, "Ikigai Taikoku to ASEAN."

20. To get the chronology of policies of the IMF, the World Bank, and Japan in response to the Indonesian economic crisis, I used the following books and reports: Kenward, *From the Trenches;* Japan International Cooperation Agency, *Report of the Fourth Country Assistance Study on Indonesia;* Satō, *Indonesia Shiryōshu;* and IMF, *IMF-Supported Programs in Indonesia, Korea, and Thailand.*

21. Regarding the US policy toward the Indonesian crisis, see John Bresnan, "The United States, the IMF, and the Indonesian Financial Crisis," in Schwarz and Paris, *The Politics of Post-Suharto Indonesia.*

22. Shiraishi, *Hōkai Indonesia wa Dokoeiku,* 75.

23. *Yomiuri Shimbun,* March 16, 1998.

24. Vice Minister of Finance Sakakibara was one of the commentators opposing conditionality.

25. Speech given by Sakakibara Eisuke (Ministry of Finance) at a seminar at the Tokyo Institute of Technology, Tokyo, July 11, 1998; interviews with some officials of the Ministry of Foreign Affairs, a Japanese delegate to the World Bank, and a US Treasury official, March 24 and March 27, 1998, Washington, DC.

26. The political situation in this period is well described in Shiraishi, *Hōkai Indonesia wa Dokoeiku,* 80–102.

27. Mcquillan and Montgomery, *The International Monetary Fund,* 171.

28. Regarding corruption under the Suharto regime, see Murai, *Suharto Family no Chikuzai.*

29. President Clinton met Wahid in Washington, DC, on November 13 and pledged to continue US assistance to Indonesia. Three days later, on November 16, Japanese prime minister Obuchi Keizō met Wahid in Tokyo and announced Japan's willingness to provide further to Indonesia. Obuchi visited Jakarta on November 27 and pledged further Japanese assistance. The IMF agreed on the additional memorandum (for implementation of loan) with the Indonesian government on November 23. On December 9, the ADB announced an additional $1–1.5 billion in assistance for medium-sized enterprises to Indonesia, and on January 20, 2000, US secretary of the treasury Summers visited Jakarta and announced continued assistance to Indonesia, mainly through international institutions (the IMF and the World Bank). On January 25, Japan exchanged a note of a 7.19 million–yen loan to Indonesia. In February, a CGI meeting was held in Jakarta, and donors pledged $4.7 billion of assistance for fiscal year 2000, of which Japan offered $1.56 billion. In April, the Paris Club approved the rescheduling of official debt of $5.8 billion. The IMF decided to offer a $5 billion loan in three years in February, signed the memorandum on

May 17, and approved a $372 million loan for economic reform assistance.

30. For instance, see Zoellick and Zelikow, *America and the East Asian Crisis,* 58–59.

31. Interview with an official of the JBIC Hanoi office, February 2, 2000, Hanoi, Vietnam.

32. Interview with an official of the Ministry of Finance, February 21, 2001, Tokyo.

33. Interview with an official of the World Bank Hanoi office, February 2, 2000, Hanoi, Vietnam.

34. Ishikawa and Hara, *Vietnam no Shijō Keizaika.*

35. Yamakage, "Nippon no Eai ASEAN Seisaku no Henyō."

36. Takahashi, Kan and Sano, *Ajia Kinyā Kiki,* 5–8.

37. For instance, see comments by Sakakibara Eisuke (Ministry of Finance) and Kakizawa Kōji (Liberal Democratic Party), *Nihon Keizai Shimbun,* February 7, 1998; and Kondō, *Kokusai Tsūka to APEC.*

38. For instance, see Krauss and Pempel, *Beyond Bilateralism.*

39. For the argument that Japan had been promoting its national interests through development aid, see Arase, *Buying Power.*

| Part 3 |
Regional Diplomacy

| 9 |

The Politics of Memory in Japanese Foreign Relations

Thomas U. Berger

The philosopher George Santayana is best remembered for having said that "those who cannot remember the past are condemned to repeat it." Sometimes it seems as if the Asian region as a whole is determined to prove the great man wrong, to demonstrate that it is precisely those who remember the past who are condemned to repeat it, especially when they remember the past differently. Sixty years after the end of World War II, Asia continues to be plagued by controversy over history and the ways in which the past is represented. Even though much of the region, as well as the rest of the world, views Japan's pre-1945 history as one of unbridled imperialist aggression and colonial oppression,[1] the general tendency in Japan itself has been to focus more on the suffering of the Japanese people during World War II than on the suffering that Japan inflicted on others.

Of course, Japan is hardly unique in this respect. Most countries, including China, Korea, and the United States, have selective views of their pasts.[2] In the context of East Asia, however, the issue of how the past is defined has become an international issue. Since the early 1980s the gap in historical views has sparked a series of diplomatic crises between Japan and its Asian neighbors, especially South Korea and China. Since August 2001, when Prime Minister Koizumi Junichirō made his first controversial visit to the Yasukuni Shrine—where the spirits of two and a half million soldiers and sailors who have died in Japan's wars since the Meiji Restoration are enshrined—tensions over history have escalated dramatically. By 2006, diplomatic relations among Beijing, Seoul, and Tokyo had all been seriously damaged, paralyzing efforts at forging regional institutions and turning what ought to be manageable territorial disputes into the foci of national passions and, potentially at least, military conflict.[3] No other issue has as great a potential to undermine the essentially liberal thrust of contemporary Japanese foreign policy. Although Japanese leaders, beginning with Koizumi, continue to avow their commitment to avoiding the mistakes of the past and to building a stronger East Asian community, their entreaties are met with suspicion because of the widespread perception that Japan remains unpenitent for its past transgressions.

This intense controversy over the past is in many ways a by-product of Japan's newfound activism in international affairs. Since 1945, whenever Japan has sought to enhance its military role, Japanese conservatives consistently have sought to rouse a sense of popular patriotism and "defense consciousness" (*aikokushin* and *bōei ishiki*). In part, this is because they believe that patriotism is the necessary complement to any expansion of the armed forces capabilities and missions; in part, it is because they hope to harness external pressures to effect changes in the domestic political environment.[4] In 2006 this same trend has been in evidence once again. Faced with the challenge of coping with a complex, post–Cold War security environment in Asia while trying to meet the heightened expectations of its US ally in the context of the war on terror, the Koizumi government has overseen one of the most dramatic expansions of Japan's military role since the 1980s, if not the entirety of the post-1945 era. As Japanese forces have been sent abroad into potentially dangerous situations for the first time since the war in the Pacific—all in the name of Japan's making "a human contribution to global security" (*hitoteki kōken*)—naturally many conservative Japanese have felt that this Japanese prime minister has a duty to pay his respects to those Japanese who gave their lives in the service of the Japanese nation in the past; it is, they argue, the functional equivalent of visiting Arlington National Cemetery.[5]

This natural Japanese tendency to stress nationalist themes at a time when the military is assuming new roles has been amplified by changes in the Japanese political system that give politicians new incentives to cater to populist sentiments on issues such as the North Korean abduction of Japanese citizens or the defense of Japanese territorial claims in the East China Sea. At the same time, the forces of popular nationalism are on the rise in China and South Korea as well, albeit for very different reasons than they are in Japan, creating the potential for a destructive, mutually reinforcing conflagration of nationalist sentiments that potentially could destabilize the Asian region.

The tension between Japan's efforts to make a contribution to international security, necessitated by its continued desire to preserve its security relationship with the United States and its efforts to build better ties with its neighbors, is the central dilemma facing Japanese foreign policy today. How well it proves capable of managing this tension has important, long-term consequences for the future of Japanese foreign policy, and for the development of the Asian region as a whole.

It is, of course, impossible to make sure predictions in the social sciences. Moreover, the "history problem," as it is widely referred to in the US State Department and media circles, is by its very nature an international issue; we cannot safely predict the outcome of the issue on the basis of developments inside of Japan alone. Other factors that lie beyond the scope of this chapter, of which the most important is the politics of history inside of China and Korea, will have important consequences for the final outcome. Nonetheless, this chapter will argue—based on an analysis of the politics of history and nation inside of Japan—that the history problem, if left unattended, could have a corrosive impact on regional affairs. But there are also grounds to believe that the situation can be rectified. Far more than is commonly appreciated outside of Japan, over the past fifteen years Japanese political leaders have made sincere efforts to come to grips with the darker aspects of Japan's recent past in order to pursue reconciliation with Japan's neighbors. These efforts have had some success, most notably in the context of Japanese-Korean relations. Despite the current mood of "apology fatigue" in Tokyo, mainstream elite opinion—especially in the business community but also in the bureaucracy and among politicians—would welcome a revival of that process. If the leaders of other Asian countries were willing to reengage in dialogue with Japan on this topic and not respond neurotically to every provocation, there is reason to believe that the history problem can be at least contained and that Asia may yet be able to remember history in ways that will not condemn it to repeat the mistakes of the past.

After a few preliminary observations regarding the history problem and the origins of the official Japanese historical narrative, this chapter explores how the politics of history were transformed after 1991. It concludes by offering some reflections on the possible directions the history problem may take in the future.

The Social and Political
Construction of Collective Memory

At its root, the history problem is the product of differences in the way collective memory—and, what is just as important, the way in which the past is represented in the official historical narrative—is constructed in Japan as opposed to how that is done in neighboring countries. In order to analyze the question of history and to offer possible solutions to it, it is necessary to consider why in general such divergences occur and what their potential political consequences may be. Fortunately, in this regard there has been an outpouring of scholarly work in recent years dealing with the concept of collective memory. Anthropologists, historians, psychologists, and sociologists have used the concept to explore a wide variety of phenomena, including the formation of national as well as subnational identity and the dynamics of public controversy over public monuments and museums as well as the establishment of narratives regarding the past.[6] Until quite recently, however, there has been relatively little study of the implications of collective memory for the study of politics and international relations.[7] The basic assumption is that the passions aroused by disputes over history are merely derivative of underlying economic and political forces. As a result, international relations analysts and practitioners have tended to neglect the history problem in Japanese foreign relations. To remedy this failing, this section will make some basic observations regarding collective memory.

To begin with, it is necessary to define the concept. Although any number of definitions are available, for the purposes of the present discussion *collective memory* can be defined broadly and simply as the ideas that a given society collectively holds about the past. The simplicity of this definition is deceptive, however, and it is worthwhile dwelling on three important aspects of collective memory: first, the relationship among collective memory, individual memory, and history; second, the often-contested nature of collective memory; and third, the relationship between memory and interests, especially the national interest. As the reader shall see, each of these points is quite relevant for the subsequent analysis of the emergence of Japan's memory of the past and the development of the history problem in East Asia.

The first point that needs to be emphasized is that collective memory is not the same as individual or societal memory. Nor should collective memory be equated with the study of the past as practiced by professional historians. Both individual memory and the study of history have some bearing upon collective memory, but they are very different things. Memory as it exists at the level of the individual is based on past experiences. Individual memory is often inaccurate and is distorted in numerous ways; nonetheless, it is based on direct, firsthand knowledge of events. Collective memory, in contrast, consists mainly of representations of the past, in the form of books, films, textbooks, monuments, museums, commemorative ceremonies, and so forth. Even though collective memory may originally have been grounded in the recollections of individuals and groups of people, it can exist independent of them. As a result, the collective memory of events can survive long after individual memory has faded and died. In addition, the necessarily artificial character of memory means that arguably it is even more liable to distortion and manipulation.

History, at least in the conventional sense of the term, is the record of what actually happened in the past, and professional historians ostensibly are committed to the positivist research project of trying to reconstruct the past as accurately as possible. The norms of the historical profession force historians to follow certain rules regarding documentary evidence, and certain accounts of the past are judged as more or less plausible based on reasoned decisions regarding their grounding in the existing historical record. This impulse is shared at least in part outside of the historical profession, but to a much more limited extent. The larger public's ability to engage in historical reconstructions of the past is necessarily far more limited than that of historians, and its commitment to accuracy and consistency is far weaker. History, it is often felt by the ordinary person and by elites outside of the academy, should serve other more immediate needs—be it to mourn the dead, promote social justice, or strengthen the sense of national solidarity.

Collective memory, in this sense, is as much about the present and the future as it is about the past. Societies do not search for the past per se; rather they are trying to define a "usable past." It should be added, of course, that historians are far from immune to the powerful pressures emanating from society to reshape their work to conform to these expectations. Many historians succumb to these pressures and produce the type of history that the public or their employers expect of them. More often, however, historians are not even aware of the extent to which existing scholarship and even the categories of analysis that they work with have already been decisively shaped by societal pressures. The main point, however, is that the historical enterprise and the construction of collective memories are fundamentally divergent enterprises and should not be equated with one another.[8]

One important component of collective memory is the way that political authorities forge the official historical narrative. The official historical narrative is deeply influenced by the collective memories of the society and in turn has a profound influence on the development of society's collective memory. Collective memory and the official historical narrative are not identical, however, and often exist in dynamic tension with one another. There are many ways in which history is evoked by the state—in the ways that political leaders talk about the past, how history is portrayed in school textbooks or in public museums and historical monuments, through the kinds of limitations that are placed on public speech, or the kinds of efforts the state makes in pursuit of rectifying historical injustices (through apologies, offers of compensation, and prosecution for past crimes). The collective memory of the society may at any given point set the parameters for the kind of historical narrative that a society can impose. This is especially so in more democratic or pluralistic political regimes. Even in democracies, however, the official narrative can have a tremendous impact on how events are remembered, and often the official narrative guides and shapes the broader societal memory over time.

Second, it is important to recognize that collective memory is rarely, if ever, monolithic. A central element of the totalitarian project is to seize control of the collective memory and tailor it to suit the interests of the regime, creating a single master historical narrative that is reflected in all official representations of the past. In more pluralistic societies, however, there is room for divergent portrayals of the past, and multiple historical narratives typically compete with one another in the public sphere. Different narratives emerge out of the very different experiences of different groups in society and are influenced by the very different needs and interests that they may be intended to serve. In this sense collective memory is contested terrain, and battles over the past and how to interpret it are a vital element in the political life of any country. Groups who were once underrepresented in the political system—for instance, women and minorities—may promote very different historical narratives once they become politically organized. Hence the fierce and ongoing debates within the United States over such issues as how to portray the Founding Fathers, who may have created the liberal democratic institutions and fought for independence from Britain, but who in many cases also were slave owners. Similarly contentious is the question of how to commemorate the soldiers of the Confederacy.[9]

Collective memory thus is a reflection of the social and political divisions of society. Although the contested nature of collective memory might seem to make it more fluid, in fact the lines of cleavage and the contending historical narratives that it creates may be just as durable as, or even more durable than, the master narratives produced by totalitarian states. France's perennial debate over how to view the French Revolution may serve as an example. More than 200 years after the revolution has ended, a fierce debate continues to rage over its meaning and what it stood for: the triumph of reason over superstition and the liberation of the individual from the shackles of the old aristocratic order, or the crushing of tradition and community in the name of a mad egalitarian ideology.[10]

Finally, although collective memory is certainly malleable and frequently manipulated by a wide variety of different interests, that malleability is not infinite and manipulation can be both difficult and costly. There are at least two reasons why this is so. First, collective memory is the foundation on which group identity rests. It is difficult to imagine a group identity that does not have some account of where that group came from and what, in historical terms, ties its members together. Although individuals have interests that are independent of those of the group as a whole, to a considerable extent the individual's membership in a group is constitutive of his or her interests. Examples of this type of thinking are readily observable in the real world. Why, for instance, should a Pakistani or Indonesian feel a sense of solidarity with the Palestinian struggle against Egypt, were it not for the belief that their common identity as Muslims somehow ties them together? Representations of history that challenge or weaken an identity are therefore seen as profoundly threatening and tend to be strongly rejected.

Second, particular policies or practices are often legitimated in terms of a particular reading of the past. For instance, during the Cold War those advocating a strong, muscular posture vis-à-vis the Soviet Union naturally favored a historical narrative that blamed the Soviet Union and its ideologically motivated desire to spread Communist ideology around the world for the origins of the East-West conflict. In contrast, opponents of the tough anti-Communist policies of the United States instead stressed US actions, such as the cutting of aid to the Soviet Union, as the cause of tensions. For either side to grant that the other side was at least partly correct would have undercut their preferred foreign policy position. As a result, how to depict the origins of the Cold War became a highly politicized and hotly contested issue throughout the Cold War period.

The foregoing observations have a number of concrete implications for the study of the history problem in Asia. First, it needs to be recognized that the problem is not simply a matter of inaccurate or differing recollections of the past or the product of misguided historical inquiry. Rather, it is the product of the very different ways in which societies choose to remember those events after they transpired. The starting point of any investigation of the origins of the history problem must begin with the exploration of how the past events came to be depicted in the collective memory of the society. Ideally, this would involve an investigation of collective memory at the level of both the official historical narrative and the broader popular and elite culture, although in this chapter the emphasis will be on the official narrative. Second, the contested and divided nature of collective memory even within a given society means that the analyst must be very careful not to take a single expression of views on history as representative of what a given society as a whole thinks. Rather, the analyst should try to gauge how broadly a particular view of history is shared in a given society or political system and remain attentive to how those views may shift or not shift over time. Third, the analyst needs to be sensitive to how interests and policy agendas may be linked to a particular historical narrative, especially through the vehicle of the official historical memory. Changes in interest can lead to openings for the reshaping of historical memory. At the same time, such changes are likely to be contentious and difficult. By focusing on controversies over history, however, the analyst probably has the best chance to see how collective memory is being reformed.

The Politics of Historical Representation in Japan, 1945–1960

Contemporary Japan's memories of modern Japanese history have been shaped decisively by the fierce ideological struggles that wracked the nation in the aftermath of its catastrophic defeat in 1945. In sharp contrast to postwar West Germany, where the dominant historical narrative that eventually emerged stressed the horrors of the Holocaust and downplayed the suffering undergone by the German civilians during the war, in Japan the reverse was true. Although there was widespread awareness of the general nature, if not the precise scale and brutality, of the atrocities committed by Japanese forces in Asia, the dominant historical narrative that emerged during the postwar period cast the Japanese people as the hapless victims of the war and downplayed any serious discussion of whether Japan should express a sense of guilt or bore any responsibility for the horrors that had been visited upon Asia.[11] Three factors were critical in producing this outcome. The first was the role played by Japan's conservative elites, who had every reason to avoid a serious pursuit of the issue of who bore responsibility for the war. Second, there were the political calculations of Japan's leftist opposition, who had their own reasons for portraying the Japanese people as the innocent victims of war. Third, Japan's geostrategic environment in the 1940s and 1950s permitted, even encouraged, Japan to avoid dealing with the issue of its responsibility for the war and colonialism.

One significant issue that cannot be avoided in this context is the question of why Japan was far less willing to acknowledge its misdeeds than was true of West Germany. In part, this question is flawed on several levels. First, the question is based on an assumed equivalence between German and Japanese atrocities during World War II. In fact, both the conditions under which they occurred and the scale of the atrocities are quite different. There was no Japanese equivalent of Auschwitz, nor did Japan seek to systematically annihilate an entire category of people defined in terms of race as the Germans did. This, however, should in no way be construed as denying the scale of destruction inflicted in the Asian theater or the brutality with which Japanese imperial forces often acted. Second, the comparison is based on an assumption of an immediate German readiness to acknowledge its misdeeds, when in fact it took decades for such an acknowledgment to emerge. Arguably it was not until 1985 that West Germany was willing to adopt a fully penitent stance on history.[12] Bearing these fundamental differences in mind, it is worthwhile paying close attention to the domestic and international political contexts in which Japanese and German collective memories developed in order to better understand the differences between them.[13]

Far more so than was the case in Germany, many members of Japan's postwar conservative leadership were directly implicated in the expansion of imperial Japan, the war against the United States, and wartime atrocities. Emblematic of this phenomenon was the reemergence of Kishi Nobusuki, who had been the head of the Manchurian railroad in the 1930s, a minister of munitions in the Tōjō government, and a signatory of the 1941 declaration of war on the United States. After the war he was purged and held briefly as a Class A war criminal before being released by the US occupation authorities. Despite this rather dubious record, Kishi returned to active politics in the 1950s and eventually became prime minister in 1957. Such a rehabilitation would have been unthinkable in the German context. It would have been as if Albert Speer had sauntered out of Spandau prison to become the chancellor of West Germany. Nor was Kishi's an isolated example. Other prominent postwar political leaders who had been held as Class A war criminals by the Allies included Shigemitsu Mamoru, who served as foreign minister in the Hatoyama Ichirō cabinet, and Kaya Okinori, who was justice minister under Prime Minister Ikeda Hayato.

Yet in the context of the Cold War, the United States had limited options. The services of men like Kishi were needed to help Japan recover from the devastation of World War II and to counter the spread of communism in Asia. Even centrist leaders such as Prime Minister Yoshida Shigeru had been ardent supporters of the Japanese empire and at best tepid opponents of the war.[14] There was a relative paucity of Japanese leaders who could be said to have genuinely suffered at the hands of the regime. In contrast, in Germany many thousands of German opponents of the Nazi regime had been killed—Jews, Socialists, homosexuals, Communists, and Christian critics of the regime, among others. Thousands more returned from foreign exile, prisons, and the concentration camps. Many of these men, including Konrad Adenauer and his Social Democratic opponent, Kurt Schumacher, became leading figures in the postwar German political system. The German victims of Nazism were naturally more inclined to pursue the issue of guilt.[15]

Japan's conservative leadership, gathered together after 1955 under the umbrella of the LDP, favored a narrative of the origins of the Pacific war that was largely exculpatory in nature, stressing the defensive motives behind the expansion of the empire and largely neglecting the issue of Japanese wartime atrocities. In propagating this view they were supported by a number of important constituencies—including veterans' organizations and organizations who represented the interests of fallen soldiers and their families (the Nihon Izokukai)—who were similarly inclined toward a positive portrayal of the Japanese armed forces and the empire that they had fought to expand and defend.[16] From the perspective of the conservatives, however, the history issue was about more than merely the accurate portrayal of the past or defending the honor of Japan's military men. Japanese conservatives felt strongly that the US occupation together with the Japanese Left had used the history issue to deal a near-lethal blow to the Japanese sense of self. Restoring the population's sense of pride in the nation's past was vital if Japan was to become a true nation. Conservatives also tended to link the history issue to national security, since they believed that a strong sense of nation was the critical psychological component needed for a successful defense policy.

Although conservative political elites bore the primary responsibility for Japan's collective avoidance of guilt, the Japanese leftist opposition also contributed to this outcome. Far more than their German counterparts, the Japanese Left held a highly idealistic view of the Soviet Union and the Communist world.[17] Few had any direct experience with Communist regimes, unlike leading German Social Democrats such as Herbert Wehner, who had gone into exile in Moscow after being forced to leave Germany. Nor were Japanese intellectuals as acutely conscious as their German counterparts were of the oppressive nature of the Communist regime in Eastern Europe.

As a result the Japanese Left was far more anti-Western and strident in its campaign against the military alliance with the United States than was true of its German counterparts. In turn, Japanese conservatives were far more adamant in their opposition to the Left. The radicalism of the Left spurred reactionary tendencies on the Right, and vice versa, resulting in a political environment far more polarized than Germany's. The Japanese Left's extremism encouraged potentially centrist Japanese, such as Ashida Hitoshi and Ishibashi Tanzan, to make common cause with far more conservative leaders such as Kishi Nobusuke and Hatoyama Ichirō and allowed the LDP to dominate Japanese party politics for nearly forty years, perhaps the longest domination of a political system by a single party in any advanced industrial country.[18]

After the occupation ended in 1952, the conservatives used their position in government to try to reverse what they saw as being the overly liberal aspects of the US occupation's reforms and in particular to defuse the historical narrative that had been established by the Tokyo War Crimes Tribunals that held Japan responsible for the war in the Pacific. Of particular importance in this regard were the efforts of the LDP government to purge Japanese textbooks of views that were overly critical of prewar Japan and to avoid any reference to the invasion of China or to atrocities that had been committed by the Japanese imperial forces.[19]

For its part, the Left in Japan, although acutely aware of Japanese atrocities during its occupation of Asia, was primarily concerned with mobilizing public opinion against the threat of a remilitarization of Japan within the context of the US alliance. By the late 1950s the leaders of the Japanese peace movement came to the conclusion that this could more easily be accomplished by focusing on the Japanese people's sense of victimization, and in particular on the potent symbols of Hiroshima and Nagasaki.[20] In this the Left was strongly encouraged by the leadership of China, which for its own purposes chose to define the Japanese people as having been victims of Western capitalist imperialism, together with the peoples of China and the rest of Asia. In this way, the Chinese leadership hoped to create a narrative that would help lure Japan out of its alliance with the United States and the West.[21] As a result, the Left and the Right entered into what amounted to a "conspiracy of silence" regarding the darker sides of Japanese history.

Finally, it is worth noting that the international context did not encourage Japan to seriously confront its past. West Germany was a divided country sitting on the front lines of the Cold War, faced with the massive presence of the "glorious" Red Army on its borders. West Germany was occupied by four countries, including Britain and France, with whom it had to reconcile itself as part of the process to bring the occupation to an end. In addition, Germany's economic reconstruction hinged upon its ability to reintegrate itself with the other advanced industrial economies of Europe. To deal with these geopolitical and geoeconomic challenges, West Germany under the leadership of Konrad Adenauer embarked on a strategy of integrating itself tightly into the West through closely knit economic and strategic multilateral structures, beginning with NATO, which was founded in 1949, and the European Economic Community, which formally got started in 1957 but whose roots can be traced back to 1951. One consequence of this strategy was that Germany had to work closely with countries that it had invaded during the war, and thus it came under heavy pressure to provide compensation for the victims of Nazi war crimes who lived in the West.[22]

In contrast, Japan found itself in a position of "splendid isolation" in East Asia. As an island nation, Japan was relatively insulated from the threat of a Communist invasion. Japan's strategic position encouraged it to adopt a military posture that aligned it with the West and the United States while at the same time minimizing the chance that it might be entangled in a land war in East Asia.[23] Unlike Germany, Japan was de facto occupied by a single nation, the United States. Economically Japan's chief trading partner was the United States. Although Japan relied on the import of strategic raw materials from other parts of Asia, it drew upon an increasingly diversified range of suppliers. Whereas in Europe a dense network developed consisting of overlapping multilateral institutions centered on NATO and the European Economic Community, in Asia a complex system of bilateral alliances emerged instead. At the core of this system was the United States, which played the role of mediator and coordinator of a very loosely integrated region. Although the United States was the dominant player in this system, Japan was number two. No other Asian country came close to Japan in terms of economic and political power. Thus, except vis-à-vis the United States, Japan held the upper hand in any dyadic relationship in which it found itself.[24] There was no nation in Asia that could come close to dealing with Japan as an equal, or even as a superior, the way that Britain or France could deal with West Germany. There was thus no compelling military, economic, or political incentive at the time for Japan to make far-reaching compromises in order to achieve reconciliation with its Asian neighbors.

In the process of normalizing its relations with other Asian countries during the 1950s and 1960s, Japan was confronted with the issue of paying compensation for the damages it had inflicted on other nations during the war. The major Western powers, following the lead of the United States, renounced any claims that their governments might levy with the signing of the Treaty of San Francisco in 1951. In bilateral negotiations with other Western-aligned Asians, beginning with the Republic of Taiwan in 1952, followed by Burma in 1954, the Philippines in 1956, Indonesia in 1958, South Vietnam in 1959, South Korea in 1965, and Malaysia in 1967, Japanese negotiators were able to hammer out ambiguously worded agreements in which they offered economic development assistance that could be interpreted as reparations, without officially having to acknowledge them as such.[25] The desperate need of these countries for funds, their limited leverage vis-à-vis Japan, as well as the recognition of Japan as a key member of the US-led alliance to contain communism in Asia, all strongly encouraged these governments to settle for limited reparations instead of holding out for more. The strongly authoritarian character of most of these governments allowed their leadership to squelch popular discontent over the issue. Popular protests were particularly fierce in South Korea, where large-scale demonstrations forced the Japanese government, as represented by Foreign Minister Shiina Etsusaburō, to offer more strongly worded expressions of remorse and larger sums of aid. But in the end the harshly authoritarian government of Park Chung Hee was able to bring the protesters under control.[26]

For very different reasons, mainland China as well chose not to pursue the issue of Japanese historical responsibility for the war. During the first half of the Cold War it did so because it hoped that by defining the Japanese people as one of the peoples victimized by Western imperialism in Asia, it could strengthen anti-American sentiments in Japan and undermine the US-Japanese security alliance. Later, after China aligned with the United States against the Soviet Union and began the process of normalizing diplomatic relations with Japan, the Chinese leadership relinquished compensation in favor of winning greater Japanese economic aid and investment.[27] There was, however, a widely recognized and unofficial link between foreign aid to China and compensation. By defining Japanese payments to China as aid rather than compensation, the Japanese government was able to avoid a politically painful and potentially debilitating debate over responsibility for the war. For its part, China received massive infusions of aid from Japan, over 20 billion dollars in the 1990s alone.

This combination of domestic and international factors removed the issue of Japanese responsibility for wartime atrocities from the international political agenda, and the official historical narrative propagated by the

Japanese state reflected a relatively conservative interpretation of modern Japanese history. The liberal textbooks of the US occupation period, which portrayed World War II as the result of Japanese aggression and at least touched on the Nanjing massacre and other atrocities, were phased out as the conservative Hatoyama and Kishi government reasserted government control over the screening of textbooks.[28] Many of the individuals who had been purged for their connection with the wartime regime were rehabilitated and were opposed to pursuing the war guilt issue any further. In a more sinister vein, beginning in the late 1950s, subtle and not so subtle pressures were brought to bear on the Japanese media to avoid raising embarrassing questions regarding Japanese wartime atrocities and in particular the role of the emperor in the pre-1945 Japanese political system. Particularly pernicious was the role played by groups in the Far Right, who reemerged in this period and who were ready to resort to violence against those they identified as their ideological opponents.[29]

Public opinion data from the late 1950s and 1960s also reflected a fundamentally ambivalent stance on the history issue. On the one hand, there was considerable popular resentment of Japan's wartime leadership,[30] and many Japanese were evidently aware that terrible things had happened in Asia during the war. On the other hand, opinion was sharply divided over whether responsibility for the war should be pursued. When asked about the war with China, only 17 percent of Japanese surveyed in 1967 felt that Japan had done something bad, and 46.5 percent felt that it was either justifiable in self-defense or otherwise unavoidable (*yamuenakatta*). Similarly, the atrocities that were committed in the war were viewed as wrongful actions by only 46.4 percent of those surveyed; 8.4 percent felt that they were justifiable acts of self-defense; 46.6 percent felt that they were unavoidable.[31] Thus, although few Japanese were willing to positively affirm the war, most Japanese were also not ready to condemn their own part in it. The war had been a terrible tragedy, one whose repetition had to be avoided. It was not, however, viewed as a terrible sin for which Japan as a nation had to atone.

The Evolution of the Japanese Debate over History During the Cold War

Despite the conservative hegemony in Japanese politics, the public debate over history did not die out during the 1960s. On the contrary, over the course of the next few decades it raged on, fed by both domestic and international trends. In addition to debates over the meaning of the war and the imperial period, Japanese foreign policy, and in particular its relationship to other Asian countries, became an important ideological battleground where the shadow of the past loomed large.

The debate continued to run along the battle lines that had been drawn in the 1950s. On the one side there were the progressive historians, usually Marxist in their ideology and supporters of the Japanese Communist or Socialist parties, who were highly critical of both the wartime regime and the contemporary conservative Japanese government. The most prominent progressive historian of the era was Ienaga Saburō, who became embroiled in a series of lawsuits brought against the Ministry of Education's textbook review system, which Ienaga accused of being an unconstitutional form of censorship.[32]

On the other side of the debate were conservative writers who were highly critical of the version of history that had been established by the Allied powers at the Tokyo Tribunal and propagated by the progressive historians. Some, like the philosopher Ueyama Shunpei, argued that the war had been nothing more than a normal conflict between sovereign states. Others, like the novelist Hayashi Fusao, went further and argued that it had been a just war against the forces of Western imperialism. The conservatives enjoyed strong support in the Japanese government as well as the more right-wing parts of the Japanese media and publishing worlds.[33]

The debate over the past intensified during the 1960s and 1970s. The Vietnam War, which was widely viewed as an unjust war by both the Left and the Right, helped fan the flames of controversy. For the conservative historians, US misdeeds in Vietnam undermined the high moral position that the United States had carved out for itself during the occupation period and reconfirmed their view that atrocities against the civilian population during wartime are an inevitable feature of military conflicts. The Left for its part viewed the Vietnam War as a new form of Western imperialism, and it was alarmed by the indirect involvement of Japan in the conflict through the presence of US military bases. The Vietnam War reinforced the Left's fear of a third world war and lent added urgency to its efforts to educate the Japanese people about the horrors of war.[34]

The reopening of direct diplomatic relations with China in the 1970s gave further impetus to the debate. For the first time in decades, Japanese scholars and researchers had direct access to sources on mainland China, and popular interest in China was heightened. *Asahi* reporter Honda Katsuichi wrote a best-selling account of the Nanjing massacre based on eyewitness accounts from the region.[35] Public opinion was focused as never before on the question of Japanese atrocities in Asia. Conservative writers such as Suzuki Akira and Yamamoto Shichihei launched a counterattack, dismissing Honda's findings as little more than Chinese propaganda.[36] Despite such rearguard actions, the times seemed to favor the progressives. A mass of writings on Japanese atrocities poured out during the 1970s, supported by unprecedented access to documents and witnesses on mainland China. Pressure on the history issue also came from Southeast Asia, especially during Prime Minister Tanaka Kakuei's visit to Southeast Asia in 1974, when anti-Japanese riots broke out on the streets of Bangkok and Jakarta. The conservative interpretation of Japan's past suffered further set-backs in the courts, as first the Tokyo District Court in 1970 and then the Tokyo High Court in 1975 ruled in favor of Ienaga Saburō. As a result, in the late 1970s, a number of textbook publishing companies began once again, as they had during the US occupation, to publish high school texts that included discussion of the Nanjing massacre and other Japanese wartime atrocities.[37]

During the 1980s the international climate changed yet again, giving fresh wind to the conservative movement. A major electoral victory by the LDP in 1980 and the coming to power of Prime Minister Nakasone Yasuhiro gave conservative politicians and bureaucrats increased leverage to pursue their agenda. The revival of US-Soviet military tensions in the late 1970s and early 1980s increased the sentiment among Japanese conservatives that a healthy sense of patriotism had to be nurtured.[38] A central objective of this campaign was to promote a more positive view of Japanese history in the Japanese school curriculum and in the public discourse. The Ministry of Education began to encourage a softening of language used to describe Japanese aggression and to downplay Japanese wartime atrocities. At the same time, a new wave of conservative revisionist literature was published, and prominent Japanese politicians such as Fujio Masayuki, minister of education in 1986, and Okuno Seisuke, director general of the National Land Agency in 1988, made provocative statements claiming that the Nanjing massacre had never taken place and that Korea had voluntarily chosen to be annexed by Japan.[39]

Perhaps the most controversial symbolic act took place in 1985, when Nakasone Yasuhiro became the first postwar Japanese prime minister to pay an official visit to the Yasukuni Shrine, dedicated to the spirits of the war dead.[40] Among those enshrined at Yasukuni were General Tōjō Hideki and thirteen other Japanese wartime leaders who had been tried as Class A war criminals by the Allied powers in the Tokyo Tribunal and who had either been executed or had died in prison.[41] At the same time, Nakasone called for the "general resolution of post-war Japanese politics" (*Sengo seiji no Sōkessan*), implicitly linking these symbolic acts to raising the Japanese defense budget to more than 1 percent of GDP.[42]

Despite the resurgence of the conservative viewpoint, however, the progressive gains of the 1970s could not be reversed. Conservative denials of Japanese responsibility foundered in the face of the mass of evidence arrayed against them. For instance, when the usually conservative veterans' organization Kaikōsha invited its members to share their experiences of the occupation of Nanjing, to the initial chagrin of its editors there was an unprecedented outpouring of acknowledgments of atrocities from former soldiers who had participated in the taking of the city. These accounts were published in 1984–1985 in the organization's journal, and the chief editor of the journal, Katokawa Kōtarō, made an emotional apology to the Chinese people.[43] International pressures as well served to prevent the official narrative from moving too sharply in a conservative direction. In the early 1980s, under intense pressure from other Asian countries, in particular China, South Korea, and Vietnam, the government was forced to leave the textbooks essentially as they were.[44] Both Fujio and Okuno became the objects of massive public controversy. In Okuno's case, he was forced to step down from his post.[45] The widespread consternation and alarm that Nakasone's hawkish stance on defense and history had provoked in both Japan and Asia similarly compelled him to back down on both issues. Opposition from within his own party forced Nakasone to abandon temporarily some of his defense policy goals. At the same time, Nakasone's desire to keep relations with China on an even keel led him to abandon any further trips to Yasukuni during his prime ministership.[46]

The End of the Cold War and Japan's Campaign to Seek Reconciliation

The end of the Cold War had an enormous impact on Japanese politics and on its position in the international system. Not surprisingly, it also strongly influenced the official Japanese discourse on history, this time moving the Japanese official historical narrative toward a more self-critical, penitent stance. The immediate impetus for an official reopening of the issue of war guilt came from the international environment. Whereas earlier Japan had been the only advanced industrial democracy in the region, by the early 1990s both democracy and industrial dynamism had spread. The region as a whole enjoyed spectacular growth rates, and Japanese trade and investment in the other Asian countries, which had been increasing steadily since the 1970s, began to skyrocket. Parallel to these developments was the gradual emergence of a network of international institutions—the Pacific Economic Cooperation Council (PECC), APEC, the ASEAN Regional Forum (ARF)—that bound Japan more closely with the rest of the region. Political democracy began to spread as well, as vibrant pluralist regimes replaced authoritarian dictatorships in South Korea, Taiwan, Thailand, and the Philippines. Even in China, the political climate became considerably more open, despite the brutal reassertion of authoritarian rule following the Tiananmen incident of 1989.

One unexpected upshot of this transformation was that popular anti-Japanese sentiments rooted in historical grievances began to be reflected in government policy, especially in China and South Korea. Freed of the constraints imposed by the East-West conflict and increasingly wealthy and prosperous in their own right, Asian governments no longer felt as dependent as they had been on Japanese support. At the same time, the pluralization of politics throughout the region created political space where such sentiments could be voiced without fear of repression. In China, the government began to actively criticize Japan's attitude on history. In part, this came as a reaction to the appearance of more openly revisionist views in Japanese politics in the 1980s. Anti-Japanese sentiment was also a reflection of growing Chinese feelings of nationalism in an era when the old Maoist ideology was rapidly losing its appeal and when rival political groups had become eager to demonstrate their nationalist credentials.[47]

Japan's changed international environment created powerful incentives for it to seek closer ties with its neighbors. As early as 1991 Prime Minister Kaifu Toshiki proclaimed that for Japan to play a larger regional role it would have to face up to its past and "severely reflect upon" (*kibishiku hansei suru*) its actions during the imperial period. Powerful factional leaders such as Ozawa Ichirō likewise recognized that Japan needed to address the "history question" more clearly and directly than it had been willing to do in the past if it were to become more engaged in world affairs.[48] And prominent Japanese business leaders publicly warned that Japan had to acknowledge its responsibility for its past transgressions if they were to expand their business activities in Asia.[49]

Domestic developments as well created the conditions for a reappraisal of the Japanese past. First and foremost, a generational change took place as many of the Japanese leaders who could be directly implicated in Japanese atrocities passed from the scene. No individual was more important in this context than the Japanese emperor Hirohito. Prior to his death, the issue of the emperor's responsibility for the war had been a taboo topic, one that occasionally was enforced violently by right-wing extremists. After his death the question could be raised in a more clear and forthright manner. Soon a spate of documents and testimonials relating to the emperor's wartime role floated to the surface.[50]

The end of the Cold War also changed the calculus of Japanese party politics. With the threat of entanglement in a larger East-West war gone, the Left became more pliant on the issue of the Mutual Security Treaty. With the disappearance of the Communist threat, conservatives and moderates for their part became concomitantly less concerned with keeping the Left out of power. As a result, in 1993, for the first time since 1948, the Japanese Socialist party entered into the government as part of a coalition of former opposition parties and defectors from the conservative LDP, united under the leadership of Hosokawa Morihiro. A broader range of views on the history issue was now represented inside the government, and Japan's new political leadership proved more forthcoming regarding public acknowledgment of Japanese responsibility for the war. In subsequent years a series of apologies was issued by senior Japanese leaders, beginning with a dramatic speech by Prime Minister Hosokawa before the Japanese Diet on August 23, 1993, in which he publicly apologized for Japanese aggression and colonial rule in Asia.[51]

The conservative perspective on the past, however, remained a politically potent force. In response to Hosokawa's apology, 105 LDP Diet members formed the Committee to Examine History (Rekishi Kentō Iinkai) to challenge the new, more progressive official view of Japanese history that the Hosokawa government sought to promote. In subsequent years similar groups formed to protest the government's new policies aimed at seeking reconciliation with Japan's neighbors over the history issue.[52] Outside of political circles, the same coalition of conservative writers and publishers that had been active in the 1960s, 1970s, and 1980s renewed its campaign against the progressives and in favor of a more positive view of Japanese history. The most prominent champion of the conservative view has been Fujioka Nobukatsu, a professor of education at Tokyo University, who took the lead in organizing various conservative scholarly groups and who founded the journal *Kingendaishi no Jugyō Kaikaku*, which has served as a showcase for conservative interpretations of modern Japanese history.[53]

As a result of these pressures, Japanese leaders' efforts at promoting a more progressive view of Japanese history have frequently been sabotaged or undercut. For instance, in 1995 the Murayama Tomiichi government sponsored a "no-war" resolution (Fusen Ketsugi) in the Japanese legislature that was originally intended as an atonement for Japanese militarism and aggression during the Pacific war. Pressures from various conservative politicians and interest groups, including members of Murayama's ruling coalition, first forced the language of the resolution to be significantly toned down, then withheld their support of the bill so that ultimately it was not passed. Instead of promoting a new consensus on the history issue and creating the image of a Japan as a nation facing up to its past, the incident had the opposite effect. It underlined the differences that continued to divide Japanese society over how to interpret the past and created the image abroad of Japan as "a nation that can't say sorry."

Despite the persistence of the conservative view, the polarity of the official discourse on modern Japanese history and Japanese responsibility for the war and the colonial period has been switched in the post–Cold War era. Public opinion polls showed that more than 50 percent of Japanese polled in 1993, after Prime Minister Hosokawa's historic speech, felt that some level of monetary compensation had to be paid to the victims of Japanese aggression and colonialism.[54] Similarly, even after the 1995 debacle surrounding the "no-war" resolution, the new Japanese diplomacy of seeking reconciliation continued and by the late 1990s appeared to have achieved some important successes, most visibly in the context of its relations with Korea. Korean president Kim Dae Jung's 1998 summit meeting with Japanese prime minister Obuchi Keizō led to a marked improvement in the atmosphere between Seoul and Tokyo when Obuchi offered an apology, and Kim Dae Jung accepted it on behalf of the Korean people.[55] Thereafter, agreements were reached on lifting the ban on the import of Japanese cultural products into Korea, fishing in disputed waters in the Sea of Japan, and the joint hosting of the World Cup soccer games. Following the successful conclusion of the soccer games in 2002, there was a marked improvement in mutual public perceptions, as reflected in both public opinion polls and an increased interest in the other country's culture.

Similar progress could be detected in terms of Japanese relations with Southeast Asia, where anti-Japanese sentiment had been quite strong in the past and where the memory of the brutality of the Japanese occupation during the Pacific war at least potentially could have made history a major diplomatic issue. Despite occasional expressions of historically based misgivings—such as Singaporean prime minister Lee Kuan Yew's famous warning that encouraging Japan to take on peacekeeping missions was akin to giving chocolate liqueurs to a reformed alcoholic—Southeast Asian perceptions of Japan became increasingly positive throughout the decade.[56]

In the context of Sino-Japanese relations there was less evidence of improvement, in part because tensions between the two countries over a range of other issues intensified, most notably in the area of national security. Chinese nuclear tests in 1995 provoked considerable consternation in Japan, as did Chinese challenges to Japan's control over the disputed Senkaku/Diaoyu Islands, claimed by both countries. Equally disturbing were Beijing's efforts in 1996 to influence the outcome of elections on Taiwan through intimidation. In a blunt warning to Taiwanese voters that China would react violently to any move toward independence from the mainland, China fired a barrage of missiles around the island, triggering a major international crisis and leading the United States to dispatch two carrier battle groups to the area.[57] Against this background of growing geopolitical tensions, Chinese efforts to raise the history issue tended to be viewed with suspicion in Japan; they were seen as blatant efforts to manipulate Japanese public opinion by a regime that itself was guilty of enormous human rights abuses in the more recent past. As a result, when Chinese leader Jiang Zemin visited Tokyo a few weeks after Kim Dae Jung, there was no comparable breakthrough on the history issue. Instead, Jiang's efforts to lecture his Japanese hosts on the need to draw the correct lessons from the past were met with a decidedly cool response from the Japanese side.[58]

In short, by the end of the 1990s, Japan appeared to have made substantial progress toward finding a new domestic and international political equilibrium on the history issue. Beginning with the election of Prime Minister

Koizumi Junichirō in 2001, however, whatever progress had been made in dealing with the history issue soon came undone. In his campaign to win the LDP nomination for prime minister, Koizumi sought to mobilize conservative support within the party by promising to visit the Yasukuni Shrine every year in his official capacity as prime minister. After being elected, Koizumi made good on his promise by visiting the shrine on August 13, despite repeated and sharp warnings from Beijing and Seoul. The visit prompted a storm of protest throughout the Asian region, particularly in China and Korea. Beijing suspended direct, bilateral meetings between the two heads of state, relying on lower-level meetings and contacts in such multilateral settings as meetings of APEC. Seoul suspended military-to-military talks between Japan and Korea, reimposed the ban on Japanese cultural items, and temporarily recalled its ambassador. [59]

Faced with the need to coordinate policies in response to the September 11, 2001, attacks and the war on terror—especially with respect to North Korea—China, Japan, and South Korea managed to patch over their differences temporarily.[60] Over the next five years, however, Japan's relations with its two most important Asian neighbors continued to spiral downward, spurred on by Koizumi's continued visits to Yasukuni and by an increase in nationalist public sentiment in all three countries. In 2003, a series of anti-Japanese incidents began to break out in China, triggered by Koizumi's continued visits to Yasukuni and the Japanese Ministry of Education's certification of revisionist textbooks. These incidents culminated in April 2005, when an Internet campaign to collect signatures opposing Japan's bid for a permanent seat on the United Nations Security Council (reportedly more than 30 million signatures were collected within a year) escalated into countrywide riots in which Japanese shops and diplomatic outposts were pelted with stones and several Japanese were injured in attacks by Chinese mobs, as reported in front-page stories in *Asahi*.[61] Although the Chinese authorities moved to contain the violence in the name of "maintaining social order,"[62] and Koizumi made a strong speech in Bandung, Indonesia, repeating Obuchi's 1995 apology,[63] relations between the two sides remained poisonous.

A similar deterioration was to be observed in Japanese-Korean relations. Kim Dae Jung's successor, Roh Moo Hyun, entered office promising that he would not seek to make history an issue between the two countries. Soon an escalating war of words between the two countries ensued, however, first over the revisionist Japanese textbooks produced and then over the Dokdo/Takeshima Islands in the Sea of Japan, a small group of thirty-three uninhabited islands controlled by Korea since 1952 but claimed by both sides. On the Korean side, a campaign began to rename the Sea of Japan the East Sea, and the issuing of a Korean postage stamp commemorating the disputed islands enraged nationalist sentiment on the Japanese side. When in March 2005 the Shimane prefectural government in Japan declared February 22 to be Takeshima Day, a major diplomatic crisis ensued. President Roh stressed that from the Korean standpoint, Dokdo, which had been incorporated as Takeshima into the Shimane prefecture in 1905, had been the beginning of the annexation of Korea and therefore had a symbolic and historical significance that far outweighed its economic or strategic importance. Japan's stance, he claimed, was an effort to legitimate its policies of expansion and colonialism in Asia. Roh went on to declare the "diplomatic equivalent of war."[64] Thereafter, China and South Korea began to work together to oppose Japan in a number of international settings, including opposing its bid for a permanent seat on the UN Security Council and frustrating it in regional summit meetings.[65]

Tensions between Japan and its two Asian neighbors took on a dangerous new dimension in 2006, as nationalist tensions threatened to spark major diplomatic and potentially even military crises involving these disputed territories. In April 2006, after Korea announced its intention to rename oceanographic features in the contested Takeshima/Dokdo area, Japan threatened to send survey ships from the Japanese Maritime Safety Agency. Korea than dispatched a flotilla of gunboats to the islands and threatened to use force if Japan sent the survey ships. Meanwhile, as of the fall of 2005, China and Japan began to engage in an escalating war of words over the definition of the Exclusive Economic Zone around the Senkaku/Diaoyu Islands. Both countries were interested in asserting their claims to the potentially large reserves of natural gas believed to lie beneath the ocean floor in the area, and both sides began armed patrols in and around the disputed area. Although last-minute diplomatic efforts, with quiet, behind-the-scenes support from the United States, managed to contain these crises, none of the three governments showed any willingness to compromise on the issue.[66]

The steady deterioration of Japan's relations with its Asian neighbors began to provoke growing concern in a variety of quarters. Naturally, the Japanese Foreign Ministry was deeply concerned over Japan's growing diplomatic isolation in the region.[67] The Japanese business community was concerned about the potential damage to Japan's rapidly growing economic interests in the region. By 2005, China had become Japan's number one trading partner, outstripping the United States, and by some estimates as much as half of the increase in Japan's economic growth since 2002 can be attributed to exports to Asia. In an effort to contain the damage caused by Koizumi's visits to Yasukuni, leaders of the major Japanese business federation, Keidanren, took the unusual step of making independent overtures to the Chinese leadership.[68] Other business leaders were even more outspoken in their admonishment, calling for the establishment of a new, secular monument commemorating Japan's war dead as an alternative to the Yasukuni

Shrine.[69] Even the United States, which has traditionally been hesitant to interfere in what it sees as an issue that should be left to Asian nations to settle, became increasingly vocal in an effort to persuade Japan to adopt a more moderate stance on the issue.[70]

What makes the deterioration of Japan's relations with Beijing and Seoul remarkable is that from the perspective of conventional paradigms in international relations there was every reason to expect the opposite. From a realist perspective, the balance of power in the region remained overwhelmingly in favor of the United States and Japan, and although cooperation on security issues between the United States and Japan increased in the context of the war on terrorism, it is difficult to detect any substantial increase in the threat that the alliance posed to either Korea or China. In strategic terms, the United States enjoyed a vast edge over China in nuclear capabilities, and although US-Japanese cooperation on ballistic missile defense could potentially negate whatever second-strike capability China might have, there is reason to believe that China was not overly concerned about a weapon system that was still not developed and that China would probably have the capacity to overwhelm anyway by the time it was deployed.[71] And although increasingly open US-Japanese defense coordination with respect to the Taiwan Strait was an annoyance from the perspective of Beijing, there was little change in the actual capabilities of the two countries to intervene, and diplomatically the two countries had acted in concert to discourage the Taiwanese government of Chen Shuibien from moving in the direction of declaring independence from the mainland. Seoul had even less reason to fear from Japan's increased defense role.

From a neoliberal point of view, trends in the region were pointing in a generally positive direction. The natural complementarity between the Chinese and Japanese economies has fed an enormous boom in economic relations between the two countries, enhancing the growth of both economies. Although competition between Seoul and Japan was fierce in many sectors, both countries were enjoying increased success in international markets in such sectors as automobiles and consumer electronics. The 1990s witnessed a sharp increase in efforts at building regional institutions, and Korean democratization at least initially had the positive effect on Japanese-Korean relations that democratic peace theory would suggest it should. And even though China remained a harshly authoritarian system, the political leadership in Beijing was increasingly technocratic in orientation and focused on increasing economic growth through cooperation with the outside world.

Although tensions over history did not entirely reverse these positive trends, they at the very least hampered further progress and created at least the potential for a dangerous reversal. Efforts at institution building in the region were overtaken by nationalist rivalries, paralyzing diplomatic relations among the capitals of the three largest and most powerful countries in the region, and the shadowboxing over the disputed territories between the three countries created the possibility of direct military clashes and a further escalation in regional tensions. If, as in the 2001 spy plane incident between the United States and China, a Chinese or Korean military plane or vessel crashed into or, even worse, fired upon a Japanese Coast Guard or Maritime Self-Defense boat, the impact on regional politics could be immense. Even though such an incident could probably be contained (as the 2001 incident was), the shift in public and elite attitudes on all sides would be large. A hardening of nationalist sentiment could be expected, and a regional arms race—long predicted, but thankfully largely avoided—could ensue, paving the way for larger-scale conflict.

Under these circumstances, Koizumi's political need for conservative support inside the LDP, combined with what is probably his personal conviction that there is nothing wrong with visiting Yasukuni, destabilized the fragile equilibrium that had emerged by the late 1990s. At the same time, political developments in South Korea and China moved in a more nationalist direction. In Korea, the perception that democratic consolidation required increased confrontation with the past, combined with a politically weak Roh Moo Hyun government that needed some nationalist appeal to bolster domestic political support, created the preconditions for renewed tensions over the past. Likewise, in China, the politically fragile Hu Jintao regime found itself besieged by grassroots sentiments that could as easily turn against Communist rule as they could against Japan. Combined with an international environment that pushed Japan toward increased activism on defense issues, all the elements were in place for a sort of "perfect storm" of nationalist sentiment.

In September 2006, Koizumi stepped down, to be replaced by another conservative LDP politician, Abe Shinzō. During the preceding campaign to choose Koizumi's successor, the history problem emerged as a central issue dividing the candidates. Two contenders, Finance Minister Tanigaki Sadakazu and former chief cabinet secretary Fukuda Yasuo, actively criticized the Koizumi administration's stance on the problem.[72] Initially Abe and other more conservative leaders sought to avoid the Yasukuni issue. Public opinion data, however, suggested growing opposition to future visits to the shrine.[73] As a result, Abe felt compelled to promise to improve relations with Beijing and Seoul while adopting a more ambiguous stance on the history issue, refusing to either confirm or deny that he planned to visit the Yasukuni shrine in the future.[74] In response, the Chinese government invited Abe to visit Beijing, and tensions over the history issue subsided.[75]

Whether these diplomatic efforts will result in a lasting settlement of the issue remains doubtful. To be sure, the leaderships in Beijing, Seoul, and Tokyo have good reason to avoid renewed frictions over the history issue. At the same time, there are powerful forces pulling in the opposite direction.

It is true that a combination of economic interests, quiet pressure from the United States, and public apprehension over worsening relations with Asia pushed Abe to defuse the history problem. As the grandson of Kishi Nobusuke, who had been imprisoned as a possible Class A war criminal by the US occupation,[76] Abe comes from a deeply conservative political background, however, and has a long history of promoting revisionist views of Japanese history, including through visits to Yasukuni. Of course, it is possible that Abe's conservative credentials will provide him with the political cover on the Right that he needs to pull off a sustained change in Japanese policy on the history issue, much as President Nixon's reputation as a "cold warrior" enabled him to change US policy on China in the 1970s. It is just as plausible, however, that Abe's conservatism in the long run may lead him to revert to form. Already by the winter of 2006 there were mixed signs regarding the strength of Japan's commitment to engage with China on the history issue.[77]

Regardless of which direction Abe decides to move in the short term, there are long-term trends that favor the reemergence of the history problem. In Japan, a new generation of leaders is taking the helm, who are both more ready to assume an active role than was true of their predecessors and less willing to back down on symbolic issues than was true of their post-1945 predecessors.[78] Similarly, in both China and Korea, there are strong currents of nationalist sentiment that could easily be reignited. Global trends, such as the emergence of norms supporting the pursuit of historical justice issues as well as pressures on Japan to assume a more active security role, likewise create points of tension around which acrimony over history could emerge. The conditions that gave rise to a perfect storm of nationalist passions in 2006 appear to persist today.

Conclusion

Japan's problem with its neighbors over history has long and complicated roots. Contrary to the popular perception that Japan suffers from a form of "historical amnesia," the past has loomed large in Japan's public life and has had a substantial impact on its domestic politics and its foreign relations. The problem, in fact, is not that there is too little memory of the past but too much. Japan remains deeply divided on the issue, with certain groups deeply committed to a progressive interpretation of the past and others to a more conservative reading. Moreover, the pressures emanating from the international system have often pulled it in conflicting directions. For much of the Cold War, the international system allowed Japan to largely avoid confronting the past and making difficult apologies and restitution for Japanese war crimes and colonialism. At other times, the prospects for achieving some measure of reconciliation on issues of historical justice encouraged Japan to try to tackle this thorny issue.

In recent years, these pressures have intensified. Democratization, increased economic interdependence, and the perception that the old "hubs-and-spokes" system of regional relations centered on the United States is no longer adequate for managing Asian regional affairs have led to an upsurge of pressure for Japan to seek some sort of resolution of historical issues. As a result, during the 1990s Japan launched a substantive—if at times troubled—diplomatic campaign to address the problem. At the same time, however, increasing tensions on security issues between Japan and some of its neighbors, most importantly China but also North Korea, have made the pursuit of reconciliation seem unprofitable. In the meantime, the continued slow pace of progress between Japan and South Korea on the historical issue has fed a growing mood of "apology fatigue" in Tokyo. Nonetheless, in the past, substantial progress had been made on the issue, at least in the context of Japanese relations with South Korea and Southeast Asia, before the current crisis over history ensued.

Whether Asia can resolve this crisis and return to the path toward greater harmony over history depends on a variety of factors that cannot be predicted with any degree of certainty. A number of things can be said with confidence. First, concrete national interests will play a crucial role if any degree of reconciliation can be achieved. Security concerns and economic factors do matter in how countries relate to one another. Without a firm foundation of mutual interest, there is little incentive to address the history issue and little prospect that political leaders will make the often difficult compromises needed to move the reconciliation process forward.

Second, common interests alone are not enough. Historical memory, although it may be malleable, is itself a reality that political leaders in the region find difficult to ignore. However much Kim Dae Jung, Roh Moo Hyun, and their Japanese counterparts may want to put the past behind them and focus on more immediate and pressing issues, the ghosts of the past have a habit of rising up and troubling the relationships among the three countries, often in unpredictable ways. Arguably, given their common economic and security interests, Japan and South Korea should have begun a dialogue on history far earlier than they in fact did. Yet, the way the issue is defined in terms of national identity and national perceptions does matter. The depth of anti-Japanese sentiment in postcolonial Korea made tackling the issue almost impossible for over a generation. Conversely, the relative absence of anti-Japanese sentiments in Southeast Asia is at least partly the result of the way in which Southeast Asian national identity has been constructed vis-à-vis the West. Likewise, the lack of democratic legitimacy on the part of authoritarian leaders such as Park Chung Hee and Jiang Zemin has made the Japanese reluctant to respond to Korean and Chinese demands for apologies and compensation.

Progress can be made only when there is a convergence of both interest and political will. Leaders have to seize the opportunity to pursue reconciliation on the past when it avails itself. In the 1990s, structural conditions made Japan far more responsive to demands for historical justice than it once was, and it is to their credit that Japanese leaders such as Hosokawa, Murayama, and Obuchi Keizō made a genuine effort to promote better relations with Japan's neighbors. To a certain extent, however, Japan has fallen victim to its own success during that period, for there has been a lack of appreciation of the extent to which reconciliation between peoples is an ongoing process that requires the sustained expenditure of political energy. Grand symbolic gestures of the sort made by Kim Dae Jung and Obuchi Keizō in 1998 have to be followed up with a series of lower-level initiatives spaced out over many years. The Japanese expectation that the issue had been resolved once and for all in 1998 proved patently false. The process had only just begun, and what progress had been made during the 1990s was then undone by a combination of ill-considered policies on the Japanese side, matched by equally ill-advised and destructive trends emerging in China and South Korea.

During the 2006 race to succeed Prime Minister Koizumi, a consensus emerged inside of the LDP and Japanese elite circles that dialogue with Japan's Asian neighbors had to be reengaged. Whether such efforts will succeed will depend on a variety of factors. The new Japanese prime minister, Abe Shinzō, will need to be willing to show greater flexibility on the history issue. How Japan chooses to deal with such a matter is, of course, ultimately a domestic political matter. Nonetheless, the Japanese debate on the topic has already pointed to a number of intriguing possibilities. So, for instance, former Japanese ambassador to the Netherlands, Tōgō Kazuhiko, has suggested the idea of at least temporarily suspending visits to Yasukuni while reopening the debate that had begun in 1992 over possible alternative commemorative sites.[79] The product of joint historical research of the sort that has been produced by Korean and Japanese historians deserves further promotion by the Japanese government, and renewed efforts should be made to pursue similar projects with China. Renewed consideration should also be given to compensating surviving Chinese and Korean forced laborers. Finally, although Japan guarantees the freedom of speech to all its citizens, including revisionist historians, this need not mean that Japanese political leaders cannot distance themselves and the state from views that they disagree with, especially when those views are inimical to the interests of the Japanese state. This is especially true since the Japanese textbook review process can give the impression of tacit state approval of such views.

Japanese efforts, however, have to be matched by an equal readiness to respond on the Chinese and Korean side. As the 1998 Korean-Japanese and Sino-Japanese summits clearly demonstrated, apologies are only likely to be productive if there is some assurance that they will be accepted by the other side. Whether the willingness to engage in such a process will in fact emerge in Beijing, Seoul, and Tokyo is uncertain.

The United States can help urge the parties along in such a direction, but only to a limited extent. The United States as well has its burdens of history that have not been fully resolved—witness the occasional US-Japanese disagreements over how to evaluate the atomic bombings of Hiroshima and Nagasaki or the intense feelings of grievance many Koreans feel toward the United States for its acceptance of the Japanese colonial takeover of the Korean peninsula. The path of quiet diplomacy is the only realistic option for Washington.

Internationalizing the problem is likewise ill advised. Differences over history are at least as complex as differences over the definition of human rights or terrorism. Trying to establish a general principle that states should always apologize for past transgressions is likely to be highly counterproductive and might well produce more tensions than it would resolve. It is highly unlikely that a neutral, international "truth commission" would be able to achieve very much in the Asian context, especially given the rather mixed performance that such institutions have had even in the context of a single state.

In the final analysis, the future of the history problem depends on political leaders in the region. The past need not be an ancient curse that condemns the region to mounting tension and ideological confrontation. Nationalist passions can be defused as well as stoked. Certainly Japan, with its essentially liberal definition of its national interests, has every reason to seek reconciliation with its neighbors. If the leaders of the other Asian nations are willing to reciprocate, there is reason to believe that sustained progress can yet be made.

Notes

1. It is worth noting that in some parts of Asia, especially Southeast Asia and to a lesser extent South Asia, things tend not to be viewed in black or white terms. Even though many in countries such as Indonesia or Myanmar view imperial Japan as having been an aggressive and expansive nation, there is also the widespread perception that Japan's imperial expansion was no worse than that of the European colonial powers and that Japan's expansion had the virtue of shattering the European hold on power in the region.

2. The United States, for instance, tends to focus far more on the 58,000 or so Americans who were killed during the Vietnam War than on the 2 million or so Vietnamese who may have died between 1962 and 1972. For a critical perspective

on US views on Vietnam, see, for instance, Loewen, "Teaching Vietnam in High School American History"; and Hunt, "War Crimes and the Vietnamese People." Russia continues to avoid dealing with the immense suffering that the former Soviet Union inflicted both on its own population and on neighboring countries before, during, and after World War II. For a fascinating analysis, see Wertsch, *Voices of Collective Remembering*. Most European countries remain similarly averse to offering official policies or compensation for the evils of colonialism.

3. For a discussion of how the history problem has fed Chinese suspicions regarding Japan, see Christensen, "China, the U.S.-Japan Alliance, and the Security Dilemma in East Asia." The history issue is commonly seen as a major factor impeding institutional development in Asia. See, for instance, Lincoln, *East Asian Economic Regionalism*.

4. In the late 1950s, the Kishi Nobusuke government began its campaign to increase Japan's military role with an attack on the power of the Communist-dominated Japanese Teachers' Union before it sought to revise the US-Japan Mutual Security Treaty. In the late 1960s, the government of Kishi's half brother, Satō Eisaku, similarly timed its efforts to reform the education system with the announcement of a more active Japanese security role designed to counter the geopolitical vacuum that might emerge from the looming US disengagement from Vietnam. In the late 1970s, Prime Minister Fukuda Takeo oversaw the reintroduction of the imperial calendar and of the Japanese national anthem "Kimi ga yo" when Japan intensified its alliance relationship with the United States. In a similar fashion, when Prime Minister Nakasone Yasuhiro visited Yasukuni in 1985, his trip came against the background of a significant expansion of the role of the SDF and a major national debate on defense and security policy. Ōtake, *Nihon no Bōei to Kokunai Seiji*.

5. I first heard this analogy being made by Komori Yoshihisa, editor-at-large of the conservative *Sankei* newspaper. It is a very common point of reference for conservative Japanese when talking to Americans.

6. The seminal work in the field of collective memory studies is Halbwachs, *On Collective Memory*. For overviews, see Wertsch, *Voices of Collective Remembering*, esp. chaps. 2 and 3; Hutton, *History as an Art of Memory;* and McDonald, *The Historic Turn in the Human Sciences*. For a discussion from a more philosophical point of view, see Hacking, *Rewriting the Soul*.

7. There are signs of change in regard to these studies. See, for instance, pioneering works by Müller, *Memory and Power in Post-war Europe;* Markovits and Reich, *The German Predicament;* Gong, *Memory and History in East and Southeast Asia;* and Starr, *The Legacy of History in Russia*. The problem of memory has emerged in a variety of other, closely related areas of political science research, notably the impact of national identity on international relations (a central topic in the new constructivist movement in the field of international relations) and the question of how to manage demands for wrongs by an earlier generation or preceding political regime (referred to as "transitional justice" in comparative politics). For an overview of constructivism, see Checkel, "The Constructivist Turn in International Relations Theory." On the issue of transitional justice, see Teitel, *Transitional Justice*. For an exploration of the extension of these norms to interstate relations, see Barkan, *The Guilt of Nations*.

8. For a highly useful overview of the debates that roil the historical profession regarding the purpose of the enterprise and the methods, see Fulbrook, *Historical Theory*.

9. See Bodnar, *Remaking America;* Kammen, *Mystic Chords of Memory*.

10. For a learned reflection on these and other issues, see Birnbaum, *The Idea of France*.

11. Yang, "The Malleable and the Contested."

12. For useful reviews, see Maier, *The Unmasterable Past;* Fulbrook, *German National Identity;* Olick, *In the House of the Hangman;* and Art, *The Politics of the Nazi Past.*

13. In the research project out of which this book emerged, no single issue excited greater and more animated discussion than the comparison of German and Japanese attitudes toward history. Although the US participants tended to assume a basic similarity between the two cases, many of the Japanese participants strongly objected, pointing out the numerous differences between the two countries and their histories. I benefited greatly from these discussions and have tried to incorporate some of the insights provided by the Japanese side in the analysis here.

14. See Ōtake, *Adenaū to Yoshida Shigeru;* and Dower, *Empire and Aftermath.*

15. The extent to which even former victims of Nazism were willing to compromise on issues of historical justice in the interests of reconstruction is striking, however. See Art, *The Politics of the Nazi Past.*

16. See Seraphim, *War Memory and Social Politics in Japan, 1945–2005,* as well as James J. Orr, *The Victim as Hero,* chap. 6.

17. See Kojima, *Hangarii Jiken to Nihon.*

18. For a comparative analysis of one-party dominant democratic systems, see Pempel, *Uncommon Democracies.*

19. Takashi Yoshida, "A Battle over History in Japan," 75–76.

20. See James J. Orr, *The Victim as Hero,* chap. 3; and Dower, "The Bombed."

21. Particularly important in this regard was the visit to Beijing of Japanese Socialist Party chairman Asanuma Inejirō in March 1959.

22. See Scharfstetter, "The Diplomacy of Wiedergutmachung."

23. For an analysis of post-1945 Japanese alliance behavior as the product of alternating fears of abandonment versus entrapment, see Tsuchiyama, "The End of the Alliance?"

24. This argument is developed further in Berger, "Of Shrines and Hooligans."

25. See *Asahi,* November 13, 1993; Shimizu, "Sengo Hoshō no Kokusaihikaku."

26. On the bilateral negotiations and the larger strategic background against which they occurred, see Cha, "Bridging the Gap."

27. See He, "National Mythmaking and the Problems of History." There may also have been some measure of competition between China and the nationalist government of Taiwan. Both governments had strong supporters inside the LDP during the Cold War, and the split between the sides led to some of the sharpest ideological battles within the party during the 1960s. Both Beijing and Taipei may have wanted to display magnanimity on the issue of war guilt in order to strengthen the hand of their respective supporters.

28. See Nozaki and Inokuchi, "Japanese Education, Nationalism, and Ienaga Saburō's Textbook Lawsuits"; and James J. Orr, *The Victim as Hero,* chap. 4. Orr noted that even the textbooks produced during the occupation period helped propagate an exculpatory historical narrative that emphasized the responsibility of a small militarist clique for the horrors of war without dwelling on the issue of whether ordinary Japanese should bear any burden of guilt. For a useful overview of the development of Japanese textbooks during the postwar period, see Okamoto, *The Distortion and the Revision of History.*

29. For an overview of the resurgence of the Far Right during this period, including their attacks on the media, see Morris, *Nationalism and the Right Wing in Japan.*

30. See Dower, *Embracing Defeat: Japan in the Wake of World War II.*

31. In general, the older, more rural, and less educated segments of the population opposed pursuing responsibility for the war, whereas younger, more urban, and better-educated Japanese tended to support it. See Yoshida Yutaka, *Nihonjin no Sensōkan,* 56.

32. For more on Ienaga's views of the war, see Ienaga, *Taiheiyō Sensō.* This book is also available in English as Ienaga, *The Pacific War.*

33. For a brief overview of this period, see Takashi Yoshida, "A Battle over History," 72–79.

34. See ibid., 78–79; and Havens, *The Fire Across the Sea.*

35. Honda, *Chūgoku no Tabi,* followed by Honda, *Chūgoku no Nihongun.*

36. See Yamamoto, *Watakushi no Naka no Nihongun;* and Suzuki Akira, *Nankin "Gyakusatsu" no Maboroshi.* For an overview of the Japanese debate, see Takashi Yoshida, "A Battle over History," 85–94; and Yoshida Yutaka, *Nihonjin no Sensōkan,* chap. 6.

37. See Nozaki and Inokuchi, "Japanese Education, Nationalism, and Ienaga's Textbook Lawsuits."

38. See Ōtake, *Sengonihon no Ideorogii tairitsu jiku,* chaps. 2 and 3.

39. Wakamiya, *The Postwar Conservative View of Asia,* 177–178.

40. In 1975 Prime Minister Miki Takeo became the first postwar Japanese prime minister to visit the Yasukuni Shrine, but he did so in an unofficial capacity. Nakasone was the first to do so in an official capacity. For an overview of the Yasukuni issue, see Safier, "Yasukuni Shrine."

41. Many other Japanese prime ministers had visited Yasukuni in the past. None had done so in an official capacity since 1978, when the names of thirteen Class A war criminals had been added to the list of those commemorated at the shrine.

42. Kamanishi, *GNP 1% Waku,* 21–22.

43. Takashi Yoshida, "A Battle over History," 91; Yang, "The Malleable and the Contested," 65–66. The findings of the study were published as Kaikōsha, *Nankin Senshi.* A third volume of documents was later published in 1993.

44. *Asahi,* July 26, 1982. See also *Shūkan Asahi,* August 13, 1982, 20, cited in Yang, "The Malleable and the Contested," 62–63; and Takashima, *Kyōkasho wa kō kakinaosareta!* 98.

45. For the announcement of Ōkuno's resignation and an analysis of the political background, see *Asahi,* May 14, 1988.

46. For a more extensive analysis of this episode, see Wakamiya, *The Postwar Conservative View of Asia,* 172–177. See also Berger, *Cultures of Antimilitarism,* 139–142.

47. This point has been strongly emphasized by a large number of observers of Chinese politics since the early 1990s. See Yang, "The Malleable and the Contested." For more detailed discussions of Chinese nationalism and the politics of the past, see especially Gries, *China's New Nationalism;* and Zhao, *A Nation State by Construction.*

48. Ozawa, *Blueprint for a New Japan,* 128–129.

49. See the forum of business leaders in *Gekkan Keidanren,* April 1992, cited in Yoshida Yutaka, *Nihonjin no Sensōkan,* 175.

50. For a well-received volume that draws heavily on these sources, see Bix, *Hirohito.*

51. For a brief overview of the politics of Japan's apology campaign of the 1990s, see Howell, "The Inheritance of War." On the political importance of the campaign to the Japanese Socialist Party, see Asano, *Renritsu Seiken,* pt. 2, chap. 3.

52. Takashi Yoshida, "A Battle over History," 96–99.

53. For more on Fujioka's views of Japanese history, see his *Kyōkasho ga oshienai Rekishi* and *Ojoku no Kingendaishi;* and Fujioka and Nishio, *Kokumin no Yudan: Reikishi Kyōkasho ga Abunai.*

54. Thirty-four percent of those polled felt that compensation was necessary, and 21 percent felt it was partially (*aru teido*) necessary, whereas only 29 percent felt it was unnecessary. Yoshida Yutaka, *Nihonjin no Sensōkan,* 3.

55. For the text of the statement and initial press reactions, see *Asahi Shimbun,* October 8, 1998, and *Shimbun Yomiuri,* October 8, 1998, 1. A cynic might observe that Kim did not go unrewarded for his tact. In return for softening his demands for an apology, Korea received an additional 3 billion dollars in aid from Japan, thus continuing a pattern of Japanese money in return for Korean circumspection that dates back to 1965.

56. See Singh, "ASEAN's Perceptions of Japan," 292. Diana Wong made the argument that in Southeast Asian countries, unlike the situation in China and Korea, the focus of national passions is the former colonial powers of the West. See Wong, "Memory Suppression and Memory Production."

57. On the evolution of Sino-Japanese relations through the 1990s, see Green, *Japan's Reluctant Realism,* chap. 3; Thomas Christensen, "China, the U.S.-Japan Alliance and the Security Dilemma in East Asia."

58. For a comparison of the Japanese reaction to the two visits, see Wakamiya, *The Postwar Conservative View of Asia,* 256–261; and Green, *Japan's Reluctant Realism,* 96–98.

59. See *Korean Herald,* August 15, 2001, 1.

60. *Asahi* satellite edition, October 22, 2001, 3.

61. *Asahi* satellite edition, April 9, 10, 11, 17, 18, and 21, 2005.

62. Joseph Kahn, "Chinese Official Orders End to Anti-Japanese demonstrations," *New York Times,* April 20, 2005. Available at http://www.nytimes.com/2005/04/20/international/asia/20china.html?ex=1271649600&en=d539df61c78c523a&ei=5090&partner=rssuserland&emc=rss (accessed May 17, 2006).

63. For the text of the speech, see the Ministry of Foreign Affairs Web site. Available at http://www.mofa.go.jp/region/asia-paci/meet0504/speech.html (accessed May 26, 2006).

64. "Kankoku Daitōryō: 'Nihon, Shinryaku o Seitōka' Takeshima Kyōkasho Hihan no Danwa" [Korean President: Statement on Takeshima and Criticism of Textbooks—'Japan Legitimizes Aggression']", *Asahi* satellite edition, March 24, 2005, 1, 2, 7.

65. "Ajia tono 'wakai' tōku [Reconciliation with Asia Remains Far Off]," *Asahi* satellite edition, May 10, 2005, 2; "APEC Meeting Sees Splits over Trade, Japan's Past," Agence France Presse, November 15, 2005. Available at http://asia.news.yahoo.com/051115/afp/051115085837.business.html (accessed November 15, 2005).

66. For an overview of the crisis over Dokdo/Takeshima, see Weinstein, "South Korea–Japan Dokdo-Takeshima Dispute."

67. "Ajia Gaikō Yuzuranu Shushō [The Prime Minister Refuses to Back Down on Asian Diplomacy]," *Asahi* satellite edition, November 15, 2005, 2.

68. On the diplomatic overtures to China of the Japanese Federation of Business (Keidanren), see "Keidanren Made Covert Trip to China Last Month," *Japan Times,* October 23, 2005. Available at www.japntimes.co.jp/cgi-bin/makeprfy.pl15?nn20051023a1.htm.

69. "Keizai Dōyūkai: Shushō Yasukuni Sanpai Saikō o [Japan Association of Corporate Executives Calls on the Prime Minister to Reconsider Making Trips to

Yasukuni]," *Asahi* satellite edition, May 20, 2006.

70. "US Lawmaker Wants Koizumi's Guarantee That He Won't Visit Yasukuni," *Asia News,* May 16, 2006. Available at http://asia.news.yahoo.com/ o60516/Kyodo/d8hkji981.html (accessed May 25, 2006). See also "Yasukuni Nichibei ni mo Eikyo," *Asahi* satellite edition, April 30, 2006, 1.

71. Urayama, "China Debates Missile Defense," *Survival* 46, no. 2 (Summer 2004).

72. "'Jimin Sōsai Sen: Yasukuni' Tōnai Semegiai [Selecting the Next LDP President: Quarrels over Yasukuni]," *Asahi Shimbun,* January 13, 2006, 2; "'Koizumi ato' e Aratana Tairitsu [New Conflicts 'After Koizumi']," *Asahi Shimbun,* June 1, 2006, 4; and "Yasukuni Key to LDP Presidency," *Daily Yomiuri,* June 9, 2005.

73. According to a survey published by the liberal *Asahi* newspaper, as much as 60 percent of the Japanese public were in favor of the next prime minister's not visiting the Yasukuni shrine. "Jiki Shushō no Yasukuni Sanpai 'Hantai' fue 60% ni [Public Opposition to the Next Prime Minister's Making a Visit to Yasukuni Increases to 60 Percent]," *Asahi Shimbun,* July 25, 2006. According to a survey from around the same time published by the more conservative *Yomiuri* newspaper, 50 percent opposed further visits. See "Yasukuni, Jiki Shushō no Sampai 'Hantai' 50% [50 Percent Oppose the Next Prime Minister's Visiting Yasukuni]," *Yomiuri Shimbun,* August 8, 2006.

As always, however, public opinion data have to be viewed with a certain degree of skepticism. Much depends both on the timing and the framing of the questions that are asked. Recent survey data seem to have been strongly influenced by revelations that Emperor Hirohito had been discomfited by the enshrinement of Class A war criminals at Yasukuni. See "Yasukuni no A Kyū Sempan Gōshi: Shōwa Tennō ga Fukaikan [The Showa Emperor Discomfited by the Enshrinement of Class A War Criminals at Yasukuni]," *Asahi Shimbun,* July 21, 2006, 1. In addition, previous surveys showed that when the question was framed in terms of whether the prime minister should stop visiting the shrine in order to avoid displeasing neighboring countries, opinion data tended to come out more strongly in favor of visiting the shrine. Evidently, many Japanese feel that they should not give in to what they see as bullying by foreign countries.

74. "Abe-shi: 8-Gatsu 15-Nichi Wa Sampai Sezu [Mr. Abe Will Not Visit the Shrine on August 15]," *Asahi Shimbun,* July 23, 2006, 3.

75. See "Nitchū, Kankei Kaizen de Itchi [Japan and China Agree to Improve Relations]," *Asahi Shimbun,* October 9, 2006, 1. For an analysis of diplomacy in the early days of the Abe administration, see Sheila Smith, "Abe Shinzo's Diplomatic Debut."

76. Abe is said to have been profoundly influenced by his grandfather, and he writes admiringly about him in his political manifesto: Abe, *Utsukushii Kuni e,* 18–29.

77. On the one hand, Abe in his New Year's address on January 1, 2007, stressed his commitment to improving relations, and changes have been made to the historical museum, the Yūshūkan, at Yasukuni. See David Pillings, "Abe Puts Relations with China as a Priority," *Financial Times,* January 1, 2007. On the other hand, proposals for removing indicted Class A war criminals from the list of those enshrined at Yasukuni soon ran out of steam after Abe visited China and Korea in the fall of 2006. See "Shibomu A-kyū Sempan Bunshi Ron [The Withering of the Debate on De-enshrining Class A War Criminals]," *Asahi Shimbun,* November 1, 2006, 1. Likewise, Abe remains noncommittal as to whether he will visit Yasukuni in the future. See "Abe Remains Ambiguous over Yasukuni Visits," *Japan Times,*

December 29, 2006.
    78. See Kenneth B. Pyle, "Abe Shinzo and Japan's Change of Course."
    79. Tōgō Kazuhiko, "A Moratorium on Yasukuni Visits," *Far Eastern Economic Review,* June 2006. Available at http:/www.feer.com/articles1/2006/0606/free/p005.html. I would like to thank Ambassador Tōgō for making an advance version of the article available to me.

| 10 |

The Role of Human Rights: The Case of Burma

Catharin Dalpino

For nearly two decades, the political situation in Burma[1] has presented a foreign policy challenge to Japan that affects Tokyo's relations with its major partners, particularly the United States; Japan's role in Southeast Asia; and, most surprising, domestic political dynamics in Japan itself. The stalemate between opposition leader Aung San Suu Kyi and the military junta in Rangoon has forced the Japanese government to give human rights a more central role in foreign policy, if only in this specific case, and has compelled some Japanese to expand their roles as "global citizens." International focus—and pressure—on Japan with respect to Burma were inevitable, given the long-standing "special relationship" between the two countries and the leverage that was assumed to follow from that relationship.

Tokyo's efforts to influence the political situation in Rangoon since the military crackdown in 1988 have tested that leverage and drawn it down. Although these efforts to promote political progress in Burma have been unsuccessful to date, like those of the United States, the European Union, and ASEAN, they have had an impact on dynamics between the Japanese state and civil society over the formulation and conduct of foreign policy. Japanese strategies to influence Burma's political dynamic, and to establish additional channels to Burmese society, have led the government to pioneer new roles for nongovernmental organizations in foreign policy. Ultimately and ironically, Burma may have changed Japan more than Japan has changed Burma.

The Struggle over "Idealpolitik"

Since the end of the Cold War, advanced democracies have tended to assume an evangelical role in the promotion of democracy, attempting to

213

advance the "wave" of political liberalization by providing aid to help new democracies take root and pressuring authoritarian regimes to allow greater political openness. In the early 1990s, with democracy apparently sweeping the globe, political freedoms were held in some quarters to be universal, rather than culturally linked to the Western experience. Japan, with its established democracy, was considered to be proof of that. In contrast to the United States and Europe, however, Japan has been more reluctant, but not completely opposed, to basing its foreign policy on universal values, especially in the Asia Pacific region.

Japan has differed from the West, particularly the United States, on both the substance and style of the promotion of democracy. By the early 1990s, the United States had established itself as a leader in "idealpolitik," with fifteen years of human rights diplomacy initiated during the Carter administration.[2] The dramatic end of the Cold War enabled US policymakers to blend the advocacy of human rights with the promotion of democracy under strong bipartisan support. This has resulted at times in a crusader's approach, setting out goals for countries that, in Tokyo's view, would be difficult if not impossible to reach in the near term. Moreover, the US Congress is increasingly inclined toward automatic policy mechanisms, such as the imposition of sanctions in dealing with gross human rights violations or democratic reversals.

By contrast, Tokyo favors a more incremental approach and one delivered at lower decibels. As a general rule, Japan opts for persuasion over coercion in dealing with the domestic affairs of another country. Moreover, Japanese policymakers tend to resist a uniform formula in this area of foreign policy, leaning more toward pragmatism and an ad hoc approach to each country. This awkwardness and distance between Japan and the West are often seen in the conduct of diplomacy. For example, US diplomats sometimes complain that Tokyo will not join Western countries in joint démarches to authoritarian governments on human rights violations but may make parallel démarches with the same points.[3]

This caution is a relative, rather than an absolute, trend in Japanese policy, however. After the fall of the Berlin wall, Tokyo was willing to depart from previous practice and take a more forward-leaning role to promote democracy in such regions as Eastern Europe and Latin America. Although structural and philosophical changes in Japanese diplomacy and aid were needed to make this shift, it was not politically controversial—both of these regions were well into widespread democratization movements. Clearly, receptivity was a key factor. Indeed, in 1992 Japan officially specified in its ODA charter that attitudes of recipient countries toward democratization and human rights would be key criteria in offering assistance.[4]

In Asia, however, Tokyo has maintained that there are more built-in brakes. Several factors account for this. First, since World War II and the attempt to forge a Greater East Asia Co-Prosperity Sphere, Japan has made a conscious attempt to detach ideology from the promotion of its foreign policy goals, not wanting to appear to force Japanese values on other cultures.[5] As an adjunct issue, some analysts point out that Japan's own political system was in part the product of outside engineering following World War II and that Japanese approach other political systems with resulting sensitivities.[6] Second, the Asian political spectrum is far broader than that of any other region, with regimes ranging from the Orwellian (in North Korea) to the newly democratic (South Korea, Taiwan, Thailand, and the Philippines). With such diversity, even democratic Asian nations are sometimes reluctant to prescribe a common democratic formula for the region. Third, for several decades after the war, Japanese ODA in Asia, particularly Southeast Asia, was closely coordinated (through a practice of "tied aid") in order to secure and protect Japan's raw goods supply and its markets. Moreover, Tokyo has vital security interests to protect in the region. Eighty percent of Japan's oil passes through the Straits of Malacca. Even by the mid-1990s, none of the littoral countries ringing the Straits—Indonesia, Singapore, Malaysia—were democracies.

It would be inaccurate, however, to conclude that Japan's reluctance to confront governments on their political practices signals agreement with those leaders. For example, at the United Nations Conference on Human Rights in Vienna in 1993, Tokyo broke with the rest of Asia to support a resolution affirming the universality of rights. This effectively positioned Japan with the West in the "Asian values" debate that followed for most of the 1990s.

Nor would it be correct to assert that Japan has always avoided a leadership role in promotion of democracy, even in Asia. It was a forceful catalyst for both peace and democratization in Cambodia for much of the 1990s. Prior to the 1991 Paris peace conference, Tokyo helped to bring Cambodian People's Party leader Hun Sen to the negotiating table with diplomatic overtures. These efforts differed from the Western policy of isolating Hun Sen at the time. Japan played a major funding and operational role in the United Nations Transitional Authority in Cambodia, which oversaw transitional elections in 1993.[7] Equally important, in 1997—following the violent breakup of the ruling coalition in Phnom Penh—Tokyo demonstrated that pragmatism could succeed where Western sanctions could not, when Japanese diplomatic efforts achieved a political reconciliation between the warring parties. This success also supported Tokyo's view that efforts to promote democracy require a case-by-case approach.

The same tactics that Japanese diplomats had employed successfully in Cambodia over a decade—reducing isolation, providing timely assistance, conducting shuttle diplomacy—proved to be far less effective in promoting political reconciliation in Burma over the same stretch of time. Moreover, the legal and external factors that helped to nurture, and sometimes force, advances in Cambodian democracy do not exist in Burma. The 1991 Paris Accords committed not only the Cambodian parties but also the regional powers to democracy in Cambodia, so that Tokyo's intervention in the 1997 regime split in Phnom Penh could have been viewed as honoring the obligations it had adopted in signing the treaty. In Rangoon's eyes, however, foreign powers who are attempting to broker political reconciliation are hardly legitimate actors.

Beyond its 1997 shuttle diplomacy, Tokyo's primary and ongoing contribution to Cambodian democracy has been in funding electoral infrastructure; indeed, Japan's willingness to fund elections has been an influential factor in their very continuation in Cambodia. Since the end of the Cold War, Japan has demonstrated that it is generally more comfortable funding the "technical" side of promotion of democracy rather than the ideological side, and Cambodia affords Tokyo regular opportunities to exercise that preference. In contrast, Japan has yet to find a Burma policy that is comfortable and even moderately successful. As a result, despite the innovations that diplomatic desperation has visited upon Japanese policy toward Burma, these new practices may not yield enduring policy paradigms in the near term. Mirroring the experiences of other advanced democracies, Japan's efforts in Burma since the 1990 election have primarily taught policymakers what does not work.

The "Special Relationship"

Without doubt, however, Japan has played a larger role in Burma's development than in Cambodia. This arose out of Japan's historic relationship with Burma, centered largely on World War II. Just prior to the war, Tokyo began to nurture Burma's nationalist movement by recruiting the Thirty Comrades, young officers who were given training in military science and anticolonialism on the island of Hainan, occupied by Japan at the time.[8] Included in the ranks of the "thirty" were Aung San and Ne Win, both of whom were to play historic roles in Burma's postindependence era. This was part of a larger Japanese attempt both to subvert the British administration and to fend off potential attacks by Chiang Kai-shek's forces, by encouraging anticolonialist uprisings that would weaken Japan's enemies. When the occupying Japanese army set up a puppet government in Rangoon—with Aung San as defense minister—they encouraged the perception among Burmese that this was the first independent postcolonial Burmese regime. A more enduring legacy of the early "special relationship" was the establishment of Burma's powerful national army, the *tatmadaw*, which was modeled after the Japanese military rather than that of Britain, the colonial power.[9]

On the Japanese side, the occupation and the large number of war dead in Burma, with some estimates as high as 190,000, gave Japan a large group of families and veterans with a strong, continuing interest in Burma. Following the war, the Japan-Burma Veterans Association was the largest international veterans' association and in due course became a powerful lobby for Japanese government assistance for Burma's development.[10]

Development assistance began with Japanese war reparations to Burma, some $250 million disbursed from 1955 to 1965. Burma was the first country in Southeast Asia to receive reparations from Tokyo; these payments were also the beginning of tied aid to Burma. Funds were used for the construction of a major hydroelectric plant and the production of light and heavy vehicles, agricultural machinery, and electrical goods. To underscore the greater benefit to the donor rather than the recipient, critics point out that all of the projects funded by reparations were implemented by Japanese corporations. They relied on components manufactured in Japan and merely assembled in Burma, without technology transfer.[11] Although Burma became dependent upon Japan as a catalyst and patron of its economic development, it was clear from the beginning that the dependency, although asymmetrical, worked both ways.

The reparations period engendered a peacetime "special relationship." A cadre of Japanese diplomats and technical advisers formed in the 1950s and 1960s, the Biruma-kichigai, or "crazy about Burma." This group was mirrored by a group of Japanese academic specialists on the country. Their interest in Burma was based as much on cultural ties as on economic interest. Japan and Burma share Buddhist values, albeit with different strains—Japanese subscribe to Mahayana Buddhism, whereas Burmese adhere to the Theravada branch of the religion. Beyond this similarity, Burma appealed to the Japanese imagination. Japanese who felt that their country had rushed too quickly into modernization admired the otherworldliness of the Burmese, who seemed determined to adhere to traditional values.[12]

Reparations, which extended into the mid-1960s, were not disrupted when General Ne Win seized power in 1962 and nationalized foreign and domestic enterprises. Following the coup, Ne Win's strongman actions did not interfere with Burma's relations with Japan for the most part; in particular, he was careful to cultivate the Japanese veterans' lobby. Tokyo's practice of separating political and economic goals, along with the Cold War environment in Asia in the 1960s, further smoothed the relationship with democratic powers that placed greater emphasis on keeping Third World regimes out of Moscow's or Beijing's orbit than on the quality of their domestic freedoms.

Ne Win's Burmese Way to Socialism decimated the country's civil service, however, and imposed policies that ultimately led to economic ruin. As a result, in the early 1970s the government reluctantly agreed to cautious measures of economic liberalization that allowed a modest opening to the international community. Already well situated in Burma, Japan played a central role in organizing an international Burma Aid Group.

Bilaterally, the reforms ushered in a new era of Japanese ODA in Burma. From 1978 to 1988, Japan gave US$1.87 billion to Burma, which comprised two-thirds of all bilateral aid to the country at that time. In that time period, Japanese aid to Burma was more than twice that of its ODA to Indonesia. Burma's strategic natural resources, particularly its oil and natural gas, supported Japan's growing economic role in the world. Most Japanese-funded projects in Burma focused on mining, manufacturing, and energy; few supported human development or health services during this period.[13]

It would be inaccurate, however, to paint Japan's relationship with Burma at this time as completely uncritical or unconditional. Ne Win's reforms proved to be halting at best and did little to put the Burmese economy on sounder footing. This was owing in no small part to rampant corruption, the government's unwillingness and inability to reduce massive and growing debt, and the regime's refusal to relax administrative or political controls. Although Tokyo was primarily concerned with the economic side of reform in Burma, in 1986 it gave Rangoon notice that no new ODA funds would be disbursed as generously until economic reform was deepened and accelerated. In particular, Japanese officials pressed Rangoon to liberalize laws that prevented foreign companies from operating in Burma, in keeping with the official practice of blending the interests of government and corporations in Japanese foreign policy.

Political Conflict in Rangoon

To be sure, Tokyo was not the only entity to display discontent over Burmese government policy and the failure of the economic system. Domestic unrest grew rapidly in Burma in the mid-1980s. Throughout the 1960s and 1970s, student demonstrations against the regime had been mounted sporadically and quickly suppressed. Burmese universities were particular targets of regime surveillance and control and were closed down by the government on occasion. In the mid-1980s, however, a student movement against the government drew strength from the participation of monks, peasants, and other disenfranchised Burmese, demanding greater reforms and an end to the Ne Win regime.

This movement came to an abrupt halt when the Burmese military killed thousands of protesters in Rangoon and other cities in August 1988. On the recommendation of the Japanese ambassador in Rangoon, Ōtaka Hiroshi, as well as considerable pressure from Washington, Tokyo followed suit with the West and suspended economic assistance to Burma in response.

Beyond the obvious moral dilemma, the crackdown created a procedural crisis for Japanese foreign policy. Japanese relations with other countries are on a government-to-government rather than state-to-state basis. This distinction seldom matters when a foreign government transfers power peacefully and according to its own defined political process. An irregular situation, particularly one involving a violent overthrow, however, necessitates a deliberate decision on whether or not to resume full and formal ties with the new government.

A debate on recognition of the reconstituted military regime, now under the control of Aw Muang and named the State Law and Order Restoration Council (SLORC), was waged in the Japanese political system in the fall of 1988. On the front lines, the Japanese ambassador in Rangoon boycotted SLORC ceremonies on the national independence day and generally maintained a critical view of the new regime. In his contact with the new regime, however, he continued to press the recommendations that Tokyo had made to Burmese officials in the mid-1980s, including liberalization of laws that affected foreign business in Burma. As in 1962, the Burmese junta saw no contradiction between domestic political control and maintaining ties with Tokyo. In late 1988, the regime introduced a law that, on paper at least, would have liberalized controls on foreign companies.[14]

In the meantime, Japanese business interests were petitioning the Japanese government to lift the suspension of aid and resume normal relations with Burma. They were represented by the Nihon-Birima Kyōkai, or Japan-Burma Association, which has remained a powerful lobby in Japanese-Burmese relations ever since. At the time, the association's chairwoman was Ōtaka Yoshiko, the wife of the Japanese ambassador in Rangoon, who was herself a friend of Ne Win. This seeming contradiction with her husband's views caused Japanese human rights advocates to question whether the ambassador's position was genuine. More likely, it indicated that, however much the Japanese might disapprove of the junta's repression in 1988, it would not alter the long-term dynamic between Japan and Burma. The Japan-Burma Association feared that withholding recognition and aid would give an opening to other Asian countries to establish preemptive relations with the new regime. In fact, Thailand became the first country to recognize the SLORC when the Thai supreme commander of the armed forces visited Rangoon in late 1988.

In February 1989, Tokyo recognized the regime in Rangoon but did not fully restore relations. ODA was resumed for ongoing projects, but Tokyo withheld funds for any new projects until Rangoon had demonstrated progress on democratization. The political situation was the ostensible reason for this conditionality, however mild, but Tokyo was equally concerned over the ability of the military regime to formulate and implement sound economic policy and to reduce the country's debt.

In the eyes of Japanese officials, this combination of carrots and sticks gave Tokyo leverage to press for further political and economic reforms. To the United States and several European governments, however, Tokyo appeared to have broken ranks with the other industrialized democracies and undermined their attempts to check a ruthless regime.[15] This impression has persisted among Western diplomats to a greater or lesser degree in the years following 1988.

Nevertheless, the Japanese approach initially appeared to be working to some extent. In 1990, the regime agreed to hold national elections, and the opposition party, the National League for Democracy (NLD), was allowed to contest for power, despite the fact that its leader, Aung San Suu Kyi, was under house arrest at the time. The conduct of the election was generally considered to have been fair, and the NLD won with a strong majority. Although the international community briefly considered that Burma was on the road to democracy, the SLORC dashed those hopes by laying the election results aside. That they would do so was less of a surprise than the fact that they had allowed a free election process to go forward in the first place.

There are no direct accounts from the SLORC to explain that decision, but their subsequent nullification of the results suggests that the military had assumed they would win at the polls. Aung San Suu Kyi and her top officers remained under detention, and in 1991 she was awarded the Nobel Peace Prize, solidifying her role as an international icon. To the West, the 1990 election had anointed the National League for Democracy as the legitimate rulers of Burma, and demands on the military regime were two-pronged: the release of Aung San Suu Kyi and other NLD leaders and dialogue with the NLD with the eventual goal of democratic government.

When relations between Burma and Japan were resumed in 1989, six grant projects and nineteen loans that had been in progress were continued. The grants constituted 80 percent of Burma's foreign assistance. By 1992, aid levels had dwindled, owing to the completion of some projects, but they still constituted the overwhelming majority of foreign assistance to Burma, since Western aid had been frozen for several years. In the early 1990s, the conditionality in Japanese aid converged with broader changes in ODA policy, to require recipients to meet markers on reduction in military expenditures; nonproliferation in nuclear, chemical, and biological weapons; and open markets and democratic governance.[16] This sea change in ODA was intended mainly for new recipients, however, primarily the former Communist countries. Ongoing aid clients, even those as draconian as Burma, were grandfathered into the new ODA policy.

Since the 1990 election results were overturned, there have been few discernible gains in Burma's political development. Under continual pressure to release Aung San Suu Kyi, the SLORC has played "dissident poker" with her and other NLD officers, releasing them or softening their detention, only to re-arrest them at a later time. For much of the 1990s, the West encouraged Japan to adhere to a hard line against the regime. Although Tokyo seldom matched the United States and Europe in this regard, a "good cop/bad cop" dynamic developed between Japanese and Western diplomats in Rangoon in pressuring the government on reforms. When Aung San Suu Kyi was released in 1995, Japan was credited as having been a leading factor in persuading the regime in Burma to accede to international demands. The regime encouraged this impression by telephoning the Japanese embassy in Rangoon to announce the decision in advance of her release.[17]

The Burma Debate

By 1996, however, it was clear that neither carrots nor sticks would induce the military regime to negotiate a power-sharing arrangement with the NLD and that the political stalemate would endure indefinitely. By that time as well, a debate within Japan on Burma policy had emerged. The main parties were the powerful Japanese business lobby, primarily the Japan-Burma Association; the Foreign Ministry; and the nascent human rights movement in Japan, which focused increasingly on international issues of Japanese foreign policy. The Japanese Diet also became involved in this debate, with both pro- and anti-engagement factions.

The Foreign Ministry's position could best be summarized as accepting the need to encourage political liberalization and reconciliation in Burma but pursuing those goals through quiet and incremental diplomacy. On balance, Tokyo places greater faith in carrots over sticks and has reinforced small incidents of relaxation by the Burmese regime with humanitarian assistance. When Aung San Suu Kyi was released in 1995, for example, Japan quickly moved to offer support for a Burmese nursing school. In some cases, however, Tokyo's definition of humanitarian assistance for this purpose has come under question. In 2001, to support secret talks between the NLD and the regime, Japan approved a $28.6 million project for reconstruction of turbines in a hydropower dam. Critics charged that the dam would benefit the regime as much as or more than the Burmese people; the Japanese government responded that the plant provided electricity to 20 percent of the nation, including many hospitals.[18]

Tokyo's approach is based not only on its assessment of what will best work in Burma but also on its position in the international community. Japan's position must be consonant not only with Western concerns for democracy and human rights but also with the policies of other Asian coun-

tries, all of which are more inclined toward compromise. ASEAN in particular has been pro-engagement in its relations with Burma, declining to
impose sanctions on Rangoon despite pressure from the West.[19] Moreover,
Japan's role in regional and international organizations has also affected its
policies toward authoritarian countries. Tokyo is a member of the ASEM, an
Asian initiative that has been sharply divided over Burma policy.[20] In international forums, Tokyo has been inclined to follow the Asian line on
Burma. For that reason, it has simultaneously urged the military regime to
establish a dialogue with the NLD while opposing attempts to censure
Burma at the United Nations Human Rights Commission.

Another point is that the Foreign Ministry's approach to Burma mirrors
Japanese policy toward other Asian authoritarian countries, most notably
China. For example, in contrast to the United States and the West, Tokyo
did not suspend assistance to Beijing following the crackdown in
Tiananmen Square in 1989. A radical shift in policy toward either Burma or
China would imply a precedent for policy in the other.

The Japanese human rights community has largely favored a harder line
and a more confrontational approach to Rangoon. The movement on
Burmese human rights has been fueled by a number of developments,
including a growing assertiveness on the part of Japanese nongovernmental
organizations, discussed below. Two more specific factors have spurred
interest in this cause: the presence and role of Burmese displaced persons in
Japan and the Japanese public reaction to Aung San Suu Kyi.

Since 1988, approximately 3,000 Burmese displaced persons have
resided in Japan. These are primarily pro-democracy Burmese students who
fled the military crackdown. They have formed a nucleus of dissidents, with
links to other Burmese exile groups in Australia, India, and Thailand. Some
of these exiles have specific political coloration: the League for Democracy
in Burma, a Japan-based group, is an overseas branch of the NLD.[21]
Moreover, these Burmese in Japan have themselves become the object of a
human rights debate, because Japan has granted very few of them the protection of refugee status. This situation is not specific to the Burmese but
reflects the broader Japanese reluctance to admit large numbers of refugees.
Since the inception of Japan's most recent refugee policy, in 1982, only a
small number of displaced persons have been given refugee status, most of
them from Indochina.[22]

A more diffuse but broader factor in Japanese human rights policy
toward Burma has been the effect of Aung San Suu Kyi on the Japanese
people. Her Asian heritage has made her more popular than other high-profile international dissidents. Moreover, the historical ties between Japan and
her father, General Aung San, reinforce present-day interest in her. The
Japanese media have kept her plight and her image alive, and the Diet has
responded to public interest in her with petitions for her release.[23] This col-

lective pressure has had an impact on the Foreign Ministry. Since 1990, Japanese diplomats have consistently urged that the junta recognize Aung San Suu Kyi as a dialogue partner and have helped maintain her international legitimacy as a result.[24] This degree of attention to an individual opposition leader demonstrates one of the difficulties democratic governments face: that of formulating effective policies in the face of such strong public interest. Like their Western counterparts, Japanese officials have fallen into the trap of defining their human rights policy in Burma almost solely in terms of Aung San Suu Kyi's treatment by the regime, drawing attention away from more deeply rooted problems in Burma's ruling elite and political system.

In contrast to the Japanese human rights community, the business community had consistently lobbied the Japanese government for the resumption of full relations and economic assistance (particularly that which could be tied to Japanese contracts) since 1988 without a significant regard for the human rights aspects of Burma's situation. By the mid-1990s, business associations began to step up direct ties with the government in Rangoon, out of impatience with the Japanese government's dilemma over this issue.

In 1994, Keidanren, the Federation of Economic Organizations, sent a large delegation to meet with top Burmese officials, which resulted in many Japanese companies' opening branch offices in Rangoon. The mission was a springboard for visits by individual Japanese companies to broaden their business contacts and projects. Notable examples included Daiwa Securities' 1994 agreement with the SLORC to help establish a stock exchange in Rangoon and the reopening of branches of the Bank of Tokyo and Fuji Bank in 1995.[25] By 1996, Keidanren had established a formal Japan-Myanmar Economic Committee.

Much of this activity has been prepositioning Japanese companies for a time when investment in Burma will be more profitable and more secure. The human rights debate over Burma has obscured the reality that the Burmese economy under the SLORC has been anything but healthy or stable. Nevertheless, most of the major Japanese companies have some representation in Rangoon at this time, however skeletal. Beyond planning for better times, the business community is increasingly concerned with the growing portion of Burmese business that has gone to other Asian countries, particularly those in Southeast Asia. With Burma's entry into ASEAN in 1996, the shares of the top-tier ASEAN countries in Burma—Singapore, Malaysia, and Thailand—have risen rapidly.

This fear that Japanese business was slipping too far behind was the likely catalyst behind Japan's breaking its own ban on new projects in Burma in the late 1990s. In February 1998 the Japanese government announced a $20 million loan for the renovation of Rangoon's Mingaladon International Airport. Once again, Tokyo tried to justify the move as a humanitarian one that would prevent air crashes, but it was sharply criticized by the United States and by Aung San Suu Kyi. In the wake of the airport uproar, Japan made a number of smaller new grants, including one intended to encourage the cultivation of buckwheat (the base for Japanese *soba* noodles) as an export commodity and a crop substitute for opium in the Burmese border provinces of the Golden Triangle.[26] By 2003, however, after the regime's re-arrest of Aung San Suu Kyi, aid was once again suspended. All of the constituent elements of Japan's Burma debate have had to contend with an essential fact: as long as the junta's actions toward the political opposition are cyclical, so will be Japanese policy.

Civil Society Weighs In:
The Rise and Role of Japanese NGOs

A counterweight to Japanese government and business interests advocating a business-as-usual approach eventually emerged in the form of a Japanese civil society movement concerned with human rights abuse in Burma and the Japanese response to the Burmese human rights situation. This group, although slow to mobilize after the 1988 crackdown in Rangoon, was led by human rights NGOs. The growth of this movement was bolstered by the growing role of Japanese nongovernmental organizations in the broader Japanese policy equation.

The development of Japan's nongovernmental sector was a function of dramatic Japanese economic growth in the 1960s and 1970s and of Japan's attempt to find a more assertive role in international affairs in the 1980s and 1990s. As in other developed countries, the Japanese NGO sector performs a range of functions, from the provision of social services to citizens' advocacy in the policy process. Corporate philanthropy has been a major catalyst in the development of NGOs in Japan. Following the interests of Japanese corporations in foreign investment, many business foundations established offices and programs abroad, particularly in Asia.

In the post–Cold War era, however, globalization and the international focus on human rights and democracy have stimulated the growth of advocacy NGOs, which tend to be smaller and more specialized. These NGOs have been particularly important in inserting human rights concerns into a foreign policy process that had previously assumed a close relationship between Japanese government and business. Building influence has been difficult in a policy climate that had traditionally been suspicious of citizens' advocacy.

As a result of both of these trends, Japanese NGOs have been able to establish themselves to the point that they are an accepted tool in Japanese diplomacy as well as actors in the national political debate. In 2002, the government established the position of Japanese ambassador in charge of NGOs and matched that with increased government support for NGOs. Policymakers had discovered that Japanese NGOs working abroad increased Japanese visibility and influence. And, as in other advanced democracies, the Japanese government found that working through NGOs allowed more assistance to be funneled directly to the grassroots level and was often a more effective use of funds.[27]

The human rights movement in Japan concerning Burma has produced an impressive range of NGOs of both kinds, those that advocate for policy change and those that support government assistance objectives abroad. This range of NGOs falls into three categories. First, the Japanese branches of international human rights watchdog groups, particularly Amnesty International, have paid particular attention to Burma. Second, a range of NGOs has emerged from the Burmese exile community in Japan. These are primarily political organizations, such as the Japanese branch of the NLD, but they also include a branch of the Burmese Women's Union and the Burma Youth Volunteer Association. Beyond their media campaigns and petitions to the Diet and executive branch, these groups are intended to serve as contacts with their counterparts in Burma; if political space in that country opens up, they would be the natural organizations through which to funnel Japanese support for Burmese civil society. A third group of NGOs is exemplified by the People's Forum on Burma, a Japanese group that provides assistance to Burmese displaced persons in Japan.[28]

No less instrumental in the Burma debate are Japanese NGOs that operate abroad and have had a presence in Burma. These have included Bridge Asia (Japan); the Organization for Industrial, Spiritual, and Cultural Advancement (OISCA) International, an umbrella group of Japanese NGOs working abroad; and the Japan International Volunteer Center (JVC), with a broad agenda including community development, peace advocacy, and emergency relief.[29] Such groups afford Japanese diplomats and other government officials greater flexibility in Burma and in Burma policy. By their use of Japanese government funds, these NGOs give the Japanese government a channel for direct contact with the Burmese people that is otherwise difficult to establish in a population under tight governmental control. They are also silent advertisements for greater pluralism, since they export Japanese civil society to some extent. Grassroots Burmese have contact with Japanese civil society organizations that have no parallel in Burma at present.

Another function, as Western governments have discovered through their extensive use of "quangos"—"quasi-nongovernmental organizations"—and NGOs that contract with government, is that Japanese NGOs provide Tokyo with a certain amount of deniability. Suspension of official ODA can be softened (and even circumvented) by the use of Japanese

NGOs to implement humanitarian and other projects in Burma. To be sure, Japanese NGOs are perceived, by the Burmese government if not the people, to be part and parcel of the official Japanese presence in Burma. In this case, the flexibility and deniability may be with the international community rather than within Burma.

Nevertheless, whatever the scenario, the use of NGOs in Japan's policy toward Burma is only likely to increase. Until the regime in Rangoon agrees to political reforms, NGOs may be the main instrument through which Tokyo can pursue some of its policy objectives. If and when the Burmese political system does begin to democratize, Japanese NGOs will provide a rapid response system that will enable Japan to expand its presence in Burma to the extent that new political space allows.

Conclusion

By now it is obvious to the external actors in Burma's political drama—Japan, the United States, the European Union, and ASEAN—that their ability to persuade or coerce the regime to adopt democratic reforms is minimal. To date, neither the Western hard line nor the Asian inclination toward compromise has proved to be effective or even to be marginally better than its opposite approach. Since Aung San Suu Kyi's most recent arrest in 2003, Japan and the West have been more in sync with a harder line toward Rangoon.

Two factors in Burma's political situation may prompt the pendulum to swing back toward a greater emphasis on engagement, however. First, since the mid-1990s China has taken advantage of the industrialized democracies' relative distance from the regime in Rangoon to strengthen its political, economic, and security relations with Burma. As a result, China has dramatically outdistanced Japan in the levels and complexities of its assistance and investments in Burma.[30] China has supplied Rangoon with $1.6 million in military aid and has created infrastructure to facilitate the two countries' trade and security cooperation. Beijing has a particular interest in establishing a strategic presence on the Bay of Bengal, and Chinese migration has changed the cultural mix of northern Burma.[31] Japan's increasing concern over strategic cooperation with China in Burma could move the government to restart a vigorous campaign to restore Japanese influence in Rangoon.

India, which has focused increasingly on Burma in its "Look East" policy since the early 1990s, is equally if not more concerned with China's growing security presence in Burma. India's democracy is as old as Japan's, and like Tokyo, New Delhi has a mixed record on democracy promotion. In recent decades, democracy on India's strategic rim—in Sri Lanka, Nepal, and Bangladesh—has brought greater instability. Although Washington has expressed hopes that India's increased attention to Burma will cause it to adopt democracy as a policy plank, there is little to support this notion in India's recent regional behavior.

Second, a shakeup in the regime structure in Rangoon in late 2004 ousted Prime Minister Khin Nyunt and moved hard-line officials into top positions of power. Than Shwe, the victor in this process, has exhibited xenophobia unusual even for a Burmese leader, to the extent that he has moved the capital from Rangoon to Pyinmana, a remote jungle outpost. The new regime has also moved to constrict and in some cases expel foreign NGOs. The reshuffle left Tokyo with weaker lines of communication with the regime and fewer channels for contact with Burmese society. Khin Nyunt had been Tokyo's primary interlocutor through much of the 1990s, as he had been for most of the external powers. As the designated contact point, foreign governments had tended to ascribe more liberal values to him than to other regime members, despite the fact that Khin Nyunt had been head of Burmese military intelligence.[32] Nearly all Japanese policy objectives—ranging from influencing the regime to reconciling with the political opposition, to advancing economic interests—will eventually require, however, that Tokyo establish closer ties with the current government in Rangoon, whatever its character.

With nearly twenty years of political stalemate in Burma as instruction, it is obvious to all actors in the Burma debate that the "special relationship" between the two countries is waning. To influence the course of political development in Burma, Japan will have to consider measures to put Japanese-Burmese relations on a new footing. That process is sure to keep the internal debate over Burma policy alive in Japan indefinitely.

Notes

1. In 1989, the military government changed the country's name to Myanmar and the capital's name to Yangon. The US government and most pro-democracy groups continue to use the name Burma, although many Asian governments have adopted the use of Myanmar. This chapter uses the names Burma and Rangoon, except when the new titles are used in the names of foreign organizations, such as the Japan-Myanmar Economic Committee of the Keidanren (the Federation of Economic Organizations).

2. "Idealpolitik" emphasizes the importance of ideologies and values in foreign policy. See Kober, "Idealpolitik."

3. Author's 2004 confidential interviews with US diplomats serving in three Asian embassies, 1993 to 2000.

4. Takeda, "Overcoming Japan-US Discord in Democracy Promotion Policies."

5. Ibid.

6. See, for example, Alston, "Transplanting Foreign Norms: Human Rights and Other International Legal Norms in Japan."

7. This position reflected not only Japanese concerns with peace and democracy but also a desire to take a more operational role in international interventions. Prior to the UNTAC process, Japan had been widely regarded by the West as the bankroll for international peacekeeping efforts—sometimes dubbed "checkbook diplomacy"—and Tokyo was anxious to have more decisionmaking power in such interventions. (Author's interview with Japanese officials and diplomats involved in the 1991 Paris Accords for Cambodia and the 1991–1993 UNTAC period.)

8. Seekins, *Japan's "Burma Lovers" and the Military Regime.*

9. Ibid.

10. Badgley, "Reconciling Burma/Myanmar: Essays on U.S. Relations with Burma," 19.

11. Usul and Debenham, *The Relationship Between Japan and Burma.*

12. Seekins, *Japan's "Burma Lovers."*

13. Ibid.

14. Usul and Debenham, *The Relationship Between Japan and Burma.*

15. Seekins, "The North Wind and the Sun: Japan's Response to the Political Crisis in Burma, 1988–1996."

16. Usul and Debenham, *The Relationship Between Japan and Burma.*

17. Author's confidential interview with Japanese diplomats serving in Rangoon in the mid-1990s.

18. Crampton, "Japanese Grant Rewards Burmese Talks."

19. In 2004, Senator Mitch McConnell, chairman of the Subcommittee on Foreign Operations, Senate Appropriations Committee, attempted to impose sanctions upon Thailand in an effort to force Bangkok to take a harder line toward Rangoon. Although McConnell's measure did not pass, it was a warning shot across the bow that ASEAN could be held liable for lack of progress in Burma.

20. For an exploration of the implications of Japan's membership in ASEM, see Isami Takeda, "A Third Stage in Europe-Asia Relations."

21. "Activists Urge Total Ban on Investments in Burma," Mizzima News Group, November 30, 2000. Available at http://www.rebound88.net/00/dec/01.html.

22. Watanabe, "Japan's Burma Refugees: Time to Change Tokyo's Status on Refugees."

23. Seekins, "The North Wind and the Sun: Japan's Response to the Political Crisis in Burma, 1988–1996."

24. Oishi and Furuoka, "Can Japanese Aid Be an Effective Tool of Influence? Case Studies of Cambodia and Burma," 902.

25. Seekins, "The North Wind and the Sun: Japan's Response to the Political Crisis in Burma, 1988–1996."

26. Seekins, *Japan's "Burma Lovers" and the Military Regime.*

27. Ochi, "NGOs Activities Are Effective Diplomacy."

28. Burma Youth Volunteer Association of Japan, press release.

29. Burma Fund, *Civil Society and Non-Governmental Organizations in Burma.*

30. Badgley, "Reconciling Burma/Myanmar: Essays on U.S. Relations with Burma."

31. Dalpino and Steinberg, "Southeast Asia Looks North: New Dynamics with China," 43–52

32. Seekins, *Japan's "Burma Lovers" and the Military Regime.*

| 11 |

Dealing with a Rising China
Mike M. Mochizuki

If history is any guide, the emergence of a new great power can lead to a cycle of hegemonic rivalry and war. The rise of China certainly presents such a systemic challenge. But is it possible to escape this trap of history and avoid the kind of international conflict that accompanied the emergence of France, Germany, Japan, or even the Soviet Union?

Because of its modest size relative to China in terms of population and territory, Japan is unlikely to play the central role in dealing with the systemic problem of China's rise. That task will surely go to the United States. As the world's sole superpower in terms of economic and military capability and the primary architect of the existing international order, the United States is likely to take the lead on the China question. The bilateral interaction between China and the United States will be the key determinant in shaping how the world handles this international power transition.

But even as a middle power that is unable to define the basic parameters of international relations, Japan will still be an important factor.[1] Its geographic proximity to China, its superior industrial and technological assets, and its military potential indeed make Japan a significant variable in the Sino-US relationship. A Japan that continues to align with the United States will enhance US leverage and help sustain its preponderant power even as Chinese capabilities grow. A Japan that sides with China, however, will weaken US leverage over China and might even undermine the predominant status of the United States in the world system. The one scenario that would dramatically diminish the Japanese factor is one in which China and the United States establish an international condominium that makes Japan strategically irrelevant.

Theorists of international relations differ regarding the best way to deal with rising great powers so as to avoid hegemonic war.[2] Some argue that effective balancing against a rising power will help to limit its ambitions and deter it from launching a war to revise the existing international order. Others argue that the primary interests of the rising power should be accommodated or appeased so that this power would have more reason to embrace the existing order and become a "stakeholder" and less cause to challenge the order through military means. Both sides of this theoretical debate stress the weaknesses of the other.

Those who advocate balancing and robust deterrence believe that accommodation or appeasement will only whet the rising power's appetite and increase its international ambitions. By the time the existing great powers find this behavior intolerable, the only recourse left will be war. Therefore, it is far better to balance against a rising power early on and contain both its behavior and ambitions.

Those who recommend accommodation or appeasement counter that balancing and robust deterrence will provoke the rising power and undermine efforts at international cooperation. Rather than embracing the existing international order, the rising power will augment its military capabilities and diplomatic position until it feels ready to militarily challenge that order. In short, a tough strategy is unlikely to yield a stable equilibrium. More probable is a vexing "security dilemma" in which efforts by one party to promote its security interests threaten the security interests of the other.[3] The outcome would then be an unstable arms spiral and an atmosphere of distrust in which even a minor spark could ignite a war.

Historians have analyzed the past on behalf of both perspectives without any decisive resolution of this debate. Therefore, instead of pursuing a strategy based on one theory to the exclusion of the other, policymakers have tended to adopt a mixed approach or a "hedging strategy" that involves both balancing and accommodation.[4] A variety of factors will affect the concrete mix between these two approaches: changes in the relative balance of power, the behavior of the rising power, the nature of the issue area, and domestic politics and perceptions regarding the rising power.

But evaluating the efficacy of a strategy toward a rising power will hinge ultimately on what kind of response that strategy evokes from the rising power itself. The danger of a mixed strategy is that one aspect of the strategy may weaken the other aspect. For example, the balancing component might undermine an effort to achieve a stable accommodation. Conversely, the accommodation element might jeopardize the deterrence function of balancing. Therefore, national leaders will have to adjust their policies in response to the actions of the rising power.

This chapter describes and explains the recalibration of Japan's policy toward China since 1972. It will show how Japan has gradually shifted from a primary emphasis on accommodation to a mixed strategy of engagement and balancing. Although this shift has resulted largely in response to China's increasing capabilities and its behavior, it also reflects a change in the politics of China policy in Japan itself. The injection of the "balancing" element suggests that the possibility of Japan's accommodating or appeasing Chinese interests to the strategic detriment of the United States has diminished. Indeed, the "balancing" aspect of Japan's policy toward China has become more pronounced as China's capabilities have increased.

To some, this shift toward "reluctant realism" in Japan's dealings with China demonstrates how a problematic history and inevitable geopolitical rivalry will mar relations between Japan and China.[5] Others even go so far as to say that Sino-Japanese relations will be so fraught with tension that the critical challenge for Washington will be to foster better relations between Tokyo and Beijing. But for Japan, the optimal outcome continues to be sustaining a close alliance relationship with the United States while developing stable ties with China.

Postnormalization Policy Regime

The 1972 normalization agreement established the basic framework for the development of Japan's subsequent policy toward China. On Taiwan, Japan declared that it "fully understands and respects" the Chinese position that "Taiwan is an inalienable part" of its territory.[6] Resisting Beijing's insistence that Tokyo terminate Japan's 1952 peace treaty with Taiwan, Japan finessed this issue by referring to the Potsdam Proclamation, which declared that Taiwan should be returned to China after World War II. Although Japan terminated its diplomatic relations with Taiwan, Zhou Enlai in the context of the normalization talks suggested China's willingness to permit Japan's economic and cultural ties with Taiwan to continue.[7]

Concerning the history issue, Japan stated that "[it] is keenly aware of and deeply reflects on its responsibility for the great injury it had inflicted in the past on the Chinese people through war."[8] China in turn "renounced its demand" for reparations from Japan.

Regarding the security dimension, the two countries confirmed that they would resolve all disputes between them through peaceful means under the principles of the UN charter and would not use force or the threat of force. They declared that the normalization of bilateral relations was not directed against a third country. In addition to agreeing not to seek hegemony in the Asia Pacific region, China and Japan stated that they would oppose attempts by another country or group of countries to establish hegemony. Although the normalization communiqué was silent about Japan's security relationship with the United States, China did not demand a revision or abrogation of the US-Japan defense pact as a precondition of normalization. Nor did it insist on excluding Taiwan from the concept of the "Far East" that defined the treaty's geographic scope for US security responsibilities. Indeed, Tokyo reassured Washington that the cessation of diplomatic relations with Taiwan would not change the position of Taiwan in the context of the US-Japan security treaty.

After his election as prime minister in 1972, Tanaka Kakuei moved swiftly to normalize relations with China in order to prevent the mobilization of strong opposition from the pro-Taiwan group within his own Liberal Democratic Party, especially members of the Fukuda faction. Despite the political controversy that the China-Taiwan issue had provoked before 1972, Japanese political elites and the public saw Tanaka's normalization effort as a great success. Even before Tanaka's initiative, pressure to move forward on ties with Beijing had been growing within the Liberal Democratic Party as well as the opposition camp. The humiliation of the July 1971 Nixon shock whereby President Richard Nixon announced his intention to visit China without consulting Japan created a political atmosphere in Japan that Tokyo should normalize relations with Beijing before Washington did so.

Moreover, there was little opposition to the normalization communiqué because the general terms did not sacrifice Japanese interests held dear by those in the right wing of the ruling LDP who had been less enthusiastic about relations with the Communist regime in Beijing. Japan did not have to weaken its defense tie with the United States. It did not have to pay reparations to China, nor did it have to acknowledge that Japan had committed a war of aggression against China or issue an unequivocal apology for its militarist past by using a less ambiguous phrase than *"fukaku hansei suru."*[9] Finally, Japan was able to continue to pursue its commercial interests in Taiwan. It was therefore not surprising that most of Japan applauded Tanaka's opening to China as a great diplomatic success.

But insofar as the normalization agreement reflected compromises and deflected conflict rather than clearly and definitively resolving various controversial issues, frictions between China and Japan inevitably emerged in the postnormalization period. As a general rule, Japanese political leaders and bureaucratic officials responsible for China policy tended to be conciliatory while sustaining the basic parameters of the normalization agreement.

Concluding a bilateral Peace and Friendship Treaty as mandated by the 1972 normalization communiqué presented one of the biggest diplomatic challenges in the postnormalization period. Two issues complicated the negotiations. One was the Senkaku/Diaoyu Islands dispute. During the normalization talks, Tanaka asked for a clarification of the territorial question, but Zhou dodged the issue by stressing that it was a minor problem that should not impede normalization. But in April 1977 when bilateral treaty discussions were under way, armed Chinese fishing boats approached the disputed islands, and some of them rebuffed Japanese coast guard orders to leave Japanese territorial waters. This incident mobilized LDP politicians opposed to the treaty in the first place to get their government to take some action against China. Fukuda Takeo, the prime minister at the time, ordered his diplomats to raise the territorial issue with the Chinese at the highest levels. To forge an intraparty consensus on behalf of the treaty negotiations, Nakasone Yasuhiro, then chairman of the LDP Executive Council, proposed the principle that Japan should protect its territorial rights and national security, but what this meant in practice was never specified.

In the end, Beijing called the incident an accident, and the Chinese fishing boats departed from the scene. Deng Xiao-ping himself told the Japanese that the disputed islands would remain as they were for the time being, meaning that China would not seek to overturn Japan's possession. Although Tokyo did not get Beijing to acknowledge Japanese sovereignty over the islands, China's conciliatory attitude was enough to restrain nationalistic opposition to the peace treaty within the LDP. Furthermore, in sharp contrast to the northern territories dispute with the Soviet Union, because Japan controlled the Senkaku Islands, the Japanese were willing to sidestep the issue with the Chinese—something they were unwilling to do with the Russians.

The other issue was China's insistence on the inclusion of an antihegemony clause. Although the notion of opposing hegemony in the Asia Pacific region was already included in the normalization agreement, the Chinese wanted this concept in the treaty as well because of their keen interest in promoting an international coalition to oppose Soviet expansionism. By contrast, Prime Minister Fukuda wanted to pursue an "omnidirectional" foreign policy, which meant an "equidistant" diplomatic stance between China and the Soviet Union. Therefore, Tokyo pressed Beijing to agree to include a disclaimer that the treaty would not affect either party's relations with third countries—similar to a phrase in the normalization agreement. When Beijing agreed to this disclaimer, Tokyo believed that it had successfully broken the link between the Peace and Friendship Treaty and the Sino-Soviet rivalry.[10]

But to the chagrin of Japanese diplomats, such was not the case. Beijing's ambassador to Japan invoked the antihegemony clause in the Peace and Friendship Treaty to ask for Japanese support for the Khmer Rouge regime in Cambodia. Shortly thereafter, the Soviet Union signed a pact with Vietnam. Washington, at the insistence of President Jimmy Carter's national security adviser Zbigniew Brzezinski, had already begun to favor a broad international coalition that included China as a means of containing the Soviet Union. The Soviet invasion of Afghanistan in January 1980 only reinforced this US strategic orientation. Around this time, the

Soviet Union began to beef up its military presence on the "northern territories" off of Hokkaido that were claimed by Japan. Some Japanese critics of China argued that the Soviet action was a direct response to the Sino-Japanese peace treaty. This turn of events made it impossible to sustain Fukuda's omnidirectional foreign policy.

Those in the conservative camp who were either opposed to or skeptical about the peace treaty with China, however, did not seek to correct this strategic tilt toward China. The fact that Prime Minister Fukuda had taken the lead on the peace treaty made it easier to contain intra-LDP criticism of China. For one thing, the Fukuda faction had many pro-Taiwan members, and this group had locked horns with the Tanaka-Ōhira partnership, which pushed ahead with normalization. But with Fukuda now at the helm, loyalty to the factional boss kept the pro-Taiwan group in check. Second, Ōhira Masayoshi succeeded Fukuda as prime minister in the fall of 1979. As one of the key architects of Sino-Japanese normalization, Ōhira was clearly in favor of good relations with China even if this came at the expense of relations with the Soviet Union. In fact, Ōhira appeared to accept Carter's strategic shift when he abandoned the notion of an "omnidirectional" foreign policy and emphatically declared that Japan was a member of the Western camp.

Finally, the shift away from an omnidirectional foreign policy to a tough stance toward the Soviet Union served the interests of conservatives who wanted to strengthen Japanese defense capabilities and promote security cooperation with the United States. Indeed, many in the pro-Taiwan group within the LDP were hawkish on defense issues and hostile to the Soviet Union. So as the Cold War between the United States and the Soviet Union intensified and Washington normalized relations with Beijing, the old cleavage between the pro-China and pro-Taiwan groups within the LDP became less relevant in foreign policymaking.

Another issue that marred Sino-Japanese relations after normalization was the problem of Japan's militarist past. The Chinese were not completely satisfied with how this issue had been treated in the context of normalization. Premier Zhou himself felt that Japan's expression of contrition in the communiqué was wanting, but Mao Zedong urged him not to allow this matter to delay normalization. Moreover, China not only refrained from demanding reparations but also conceded Japan's point that China did not have a "right" to demand reparations. After normalization, the history issue emerged because of developments within Japan. The most contentious was the textbook controversy. The Japanese press reported in 1982 that the Education Ministry had compelled a progressive scholar to tone down his characterization of Japanese military action against China in high school textbooks. Rather than use the word *aggression,* the textbook screeners, according to press reports, got the author to substitute the word *advance.* As it turned out, the media story was incorrect. The official reviewers had only suggested the revision, but the author had refused. Nevertheless, the Chinese government launched a vigorous campaign criticizing Japan and warning of the revival of Japanese militarism. Rather than refuting these charges, Prime Minister Suzuki Zenkō was apologetic, and in November 1982 the Education Ministry approved new textbook guidelines that stated that "necessary consideration from the viewpoint of international understanding and international cooperation will be given to the treatment of modern and contemporary history regarding relations with the neighboring countries of Asia."[11]

Another example of Japan's conciliatory behavior on the history issue was the question of official prime minister visits to the Yasukuni Shrine. In August 1985, Prime Minister Nakasone Yasuhiro visited the shrine in his official capacity to commemorate the fortieth anniversary of Japan's surrender to allied forces. This gesture provoked anti-Japanese student demonstrations in China and placed Hu Yaobang, chairman of the Chinese Communist Party and a strong supporter of friendly Sino-Japanese relations, in a difficult political position at home. The Chinese government sharply criticized Nakasone's visit to Yasukuni, and Hu called on Japan to evaluate history correctly. To avoid jeopardizing Hu's political position in China, Nakasone cancelled his plan to make another official homage and stated in the National Diet that future visits would be made on a case-by-case basis. He in fact did not make another visit in his official capacity as prime minister. Furthermore, when his education minister, Fujio Masayuki, complained in July 1986 that Japanese textbooks were portraying national history in too negative a light, Nakasone fired his cabinet member so as to mollify the Chinese.[12]

These examples of yielding to the Chinese on the question of history naturally irritated many of the traditional nationalists in the ruling LDP. Nevertheless, Japan's top political leaders were able to keep these sentiments in check in order to prevent a deterioration of relations with China.

The main pillar of Japan's accommodative policy toward China dealt with economics. There was an implicit understanding that in exchange for forgoing its demand for reparations, China would receive economic assistance from Japan. Tokyo met these expectations by providing a series of three generous yen loan packages: ¥330 billion for 1979–1983, ¥470 billion for 1984–1988, and ¥810 billion for 1989–1993. The last government package announced in 1988, which entailed a dramatic increase over the previous two, was the handiwork of then finance minister Takeshita Noboru. As successor to Tanaka and Ōhira as the party boss in charge of China policy, Takeshita sought to use the large jump in aid to soothe Beijing about Japan's trade surplus with China as well as the history issue. In addition to the yen loan programs that fell under the rubric of official development assistance, Japan provided large amounts of capital on a concessional basis through the Japan Export-Import Bank. The Export-Import Bank funds came from the Fiscal Investment and Loan Program, which stood outside the regular budget process.

Despite the vast funds that poured into China, there was virtually no political opposition in Japan. Most conservative politicians and the business community felt that economic aid to China served Japan's long-term economic interests. Others felt that using this aid to promote economic interdependence between China and Japan would serve the political-security objective of preventing China from becoming a hostile power. Those on the liberal side of the political spectrum felt that this aid was the least that Japan could do to atone for its past behavior. This broad political consensus insulated the officials in charge of disbursing the aid from external scrutiny or interference. This did not mean, however, that the Japanese were entirely happy with the bilateral economic relationship. They frequently complained about how unfavorable China was for direct investments. They were dismayed at how abruptly Chinese authorities could cancel large projects or change the economic rules of the game. Although these negative experiences tended to restrain Japanese investments in China, they did not cause the business community or the political world to question seriously the aid programs for China.

The Taiwan issue did not pose much of a complication in Sino-Japanese relations in the postnormalization period. The Japanese were generally satisfied with the separation of politics and economics. While mollifying Beijing by carefully minimizing political contacts with Taipei, the Japanese expanded their commercial and industrial ties with Taiwan with hardly any interference from China. The one Taiwan-related issue that did cause bilateral problems was the Kokaryo student dormitory, located in Kyoto. When Japan's judicial system in 1986 and 1987 upheld court rulings on Taiwan's ownership of this historic dormitory, Beijing charged that Japan was violating both the 1972 normalization agreement and the 1978 peace treaty. Deng Xiao-ping stepped up the negative rhetoric by accusing Japan of being a "chauvinist country" and warning of "growing Japanese militarism." Although Prime Minister Nakasone reassured China by reaffirming Japan's one-China policy, a high-ranking Japanese diplomat vented his frustration over Deng's inflammatory remarks by stating that the Chinese leader had become "hard-headed" with age. Beijing responded with a new round of sharp criticisms of Japan. In the end, top Japanese political leaders and foreign ministry officials, including the prime minister himself, had to apologize for the diplomat's indiscretion.[13]

All of the above episodes demonstrate how willing Japan was to back down in the face of Chinese criticisms. This conciliatory behavior reflected a powerful consensus among Japanese political and bureaucratic elites that

China for historical reasons was a special country requiring special treatment. Although some Japanese nationalists found this "kowtowing" humiliating, their irritation was contained because in terms of substance, neither national security nor economic interests were compromised. The factional structure of the ruling LDP and a "pro-China" opposition camp (especially the Socialist Party and the Kōmei Party) also helped to keep the nationalist Right in check.

The Post-Tiananmen Transition

For the most part, Japan's response to the June 1989 Tiananmen massacre was a continuation of its accommodative policy. Compared to the strong public outcry in the United States, Japanese public reaction was much more muted. Political leaders argued that "the heavy burden of the past" made it difficult for Japan to criticize China or impose economic sanctions. The Foreign Ministry suggested that it would be better to keep economics and politics separate because Japan's promise to assist China's economic development was distinct from humanitarian questions. When the United States and other Western nations began to move clearly in the direction of sanctions, however, Tokyo fell in step by deciding to freeze its third yen loan package to China.[14]

Within a few months after the imposition of sanctions, Japan began to explore how to revive relations with China by dispatching high-level political delegations that included numerous LDP politicians to Beijing. According to some analysts, Japanese leaders may have been trying to gain a diplomatic advantage by moving ahead of the United States in developing better relations with China. Others argue that Japan was simply trying to prevent China from becoming internationally isolated—something that would serve neither Japan's nor the world's interest. By spring 1990, the ruling LDP, the business community, and even bureaucratic agencies such as the Ministry of Finance were clamoring to unfreeze the yen loans to China. The only obstacle that stood in the way was the United States. At a time when US-Japanese economic relations were tense, the last thing Japan wanted to do was to add another contentious issue to the bilateral agenda: China policy. Tokyo therefore waited until the moment was ripe to make its move.

In June 1990, China agreed to allow dissident Fang Lizhi and his family to leave China, and the United States extended most-favored-nation trading status to China. These developments, plus the release of the final report of the US-Japan Structural Impediments Initiative talks, gave Japan the green light. At the G7 summit in July 1990, Prime Minister Kaifu Toshiki announced Japan's intention to resume its aid to China. Four months later, the cabinet formally restored the yen loans.[15] Although the administration of George H.W. Bush too wanted to normalize relations with Beijing, it was hampered by severe domestic political constraints. The Kaifu government faced no such internal opposition. This contrast in domestic politics allowed Japan to play the "good cop" to the US "bad cop" vis-à-vis China after Tiananmen. In fact, many officials in the Bush administration appreciated the role that Japan played in engaging China.

After the restoration of the yen loans and China's appreciation for Japan's help in bringing China back into the international community, Sino-Japanese relations took an upswing. Instead of warning of a revival of Japanese militarism, Beijing did not criticize Japan's decision to participate in UN peacekeeping operations. In fact, President Yang Shangkun stated that China would welcome a greater Japanese contribution to regional peace and development. This positive trend culminated in Emperor Akihito's historic trip to China in October 1992. The trip's success created another China boom in Japan. For example, Kakizawa Kōji, who later became foreign minister in the short-lived Tsutomu Hata cabinet, heralded the arrival of a "new stage" in Sino-Japanese relations in which friendship between Japan and China would become the foundation of East Asian stability comparable to the Franco-German partnership for Western Europe.[16] On the economic front, after many years of hesitation, Japan's direct investments in China finally began to take off. Japanese firms were now attracted by the increasing ability of Chinese consumers to buy high value-added products.[17]

Despite this newfound warmth in Sino-Japanese relations, there also emerged in Japan a significant undercurrent of uneasiness about China that later manifested itself in a less conciliatory posture toward China. This new undercurrent derived from changes at both the international and domestic levels.

At the international level, the end of the Cold War dissolved the notion that China served a strategic purpose of balancing against a common adversary: the Soviet Union. As the Soviet military threat to Japan dissipated while China began to burst with economic energy, it was only natural that Japanese defense analysts started to focus on China as a possible future military threat to Japan. Many LDP politicians found alarming China's 1992 territorial waters law, which unequivocally treated the disputed Senkaku/Diaoyu Islands as Chinese territory. Moreover, Chinese vessels started to intrude in waters close to the islands with greater frequency.

Compared to the reaction of the United States, the Tiananmen massacre did not seem to have much of an impact on Japanese elite views of China. In general, Japan's leadership class appeared to appreciate more the need to maintain internal order in China than the political aspirations of China's democracy movement. But the massacre did have a negative impact on Japanese public attitudes. According to opinion surveys conducted by the

Prime Minister's Office, those Japanese who had friendly feelings toward China plunged from close to 70 percent in 1988 to just above 50 percent right after Tiananmen. Since then, the percentage of those who harbor positive feelings toward China not only has failed to recover to pre-1989 levels but also has generally been on a downward slope. In the same surveys, the percentage of those who did *not* have friendly sentiments toward China jumped from about 25 percent in 1988 to over 40 percent in 1989. In 1996, the percentage of Japanese having negative views of China exceeded those with positive views for the first time since the Japanese government began to conduct these annual surveys in 1978.[18] With this shift in public opinion, those politicians who had been more critical of China than most of their colleagues found a more congenial domestic context in which to vent their frustrations about China.

At the same time, Taiwan's democratization projected a sharp contrast to the repressive tactics of the mainland regime. Although the Japanese government has not conducted opinion polls about Taiwan, there can be no doubt that public views about Taiwan improved considerably as it democratized. In the past, liberal-minded Japanese saw the pro-Taiwan group in the LDP as sympathizers of a reactionary regime. But after Tiananmen, the pro-China group lost its superior moral position relative to the pro-Taiwan lobby. So, unlike the situation during the postnormalization period, pro-Taiwan politicians could now be less shy about expressing their point of view.

In short, the end of the Cold War and the stark juxtaposition of mainland China and Taiwan altered the general political climate for policymaking on China. This change was clearly evident regarding the decision about the imperial visit to China. Despite the overall upward trend in Sino-Japanese relations, there was a remarkable level of opposition in the LDP to the trip. Some conservatives expressed concern that the Chinese might insult the emperor by pressing the history issue. They also found irritating the growing calls within China that war reparations should be sought from Japan. Others reacted strongly against the 1992 Chinese territorial law. In the end, Beijing saw how politically delicate the imperial visit to China had become in Japan, so the government carefully refrained from making hostile remarks that might undermine Prime Minister Miyazawa Kiichi's efforts to forge the necessary LDP consensus for the trip to go ahead. As it turned out, the emperor's trip went extremely well, with the Chinese being gracious hosts. Nevertheless, the intense domestic debate about whether the emperor should go to China demonstrated that the robust political consensus in favor of an accommodative policy toward China had begun to fray.

The making of China policy became further complicated by the dramatic political changes that swept Japan in 1993 and after. First, the 1993 LDP defections and the formation of splinter groups from the conservative camp gave greater voice to those who had been critical of the government's style of dealing with China. For example, Ozawa Ichirō, who was one of the prime instigators of the 1993 LDP split, advocated a more frank and less obsequious approach to China. He believed that China should not be allowed to stand in the way of Japan's assuming a larger international security role. Nor should Japan shy away from criticizing Beijing's authoritarian politics. Although Ozawa's Liberal Party shrank in size, the fact that he and his followers stood outside the ruling LDP allowed them to be less restrained in pressing the Japanese government to be less conciliatory toward China. Similarly, the more progressively oriented LDP splinter group, the New Party Harbinger (Shintō Sakigake), provided a platform for criticizing China from a liberal and pacifist perspective. The existence of such groups outside the LDP in turn encouraged those in the LDP who favored a tougher China policy.

Second, the post-1993 flux in party politics transformed opposition politics. The largest opposition party, the Japan Socialist Party, initially joined forces with the LDP splinter groups, the centrist Kōmei Party and Democratic Socialist Party (DSP), and the New Japan Party to form a non-LDP governing coalition. After the passage of the electoral reform legislation in spring 1994, however, the JSP switched gears and allied with the LDP to form an unprecedented conservative-Socialist coalition government, with Murayama Tomiichi becoming the first Socialist prime minister since 1948. Insofar as the JSP, which changed its name to the Social Democratic Party of Japan in 1996, had traditionally supported good relations with Communist China, its participation in the ruling coalition from 1993 to 1998 provided a voice for foreign policies that would help to keep ties with China on an even keel. But the SDPJ suffered at the ballot box under the reformed electoral system and declined into a marginal political force. In its place, the Democratic Party of Japan emerged as the largest opposition party. The DPJ's core consisted of politicians who had split off from the LDP, those who had been affiliated with the former DSP, and a group from the SDPJ who had turned to the DPJ for electoral survival. Compared to the SDPJ, the DPJ has been a much less stalwart voice for friendship with China through conciliatory policies. For example, in December 2005, then DPJ leader Maehara Seiji noted that China's military buildup and modernization posed a "realistic threat" to Japan.[19]

Third, changes within the LDP itself steered Japan toward a less accommodative posture toward China. Most of the key LDP architects and supporters of "friendship diplomacy" had left the political scene. After the passing and retirement of LDP veteran politicians such as Takeshita Noboru, Hashimoto Ryūtarō, and Nonaka Hiromu, persons of comparable clout have not emerged to press the ruling party toward maintaining friendship with China. Moreover, revisions in the electoral system and political funding laws in order to strengthen the political party as the key unit of political competition diluted the power of the faction bosses over their members. This weakening of the LDP factional system made it virtually impossible to rely on the factions' leaders to get rank-and-file LDP Diet members behind a particular China policy. As a result, discussions about China policy became much more unruly, and nationalistic LDP politicians found more opportunities to demand that Japanese diplomats be more assertive toward China.

In addition to this transformation in party politics, attitudinal changes within the bureaucracy have reinforced the trend toward a tougher China policy. Officials responsible for security policy, whether in the Ministry of Foreign Affairs or the Defense Agency, have increasingly emphasized the potential threats of Chinese military modernization to Japan. Diplomats responsible for relations with the United States have tended to favor stronger ties with Washington even though they may complicate interactions with Beijing. The attitudinal shift has been reflected even in the so-called China school of Japanese professional diplomats. These officials with Chinese-language training and specialization in Chinese affairs had heretofore supported a softer line toward China. But the younger generation of this "China school" has been much less tolerant of Chinese verbal attacks against Japan and more predisposed to treat China like a normal country. For them, China is no longer a special country requiring special treatment.[20]

Engaging and Balancing China

By the time Koizumi Junichirō became prime minister in spring 2001, the "friendship diplomacy" framework was no longer operative.[21] A prime minister's task force that had been appointed to recommend Japan's foreign policy strategy concluded in 2002 that Japan's relations with China would involve a mix of "cooperation and coexistence" on the one hand and of "competition and friction" on the other.[22] Although Japan was not about to abandon its policy of engaging China, it intended to articulate its views and interests to China frankly. Japanese political leaders and officials now believed that it was far better to seek an equilibrium in Sino-Japanese relations based on common interests and mutual respect of differences than on the "illusion of friendship." Therefore, Japan has shifted to a dualistic strategy of engaging and balancing China.

The History Question

The shift in Japan's diplomacy toward China was perhaps most dramatically reflected regarding the question of history. In the early 1990s, Japanese leaders did take important steps toward trying to achieve historical reconciliation with neighboring countries, including China. Beginning with Prime Minister Hosokawa Morihiro's candid remarks in fall 1993 that Japan's military conflict in East Asia was a war of aggression, the Japanese government became more willing to acknowledge the nation's militarist past in a straightforward manner. Indeed, the statement of contrition issued by then prime minister Murayama Tomiichi in August 1995, with the approval of the cabinet, contrasted sharply with previous ambiguous apologies made by Japanese political leaders.[23] Moreover, middle school as well as high school textbooks began to contain clear references to Japan's past militarism and the atrocities committed by its military.

With these steps, many Japanese came to feel that they had sufficiently atoned for their country's militarist past. Some nationalists felt that Japan had even gone too far. A movement of nationalist scholars argued that Japanese young people were now being taught a "masochistic view" of national history. So, in response, this movement produced alternative textbooks that accentuated the positive aspects of Japanese history while downplaying the atrocities committed during the militarist era.[24] By the late 1990s, most Japanese were no longer burdened by guilt about the past when viewing China. Many, in fact, believed that Chinese leaders were using the history issue to gain diplomatic leverage over Japan and were promoting anti-Japanese nationalism in China in order to legitimize their grip on power after the Tiananmen massacre.[25]

In preparation for President Jiang Zemin's historic trip to Japan in 1998, Foreign Ministry officials managed to get political approval for a written acknowledgment that Japan had perpetrated a war of aggression against China in the past. Such a written statement in an official diplomatic document would have been unthinkable even during the heady days of Sino-Japanese normalization of the 1970s. But there were clear limits to how far Japan could go. When South Korean president Kim Dae Jung got from Japan a written apology for the past using the unequivocal word *owabi* (apology) instead of the ambiguous *hansei* (self-reflection), President Jiang sought the same. But when Jiang was not prepared to state that he would put the past behind him as Kim had agreed to do, Prime Minister Obuchi Keizō refused and decided to express only an oral apology using the term *owabi*. Although this was the prime minister's personal decision reflecting his sensitivity to President Kim's courageous stance on the history question, Obuchi's tough stance toward China won praise at home.

Miffed by Obuchi's refusal, during his stay in Japan Jiang used many an occasion to lecture the Japanese about the past—even at the state banquet hosted by the Japanese emperor. But instead of appealing to the public's sense of guilt, Jiang's behavior only irritated the Japanese.[26] Even the liberal-oriented newspaper *Asahi Shimbun* thought that the Chinese leader had gone too far. The politics of China policy in Japan had clearly changed. China could no longer effectively use the so-called history card to make Japan conciliatory.

During the Koizumi prime ministership, his repeated pilgrimages to the Yasukuni Shrine constituted perhaps the most controversial issue in Sino-Japanese relations. Despite strong protests from Beijing, Koizumi refused to concede, in sharp contrast to Nakasone back in 1985.[27] Koizumi declared that his shrine visits were a personal expression of mourning for the Japanese war dead who had sacrificed their lives for their country. He insisted that by going to Yasukuni, he was not denying Japanese aggression against China, nor was he honoring Class A war criminals who had been enshrined at Yasukuni in 1978. Although many LDP leaders, senior diplomats, and influential business executives counseled Koizumi to refrain from further shrine visits, the more Beijing protested, the more the Japanese public appeared to support Koizumi for standing up to China. Many Japanese began to feel that China was behaving rudely by refusing to hold summit meetings with Japan just because of the Yasukuni issue.

From Koizumi's perspective, he probably believed that he was being conciliatory on the history issue. For example, to repair the diplomatic damage caused by his first visit to Yasukuni in August 2001, Koizumi made a historic stop at the Marco Polo Bridge, the site of the military clash that triggered the second Sino-Japanese war in 1937, and viewed the exhibits in the Memorial Museum of Chinese People's Anti-Japanese War. Expressing his "heartfelt apology and mourning," he vowed that Japan had learned the lessons of the past and that it must "never again fight a war."[28] Unlike Nakasone's shrine pilgrimage on August 15, 1985, Koizumi emphatically stated that his visits were undertaken in a private capacity. And to accommodate Chinese feelings, during his first five shrine pilgrimages as prime minister he refrained from going to Yasukuni on August 15, the day of Japan's surrender and of China's liberation from Japanese rule, although he had promised to go on that solemn day when he was campaigning for the top political office back in spring 2001. But when these considerations did not stop China from criticizing him, he culminated his tenure in office by making his sixth and final visit to Yasukuni on August 15, 2006. A *Mainichi* newspaper poll taken after this visit indicated that 50 percent of those surveyed supported Koizumi's action, whereas 46 percent opposed it.[29]

Economic Relations

The economic dimension of Japan's policy toward China has also undergone substantial change. During the heyday of "friendship diplomacy," Japan saw China as an economically backward country that Japan could help develop by providing ODA. In the minds of some, this ODA to China also served as a way to win China's friendship by compensating for the wrongs Japan had committed against China in the past. But by the late 1990s, domestic criticisms against Japan's generous aid programs had mounted. Some complained that the Chinese expressed hardly any gratitude for this assistance, and others claimed that Japanese aid had been indirectly helping China to modernize its military capabilities. Critics pointed out that the sharp increase in Chinese military expenditures made aid to China a violation of Japan's principles on official development assistance. The calls for a thorough review of economic aid to China came not only from nationalists in the LDP but also from progressive politicians in the opposition camp. The ballooning national budget deficit reinforced this sentiment. With Japan's economy stagnating and China's economy booming, why should Japan continue to provide aid to China—an emerging economic competitor of Japan? Because of this growing pressure, Foreign Minister Kōno Yōhei informed his Chinese counterpart in May 2000 that Japan would be reassessing its future assistance programs. After a multiyear dialogue between Japan and China, in March 2005 the ruling LDP approved a government plan to terminate the concessionary yen loans to China by 2008— the year of the Beijing Olympics.[30]

In addition to this phasing out of Japanese economic assistance to China, Japan departed from its long-standing practice of separating economics and politics in its dealings with China. The new politics of China policy became clearly evident in Japan's response to China's nuclear tests in 1995. After the May 1995 test, Tokyo protested by scaling back its grant economic aid to China. But when China detonated another nuclear device in mid-August, right after the fiftieth anniversary of the Hiroshima and Nagasaki atomic bombings, Japanese reaction was more severe. A number of Diet members pressured the Foreign Ministry to reduce the yen loans as well as to completely suspend the grant aid. Put on the defensive, the ministry decided to freeze all of the grant aid scheduled for 1995. What was striking about this episode was that right-wing nationalists and left-wing pacifists had formed a tacit coalition in favor of sanctions. Moreover, some Foreign Ministry officials in the so-called China school did not vigorously oppose the harsher measures. In fact, it was a China specialist in the MOFA's Economic Cooperation Bureau who backed the grant aid freeze within the bureaucracy. Beijing criticized the action by raising the history issue. Then Premier Li Peng declared that "Japan should never try to apply pressure on China by economic means" when "Japanese militarist aggression inflicted such great damage upon China as to dwarf the Japanese government credits so far extended."[31] But in Japan's new political climate, Li's statement—rather than appealing to Japan's sense of guilt—only infuriated the Japanese further.

More recently, in March 2006, Japan temporarily put on hold the provision of new yen loans for China. Bilateral conflicts about oil and gas drilling in the disputed EEZ in the East China Sea and about Koizumi's Yasukuni visits prompted Tokyo to use economic aid for diplomatic leverage. But soon after Japanese foreign minister Asō Tarō and Chinese foreign minister Li Zhaoxing agreed during a May 2006 meeting in Qatar to resume bilateral security dialogues as well as promote economic and trade relations, Japan lifted its momentary freeze on yen loans.[32]

Japan also started to compete with China in terms of economic regionalization. Although Japan helped to trigger the regional "bandwagon" in favor of bilateral free-trade agreements by launching FTA studies and negotiations with South Korea and Singapore in 1998 and 1999 respectively, China shocked Japan by responding swiftly in 2000 by proposing an FTA with the ASEAN states.[33] Moreover, China seized the regional initiative by pushing for an East Asian community consisting of the ten ASEAN states plus China, Japan, and South Korea—the so-called APT grouping that emerged in the wake of the 1997 regional financial crisis. But this formulation has worried Japan that with the United States excluded, China's influence would become too great and regional economic rule making and institution building would be more consonant with China's interests than with Japan's. Therefore, Japan has opted to counter Chinese influence by pressing for the inclusion of Australia, New Zealand, and India in an expanded East Asia summit for regional community building. It has also proposed an Economic Partnership Agreement among the APT countries and Australia, New Zealand, and India.[34]

This Sino-Japanese competition regarding economic regionalism does not necessarily preclude cooperation. A case in point is regional financial cooperation. Japanese finance officials understand that China shares with Japan a keen interest in regional financial stability. Although China originally joined the United States in opposing the Japanese proposal for the creation of an Asian Monetary Fund, Japan's finance officials have worked assiduously to get the understanding and support of their Chinese counterparts to develop multilateral arrangements to help stabilize capital flows. These efforts have begun to pay off, as suggested by the growing support for financial cooperation in the APT dialogues.

Japan now has a growing economic stake in China. Despite all the initial concerns that foreign direct investment (FDI) in China might hollow out the Japanese economy, the net effect of China's economic boom has been positive for Japan. Much of the growth in Japanese exports has been directed into the Chinese market. In 2003, Japanese FDI in China surpassed that of the United States.[35] Japan's recent economic revival is in part a result of the commercial benefits Japanese businesses are reaping in the China market.

In addition, Japan is acutely concerned about how China deals with its worsening environmental pollution problem. Numerous studies show that pollutants from China can endanger the health of Japanese through acid rain and other effects. Consequently, since the 1990s, Tokyo has emphasized helping China to enhance its ability to control and reduce pollution. During the 1997 bilateral summit, Prime Minister Hashimoto Ryūtarō proposed the Japan-China Joint Initiative on Environment Toward the Twenty-first Century, which consisted of two pillars. One involves an environmental model-city concept whereby bilateral expert committees recommend air pollution control measures for adoption in various Chinese cities. Depending upon their effectiveness, these measures could then serve as a model for other urban areas in China. The other pillar has been the development of an environmental information network to promote information exchange in China about antipollution measures.[36] Not surprisingly, when Japan lifted its freeze on new yen loans to China, most of the projects that Japan decided to fund related to the environment.

Security Policy

The balancing element in Japan's new approach to China is perhaps most evident in the security realm. Japan has reaffirmed and redefined its defense relationship with the United States so that the alliance can function during a regional security crisis as well as for the defense of Japan. The primary impetus for this move to tighten the alliance was Japan's clumsy response to the Gulf crisis of 1990–1991 and concerns about a military crisis on the Korean peninsula. But there can be little doubt that the Chinese missile tests and large-scale military exercises across the Taiwan Strait in March 1996 motivated Japanese leaders to be more energetic in enhancing defense cooperation with the United States. A month later, Prime Minister Hashimoto Ryūtarō issued a joint security declaration with President Bill Clinton and agreed to revise the 1978 Japan-US defense cooperation guidelines.

As to be expected, Beijing did not welcome this initiative. In the post-normalization period, Chinese leaders had expressed mild support for the US-Japan alliance because it served to contain Japanese rearmament and to balance against the Soviet threat. But with the Cold War over, China felt that a stronger US-Japan alliance was unnecessary. Indeed, an alliance that could function well in a regional security crisis might threaten Chinese interests—especially regarding Taiwan. If Taiwan believed that Japan as well as the United States would actively come to its defense, Chinese analysts feared that Taipei would be less willing to accept Beijing's terms in cross-strait talks and that, at worst, Taipei would be encouraged to move toward formal as well as de facto independence.[37] Furthermore, the very notion that Japan might assist US military intervention over Taiwan was anathema to many Chinese, especially those in the military, for historical reasons. China therefore pressured Japan to explicitly exclude Taiwan from the geographic scope of the new guidelines that were announced in the fall of 1997.

The issue provoked an intense debate within Japan.[38] Dovish politicians and commentators argued that Japan should state firmly that it would not assist military intervention during a Taiwan crisis. This sentiment was not limited to those in the opposition camp. In fact, there were reports that then LDP secretary-general Katō Kōichi had told both Chinese and Americans that the guidelines should exclude Taiwan. Hawkish politicians such as then chief cabinet secretary Kajiyama Seiroku felt otherwise. He stated in a television interview that Japan should provide logistical support to US forces if they were being deployed to defend Taiwan from a Chinese invasion. Ozawa Ichirō in the opposition camp concurred.

In the end, the Japanese government finessed this issue. It painfully argued that the notion of "contingencies in areas surrounding Japan" contained in the guidelines was not geographic in nature. In so doing, officials left ambiguous whether or not Japan would provide rear-area support during a Taiwan contingency. When Takano Norimoto, director-general of MOFA's North American Bureau, "slipped" by suggesting that Taiwan might apply because it fell within the scope of the "Far East" concept articulated in the US-Japan Security Treaty, Prime Minister Hashimoto had him fired to placate the Chinese. Hashimoto also publicly stated that Japan not only continued to adhere to its "one-China" policy but also did not support the independence of Taiwan. One might interpret these verbal maneuvers as proof that Japan was sticking to its conciliatory approach to China. But just as important was the fact that Japan refused to exclude Taiwan from the guidelines. It left open the possibility that Japan might aid US forces during a Taiwan crisis—and that was enough to alter Chinese strategic calculations.

Soon thereafter, Japan took the matter a step further. After North Korea's August 1998 Taepodong missile launch, Tokyo became more supportive of collaborating with the United States on theater missile defense research and development. Although the immediate catalyst for this policy shift was again North Korea, the initiative had profound consequences for the Taiwan question. The favored advanced missile defense system in Japan's defense establishment is a naval one that can be deployed on Aegis-equipped destroyers. But the problem with this system from China's perspective is its mobility, which makes it possible, at least in theory, for Japan to deploy these systems near Taiwan to defend the island from Chinese ballistic missile threats. Of course, the decision by Japan to cooperate with the United States to research and develop missile defense is a far cry from actually acquiring and deploying a naval missile defense. In addition to strong Chinese opposition to such a course, there remains a myriad of domestic political and legal obstacles. But as in the case of the guidelines controversy, Tokyo has left open the possibility that Japan could in the future have sea-based systems.

In addition to the Taiwan question, Japan's security relations with China have become complicated because of the overlay of the Senkaku/Diaoyu Islands territorial dispute and energy competition in the East China Sea. Although Beijing and Tokyo have disagreed about the demarcation of the EEZ in the East China Sea for some years, the dispute has escalated because of China's growing energy needs and the prospect that the seabed in the East China Sea may contain large natural gas reserves. Bilateral negotiations on this matter have become deadlocked, and the specter of a military clash is beginning to emerge. A submerged Chinese nuclear submarine was detected in November 2004 in Japanese waters near Okinawa's Ishigaki Island.[39] In early September 2005, Japanese P3-C patrol planes observed a group of five Chinese warships in the contested EEZ area. Around this time, Chinese military reconnaissance aircraft also intruded into the Japanese Air Defense Identification Zone (ADIZ), causing Japanese interceptor fighters to scramble.

According to a September 2005 report in the *Asahi Shimbun*, the Ground Self-Defense Forces (GSDF) have been engaging in a top-secret study of various military contingencies and the appropriate GSDF response to them. The two hypothetical contingencies involving China concern the East China Sea and Taiwan. In the former contingency, the study hypothesizes a deterioration of Sino-Japanese relations and intensification of the resource issue near the Senkaku Islands, causing China to seize some of Japan's outer islands in the area. In this case, Japan would respond by dispatching SDF from Kyushu to Okinawa (the main island and the southern islands such as Ishigaki Island). If Chinese troops were able to land on any of the outer islands (including the Senkakus), then the GSDF would take back the islands after maritime and air SDF operations.[40]

This incipient Sino-Japanese security competition, however, has not diminished Japan's interest in engaging China. By engaging in security dialogues with China, Japan wants to encourage greater military transparency and develop confidence-building measures.[41] During the 1998 bilateral summit, Jiang Zemin and Obuchi Keizō agreed to expand bilateral security dialogues and defense exchanges. Koizumi's visits to Yasukuni caused China to put these exchanges on hold temporarily, but Defense Minister Ishiba Shigeru visited China in September 2003 (the first such visit by a Japan defense minister since 1998). The trip yielded an agreement to enhance defense exchanges, including mutual visits of naval ships. Moreover, in May 2005, the two countries launched a comprehensive "strategic dialogue" to deepen bilateral relations as well as to discuss the management of potential crises.[42]

The Taiwan Question

Since Taiwan's democratization, Japanese have felt a growing affinity toward Taiwan, in sharp contrast to the increasing negative attitudes toward mainland China. In some circles, Lee Teng-hui, the first democratically elected president of Taiwan and a fluent speaker of Japanese, is a hero. Many Japanese now favor deepening interactions between Japan and Taiwan.

Nevertheless, there is little Japanese support for moving away from a one-China policy, and Japanese leaders have repeatedly reaffirmed it. In August 1997, then prime minister Hashimoto emphatically declared that in addition to understanding and respecting China's position that "Taiwan is an indivisible part of the People's Republic of China," Japan does not support Taiwan's independence.[43] In the Joint Declaration issued during the November 1998 summit between Jiang Zemin and Obuchi Keiz, Japan reiterated "its understanding that there is one China" and noted that it "will continue to maintain its exchanges of private and regional nature with Taiwan."[44]

One indicator of how far Japan has been willing to test the limits of Chinese tolerance and Taiwanese expectations regarding Japanese exchanges with Taiwan has been the issue of mutual visits of political dignitaries between Taiwan and Japan. During the October 1994 Asian Games held in Hiroshima, Japan withdrew an invitation to Taiwan president Lee Teng-hui to attend the opening ceremonies while permitting Taiwan deputy premier Hsu Li-teh to do so. Japan also denied a visa to Taiwan presidential office secretary-general Chang Chun-hsiung, who wished to attend Prime Minister Obuchi's funeral in June 2000.

Even after Lee Teng-hui's retirement, the possibility of his visiting Japan has been a sensitive issue for Beijing because of Lee's support for Taiwan independence and his popularity in Japan. But after strong domestic political and public pressure, Japan's Foreign Ministry did permit Lee Teng-hui to visit Japan in April 2001 for a medical checkup. In justifying this visit on "humanitarian" grounds, however, the ministry imposed tight restrictions on Lee's activities while in Japan. And it was successful in discouraging Lee from applying for a visa to attend a student festival at Keio University in the fall of 2002.[45] But in December 2004, the Japanese government decided to allow Lee to make a weeklong trip to Japan as a "tourist" despite protests from Beijing. To placate China somewhat, Chief Cabinet Secretary Hosoda Hiroyuki took the unusual step of urging the media not to cover the Lee visit as well as announcing that no Japanese politicians would make contact with Lee while he was in Japan.

Japan has also accommodated China's concerns about visits by high-ranking Japanese officials to Taiwan. For example, when LDP Diet member

Mizuno Kenichi wanted to visit Taiwan after becoming parliamentary secretary of foreign affairs (a third-level political appointee), Foreign Minister Kawaguchi Yoriko refused the request even though Mizuno had visited Taiwan in December 2001 as a Diet member. But when prominent Japanese politicians do not hold a top-level official post, they have frequently visited Taiwan. These visits, however, do not indicate that there is increasing Japanese political support for Taiwan independence. As evident in the large overlapping memberships in "pro-Taiwan" and "pro-China" Diet member associations, most political leaders would like to encourage dialogue across the Taiwan Strait and to have the growing commercial interactions between the mainland and Taiwan ease cross-strait tensions.

During the 1990s, Taiwan was an attractive economy for production outsourcing by Japanese firms reeling from the domestic economic downturn. Moreover, from 1997 to 2000, Taiwan was also Japan's second-largest export market after the United States. But after China really hit its economic stride, Japan's exports to China quickly eclipsed those to Taiwan.[46] Nevertheless, Taiwan has linked up with Japan on big-ticket projects such as bullet-train and rapid transit systems.[47] Understandably, for both political and commercial reasons, Taipei has made overtures to Tokyo as well as Washington about negotiating a free-trade agreement, but Tokyo has been cool to the idea because of concerns about Beijing's reaction.

The prospect that Japan could become involved in a Taiwan military contingency has been the most contentious Sino-Japanese issue regarding Taiwan. From Beijing's perspective, Japan's willingness to actively support US operations to defend Taiwan not only complicates Chinese military planning but also encourages pro-independence forces in Taiwan. Caught in the dilemma between being a close ally of the United States and avoiding a further deterioration in relations with China, Japan has continued to follow essentially a policy of "military ambiguity." At least officially, Japan has stated that there is no need to prepare for a Taiwan crisis with joint Japan-US military planning.[48] But in February 2005, Japan took the controversial step of declaring in a joint security statement with the United States that the two countries seek to "encourage the peaceful resolution of issues concerning the Taiwan strait through dialogue." Although both countries had separately made similar statements about Taiwan before, what was significant this time was that Japan and the United States articulated together their common strategic objective regarding Taiwan in the context of increasing bilateral defense cooperation. Not surprisingly, Beijing protested sharply that the joint statement meddled in China's internal affairs and hurt China's sovereignty.[49] But if the pro-independence movement in Taiwan fades over time, as some analysts predict, the role that Japan might play in a Taiwan Strait crisis could diminish as a controversial issue between Japan and China.[50]

Conclusion

In response to the rise of China, Japan has gradually moved away from its "friendship diplomacy" under which Tokyo had tended to be conciliatory toward Beijing in order to contain bilateral frictions. After the 1989 Tiananmen incident and the consequent economic sanctions imposed on China by the advanced industrial democracies, Japan took the lead in reengaging and reintegrating China into the international community. At the same time, the Chinese leadership's brutal repression of the student democracy movement dramatically changed Japanese public attitudes toward China in a negative direction. Furthermore, the use of nationalism by Chinese leaders to legitimate their rule at home had the effect of intensifying anti-Japanese feelings among Chinese citizens. The massive Chinese demonstrations against Japan in spring of 2005 and the Chinese Internet petition campaign to block Japan's effort to secure a permanent seat on the UN Security Council are the dramatic manifestations of this new nationalism.

In the context of Japanese political changes in the post-1993 period, the deterioration in mutual public sentiments between China and Japan as well as China's economic rise and Japan's economic stagnation made it impossible to sustain the "friendship diplomacy" paradigm that had been forged with bilateral normalization in 1972. By the late 1990s, Japan's policy had clearly shifted to a mixed approach of both engaging and balancing against China. While seizing the commercial opportunities presented by China's booming market, Japan is now hedging against a possible threatening China.

Sino-Japanese relations now manifest a combination of centrifugal and centripetal forces. Frictions about the history question, mutual suspicion about each other's strategic intentions, territorial disputes, and competition over potential energy sources in the East China Sea threaten to drive the two countries farther apart. Increasing economic interdependence and common concerns about transnational issues such as environmental degradation are steering the two countries to maintain a cooperative relationship.[51] In some sense, Japan's moderate balancing against China by beefing up its alliance with the United States can contribute to regional stability by deterring and constraining China. But if the centrifugal forces are not checked, then Sino-Japanese tensions could deteriorate further and contribute to regional destabilization—an outcome that neither the United States nor the rest of Asia wants.

Whether Japan's relations with China will slide into a downward spiral or stabilize in a new equilibrium will depend greatly on how leaders on both sides deal with each other and manage their respective domestic politics. Even as Sino-Japanese relations have gotten more troublesome since the mid-1990s, working-level officials in both Tokyo and Beijing have developed bilateral dialogues and mechanisms to solve problems and contain conflicts. And as Japan has become more assertive and less accommodative toward China, China has shown some signs of becoming somewhat more conciliatory toward Japan. Beijing has certainly wanted to avoid driving Japan closer to the United States in an alliance to contain China.[52] But given the complex and contentious issues between Japan and China, strong and courageous leadership at the top in both countries is also required to prevent a downward spiral.

Some have argued that Japan and China should strike a grand bargain to establish "a new era of cooperative and forward-looking bilateral relations."[53] Such a bargain could involve Japan's finding some way to mourn its war dead without inflaming Chinese emotions and China's agreeing to get beyond the history issue and to be more future oriented. To reduce mutual mistrust about strategic intentions, it could encompass more intensive and meaningful security dialogues to promote confidence-building measures and transparency. A grand bargain could also mean greater bilateral cooperation to address common concerns about energy security and efficiency, environmental protection, and social equity while managing bilateral economic frictions amicably. Finally, it could address how Japan and China might work together to build an East Asian community rather than becoming regional rivals. Such a bargain can only be struck if Japan and China's top leaders meet regularly to discuss their mutual interest in such a bargain and to map out a way to achieve it, given their respective domestic constraints.

Prime Minister Koizumi's persistent visits to the controversial Yasukuni Shrine made it difficult for Chinese leaders for domestic political reasons to agree to reciprocal visits by the top leaders of both countries. So much will depend on how his successor, Abe Shinzō, decides to deal with China. Abe is known for his hawkish views on defense policy, his conservative views about Japan's past history, and his tough rhetoric regarding China. At first glance, this might not augur well for a bilateral grand bargain. Precisely because of his nationalistic credentials, however, Abe may have the freedom to maneuver domestically to reach out to China. In fact, by refusing to state publicly whether or not he would go to the Yasukuni Shrine, Abe succeeded in arranging a summit meeting in Beijing with Chinese leaders on October 8, 2006—two weeks after becoming prime minister.

This October 2006 summit dramatically improved the atmosphere of bilateral relations. In the postsummit joint press statement, Japan and China declared that "promoting the continuation of sound and stable development of the Japan-China relations is fundamental in the interest of both countries" and that "contact and dialogue between the leaders were greatly significant for sound development" of bilateral relations. Among other things, the two sides agreed "to make the East China Sea a 'Sea of Peace, Cooperation, and Friendship,'" to enhance mutual trust in the area of security through dialogue and defense exchanges, and to commence joint research of history by Japanese and Chinese scholars.[54] It remains to be seen whether Prime Minister Abe can build on this auspicious start to stabilize Japan's relations with China. A lot will hinge on whether or not Abe decides to forgo making pilgrimages to Yasukuni while in office.

Notes

I would like to thank the Smith Richardson Foundation for its support of my project on Japan-China-US relations, from which this chapter is drawn.

1. On the international role of middle powers, see Cooper, *Niche Diplomacy: Middle Powers After the Cold War.* For an application of the middle power concept to Japan, see Soeya, *Nihon no "Midoru Pawā"Gaikō.*

2. For a recent examination of the theoretical debate about balance of power and power transitions, see Paul, Wirtz, and Fortmann, *Balance of Power: Theory and Practice in the 21st Century.*

3. Herz, "Idealist Internationalism and the Security Dilemma"; and Jervis, "Cooperation Under the Security Dilemma."

4. For an argument that the United States should pursue such a mixed approach toward China's rise, see Thomas J. Christensen, "Fostering Stability or Creating a Monster? The Rise of China and U.S. Policy Toward East Asia." For a discussion of the strengths and weaknesses of a "hedging strategy," see Medeiros, "Strategic Hedging and the Future of Asia-Pacific Stability."

5. Green and Self, "Japan's Changing China Policy: From Commercial Liberalism to Reluctant Realism."

6. "Joint Communiqué of the Government of Japan and the Government of the People's Republic of China," September 29, 1972. Available at www.mofa.go.jp/region/asia-paci/china/joint72.html.

7. Ogata, *Normalization with China,* 53–55.

8. This is my translation of the official Japanese-language version of the 1972 normalization communiqué that I believe is more accurate than the Japanese government's translation. See Note 9.

9. The Japanese government's English translation of the communiqué stated the following: "The Japanese side is keenly conscious of the responsibility for the serious damage that Japan caused in the past to the Chinese people through war, and deeply reproaches itself." But in the original official Japanese version, the English clause "deeply reproaches itself" corresponds to "*fukaku hansei suru.*" Rather than conveying the notion of self-reproach or self-rebuke, the word *hansei* refers to a milder notion of "self-examination" or "self-reflection." In fact, when rendered into Chinese, this expression does not constitute an unequivocal apology to China.

10. Ogata, *Normalization with China,* 87–93.

11. Takahashi Shiro, *Rekishi kyoiku wa kore de yoi no ka,* 164–165.

12. Ijiri, "Sino-Japanese Controversy Since the 1972 Diplomatic Normalization," 69–73.

13. Ibid., 73–76.

14. Tanaka Akihiko, *Nit-chu Kankei 1945–90,* 173–177.

15. Ibid., 181–186.
16. Kakizawa, "Tennō hō-Chū go no Nit-Chū kankei."
17. Harwit, "Japanese Investment in China," 983–984.
18. Annual survey data from Japan prime minister's office. Available at htto://www8.cao.go.jp/survey/h16/h16-gaikou/images/z05.gif.
19. Oda, "Maehara Right About China Threat," 4.
20. See, for example, Chiba and Xiang, "Traumatic Legacies in China and Japan: An Exchange"; Chiba, *Nit-chū taiken-teki sōgo gokai;* and Sugimoto, *Tai-chi no Hōkō.*
21. Self, "China and Japan: A Façade of Friendship"; Sasajima, "Japan's Domestic Politics and China Policymaking"; and Komori, *Nit-chū yūkō no maboroshi.*
22. Prime Minister's Task Force on Foreign Relations, "Basic Strategies for Japan's Foreign Policy in the 21st Century: New Era, New Vision, New Diplomacy," November 28, 2002. Available at http://www.kantei.go.jp/foreign/policy/2002/1128tf_e.html.
23. Wakamiya, *The Postwar Conservative View of Asia,* 179–180, 247–248, 253–256.
24. Rose, *Sino-Japanese Relations,* 50–68.
25. Shimizu, *Chūgoku wa na-ze "Han-Nichi" ni natta ka.*
26. Wan, *Sino-Japanese Relations,* 129–130.
27. Yomiuri Shimbun Seiji-bu, *Gaikō o Kenka ni shita Otoko,* 222–262.
28. "Koizumi to Mend Ties in Beijing," *Daily Yomiuri,* October 8, 2001.
29. "Shushō Yasukuni Sanpai: Hyōka 50%, Hihan 46% [Prime Minister Yasukuni Pilgrimage: 50% Appreciation, 46% Criticism]," *Mainichi Shimbun,* August 17, 2006.
30. Wan, *Sino-Japanese Relations,* 262–286.
31. Quoted in Kojima, "Japan's China Policy," 35.
32. Reiji Yoshida, "New Yen Loans to China Are Put on Hold for Now"; and Nakata, "China Détente Spells Yen 74 Billion in Loans."
33. Tsugami, *Chūgoku no Taitō,* 210–216; and Munakata, "Has Politics Caught Up with Markets?" 147–151.
34. Hitoshi Tanaka, "The ASEAN+3 and East Asia Summit: A Two-Tiered Approach to Community Building"; "Chūgoku ni taikō—Shin Tsūshō Senryaku [Countering China—A New Trade Strategy]," *Asahi Shimbun,* July 28, 2006, 10.
35. Taniguchi, "A Cold Peace: The Changing Security Equation in Northeast Asia," 445–446.
36. Hughes, *Japan's Security Agenda: Military, Economic, and Environmental Dimensions,* 229–231.
37. Garrett and Glaser, "Chinese Apprehensions About Revitalization of the U.S.-Japan Alliance"; and Wu, "The End of the Silver Lining: A Chinese View of the U.S.-Japanese Alliance."
38. Drifte, *Japan's Security Relations with China Since 1989,* 94–101.
39. National Institute for Defense Studies Japan, *East Asian Strategic Review 2005,* 105–106; and Abe Junichi, *Chūgoku Gun no Hontō no Jitsuryoku,* 183–188.
40. "'Chūgoku no shinkō' mo sotei [Hypothesizing Even a 'Chinese Attack']," *Asahi Shimbun,* September 26, 2006, 1.
41. Morimoto, "Nit-chū Bō-ei Kōryū no Genjō to Kadai," 273–289.
42. National Institute for Defense Studies Japan, *East Asian Strategic Review 2006,* 113–114.
43. Hashimoto, "Seeking a New Foreign Policy Toward China."

44. "Japan-China Joint Declaration on Building a Partnership of Friendship and Cooperation for Peace and Development," November 26, 1998. Available at http://www.cn.emb-japan.go.jp/bilateral_e/bunken_1998sengen_e.htm.

45. Noble, "What Can Taiwan (and the United States) Expect from Japan?" 2–3.

46. Ibid., 8, 10.

47. Rahman, "Japanese Groups Win Taiwan Rail Deal"; "Three Firms Win Taiwan Rail Bid," *Japan Times,* December 10, 2005.

48. Soeya, "Taiwan in Japan's Security Considerations," 144–146.

49. "Joint Statement of U.S.-Japan Security Consultative Committee," February 19, 2005. Available at http://www.mofa.go.jp/region/n-america/us/security/scc/joint0502.html; and Yardley and Bradsher, "China Accuses U.S. and Japan of Interfering on Taiwan."

50. Ross, "Taiwan's Fading Independence Movement."

51. Roy, "The Sources and Limits of Sino-Japanese Tensions." For an argument that economic interdependence is insufficient to sustain cooperative Japan-China relations, see Yahuda, "The Limits of Economic Interdependence."

52. Mochizuki, "China-Japan Relations: Downward Spiral or a New Equilibrium," 140–142; and Mochizuki, "Terms of Engagement: The U.S.-Japan Alliance and the Rise of China," 101–114.

53. Hitoshi Tanaka, "Japan and China at a Crossroads," 4.

54. "Japan-China Joint Press Statement," October 8, 2006. Available at http://www.mofa.go.jp/region/asia-paci/china/joint0610.html.

| Part 4 |
Conclusion

| 12 |

The Pragmatic Liberalism of an Adaptive State

Thomas U. Berger

Since the end of the Cold War, and even more so since the terrorist attacks of September 11, 2001, Japan's role in the world has been in flux, changing in ways that have often surprised longtime observers of Japanese defense and foreign policy. The chapters in this book have documented some of the critical dimensions of these changes. Together with recent findings by other researchers and analysts, they strongly suggest the need for a new take on Japan's approach to international relations and for a new paradigm for analyzing Japanese foreign policy.

Although it still may be premature to pass definitive judgment on the question of what kind of actor in world affairs Japan will eventually become, the broad outlines are coming into view. Three points are worth pointing out. First, there is little doubt that Japan—long viewed as a largely passive presence in international politics—is becoming a more active player, one with a greater capacity for adaptation and independent action than many observers had once thought likely or even possible. Japan's ongoing campaign for a permanent seat on the United Nations Security Council, its active participation in tsunami relief activities in December 2004, and above all its increasing international security role across a wide variety of settings—its willingness to dispatch peacekeepers to Iraq and provide logistical support in the Indian Ocean, its new assertiveness on territorial issues, its willingness to take the lead at the United Nations to push for sanctions on North Korea following Pyongyang's missile tests in July 2006—all provide powerful evidence of a new activism in international affairs on the part of the world's second-largest economy.

Second, it is clear that many of the taboos that have long constrained post-1945 Japanese policy in the area of military security are fast evaporating. To call this trend part of a "normalization" of Japanese security policy would be misleading, however, for the term is often construed as meaning that Japan will become as uninhibited with regard to the use of force as other great powers such as France or Great Britain, nations that routinely send forces on combat missions across the globe. In comparison, Japan remains relatively restrained in its use of military instruments for pursuing its national interests and is likely to remain so for some time to come. Japanese public opinion remains strongly resistant to allowing Japanese forces to engage in actual combat, and the Asian regional reaction to a militarily assertive Japan is bound to be strongly negative. Nevertheless, whereas once the military was viewed as a quasi-illegitimate institution and Japanese leaders actively avoided any mention of the use of force beyond the minimum needed for its territorial defense, today the Japanese armed forces are integrated into the policymaking process, Japanese leaders openly discuss using force to defend Japan—including launching preemptive strikes against North Korean missile bases and challenging intruders who enter Japanese waters—and Japan is increasingly willing to use its forces for a wide variety of noncombat missions, including international peacekeeping, disaster relief, and the provision of logistical support for its allies.

Third, even though Japan is more comfortable with the use of force than it has been in the past, at the same time, Japan increasingly exhibits a more cosmopolitan, even liberal attitude toward the outside world than it usually is given credit for. Historically, Japan has had a very realpolitik view of international politics—one that understood international relations largely in terms of the distribution of power, above all military power, and stressed maintaining national autonomy and independence.[1] The quest for power was a major motivation behind the creation of Japan's pre-1945 empire. Similarly, Japan's decision after 1945 to forgo rearmament and rely on the United States for security in good part was motivated by a hard-nosed calculation of national interest—Japanese security during the Cold War could be secured better by aligning itself with Washington than by relying on its own resources.[2] Thereafter, Japanese foreign policy was largely oriented toward protecting Japanese national interests, especially economic interests, while minimizing the price it would have to pay to support the international order, a stance that has often been criticized in the United States and elsewhere as a form of free riding.

Today, however, Japan is making a serious effort to contribute to the international system, not only economically but in the diplomatic and security spheres as well, and what motivates its doing so is an essentially liberal philosophy of international relations, one that stresses building international institutions and deepening economic and social ties between nations, including potential adversaries, as ways of creating an international system that is inherently more cooperative and peaceful than it has been in the past.[3] Even as Japan expands its military role, it does so primarily as a way of bolstering the international security order, not as a way of maximizing its own national power, and it sees force as a necessary, but costly, instrument of achieving its objectives. Japanese liberalism is thus of a far less muscular variety than that often espoused in the United States, a sort of "defensive liberalism" as opposed to what could be termed as the "offensive liberalism" that has been espoused in the United States from Woodrow Wilson on.[4] Japan's version of liberalism is even more distant from the aggressive foreign policy of the Bush administration after September 11, which essentially fuses a hard realist position—emphasizing military power and downplaying the importance of multilateral institutions—to liberal goals couched in moralistic language.[5]

This nascent liberalism has always been a very visible feature of post-1945 Japanese public discourse on foreign policy. Yet it is only in recent years—arguably since the early to mid-1990s—that this discourse has had much of a visible impact on Japanese foreign policy beyond providing an excuse to avoid military burden sharing. Today, however, under the banner of making a "contribution to the global order" *(kokusai kōken)*, it informs Japanese diplomacy on multiple levels, including its policies on the environment and overseas development assistance as well as military security. This essentially liberal stance belies Japan's reputation as a self-interested actor intent on expanding its own economic and political power at the expense of others.[6] It is equally at odds with the recently popular contention that Japan is slouching toward a grudging acceptance of some form of realpolitik, usually equated with becoming a "normal nation."[7]

What we see instead is a Japan that is trying—within the constraints of an imperfect regional environment and while laboring under the burden of significant domestic social, economic, and political problems—to contribute to the creation of a more liberal Asian regional and international order. In short, Japan is struggling to play a role in the international system more akin to that of West Germany or the Netherlands than to the foreign policy stance of Britain or France, despite the fact that Japan is faced with an East Asian regional context that differs radically from that of Western Europe.[8] Robert Kagan, in his insightful analysis of transatlantic relations in which he stated that "Americans are from Mars and Europeans are from Venus," argued that the United States has an essentially realist approach to foreign policy, whereas West Europeans have a liberal one.[9] Borrowing Kagan's imagery, it is possible to describe Japan as a would-be Venusian trapped in a world of Martians.

This chapter will develop this model of Japan as a "liberal adaptive state," contrasting it with the existing models that dominate the literature on Japanese foreign policy, and will spell out in more detail the changing domestic political environment in which Japanese policy is made and the ways in which that environment is influencing Japanese behavior in the areas of national security and foreign economic relations. In closing, some final thoughts will be offered on the practical policy implications that the emergence of Japan's adaptive state may have for the world, and for US foreign policy in particular, and on the direction in which Japanese policy may develop in the future.

Contrasting Models of Japanese Foreign Policy

For more than thirty years the central puzzle in the study of Japanese foreign policy has been why Japan has chosen to play a relatively passive role in international affairs despite its impressive economic, political, and potentially military power. By almost any measure, Japan should be one of the world's leading powers. Even after a decade of economic stagnation, Japan remains the world's second-largest economy,[10] and the most technologically sophisticated after that of the United States. Japan has been the second-largest financial contributor to international institutions such as the United Nations and the International Monetary Fund, and it has consistently ranked among the world's top three trading powers as well as one of the top providers of overseas development assistance. Despite their relatively small size, the Japanese Self-Defense Forces are arguably the most sophisticated and capable in East Asia.[11] Were Japan to choose to do so, there is little doubt that it could become the largest military power in the region as well, replete with nuclear capabilities second only to those of the United States.[12]

Because of its impressive resources and capabilities, since the 1970s successive waves of analysts have predicted that Japan would soon emerge as an active and central player in international affairs.[13] Yet, until the start of the twenty-first century, on balance Japan remained a relatively passive actor in the international system, more a presence than a power. Although Japan participated in the full array of international institutions, with few exceptions it rarely initiated new projects or exercised leadership on controversial issues,[14] preferring instead to shape outcomes through behind-the-scenes negotiations—a diplomatic style that Alan Rix has aptly called "leading from behind."[15] Although Japan ranked among the top three trading nations of the world, it had little visible influence in shaping the global trading regime. Despite the fact that Japan's armed forces are a critical component in the balance of power in Asia, until recently Japan has assiduously maintained a low profile on security issues and remains to this day extraordinarily circumspect in the exercise of military power. In short, although Japan may have had the resources to make the transition from a passive participant to an active player in world affairs for a long time, by and large it has been content to follow a foreign policy agenda set by others. As the eminent Japanologist, Nathaniel Thayer, has put it, Japan has been sitting at the crossroads of history for half a century.[16]

There have been numerous attempts to explain this peculiar Japanese penchant for passivity. Broadly speaking, two main schools of thought have emerged. First, there is the view that Japan is a "reactive state," one whose policies are largely made on a reactive basis and one that lacks anything that could be termed a grand strategy.[17] The chief alternative view is the thesis that Japan's passivity is in fact the product of a rational calculation of national interest; Japan prefers to let others take the lead in world affairs while it quietly builds its strength and cultivates influence. For the purposes of the discussion here, we will label this second point of view the "strategic state" thesis. Each school of thought is rooted in strikingly different inter-pretations of the Japanese political system, its conception of national inter-est, and the kind of trade, foreign economic, and national security policies that it produces.

The reactive state thesis was first advanced by Kent Calder, currently professor at the Johns Hopkins School of Advanced International Studies. Calder presented a vision of a highly fragmented and pluralist Japanese political system, one so riddled by bureaucratic rivalries, so penetrated by societal interest groups, and so paralyzed by factional infighting that it has been virtually impossible to even articulate, much less implement, anything that could be likened to a grand strategy.[18] Were it not for external pressure (*gaiatsu*), Calder contended, the Japanese system would be virtually immo-bile. Various other analysts, both inside Japan and outside, have offered similar analyses, although they differ on the causes of Japanese immobil-ism.[19] Some (including Calder) have stressed the role of political institu-tions—that is, the compartmentalized structure of the Japanese bureaucracy, the factionalized nature of Japanese political parties, and the role of strong interest groups that are deeply ensconced in the policymaking process.[20] Others have emphasized the role of ideas and deeply rooted aspects of Japanese political culture, especially the strength of strong antimilitary norms[21] and a deeply entrenched ideology of state-led socioeconomic man-agement,[22] as the key factors inhibiting the development of a coherent Japanese grand strategy.

Regardless of whether they emphasize formal political institutions or more nebulous social norms and ideals, the adherents to the reactive state view of Japanese foreign policy share an image of Japan as essentially a rudderless ship pursuing a hodgepodge of variegated policies that reflect the diverse domestic political interests and often contradictory international pressures that have impacted on the Japanese policymaking system since 1945.[23] This highly pluralistic political system, in which well-connected interest groups have de facto veto power over different aspects of public policy, called "patterned pluralism" by some[24] and "the refractive state" by others,[25] has the virtue of giving societal actors influence in the domains that affect them most. To the extent that the number of actors incorporated into the Japanese system has grown over time, it should be hailed as a positive development, one that strengthens Japanese democracy.[26] At the same time, however, it comes at the cost of being able to pursue a consistent, strategic vision.

In the area of trade and foreign economic relations, this decisionmaking system has produced a parochial protectionist stance on foreign economic issues, one that favors protecting domestic economic interests, especially those of politically well-connected producer groups in the agricultural, retail, construction, and manufacturing sectors, while frustrating attempts to liberalize the economy or promote broader Japanese economic interests on the global or regional level.[27] In the sphere of defense and national security policy, Japanese policy has been a haphazard compromise aimed at satisfying US demands for increased burden sharing while avoiding antagonizing a basically antimilitary Japanese public. That this system has worked reasonably well in the postwar period is largely owing to a combination of good luck and the largesse of the United States.

In contrast, the strategic state interpretation of Japanese foreign policy views Japan as ruled by a network of elites, above all conservative party politicians, business leaders, and bureaucrats. In some versions of the strategic state thesis, these groups are seen as working together as a well-oiled machine, sometimes referred to as "Japan, Inc."—or what in the US context used to be referred to as "the power elite."[28] In others, they are seen as a looser network of groups that often disagree and compete with one another but that nonetheless are united by a general ideological consensus on national strategy and their common desire to further Japanese national interests.[29] In either case, the strategic state line of reasoning argues that Japan's apparent passivity in international affairs is the product of a strategic calculation that at least for the time being, Japan is better off allowing other countries—namely the United States—to take the lead on security and other costly issues while Japan concentrates on building its economic and technological strength and quietly increasing its diplomatic influence.

Many adherents of the strategic state school contend that Japanese leaders are motivated by a conception of national power that differs fundamentally from that held by the United States. They argue that Japan, because of its peculiar position in the international system and different historical experiences, places special emphasis on technological and economic prowess, as opposed to the classic realist conception of power as essentially military strength, the view favored by US policymakers. Richard Samuels of MIT has labeled this peculiar Japanese weltanschauung as "mercantile realism."[30] Drawing on the liberal tradition in international relations, others, such as Richard Gow, Reinhard Drifte, and Joseph Nye, preferred the decidedly more innocuous-sounding term *comprehensive security*.[31] These strategic state analysts argue that the Japanese approach to building its national power is better adapted to the realities of the modern age, when economic strength and technological prowess are of increasing importance, whereas military power is of decreasing utility owing to a combination of factors, including increased economic and political interdependence,[32] declining willingness on the part of prosperous populations to wage war,[33] and the spread of nuclear weapons, which makes great power conflict prohibitively costly.[34]

Yet other strategic state analysts argue that Japanese actions can be explained without reference to any new conception of security and power. According to these commentators, Japan's approach to foreign policy and national security is perfectly intelligible from the standpoint of conventional realist models of foreign policy behavior—not the aggressive power-mad sort of thinking sometimes associated with the term *realpolitik* but rather a more moderate, defensive realism that sees states pragmatically balancing military power to maintain their security rather than blindly trying to maximize their military power at every opportunity.[35] From such a perspective, Japan's approach to national security seems perfectly reasonable for a large middle-ranking power that faces no immediate security threats and has had the luxury of having the world's leading superpower committed to protecting its vital interests. During the Cold War, Japan's minimalist stance on foreign affairs was a perfectly logical form of free riding. As long as Japan could rely on the United States to take the lead in maintaining order in Asia, there was little reason for Japan to expend the resources and political capital to develop the capabilities needed for it to do so on its own.[36] Japan's efforts on defense were carefully calibrated to be just enough to contain US pressures on burden sharing while minimizing the economic burden of defense on the Japanese economy. This strategy has helped ensure the maintenance of Japan's free ride on the security order underwritten and paid for primarily by the United States. At the same time, it has preserved enough military capacity to serve as a hedge that would allow Japan to rapidly reemerge as a great military power should that free ride come to an end or the US strategic guarantee become ineffective.[37] Since the end of the Cold War, as the US commitment to Japanese security has weakened with the disappearance of the Soviet Union, naturally Japan has been forced into a more activist stance, moving from a parochial focus on territorial defense and the espousal of pacifist ideals toward a more openly realist stance.

Strategic state analysts, both of the "comprehensive security/technonationalist" and "defensive realist" varieties, tend to agree that Japan's low-profile approach to regional diplomacy and trade similarly can be seen as a calculated and effective way of achieving its strategic goals at a minimal cost to itself. Japanese regional diplomacy and foreign aid policies, it has been argued, are designed to bolster its access to foreign markets while helping Japanese companies win foreign contracts and solidify a Japanese sphere of political influence in countries such as Malaysia and Thailand.[38] Japanese trade policy is an example of successful mercantilism in action. Taking advantage of the free-trade system created by the United States, Japan could export freely to the West while locking foreign competitors out of the Japanese domestic market and facilitating Japanese access to foreign markets and technology in ways that would ultimately enable Japan to assume a permanent position of economic leadership in Asia and the world. The metaphor used to describe Japan's efforts to create an international and regional economic hierarchy was that of "flying geese," with Japan occupying the position of the lead goose behind which all the others would follow.[39]

The reactive state and the strategic state interpretations of Japanese foreign policy are very much the products of the debates over Japan that raged in the US press and academy from the late 1970s into the mid-1990s. They were reflective of a mood of declining US self-confidence and a sense that Japan had become "number one."[40] To some degree, they described different eras in Japanese foreign policymaking. The vision of Japan as a strategic state had a certain degree of plausibility in the 1950s and 1960s, when the Japanese political system was more clearly dominated by a relatively small set of elites. From the 1970s on, however, the reactive state analysis would seem to more closely fit Japanese policymaking.[41] Today, however, in the early twenty-first century, both paradigms are clearly in need of some modification.

After a decade of political turmoil and bureaucratic restructuring, the strategic state vision of a closely knit elite running Japanese foreign policy seems fairly improbable. Likewise, the idea that Japan's emphasis on economic power and behind-the-scenes diplomacy would allow Japan to assume the role of a de facto regional or even global hegemony seems faintly ridiculous today in light of Japan's diminished economic fortunes, the continued weakness of Asian regional institutions, and the relative decline of Japanese influence inside of Asia.[42] Moreover, the reemergence of serious military issues both in Asia and, after September 11, on a global scale suggests that the claims of a new, superior Japanese approach to international affairs were more than a bit exaggerated. And even though the "defensive realist" variant of the strategic state analysis of Japanese defense policy in certain respects has become more relevant today than was true in the past, it tends to suggest that Japan is seeking a more autonomous defense posture, when in fact Japan clearly prefers multilateral (or at least enhanced bilateral) solutions for its security problems.

On balance, the reactive state would appear to be more relevant today than is the strategic Japan interpretation. Japanese foreign policymaking continues to be often quite fragmented, and the role of pressure groups in paralyzing reforms in certain areas—for example, in blocking free-trade agreements that would threaten the interest of Japanese farmers—continues to loom large. Nonetheless, it is equally clear that the reactive state hypothesis underestimated the Japanese capacity to respond creatively to changes in the international system, often in ways that contradicted the expectations of analysts. For instance, Peter Katzenstein, among others, claimed that the institutional and normative impediments to policymaking were greater in the realm of defense and national security than in trade and foreign economic policymaking.[43] Yet, over the past decade it is precisely in the area of defense and national security where the greatest changes in Japanese foreign policy are most apparent,[44] whereas Japanese efforts to use its economic power to advance its national interests appear relatively ossified.[45] In addition (as will be spelled out in more detail below), the reactive state vision tended to overlook the way in which essentially liberal goals have increasingly come to shape the Japanese approach to international relations over the past two to three decades. These liberal instincts have given Japanese foreign policymaking a higher degree of coherence and consistency than a purely garbage can model of policymaking would lead us to expect.

Today a new generation of research is emerging, of which the chapters in this book are part, that suggests the need for a new way of looking at and analyzing Japanese foreign policy. For the purposes of the present discussion, we will label it the "adaptive state" model, one that builds on earlier attempts at analysis while trying to go beyond them and adjust them to take into account new developments. (see Table 12.1 for a summary of the characteristics of the three models). Like the reactive state school, the adaptive state model sees the Japanese political system as basically democratic, but fragmented and prone to paralysis. As will be described in greater detail in the next section, the social-bureaucratic coalitions described in the reactive state literature appear to be breaking down. As a result, there is greater fluidity in Japanese policymaking than was true in the past, and the Japanese state has proven capable of instituting gradual reforms that over time have led to fundamental shifts in the Japanese approach to foreign policy. This process of adaptation is clearly visible in a number of different areas, particularly foreign policy and Japanese defense and national security policy.

Like some variants of the strategic state school, the adaptive state paradigm argues that what gives Japanese foreign policy an underlying sense of direction and purpose is a vague but widely shared political consensus among Japanese elites and the broader public on what Japan's mission in the world should be. That sense of mission, however, is quite different from the one posited by most strategic state analysts. Rather than a technonationalist defensive realist vision of a Japan using its relative strengths

Table 12.1 Contrasting Models of Japanese Foreign Policy

	Reactive State	Strategic State	Adaptive State
Japanese political system	Patterned pluralism	Elitist; "Japan Inc."	Pluralist
Japanese policymaking	Fragmented and prone to paralysis; reliance on *gaiatsu*	Opaque but efficient	Fragmented; gradualistic
Underlying conception of national interest	Narrow national interest; antimilitarist	Technonationalism or defensive realism	Low-key; liberalism
Trade and foreign economic policy	Protectionist-mercantilist	Strategic trade—aggressive mercantilist; the "flying geese"	Incomplete liberalism
Defense and national security	Limited national capacity; alliance-centric	Free riding; surreptitious building of major military power	International contribution within shifting limits

in economics and technology in the pursuit of enhanced national power and eventual hegemonic status, we argue that since the 1990s Japan has come to be guided by an essentially liberal view of international politics. By liberal what we mean here is not necessarily liberalism in the sense that it is used in US political discourse, that is, of support for welfare programs and an activist government that seeks to promote equality and social justice through affirmative action and other programs (although such views enjoy considerable support in Japan). Rather, what is meant here is liberalism in the sense that the term is used by international relations scholars, that is, a belief that progress in international affairs is both possible and necessary and that Japan can contribute to a progressive shift in international relations by building strong multilateral institutions, promoting international trade and commerce, and fostering the spread of democracy and human rights.[46]

Continued regional tensions have set limits to what a purely liberal approach to foreign policy can achieve, and early post–Cold War ideas about the creation of an East Asian regional community have been put on hold. Moreover, domestic political factors continue to inhibit Japan's room for maneuver in a number of important ways—for instance, on trade policy. Nonetheless, significant changes in the domestic political context in which Japanese policy is made, as well as in Japanese defense and foreign economic policies, are readily identifiable.

The Changing Domestic
Context of Japanese Foreign Policy

The end of the Cold War triggered a major transformation of Japanese politics, economy, and society exceeded in magnitude only by the opening of Tokugawa Japan following the arrival of Commodore Matthew Perry's black ships in 1854 and by the defeat of imperial Japan in 1945.[47] As in the past, the period of upheaval and turmoil that followed the triggering event has lasted for more than a decade, and it is only now, in 2006, that the dust is beginning to settle. Although it is impossible to offer more than a scant outline of what has transpired over the past decade, it is worth briefly highlighting here some of the most salient developments in the domestic economic, political, and socioeconomic spheres and elaborating on their implications for Japanese foreign relations.

From an outsider perspective, the most dramatic changes in Japan have taken place on the economic front. Prior to the early 1990s, the Japanese economy had appeared an inexorable juggernaut, outstripping its competitors in the West and Asia. For much of the 1980s and 1990s, it was widely believed that it was through the strength of its economy that Japan would exert influence on world affairs.[48] By the start of the twenty-first century, the dominant image of Japan had reversed itself almost entirely. Following the bursting of the Japanese stock and real estate bubble in 1991, Japan entered a period of nearly a decade of stagnation and relative decline during which its economy grew at less than 1 percent a year. The much-vaunted Japanese economic model proved to have feet of clay, and after a decade of painful reform and cost cutting, Japanese corporations have only begun to recover from aftereffects of what has been called "Japan's lost decade."[49] This reversal of fortunes has had far-reaching consequences for Japanese foreign policy.

The most obvious result of Japan's tightened economic circumstances is the reduced amount of resources it has available for defense and foreign policy. Despite increased Japanese concerns about security threats in its area, the Japanese defense budget has been decreasing instead of increasing in recent years, as the Japanese Ministry of Finance has fought a tough rearguard action to limit defense outlays. Likewise, as Juichi Inada points out in Chapter 8, Japanese readiness to provide funds for overseas development assistance has declined considerably, leading to substantial reductions in such unpopular programs as grants to China.

On a more subtle level, as Edward Lincoln reminds us in Chapter 6, the decline in Japanese economic fortunes has also reduced one of its critical "soft power" assets, the attractiveness of its economic model. Prior to the bursting of the bubble, developing countries around the world looked to

Japan for inspiration, and the Japanese government itself actively sought to promote its state-led model of economic development through the World Bank and other institutional forums.[50] Since the collapse of the Japanese economic miracle became apparent in the mid-1990s, and even more so after the other rapidly growing, Japanese-inspired Asian development states ran into severe economic problems in 1997–1998, the Japanese model has been largely discredited. At the same time, Japanese confidence in the virtues of their own system has been shaken. The unmistakable groundswell of Japanese nationalism in the 1980s, fueled by Japan's tremendous post-1945 economic growth, has been replaced by a palpable mood of anxiety about the state of the Japanese system and a general turning inward on the part of the Japanese public and political leaders.[51]

As Lincoln points out, however, not all the implications of Japan's economic decline have been negative. First and foremost, Japan today is perceived as a status quo power in the West, and the rising tide of so-called Japan bashing that poisoned Japanese relations with the United States and the West in general in the 1970s and 1980s has largely disappeared, despite the persistence of a huge imbalance in the terms of trade between Japan and most of the outside world.[52] Second, as Lincoln explains, the Japanese economy is becoming more open to the outside world, and the Japanese corporate sector, as well as Japanese society in general, is becoming internationalized and capable of operating effectively in the outside world.[53] Lincoln mentions that whereas in the early 1980s only 2 million Japanese visited the outside world every year, by 2003 that number had swelled to 16 million, including 835,000 living abroad on a long-term basis. Japanese assets abroad continued to grow, to $2.9 trillion by 2002. At the same time the number of foreigners living and investing in Japan has increased considerably, albeit from a relatively modest base.

In addition, as Mike Mochizuki points out in Chapter 1, the decline in Japan's economic power has encouraged an increased sensitivity in Tokyo to the importance of other instruments of power beyond the economic, including political, military, and diplomatic, and an increased maturity on the part of Japan about the goals and objectives that it can hope to achieve. When Japan's financial coffers run dry, Japanese politicians are less inclined to write a check every time a new international problem emerges. And when it is clear that Japan cannot change the world through the power of its miraculous economy, political leaders in Tokyo are more inclined to look for other ways to pursue its interests. In a very real way, Japan's diminished economic prospects are inducing it to take a more mature and balanced approach to international affairs.

Changes in the condition of the Japanese economy have been paralleled by equally dramatic changes in the Japanese political system, as described by Masaru Kohno in Chapter 2. Among the most important, yet least appreciated, of these changes is how Japan's economic failings have undermined the authority of the Japanese bureaucracy. Once held to be nearly infallible, Japanese officials acted as behind-the-scenes manipulators of the Japanese political system, setting the agenda and range of options available to Japanese politicians while carefully safeguarding the parochial interests of their respective institutions. Since the late 1980s, however, the reputation of Japanese bureaucracy has been shaken by an endless series of scandals: the mismanagement of the economy by the Ministry of Finance, the diffusion of acquired immunodeficiency syndrome (AIDS) through the blood supply as a result of lax supervision by the Ministry of Health and Welfare, the misuse of ministry funds by officials in the Ministry of Foreign Affairs; the list could easily be expanded. Even though the bureaucracy in Japan remains central to the policymaking process far more so than is the case in the United States, over the past decade its authority has been shaken and its ability to shape political decisionmaking sharply curtailed.[54]

The other central development in Japanese politics has been the turmoil in the Japanese party system. For nearly four decades, the conservative LDP held the reins of power alone while a colorful and rambunctious assortment of opposition parties, led by the Japanese Socialist and Communist Parties, agitated from the sidelines of the political process, occasionally blocking unpopular policies and serving as a mouthpiece for popular discontent without ever being able to topple the LDP. This more or less stable state of affairs collapsed in the early 1990s. The LDP was ousted in 1993 by a disparate alliance of old and new opposition parties, including a sizable number of rebels who had defected from the LDP. The opposition was unable to hold on, and in a few years LDP was able to return to power. Since 1993, however, the LDP has been forced to rule in coalition with members of the former opposition. Over the past few years its chief partner has been the Kōmei Party (the lay Buddhist Clean Government Party; CGP), a party that tends to resist a more robust defense policy and to support more active policies to assist weaker socioeconomic groups and sectors in Japan. At the same time, the old leftist opposition parties collapsed and were replaced by a left-of-center Democratic Party of Japan that was led for the most part by former LDP politicians.[55] As a result, the degree of ideological polarization has declined significantly since the end of the Cold War, and the possibilities for reform and compromise have increased proportionately.

An additional, noteworthy change in the way Japanese parties operate is the impact of a new electoral system that was introduced in 1994. Under the old multiseat electoral system, Japanese politicians were able to win election with a relatively small percentage of the popular vote, usually a bit over 20 percent. Consequently, as long as they were able to keep a core group of supporters satisfied, typically through the provision of public goods in the form of railroads, schools, and targeted subsidies, the average

Japanese Diet member could ensure his or her reelection. The powerful factions within the LDP became well-honed patronage machines that dominated the political agenda. Issues of ideology and larger national interest played a decidedly secondary role from the point of view of politicians, and the tendency was to leave such issues to the Japanese bureaucrats.

Under the new system, the majority of parliamentarians[56] have to win the plurality of the vote in their electoral district, much as in the United States. As a result, for the first time candidates for office find themselves under pressure to craft a political message that goes beyond their core group of supporters. Factions have become considerably less important than they once were to the career of Japanese politicians, and the ability to articulate coherent rationales for their domestic and foreign policy proposals has taken on a new significance.[57] At the same time, the Japanese public has become more engaged in foreign policy than was true in the past, partly as a result of an increased sense of threat in the form of North Korean agents and missiles but also because of increased exposure to the outside world thanks to tourism, travel, and migration.[58] The Japanese, to put it simply, are becoming more cosmopolitan and outward looking. At times this leads to a certain emotionalism in Japanese foreign policymaking and to an apparent resurgence of nationalist sentiments on symbolic issues, as I described in Chapter 9 with reference to the issue of history. Yet given the essentially liberal sentiments of the Japanese public, it also feeds an increased idealism in the Japanese populace on such issues as human rights and development assistance.[59]

These upheavals in the bureaucracy and the party political system initially paralyzed the Japanese political system. For more than a decade Japanese politicians and officials found themselves almost entirely focused on the task of trying to cope with these momentous changes in the political and economic environment. As a result, for much of the 1990s Japan arguably was even more of a reactive state than it had been at the time Kent Calder invented the phrase. Today, Japan is still in transition, but there are clear signs that it is beginning to grope its way toward a new strategic consensus. Certain issues that had long been neglected, such as the question of whether Japan would apologize for the atrocities of the imperial era, could be raised with the change in the political actors participating in government (see Chapter 9). At the same time, the weakening of the bureaucracy, the collapse of the old Japanese left-wing opposition, and the resulting increase in the Japanese prime minister's room for maneuver allowed for the relaxation (though by no means elimination) of many of the taboos and institutional safeguards that historically had hampered Japanese policymaking, especially in the area of defense and national security (see the next section).

Perhaps the single most important manifestation of this new fluidity in Japanese thinking on defense is the new debate on revising the Japanese constitution, reviewed by Jitsuo Tsuchiyama in Chapter 3. Although the constitution was written (in bad Japanese!) by the US occupation authorities and forcibly imposed on Japan in 1946, the Japanese constitution, including its famous "antiwar" Article 9, has survived unchanged for sixty years.[60] Repeated efforts by Japanese conservatives to revise the constitution were all stymied by bitter resistance from the Japanese opposition and a general unwillingness on the part of the broader public to tamper with a system under which Japan enjoyed unparalleled peace and prosperity. Today, constitutional reform is supported by all the major political parties and backed by public opinion polls that indicate the majority of Japanese feel that the time has come to consider far-reaching changes. Yet, as Tsuchiyama points out, continued disagreements about what should be changed and deep differences among the key players virtually ensure that the end product will be a compromise between those who wish to preserve the constitution as it essentially is today and those who aspire to a far-reaching revision of all its provisions, including Article 9.

Finally, on a broader social and cultural level, Japanese society as well has undergone profound changes during the past decade. The collapse of the Japanese miracle has inflicted profound damage on the fabric of Japanese society and in the morale of the Japanese nation. Where once Japanese society was renowned for its order and discipline, in recent years there has been an upsurge in various forms of social malaise, including juvenile delinquency, rejection of the traditional corporate "sarariman" lifestyle, and even suicide. Perhaps most worrying for Japan's long-term future has been the collapse of the Japanese birthrate and the encroaching aging of the Japanese demographic structure. Japan's economic and political crises are thus translating back into a social and spiritual one as well.[61]

In this environment there has been much comment about the emergence of a new, frustrated sense of nationalism, embodied on the political scene by Ishihara Shintaro, elected the governor of Tokyo in 1999, and on the pop culture scene by manga (comics) writer Kobayashi Yoshinori and popular novelist Fukui Harutoshi. These so-called Japanese neoconservatives tap traditional Japanese right-wing ideas that glorify the Japanese nation and defend imperial Japan's record in Asia and package them to appeal to the sensibilities of modern audiences. Prime Minister Koizumi's insistence on visiting the Yasukuni Shrine, as well as Japan's willingness to overturn old taboos regarding defense, are taken as further indications that a new, more assertive Japanese attitude toward the outside world is on the rise.[62]

As I argue in Chapter 9, however, a certain degree of caution is in order when confronted with these claims of a new Japanese nationalism. Reviewing Japanese debates over history—arguably the most central element in the definition of any national identity[63]—I point out that despite the common perception that Japan suffers a form of historical amnesia,[64] post-

1945 Japan has long been riven by deep and bitter divisions over how to interpret its past. In this sense, Ishihara, Kobayashi, and Fukui are just the latest representatives of a current in Japanese politics that has always been there, and the Far Right today arguably is no stronger than it was during the Cold War when a right-wing student assassinated the secretary general of the Japanese Socialist party, acclaimed Japanese novelist Yukio Mishima took over the GSDF headquarters in Ichigaya and called on the Japanese army to revolt, and leading Japanese intellectual Shimizu Ikutarō publicly advocated the acquisition of nuclear arms.

Since the end of the Cold War, changes in Japanese politics, together with increased pressures from an ever more tightly integrated East Asia, have meant that Japan has been seeking some way to harmonize its views on history with those of its Asian neighbors. Over the past few years, this ongoing process has generated considerable frictions. Yet at the same time significant progress has been made on the issue of history in Japanese relations with some of its neighbors, most notably in Southeast Asia and to a lesser extent in Korea. Certainly Japan has been far more responsive to foreign pressures than it is given credit for. Although nationalism is and has been a force in Japanese politics, it would be a mistake to interpret recent developments as evidence of a right-wing triumph. Instead, what we seem to be seeing is a long and difficult process in which Japan is being pushed to find ways of defining its national identity that fit in with those of its neighbors. That this can be the source of considerable frictions can be seen in the experiences of such countries as Austria, which has been forced to adjust its views on history since joining the EU, and Russia, whose relations with its neighbors are soured by its refusal to face up to its Soviet past.[65]

In Chapter 10, Catharin Dalpino sheds light in a rather different way on the continued diversity of views in Japanese society and its impact on Japanese foreign policy. For decades, Japanese foreign policy by and large has been the preserve of the relatively small number of Japanese officials and politicians who make up the Japanese foreign policy establishment. Except in a very broad and general way, public opinion has traditionally had only limited impact on the making of different aspects of Japanese foreign policy. Certainly any liberal public sentiments concerning such issues as human rights, the environment, and development had little impact on government policies beyond the Japanese home islands.[66]

This state of affairs has begun to change, however, as an increasing number of nongovernmental actors are emerging in Japan and reshaping Japanese politics on all levels, including foreign policy.[67] As Dalpino documents, Japanese human rights organizations are placing growing pressure on the Japanese government to pay attention to human rights issues, complicating Japanese relations with Burma and Southeast Asian nations in general. Recent media and public attention given to the plight of North Korean refugees in China and the fate of Japanese citizens abducted by North Korean agents provides further evidence that public concerns over human rights issues are increasingly shaping Japanese foreign relations, much to the consternation of the professional Japanese foreign policy establishment.

To sum up, since 1991 the domestic context in which Japanese foreign policy has been made has been shaken to its core. Yet the Japanese system has proven itself resilient and capable of adapting. Although the pace of reform has often seemed glacial, gradually a very different Japan is emerging, one that is both more internationally oriented and increasingly better prepared to play a strategic role in world affairs. At times, this new Japan is also likely to be more volatile and emotional than was true in the past. As a result of the changes in the Japanese political system detailed above, the room for public sentiment to intrude on the diplomatic agenda is greater than ever—as can be seen most clearly in the emotional debates between Japan and its neighbors over the "problem of history." Yet as the next two sections will detail, in the main the policies that the Japanese political system is producing can best be described as informed by the spirit of pragmatic liberalism, rather than by some sort of angry and reactive nationalism.

Defense and National Security Policy

No area of Japanese foreign policy has undergone a greater change over the past few years than defense and national security policy. Prior to the 1990s, popular Japanese thinking about defense—to the extent that most Japanese thought much about the issue at all—was characterized by a kind of naive and parochial idealism that Inoguchi Takashi described as the ideology of "prosperity in one country" (*ikkoku han-ei shugi*).[68] While the rest of the world grappled with the enormous security dilemmas created by the Cold War, and while Asia was wracked by often bloody conflicts fueled by ideology and nationalism, Japan—safe in the cocoon created by its alliance relationship with the United States—clung to its self-image as a principled pacifist nation insulated from the turmoil and strife surrounding it.[69]

This image was, of course, in large measure an illusion, as many Japanese policymakers and even much of the general public realized. Yet, it was a comfortable illusion, one that influenced actual Japanese defense policy for more than a decade. Behind it stood two hard-nosed political calculations. First, Japanese policymakers believed that greater involvement in security affairs beyond the minimum required for maintaining ties to the United States ran the serious risk of embroiling Japan in costly entanglements abroad while provoking a regional backlash. They feared that giving in to US demands for greater burden sharing could lead to Japanese forces fighting alongside US and other allied forces in Korea, Southeast Asia, and possibly even mainland China. In addition, if Japan were to build more substantial forces even within the context of the alliance with the United States, it would alarm its Asian neighbors and spark a costly and dangerous regional arms race.[70] Second, Japanese politicians, including many inside the conservative Liberal Democratic Party, were convinced that efforts to strengthen Japan's military would be overly costly politically because of the presence of powerful antimilitary sentiments in the Japanese public and political system.[71] As a result, for much of the Cold War, Japanese defense policy seemed to be a carefully calibrated exercise in maintaining just enough forces to satisfy US demands on burden sharing without provoking either the Japanese public or Japan's Asian neighbors.

The end of the Cold War shook the very foundations on which these calculations of Japanese interest were based. The disappearance of the Soviet military threat meant the primary rationale for the US military commitment to Asia had disappeared. Although the United States continued to have an interest in regional stability, the value of its military assets relative to the costs had declined now that its old Soviet nemesis had disappeared. As a result, the price that had to be paid for maintaining the security relationship with the United States went up. At the same time, as detailed in the previous section, the collapse of the old pacifist left-wing opposition reduced some of the principal domestic political barriers to a more active Japanese defense and security policy. Thus, the domestic political cost of an enhanced security role had gone down. The net result of these changes was that a major restructuring of Japanese security relations had become inevitable.

At first, the political leadership in Tokyo was slow to react. Many in Japan hoped that the end of the Cold War meant that Japan could wean itself off of its dependence on the United States in favor of regional collective security arrangements. By the mid-1990s, the emergence of new security threats in North Korea and China, as well as new demands for increased burden sharing from the United States, led to a far-reaching reformulation of Japan's approach to defense and national security across all its different dimensions: in the management of its alliance with the United States, in the structure and mission of the Japanese armed forces, and in the way Japan dealt with other regional powers.[72] September 11 and the war on terror helped further accelerate these changes.[73]

As during the Cold War, Japan's security relationship with the United States remains the solid bedrock—the "great black pillar," to use the Japanese expression—on which Japanese security policy is based. Although Japan has sought to supplement the Mutual Security Treaty by promoting multilateral regional security institutions such as the ARF, the primacy of the alliance with the United States is not in question.[74] Yet, in order to keep its security relationship with the United States viable, Japan has greatly upgraded the contribution it makes to the international security order. In the past, despite a rhetorical commitment to supporting international and Asian regional stability, Japan's military role was largely restricted to the defense of Japanese territory. Although the JSDF could cooperate with the United States to defend Japan from foreign attack, they were forbidden to support US forces for any other purpose.

After the 1996 Japan-US Joint Declaration on Security and the 1997 Guidelines for US-Japan Defense Cooperation, Japan moved systematically to increase its role in international security, improving the interoperability of US-Japanese forces and authorizing its defense forces to offer logistical support for US forces in the event of a military contingency. Such support was to be in "the areas around Japan" (*Nihon no shuhen*), a highly ambiguous term that was deliberately chosen to allow future governments extensive room for interpretation. These developments set the groundwork for further legislation after the September 11 attacks, allowing Prime Minister Koizumi to dispatch Japanese military forces to the Indian Ocean in support of Operation Enduring Freedom in Afghanistan and to send a contingent of Japanese Ground Self-Defense Forces to assist in the reconstruction of Iraq.[75]

Although Japan continued to eschew participation in combat operations, and the Japanese government insisted that under the existing interpretation of Article 9 of the constitution it was barred from participating in traditional military alliances, Japan essentially moved into what former US ambassador to Japan Michael Armacost described as an "off-shore support role" for US military operations on a global scale.[76] This trend appears set to continue in the future, receiving further reinforcement from the recent frictions between Japan and its neighbors over issues of history and territorial rights as well as from Japan's decision to participate in a US-sponsored ballistic missile defense system for Asia, which will require extensive integration of US and Japanese command and control systems.[77] The chief justification for this strengthening of the alliance is the argument that the US-Japanese alliance not only serves the interests of the two countries but also is a vital component in maintaining the stability of the East Asian region. The thinking behind Japan's new activism on defense is thus more Wilsonian than Bismarckian in character, rooted in a liberal commitment to fostering a just, stable, and peaceful international order rather than a desire to maximize national power to ensure national survival.

Changes in the alliance have been paralleled by equally far-reaching changes in the Japanese defense establishment. Since the end of the Cold War, the Japanese Self-Defense Forces have taken on a widening range of missions. Some of these have been spurred by the changes in the alliance. For example, in 2003 the Japanese Diet passed a far-reaching package of emergency laws that would allow the Japanese armed forces to respond more effectively in the event of a military crisis and to coordinate their efforts with the US forces stationed in Japan.

Other missions, such as Japanese participation in United Nations Peacekeeping Operations or JSDF participation in relief operations following the 2004 tsunami disaster, are designed to support international security beyond the scope of the US-Japan alliance. As described by Go Ito in Chapter 4, since 1992 Japan has joined a growing number of international peacekeeping missions, including those to such troubled regions of the world as Cambodia, Mozambique, and East Timor. These new missions have required the acquisition of new equipment, including air- and sealift capacity, in-air refueling capabilities, and intelligence satellites, in order to move and maintain forces at considerable distance from Japan. They have also spurred the development of new command and control organizational structures designed to enable the JSDF and the Japanese government to respond to military security crises. These capabilities are by and large along the lines of what Michael O'Hanlon suggests in Chapter 5 as being the kind of military establishment that can contribute to international peacekeeping missions without constituting a threat to its neighbors.

These changes in Japanese defense policy have necessarily had an impact on Japan's relations with its neighbors. Predictably, they have spurred fears of Japanese remilitarization in many quarters, especially in China and the two Koreas. To allay these suspicions, Japan has continued to try to engage its neighbors through trade and diplomacy. As Mike Mochizuki describes in Chapter 11, despite tensions over such issues as the comprehensive test ban treaty, the Senkaku/Diaoyu Islands, and the Yasukuni Shrine, the Japanese government has striven to keep its relations with Beijing on an even keel. Japan continues to provide large—albeit declining—quantities of foreign aid to China. Japan and China have taken steps to improve communications between their armed forces and to improve cooperation on security issues. Above all, Sino-Japanese trade has grown at a prodigious rate over the past decade, to the point at which China has overtaken the United States as Japan's largest trading partner. Although Japanese willingness to confront Beijing over sensitive issues, most notably Yasukuni, has increased in recent years, the basic strategy remains a liberal one of engagement and diplomacy, with the long-term goal of integrating China as a peaceful member of the international community, rather than a realist project of seeking to contain the power of a dangerous regional rival. Japanese policy toward other Asian countries shows similar tendencies, even with respect to North Korea, which it has repeatedly sought to engage through bilateral and multilateral talks.[78]

In sum, Japan is emerging from its postwar pacifist cocoon to become an important military as well as economic power. It is doing so, however, not as a player in the balance-of-power game in Asia but as a regional stabi-

lizer seeking to strengthen a regional and global security order that is struggling to adjust to the end of the Cold War, the emergence of China, and the
development of new security threats such as terrorism, nuclear proliferation,
and the problem of failed states. Moreover, it is important to remember that
Japan remains relatively reluctant to utilize force. Despite the hope in some
quarters that Japan might become the Far Eastern equivalent of Great
Britain—a trusted ally that could be counted on to fight side by side with
the United States in times of need—Japan continues to refuse to engage in
combat operations and prefers maintaining a low profile on security issues
in general.[79] JSDF ships in the Indian Ocean provided fuel for coalition
forces fighting in Afghanistan; they did not launch missile strikes on Kabul.
Japanese troops in Iraq are restricted to humanitarian missions; they are
expressly forbidden from engaging in combat unless they themselves are
directly engaged. In both instances, Japan joined the United States in the
name of strengthening the international order and in order to increase
Japanese influence in Washington. The long-term goal is not the enhancement of Japanese power but the creation of an international system that will
be protective of Japanese interests. While Japan is adapting to its changed
security environment, it is trying to do so in a way consonant with its essentially liberal instincts.

Foreign Economic Policy

On the whole, changes in Japanese economic relations with the outside
world have been less dramatic than in its defense and national security policies. On the surface, this might seem somewhat surprising, given the dramatically altered circumstances in Japan's economic fortunes discussed earlier in this chapter. Yet, on a fundamental level the factors that have shaped
Japan's economic relations with the outside world have changed less than
have the structural parameters of its defense and security policies. Two factors in particular—Japan's geoeconomic position as a resource-poor island
nation and its historical legacy as a late developer—stand out for the critical
role they have played, both in the past and the present, in determining the
way Japan's economy is integrated into the outside world.

As Japanese commentators are fond of pointing out, Japan is a
resource-poor island nation that has to import the raw materials (above all,
oil and gas) needed to maintain an advanced industrial economy with a high
standard of living. In the pre-1945 era, this basic reality led Japan to seek to
secure direct control over markets and raw materials through imperial
expansion, a strategy that increasingly brought it into conflict with its
neighbors and ultimately resulted in its catastrophic defeat in World War
II.[80] After 1945, Japan moved instead in a liberal direction, seeking to meet

the needs of its economy through trade and cooperation with outside countries rather than through conquest and coercion. This strategy unfolded on three levels: global, regional, and bilateral.

On the global level, after 1945 Japan moved swiftly to integrate itself into the new global trading regime. In 1955, with the critical support of the United States, Japan joined the GATT, precursor to today's WTO. In 1964 Japan joined the OECD. From 1973 to 1979, Japan hosted the sixth round of GATT tariff negotiations (the so-called Tokyo round), and by the early 1980s Japan had removed most of the significant formal barriers to trade, reducing them to a level roughly comparable with that of other advanced industrial countries. In 1975 Japan became one of the founding members of the Group of Six (G6) (precursor to today's Group of Eight [G8] forum) and a central player in managing the world's financial system. Although Japan was generally regarded as a passive participant in international forums, it tried to play the role of "good citizen," joining all the major clubs and abiding by their rules.

On the regional level in Asia, beginning in the 1960s Japan sought to promote the multilateral institutions aimed at reducing barriers to trade and investment. Japan was able to score some successes on this front and is credited with having been one of the primary movers behind the creation of the ADB, the Pacific Basic Economic Council (PBEC), and the PECC. Nonetheless, other Asian nations' fear of economic domination, together with lingering memories of prewar Japan's efforts to carve out its own sphere of influence in the region—comparable to the Greater East Asian Co-prosperity Sphere—set sharp limits to what could be accomplished on the regional level.

Finally, on the bilateral level Japan's geoeconomic circumstances made it strongly inclined to cultivate close relations with the countries that it depended upon for the supply of food, energy, and other vital resources. By far the most important bilateral relationship was with the United States, which emerged as Japan's most important export market as well as principal supplier of technology. In addition, Japan has assiduously sought to promote ties to other important economic partners, including Europe, China, Southeast Asia, and the Middle East. In fact, Japan has sought to stay on good terms with virtually every country in the world—a policy referred to as "omnidirectional diplomacy" (*zenhōi gaikō*)—even though doing so has at times created tensions with the United States over such issues as trade with China (before 1972) and Iran (after 1979).

The other key factor that has shaped Japan's economic relations with the outside world is the cultural and institutional legacy of its emergence as a late industrializing state.[81] When Japan began to participate in global politics in the mid-nineteenth century, it did so as a relatively weak and economically backward state.[82] Japanese leaders at the time felt they could not afford to wait for Japanese society to catch up with its competitors in the West and embarked on a massive modernization program aimed at accelerating the process of development through massive state intervention.

Compared to other late developers—such as Russia, Turkey, and many Latin American nations—Japan proved singularly successful in this endeavor. Its success can be attributed to a number of factors, including such favorable preconditions for industrialization as a relatively well-educated population, a unified domestic market, and relatively strong domestic political institutions.[83] In addition, Japan's success was due to the formation of a close partnership between the government and society that enabled Japan to concentrate resources in areas with a high potential for growth without succumbing to the perils of bureaucratic red tape and politically motivated rent seeking.[84] During the run-up to the Pacific war, this intertwining of the public and private spheres intensified, culminating in the formation of an enduring partnership between business and government sometimes referred to as the "1940 system."[85] Market mechanisms in Japan were maintained, and the management of business enterprises remained in private hands. At the same time, the Japanese government promoted business expansion through the provision of public funds, the sponsorship of cooperation between businesses at least at the research and development stages, the formation of cartels, and the protection of Japanese business interests vis-à-vis the outside world.[86]

The historical legacy of Japan's late industrialization in many respects lay at cross-purposes with its post-1945 promotion of international trade as a way of coping with its economic vulnerability. At the same time as Japan sought to integrate itself into the global trading regime and emerged as a major exporting power, the Japanese state and its allies in the business world created a system of nontariff barriers that made it extraordinarily difficult to import foreign goods other than those goods it could not produce itself and made it close to impossible for foreign multinationals to establish more than a foothold in the Japanese market except on terms dictated by their Japanese business competitors.[87] These barriers were enforced in part through laws and regulations implemented by a powerful bureaucracy and in part through a cartelized industrial structure that had been fostered by the Japanese style of economic development.[88] Edward Lincoln refers in Chapter 6 to this state of affairs as the "asymmetrical" character of Japan's economic relations with the outside world.

During the Cold War, this peculiar Japanese model of economic management became a growing source of tension with its trading partners, leading to bitter disputes over trade and investment that threatened to undermine Japan's relationship with even its closest ally, the United States. During the 1980s and into the 1990s much of the Japanese foreign policy establishment's energies were dedicated to managing the contradictory pressures generated by Japan's extreme dependence on outside markets and the world trading system, on the one hand, and Japan's deeply engrained preference for managed trade and state-led economic growth, on the other.

After the Cold War ended, these two structural determinants of Japan's approach to managing its economic relations with the outside world remained more or less intact. Japan certainly did not become any less dependent on trade than it had been in the past. And although the collapse of the bubble economy helped erode Japanese confidence in the superiority of its economic system, large sectors of the Japanese economy—especially agriculture, construction, and retail—had become dependent on government support and were unwilling to give up their privileged position. The increased competitiveness of the Japanese political system following the fall of the LDP, and the natural desire of Japanese politicians to reduce the pain incurred by the collapse of the Japanese economic bubble, made it all the more difficult for would-be economic reformers. As Steven Vogel, among others, has pointed out, although a certain measure of deregulation of the Japanese economy was in fact realized in the 1990s, it was soon followed by a new wave of reregulation.[89]

Since 1991, however, powerful forces have slowly but surely changed the terms on which the Japanese economy is integrated into the international system. Three developments in particular deserve attention: the increased internationalization of the Japanese economy as a result of external pressure and internal reforms, the increased importance of Asia to the Japanese economy, and Japan's improving ability to use the international trading system to protect its economic interests.

First, as Edward Lincoln explains in Chapter 6, despite the apparent intractability of Japan's asymmetrical relationship with the outside world, it is in fact slowly opening up. In part, this is simply a matter of Japan's bowing to financial necessity, as moribund Japanese firms such as Nissan or the Long Term Credit Bank are forced to look to outside partners to survive. More important, Japan's willingness to open itself to outside forces is also a product of an intellectual sea change. After more than a decade of economic misery, Japanese politicians, bureaucrats, and business leaders are keenly appreciative of the need to reform and modernize Japan on multiple levels. Although they face significant barriers to doing so and the rate of progress is glacial, there has been perceptible improvement. These trends have helped reduce the severe trade-related tensions that have historically afflicted Japan's relations with the outside world.

A second important development is the increased economic importance of Asia to the Japanese economy. Even though the outward flow of Japanese investment to Asia has slowed from its peak, an increasing share of Japanese trade is conducted with other Asian countries, especially China. By 2002 the Asian region accounted for a larger percentage of Japanese imports than did the United States and Europe combined and almost as large a share of Japanese exports (although the United States remained Japan's single largest trading partner).[90] The increased importance of the region to Japan has led Japan to sponsor the development of new regional frameworks, such as APEC and the APT framework. At the same time, the region itself has become more open to the creation of such institutions—both because of the growing importance of trade to the region's economies and because the fear of Japanese domination has receded with the decline in Japanese relative power and the emergence of other regional economic powers, most importantly that of China.[91]

Japan's new Asian orientation has not, however, translated into support for an exclusionary pan-Asian bloc, as feared by some commentators. Instead, as Juichi Inada points out in Chapter 8 in his analysis of Japan's role in the 1997–1998 East Asian financial crisis, when push comes to shove, Japan continues to try to reconcile its regional interests with its commitments to the global trading regime. Even when Japanese policymakers have strongly different ideas over how to proceed—as was the case in 1997–1998, when Finance Minister Miyazawa Kiichi proposed an Asian Monetary Fund that would have been more generous in bailing troubled Asian economies out of their monetary misery than was true of the IMF—in the end they have subordinated their efforts to the financial rescue program organized by the IMF and the US Treasury Department. Subsequent Japanese efforts to foster a cooperative approach to managing currency fluctuations—the Chiang Mai Initiative and the APT framework—were similarly timid and made largely contingent on support from the global monetary authorities based in Washington.[92]

Japan's relatively cautious approach to regional integration has its roots in a number of different factors. For one thing, as both Juichi Inada and Yoshiko Kojo argue in their chapters, Japan has no clearly developed intellectual approach to economic management that it can offer in place of the "Washington consensus" that governs the global international system. In addition, Japan's growing rivalry with China for regional leadership, as well as considerable potential for instability in the Chinese, Japanese, and other Asian economies, places sharp limits on the extent to which Asian governments are prepared to commit themselves to institutions that could restrict their room for maneuver in the event of a crisis.

The third development is that Japan has proven adept at using international institutions to pursue its own interests. One particularly clear example of this is provided by Japan's successful use of the WTO's dispute resolution mechanism to fend off US accusations of dumping and unfair trade, beginning with the landmark Fuji-Kodak case of 1995.[93] On the regional level Japan was similarly able to block a US effort to use early voluntary sector liberalization talks inside of APEC as an instrument for prying open

Japanese markets.[94] As Yoshiko Kojo demonstrates in Chapter 7, however, multilateral institutions can be a double-edged sword. In the context of the negotiations over the BIS accords governing international lending, the Japanese government was able to win concessions regarding how to calculate the minimum reserves that banks are required to hold in order to operate on international financial markets. After the Japanese financial bubble burst in 1992, however, Japanese banks had a great deal of difficulty meeting the minimum capital reserves requirement imposed by the BIS accords, feeding a general erosion of their competitiveness on international financial markets. Even worse, efforts by Japanese banks to meet the BIS requirements were believed by many in Japan to have contributed to the development of a massive downturn in domestic lending, thus helping usher in more than a decade of economic malaise.

In sum, despite certain fundamental continuities in Japan's economic position in the world, over the past decade significant changes have taken place. Japan's foreign economic relations with the outside world are both deeper and less fraught with tension than they were before the mid-1990s. Although the Japanese market remains relatively closed, it has opened tremendously compared to the past. Japan's economic ties with its neighbors are burgeoning, despite continued tension over history and other issues. And Japan continues to make excellent use of international institutions to safeguard its access to global markets while managing the painful adjustment costs that integration into the world economy can impose. The overall picture is one of gradual, if still incomplete, liberalization and is reflective of a slow, adaptive process whereby Japan—once viewed as one of the world's most savage economic predators—is increasingly viewed as a normal, law-abiding member of the international economic community.

Conclusion

Japanese foreign policy is often pilloried as being parochial and unimaginative, both by commentators abroad and even more so by ones inside of Japan.[95] Yet, if one looks back on the history of Japan over the past fifty years, it would seem that Japan has been remarkably successful with its allegedly unimaginative approach to foreign policy. Time and again, Japan has managed, in its own low-key way, to adapt to a series of often quite serious foreign policy challenges. In the immediate aftermath of the war in the Pacific, Japan was a broken pariah state, occupied by a foreign power, dependent on outside support for its economic survival, and shunned by its neighbors. Yet, by cleverly aligning itself with the United States while avoiding entanglement in regional confrontations, it managed to reintegrate itself into the global community by the early 1960s and to engineer an export-led expansion of its economy unprecedented in its size and scale. During the first half of the Cold War, Japan was disparaged for its supposedly myopic focus on economic growth, so much so that when Prime Minister Ikeda Hayato visited France in the 1960s, French president Charles de Gaulle famously dismissed him as a mere "transistor salesman." By the late 1970s, however, de Gaulle's successor, Valéry Giscard d'Estaing, was looking to Japan to help manage an increasingly volatile global economy, and in the 1980s Japan under Prime Minister Nakasone was a respected and much-relied-upon ally in coping with the Soviet military buildup of the late 1970s through early 1980s.[96] At the end of the Cold War, and especially after the first Gulf War, Japan was reviled as an economic predator and as a free rider on the global security order underwritten by the United States. A decade later, however, tensions over trade have subsided, and US officials have showered Japan with praise for its assistance in the war on terror. In the end, it would be hard not to conclude that either Japan has been remarkably lucky for more than half a century, or Japanese foreign policy is more astute than it is generally credited as being.

As argued in this chapter, the secret behind Japan's success in managing its foreign relations is its underappreciated capacity to adjust to changes in the international environment. At each juncture in its history, Japan has slowly, but judiciously, implemented pragmatic changes in its foreign policy that have allowed it to meet new challenges. The overall change in Japanese policymaking has been in a generally liberal direction, gradually opening up the Japanese economy to the outside world and an increasing Japanese participation in global and regional economic and security institutions.

On balance, this strategy has been successful not only for Japan but for Asia as a whole. Since the Sino-Vietnamese clashes of 1979 there have been no major, militarized conflicts in the Asian region. International and Asian intraregional trade and investment have grown exponentially. Asian regional institutions have multiplied both in number and in the range of issues that they deal with.[97] Finally there has been a slow, but significant, spread of democracy in the region and some improvement in human rights conditions generally.[98] Of course, Japanese policy alone cannot claim credit for these successes. But there can also be little doubt that Japan has played a key role in helping make this general transformation—this pacification of the Asia Pacific region—possible.

That this strategy has worked in the past, however, provides no guarantee that it will continue to work in the future. Two factors loom large in determining the long-term future of Japan's liberal adaptive state. First, there is the question of whether China can be peacefully integrated into the international system. And second, there is the potentially even more portentous question of the future shape of the US role in world affairs.

Many Japanese watch the rise of China with a mixture of awe and trepidation. As Mike Mochizuki explains in Chapter 11, the economic benefits of China's spectacular growth are already readily apparent and likely to grow exponentially in the future. A peaceful, prosperous China—one that over time moves in a more democratic direction and remains committed to maintaining a cooperative relationship with its neighbors—could transform the region, and indeed the world. Were such a China to emerge, many of the strains that beset Japanese policymaking today would disappear, and the prospects for creating a genuinely liberal international order in Asia, one comparable to the state of affairs obtaining in Western Europe, would be improved immensely.

At the same time, the emergence of strident Chinese popular nationalism (with its particularly virulent anti-Japanese overtones), the brittle character of Chinese political institutions, and the rapid growth in the Chinese defense budget suggest the possibility of a very different future. An overtly hostile, powerful China could pose a serious threat to Japan's national security and a fundamental challenge to Japan's liberal instincts. Almost as bad would be a weak, fragmented China whose internal chaos would inevitably spill out over its borders and could have serious negative repercussions for all of its neighbors, including Japan, in the shape of lowered regional economic growth, refugees, proliferation of the technology for weapons of mass destruction (WMD), and potentially increased geopolitical rivalries.[99] In either instance, it would be much more difficult to forge the kind of Asian-Pacific community that many in Japan continue to hope for and potentially could create the conditions for a complete rethinking of the fundamentally liberal premises on which Japanese foreign policy today is based.[100]

Even more important to the long-term viability of the Japanese approach to foreign policy will be the stance of the United States. By and large, Japanese policymakers and opinion leaders acknowledge that the alliance with the United States has served Japan's best interests. It is thanks to the United States that Japan has been able to avoid facing difficult issues such as providing for its own nuclear security or having to defend its vital sea lines of communication. Despite the often virulent criticism that has been heaped on it by many liberals—both inside and outside of Japan—US policy has, judging by its results over time, moved Asia in a decidedly more liberal direction. In a very real way, Japan's preference for a liberal approach to international relations has been made possible by the US willingness to use its power to build a more liberal world, even though the commitment of the United States to liberal principles has often been questioned and its liberalism has been of a decidedly more muscular, Wilsonian nature.[101]

In the context of the war on terror, however, the United States has moved into a proactive mode regarding terrorist threats, seeking to disrupt terrorist networks internationally and engaging in preventive (not preemptive) attacks on states that it fears could provide terrorists with WMD. As the 2002 "National Security Strategy of the United States of America" puts it, "the greatest threat our Nation faces lies at the crossroads of radicalism and technology."[102] Although the United States has continued to look to its allies to help it deal with the terrorist threat, its willingness to act independently of international institutions and alliance structures, relying instead on "coalitions of the willing," has engendered considerable tensions with many of its traditional allies and foreign policy partners. The run-up to the war on Iraq sparked a major crisis between the United States and the continental European powers and inflicted lasting damage on NATO.[103] Likewise, relations between the United States and South Korea have been under unprecedented strain over differences on how to deal with Pyongyang's nuclear weapons program.[104]

Although it is far from clear whether these tensions will continue or even worsen in the future, as predicted by some observers,[105] there is the very real possibility that the United States will find itself increasingly at odds with the institutional structures that it helped build. Although so far the types of tensions that manifested themselves in the transatlantic relationship have not appeared in US-Japanese relations—and in fact the trend would seem to be in the opposite direction—appearances are deceiving on this score. Japanese concerns regarding the threat from North Korea, together with an exceptionally pro-US, pro-defense Koizumi administration, encouraged Japan to display an unusual degree of solidarity with the United States. The new government of Abe Shinzō is set to continue this trend. Japanese public and elite opinion, however, remains skeptical about becoming too deeply entangled in US strategic designs, and decisions such as the dispatch of Japanese forces to Iraq or the provision of logistical support for US-led forces in the Indian Ocean are deeply unpopular.[106] Although the Japanese public reluctantly supported the Koizumi government's strongly supportive stance on defense cooperation with the United States, that support was fragile. It could easily have been disrupted in the event of a setback (such as the massacre of Japanese peacekeepers), and it was contingent on a number of factors, most notably the sense of threat from North Korea[107] and the presence of a pro-defense, pro-US prime minister in Tokyo.[108]

Two possibilities suggest themselves. The first is that the current spate of crises in alliance relations is a passing phase and that eventually a new modus vivendi will be worked out between the United States and the rest of the world, one that will see continued efforts on the part of the United States and other democratic nations to build a cooperative international order capable of managing the problems of global society. In this case, although the US-Japanese partnership may continue to go through periodic ups and downs, Japan's basically liberal approach to world affairs will be revalidated. The second, decidedly more negative, possibility is that disagreements between the United States and its traditional partners will deteriorate, leading eventually to a general unraveling of the international alliance system that it has built, including its relationship with Japan. Under such circumstances, the generally liberal approach that Japan has adopted toward the world will come under enormous strain, especially if at the same time Japan's relations with China continue to deteriorate, and a general abandonment of the liberal premises of post-1945 Japanese foreign policy would probably become inevitable.

What is the practical upshot of the foregoing analysis? Two sets of conclusions seem evident, one focusing on the US perspective, the other on the Japanese. First, from the point of view of US policymakers, there is both good and bad news. The good news is that Japan is capable of change and that it is likely to see its interests as largely congruent with those of the United States. Fears that Japan may drift away from the alliance, possibly in the direction of some sort of pan-Asian neutralism or even worse a belligerent nationalism, which seemed perfectly plausible a decade ago, seem rather overblown today.[109] Instead, Japan has strengthened its strategic partnership with the United States and is playing a valuable support role for US diplomacy and military operations both in Asia and beyond. With proper management, this is a trend that can be sustained for some time to come.

The bad news, from Washington's point of view, is that there are limits to how fast this process can be accelerated. There remains a very real danger that in a future security crisis, perhaps over the Korean peninsula, Iran, or the Taiwan Strait, Japan may balk, leading to a renewal of the types of alliance crises that we had in 1991, over the first Gulf War, and in 1994, during the first round of the North Korean nuclear crisis. Much will depend on the leadership in Tokyo. Not every Japanese prime minister is likely to be as forthcoming as Koizumi. Also, much will depend on the circumstances under which the crisis develops. On the one hand, if it is perceived that tensions have mounted as a result of provocations from North Korea, China, Iran, and others, then the likelihood of Japanese support is much greater. On the other hand, if Tokyo believes that the United States is the initiator of hostilities, the possibility of Japanese defection in a crisis is much higher. In short, legitimacy matters and cannot be taken for granted. If the United States is not careful, it can inflict the same kind of damage—or even greater damage—on its transpacific relations that it experienced in its transatlantic ones during the 2003 Iraq war.

In this context, it is important that Washington recognizes that there is a Japanese preference for working inside multilateral institutions for both geopolitical and ideological-historical reasons. Geopolitically, it makes sense for Japan to seek to use institutions as a way of preventing its strategic agenda from being dominated by the much larger and stronger United States. Ideologically, Japan's penchant for multilateral institutions is grounded in the deeply grounded liberalism of its adaptive state.[110] The creation of new multilateral security institutions should be an important, long-term goal of US foreign policy in the Asia Pacific region. Likewise, the United States should appreciate Japanese sensitivities on this issue and should not needlessly quash Japanese ambitions regarding institution building, as it did in 2005 with respect to the Japanese bid for a seat on the UN Security Council. Fortunately, there are signs that this is well understood in Washington, as reflected in the continued development of the Proliferation Security Initiative and the general tacit US acceptance of the Chiang Mai Initiative and other Japanese efforts to strengthen its institutional ties with the region.

A further issue that the United States will need to tackle in this regard is the issue of history in the Asian region. Although arguably there are some benefits to the United States from the current tensions between Japan and its Asian neighbors over the issue of history—insofar as the more alienated Japan is from its neighbors, the more dependent it is on the United States—in the long run the United States cannot afford to be overly sanguine about the current state of affairs. The deterioration of Japanese relations with China and South Korea has reached the point at which the prospect of military clashes over what should be manageable disputes over maritime boundaries no longer seems implausible. There is a certain irony here. For much of the last six decades, Japanese critics of the Mutual Security Treaty have complained that the United States might drag Japan into an unnecessary war in Asia. Yet today, for the first time, it is the United States that faces the possibility that it might be entangled in a militarized conflict through its alliance with Japan. Even if actual military conflict can be avoided, tensions over history have unfortunate spillover effects. The US alliance with South Korea has been weakened by disputes over history, and even political leaders in the United States who otherwise might be sympathetic to Japan become critical of it (rightly or wrongly) because of what is perceived as revisionist tendencies in its stance on history.

The US government would be foolish to intervene directly in the issue. The United States as well is potentially the target of much criticism over the past (Hiroshima, No-Gun Ri, and the colonization of the Philippines come readily to mind), and it has no interest in validating an international norm that could come back to haunt it. Yet, the United States needs to make clear, through quiet diplomacy and in the context of semiofficial "track two" discussions, that the issue is of concern to the United States and that we hope for its resolution. The United States should avoid taking sides on any particular issue (such as how many people actually died in Nanjing in 1937), but it should seek to promote dialogue and encourage Japanese leaders to remain engaged with the topic. The United States might also try to set an example by pursuing an active campaign of public diplomacy to deal with its issues of history in Asia.

From the Japanese perspective, the important thing is to recognize that Japan does in fact have a unique profile in international affairs. The long-standing critique of the lack of Japanese "agency" in international affairs, which argues that Japan is not an independent actor in international affairs and has no agenda of its own, is no longer valid, if it ever was. In fact, it is possible to discern a distinctively Japanese approach to international relations and with it a Japanese "liberal" set of values. Japan should seek to articulate its position more clearly in a way that is persuasive both to its own public and to international society in general. The United States should expect and encourage it to do so.

In so doing, however, Japan must become more realistic about the short-term limits of liberalism, both in the context of contemporary East Asia and on the global level. The Asian region continues to be beset by deeply rooted historical grievances and serious clashes of interest over geopolitical issues. Although trends in the region are moving in a favorable (that is, liberal) direction, it will take time to overcome the deep animosities that continue to persist in the region. The situation is even cloudier on the global level, and despite the omnipresent talk of a "global civil society" and the constant calls for "global governance," it will be some time before reality catches up with rhetoric. Japanese politicians should therefore be careful about the hopes and expectations that they place on the United Nations and regional institutions, even while they can and should continue to promote them. In the meantime, Japan should continue to increase its contribution to the international order, both economically and in the area of human rights and military security. Aligning its diplomatic efforts more clearly with the liberal ideals and values held by much of its own population—as well as the peoples of democratic societies—will increase the internal and external legitimacy of its new engagement with the outside world.

Japan's antimilitary animus continues to represent a serious obstacle to Japanese efforts in the area of military security. Nonetheless, Japan can continue to work to overcome these obstacles by expanding its role in providing logistical support for multilateral peacekeeping operations and by strengthening its ability to defend its own territory. Particularly promising is the area of international disaster relief, in which the Japanese Self-Defense Forces have considerable expertise and for which there is broad popular support. Eventually, Japan will need to reconsider the ban on collective self-defense, although whether it needs to do so through constitutional revision or whether it can manage this through a reinterpretation of the constitution is an issue that ultimately will have to be resolved through the domestic political process.

Finally, on the economic front, Japan needs to continue moving in the direction of increased liberalization of its economy, especially by reducing barriers to imports—including the sensitive area of agricultural imports—and on overseas investment by government entities. This is one area where Japanese domestic and foreign policy interests clearly coincide. Although conditions have improved greatly over the past decade or so, Japanese consumers continue to pay overly high prices for many products, preventing the freeing up of resources that could be more effectively invested elsewhere in the Japanese economy. Limits on Japanese investment prevent Japan from improving the rate of return on publicly invested funds (such as postal savings accounts), exacerbating the financial strains that an aging population will place on public coffers. At the same time, by further integrating Japan into the global economy, Japan will enhance its political leverage abroad. Japanese leadership on agricultural subsidies would be especially welcome at a time when the World Trade Organization talks would appear to have reached an impasse.

If the political leaders in Tokyo and Washington are able to achieve these goals, coordinate their visions of Asia's future, and turn those visions into concrete plans for coordinated action on such important issues as integrating China into the international community and managing tensions on the Korean peninsula, then the prospects for sustained peace and progress in the Asia Pacific region are excellent.

Notes

This chapter has benefited from considerable discussion and advice from a large number of people, including my two fellow editors, Mike Mochizuki and Jitsuo Tsuchiyama; Itō Kenichi of Japan Forum for International Relations; former ambassador Tōgō Kazuhiko; Richard J. Samuels of MIT; the members of the Aoyama University International Relations study group; and my fellow contributors to this book. Two anonymous readers appointed by Lynne Rienner were also of great assistance in helping to sharpen and more tightly focus the arguments made here.

1. Classic formulations of the realist position are found in Morgenthau, *Politics Among Nations*; and Waltz, *Theory of International Politics*. For a more recent statement, see Mearsheimer, *The Tragedy of Great Power Politics*.

2. Tsuchiyama, "The End of the Alliance?"

3. On the core ideas of liberalism, see Doyle, *Ways of War and Peace*, as well as Moravcsik, "Liberal International Relations Theory." For an overview of the evolution of international relations theorizing in the Western tradition, see Knutsen, *A History of International Relations*.

4. This distinction between offensive and defensive liberalism plays off of the debate in international relations over "offensive" versus "defensive" realism. Defensive realists see states as pursuing power only insofar as it is needed to balance power and maintain their own autonomy and security. Offensive realists, on the other hand, view states as power maximizers, seeking to expand their power at every

opportunity. For an overview of the debate and how it relates to liberalism, see Jervis, "Realism, Neoliberalism, and Cooperation." Mearsheimer, *The Tragedy of Great Power Politics,* is a strongly argued version of the offensive realist position. Walt, *The Origins of Alliances,* and Van Evera, *The Causes of War,* are important expositions of the defensive realist argument. By extension, defensive liberals are more cautious about exercising their power—economic and diplomatic as well as military—to reshape the international system in a liberal direction. They believe that long-term trends favor the emergence of a liberal international order and that the vigorous application of power to accelerate its emergence is likely to be both costly and counterproductive. Offensive liberals, on the other hand, are more confident about their ability to re-create the world and advocate the use of power, including, if necessary, military power, to speed the emergence of a liberal international system.

5. For a discussion by a former neoconservative in debates on US foreign policy, see Fukuyama, *America at the Crossroads.* For an analysis from a more liberal perspective, see Daalder and Lindsay, *America Unbound.*

6. See, for instance, Peter Katzenstein's contention that Japan has an essentially norms-driven, communal view of domestic politics but a Hobbesian, realpolitik view of international relations, a stance that he sees as being the opposite of that of West Germany's. Katzenstein, *Cultural Norms and National Security,* 498–537.

7. See Green, *Japan's Reluctant Realism.*

8. There is something of a debate on how to characterize the East Asian region. Some analysts, most notably Aaron Friedberg, have argued that the Asian environment is basically a realist one, characterized by great power competition and inherently prone to war. See Friedberg, "Ripe for Rivalry." More recent analyses suggested that East Asia is far more stable than Friedberg's portrayal suggested. Muthiah Alagappa, for instance, pointed out that there had been no major interstate conflict since 1979, and Amitav Acharya argued that in Southeast Asia at least there had emerged a security community based on ASEAN. See Alagappa, *Asian Security Order,* chap. 1, and Acharya, "Collective Identity and Conflict Management in Southeast Asia." The net assessment is that Asia today is not the equivalent of Europe before 1914. The balance of power favors the United States and its allies too much, and regional elites—including those in China—desire a stable international environment in order to concentrate on the economic development that they believe essential to regime survival. At the same time, however, there remain many real tensions, especially over nationalist issues such as the status of Taiwan or territorial disputes in the South China Sea, and Asia today collectively is a far more dangerous and conflictual place than, say, Western Europe. See Berger, "Set for Stability?"

9. Kagan, *Of Paradise and Power,* 3.

10. The Chinese economy is larger than that of Japan, if adjusted for purchasing power parity (PPP). Calculated in PPP terms, the Chinese economy in 2004 was approximately 6 trillion dollars, compared to 4 trillion for Japan. Calculated in nominal GDP terms, however, the Japanese economy is much larger than that of the Chinese—4 trillion versus 1.5 trillion. Which statistic provides a more accurate reflection of economic productivity and national power depends on what one is trying to measure. On the one hand, economic data calculated in terms of PPP values are a better gauge of the overall ability of the economy to produce all types of goods and services, from rice, chickens, and haircuts; through bricks, mortar, and medical services; to advanced computer circuits and cutting-edge design work. On the other hand, nominal GDP data may better capture the relative technological sophistication of what is produced. The Japanese economy produces more things that are relatively scarce and valuable than does the Chinese. At the same time, since currencies are

prone to erratic fluctuations, and the Chinese yuan is not freely traded, the measure is very rough indeed.

11. For an interesting analysis that stresses the considerable military capabilities that Japan has already acquired, see Lind, "Pacifism or Passing the Buck."

12. For a brief review of Japan's ability to go nuclear, see Harrison, *Japan's Nuclear Future*, chap. 1. For discussions of Japanese thinking on the topic, see Self and Thompson, *Japan's Nuclear Option*.

13. For an overview of the first wave of books making such predictions in the early 1970s, see Barraclough, "Watch out for Japan."

14. An obvious exception would appear to be international environmental policy, especially with respect to global warming. Yet, as Miranda Schreurs has argued, Japanese activism on environmental issues may be more a result of its lack of initiative in other issue areas than a clear example of a new trend in Japanese foreign policy. See Schreurs, *Environmental Politics*.

15. Rix, "Japan and the Region: Leading from Behind." Reinhard Drifte made much the same point when he argued that Japan engaged in "leadership by stealth." See Drifte, *Japan's Foreign Policy for the Twenty-First Century*, 14, 173–174.

16. I would like to thank Professor Thayer for his insight on this point.

17. On the concept of grand strategy, see Rosecrance and Stein, *The Domestic Bases of Grand Strategy*.

18. Calder, "Japanese Foreign Economic Policy Formation." Calder developed this argument further in a book, *Crisis and Compensation*. He updated his argument without fundamentally rejecting its basic premise in "Japan as a Post-Reactive State?"

19. See, for instance, Lincoln, *Japan's New Global Role;* Hellmann, "Japanese Politics and Foreign Policy"; Hellmann, "The Confrontation with Realpolitik"; Blaker, "Evaluating Japan's Diplomatic Performance"; Miyashita, *Limits to Power: Asymmetric Dependence;* and Katzenstein and Okawara, *Japan's National Security*.

20. See, for instance, Curtis, *The Japanese Way of Democracy;* Richardson, *Japanese Democracy;* and Muramatsu and Krauss, "The Conservative Policy Line and the Development of Patterned Pluralism."

21. See Berger, *Cultures of Antimilitarism;* Hook, *Militarization and Demilitarization;* and Katzenstein, *Cultural Norms and National Security*.

22. See Gao, *Economic Ideology and Japanese Industrial Policy;* and Tett, *Saving the Sun*.

23. The net result is quite familiar to students of organizational behavior and is referred to as the "garbage can" model of decisionmaking. See Cohen, Marsh, and Olsen, "A Garbage Can Model of Organizational Choice."

24. See Muramatsu and Krauss, "The Conservative Policy Line."

25. See Curtis, *The Logic of Japanese Politics*, 9–10.

26. Many other authors offer similar analyses. See, for instance, Richardson's description of Japan as a "bargained distributive democracy" in *Japanese Democracy*, chap. 10. For an overview, see Frank Schwartz's expert exposition of what he terms "neopluralist" interpretations of Japanese politics. Schwartz, *Advice and Consent*, esp. chaps. 1 and 7.

27. That this system has impeded Japanese efforts at domestic reform is the main argument of Pempel's *Regime Shift*. On its negative impact on Japanese foreign economic policy, see Edward Lincoln in Chapter 6 of this book, and Lincoln, "Japan: Using Power Narrowly."

28. See Johnson, *MITI and the Japanese Miracle;* Johnson, *Japan: Who Governs?* and Fallows, *Looking at the Sun*. The term *power elite* with reference to

the United States was popularized in the writings of C. Wright Mills. See especially his highly influential book entitled, appropriately enough, *The Power Elite*.

29. See van Wolferen, *The Japanese Enigma;* and Samuels, *"Rich Nation, Strong Army,"* especially his subtle discussion of the relationship between ideology and strategy, 337–341.

30. See Heginbotham and Samuels, "Japan," 98–99, as well as Heginbotham and Samuels, "Mercantile Realism and Japan's Foreign Policy." On technonationalism, see Samuels, *"Rich Nation, Strong Army."*

In his more recent writings, Samuels has emphasized that this "mercantile realism" is an ideological consensus that emerged after World War II and provided a domestic political basis around which an otherwise fractious governing coalition of conservative elites could be formed. That consensus, however, is in the process of dissolving (see Samuels, *Securing Japan*). In this sense, Professor Samuels's more recent writings have moved away from the "strategic actor" model in which his earlier work appeared to fit. I would like to thank Professor Samuels for sharing an advance copy of the first chapter of *Securing Japan* as well as for his comments on this chapter.

31. Chapman, Drifte, and Gow, *Japan's Quest for Comprehensive Security*.

32. "Complex interdependence" refers to a world in which states are tightly linked together by ties of trade, commerce, communication, and so on. See Keohane and Nye, *Power and Interdependence: World Politics in Transition*.

33. Some link this to the spread of liberal democracy. Others tie it to demographic changes, especially the decline in the size of families, which makes the loss of even a single child more costly for the long-term fortunes of the household than was true in the past.

34. For a concise summary of the argument that the international system is changing in ways that favor economic over military power, and thus the Japanese over the US approach to international politics, see Rosecrance, *The Rise of the Trading State*. For a broadly similar argument made from a decidedly different political viewpoint, see Luttwak, "From Geopolitics to Geoeconomics."

35. This concept of balance is the central argument of Michael Green's *Japan's Reluctant Realism*. See also Hughes, *Japan's Security Agenda* and "Japan's Reemergence"; and Cha, "Defensive Realism and Japan's Approach to Korean Reunification."

36. For an early articulation of this point of view, see Weinstein, *Japan's Postwar Defense Policy*. For a more recent exposition, see Pharr, "Japan's Defensive Foreign Policy," especially 236 ff.

37. Johnson, "La Serenissima of the East." Additional functions of the Japanese military were seen to be a hedge against the collapse of the security relationship with the United States and a tool for prying technology from the United States. See Samuels, *"Rich Nation, Strong Army."*

38. On aid policies, see Arase, *Buying Power*. On Japan's regional alliances, see Hatch, *Asia in Japan's Embrace*. See also Bernard and Ravenhill, "Beyond Product Cycles and Flying Geese." For an application of this general view of Japanese efforts to strengthen East Asian regional institutions, see Katzenstein and Shiraishi, *Network Power*. On Japanese efforts to cultivate close ties with oil producers, even at the cost of potentially undercutting US strategic objectives, see Samuels and Heginbotham, "Japan's Dual Hedge."

39. Perhaps the single best known exemplar of this view is Prestowitz, *Trading Places*. For a theoretical argument by an economist as to why this type of trade policy can be successful, see Krugman, *Strategic Trade*.

40. The term *Japan as number one* was popularized by Ezra Vogel's best-selling *Japan as Number One.*

41. A certain parallel can be seen here with the evolution of Japanese industrial policy. See Noble, "The Japanese Industrial Policy Debate."

42. On Asian regionalism in general, see Lincoln, *East Asian Economic Regionalism.* On Japanese lack of influence in Asia despite its foreign aid programs and network-building efforts, see MacIntyre, "Japanese and American Strategies in Asia."

43. See Katzenstein, *Cultural Norms and National Security.*

44. See Green, *Japan's Reluctant Realism;* and Hughes, *Japan's Re-emergence.*

45. Lincoln, "Japan: Using Power Narrowly."

46. See Note 1.

47. For an analysis of how changes in the international environment triggered domestic change in Japan, see Pyle, "Profound Forces in the Making of Modern Japan."

48. See Lincoln, *Japan's New Global Role;* Rosecrance, *The Rise of the Trading State;* Calder, *Japan's New Role in Asia;* Encarnation, *Rivals Beyond Trade;* Thurow, *Head-to-Head;* Garten, *A Cold Peace;* and Huntington, "Why International Primacy Matters."

49. A substantial literature has developed on the causes of Japan's lost decade, one that rivals in size the older literature on the reasons for its then-phenomenal success. Lincoln, *Arthritic Japan;* Grimes, *Unmaking the Japanese Miracle;* Katz, *Japan: The System That Soured;* Callon, *Divided Sun;* and Alexander, *In the Shadow of the Miracle.*

50. See Wade, "Japan, the World Bank, and the Art of Paradigm Maintenance," 3–36. For a spirited defense of the Japanese model of development by a senior Japanese official, see former Ministry of Finance vice minister Eisuke Sakakibara's *Beyond Capitalism.*

51. Contrast Sakakibara, *Beyond Capitalism,* with his more recent writings on the Japanese economy, *Structural Reform in Japan.*

52. For a more detailed analysis, see Bergsten, Ito, and Noland, *No More Bashing;* and Lincoln, *Troubled Times.*

53. For other recent studies that emphasize these same points, see Katz, *Japanese Phoenix;* and Vogel, *Japan Remodeled.*

54. See Curtis, *Policymaking in Japan,* esp. chap. 1; Muramatsu, "An Arthritic Japan?"; and Kato, "Reforming the Japanese Bureaucracy." For a broader analysis that incorporates changes in the role of the bureaucracy with other developments in the Japanese political system, see Pempel, *Regime Shift.*

55. For an overview of changes in the Japanese party landscape, see Curtis, *The Logic of Japanese Politics;* and Hrebenar, *Japan's New Party System.* For an entertaining but well-informed and scholarly account of the collapse of the LDP-led system, see Jacob Schlesinger, *Shadow Shoguns: The Rise and Fall of Japan's Postwar Political Machine* (New York: Simon and Schuster, 1997).

56. Of the 480 seats in the Japanese lower house (the dominant of the two Japanese representative bodies), 300 are elected from mid-sized electoral systems, and an additional 180 are elected using a proportional representation system.

57. I would like to express gratitude to Professor David Arase of Pomona College for helping elucidate this argument.

58. In the late 1980s Japanese Diet members interviewed by the author were unanimous in their view that defense and foreign policy do not translate into votes.

Today, things seem quite different, and even quite ordinary farmers in rural districts ask their representatives pointed questions about foreign affairs. I would like to thank Shintaro Ito, parliamentary vice minister for foreign affairs, for his insight on this point.

59. See also Wan, "Tensions in Sino-Japanese Relations: The Shenyang Incident." I am also grateful to Professor Gilbert Rozman of Princeton and Ambassador Kazuhiko Togo for sharing their wisdom on this topic.

60. See Kataoka, *The Price of a Constitution.*

61. See Kelly and White, "Students, Slackers, Singles, Seniors, and Strangers." For a more journalistic account, see Nathan, *Japan Unbound.*

62. See Nathan, *Japan Unbound;* and Matthews, "Japan's New Nationalism."

63. The burgeoning constructivist literature in international relations has strangely neglected to focus on historical narratives and their role in giving content to the norms and values constructivists emphasize in their writings.

64. See Chang, *The Rape of Nanjing;* and Hicks, *Japan's War Memories.*

65. See Art, *The Politics of the Nazi Past;* and Wertsch, *Voices of Collective Remembering.* On the possible global dimensions of this phenomenon, see Barkan, *The Guilt of Nations.*

66. See Arase, "Japanese Policy Towards Democracy."

67. Pharr and Schwartz, *The State of Civil Society in Japan,* esp. chaps. 2, 5, and 14.

68. Inoguchi, *Tadanori to Ikkoku Haneishugi o Koete* [Beyond Free-Riding and One-Country Prosperity: World in Transition and Japan].

69. See, for instance, Thomas Havens's description of Japan's response to the war in *The Fire Across the Sea.*

70. For an analysis of the logic behind the fear of entanglement, see Tsuchiyama, "The End of the Alliance?" Regarding fears of a regional backlash, see Midford, "Japan's Leadership." For the implications of this point of view with respect to Japanese nuclear weapons, see Self and Thompson, *Japan's Nuclear Option.*

71. Berger, *Cultures of Antimilitarism.*

72. For an excellent overview of the changes in Japanese thinking about defense in the 1990s, see Cronin and Green, *The U.S.-Japanese Alliance;* and Green, *Japan's Reluctant Realism.*

73. See Hughes, *Japan's Re-emergence,* chap. 5; and Midford, "Japan's Response to the War on Terror." For contrasting views written from more of a "reactive state" perspective, see Katzenstein, "Same War, Different Views"; and Leheny, "Tokyo Confronts Terror."

74. For a general discussion, see Berger, *Redefining Japan.*

75. For an excellent review focusing on the political side of the relationship, see Rapp, "Paths Diverging?" For a perceptive and informed analysis of the domestic political background behind many of these developments, see Fujita, "Japan in the War on Terrorism." See also Hughes, *Japan's Re-emergence;* and Midford, "Japan's Response."

76. I would like to express my thanks to Ambassador Armacost for his insight on this issue.

77. On the implications of a ballistic missile defense system for the alliance, see Cronin, Giarra, and Green, "The Alliance Implications"; and Swaine, Swanger, and Kawakami, *Japan and Ballistic Missile Defense.* On its possible implications for regional relations, see Urayama, "China Debates Missile Defense."

78. In the summer of 2006, despite North Korean efforts to exclude Japan from the six-power talks and a general atmosphere of distrust and hostility between Pyongyang and Tokyo, Prime Minister Koizumi indicated that he would like to normalize relations between the two nations before the end of his term in 2006. See *Daily Yomiuri* (English-language version), July 20, 2005. Available at http://www.yomiuri.co.jp/dy/world/20050720TDY01005.htm. Talks resumed in the winter of 2006, despite the lack of tangible progress after three years of negotiations.

79. In 2000 an influential commission headed by Richard Armitage and Joseph Nye held Great Britain up as a model of what Japan should become as a US ally. See Institute for National Strategic Studies, *The US and Japan: Advancing Towards a Mature Partnership.* Many of the commission members joined the Bush administration the following year. For an assessment of progress made in achieving the goals of the commission, see Cossa and Glasserman, *Has Japan Become the Great Britain of Asia?*

80. See Crowley, *Japan's Quest for Autonomy;* and Barnhart, *Japan Prepares for Total War.* For a good overview, see Beasley, *Japanese Imperialism.*

81. Gerschenkron, *Economic Backwardness in Historical Perspective.*

82. Of course, Japan had had a long and complex history of relations with the outside world stretching back to at least the sixth century AD. It was not until the sixteenth century that a truly global international system as such came into being. Moreover, after a period of intense interaction with the West, by 1633 Japan had moved to sharply restrict relations with the West and with its Asian neighbors as well.

83. On the preconditions of Japan's rapid growth, see Smith, *The Native Sources.*

84. On the close relationship between the Japanese state and Japanese society in general, see Garon, *Molding Japanese Minds.* There is a substantial literature on the origins of the Japanese development state. For a theoretically sophisticated explanation of how state intervention may be successful in fostering economic growth under certain circumstances, see Rodrik, "Getting Intervention Right."

85. Noguchi, *1940-nen Taisei.*

86. There exists a vast literature on Japanese industrial and economic policy. For good reviews of the system in its heyday, see Gao, *Economic Ideology and Japanese Industrial Policy;* Gerlach, *Alliance Capitalism;* Okimoto, *Between MITI and the Marketplace;* Samuels, *The Business of the Japanese State;* and Tilton, *Restrained Trade.* For an excellent set of essays reviewing the development of the Japanese development state and putting it in comparative context, see Woo, *The Developmental State.*

87. See Lincoln, *Japan's Unequal Trade;* and Mason, *American Multinationals and Japan.*

88. See Gerlach, *Alliance Capitalism.*

89. Vogel, *Freer Markets, More Rules.* See also Carlile and Tilton, *Is Japan Really Changing Its Ways?* and Katz, *Japanese Phoenix.*

90. See Sasaki and Koga, "Trade Between Japan and China."

91. As Donald Crone has pointed out, regional integration in East Asia has developed under conditions not of hegemony, as in the West, but of multipolarity. See Crone, "Does Hegemony Matter?" On Japan's approach to regional integration, see Terada, "The Origins of Japan's APEC Policy"; Yamada and Tsutomu, "Japan's Approach to APEC"; Katzenstein and Shiraishi, *Network Power;* Ashizawa, "Japan, the United States, and Multilateral Institution-Building."

92. For a rather different assessment, see Katada, "Japan's Counterweight

Strategy." I would like to express my appreciation to my colleague, William Grimes of Boston University, for helping explain the complexities of Japan's strategy for dealing with the region.

93. See Pekkanen, "At Play in the Legal Realm."

94. See Krauss, "The United States and Japan."

95. See, for instance, Blaker, "Evaluating Japan's Diplomatic Performance."

96. See Thayer, "Japanese Foreign Policy During the Nakasone Years."

97. For a brief overview, see Pempel, "Introduction," esp. 12–19.

98. In 1980, there was only one democracy—Japan—in the East Asian–Southeast Asian region, a total of fifteen countries (excluding Australia, New Zealand, and Russia but including Taiwan). By 2005 there were six, including Indonesia, the Philippines, South Korea, Thailand, and Taiwan. Although human rights abuses remain many and rampant, on the whole there has been significant improvement in many countries, including most importantly China. For a general discussion of the prospects for human rights in East Asia, see Berger, "Ripe for Rights?"

99. For a discussion of Chinese instability, see Pei, "China's Governance Crisis"; and Shambaugh, *Is China Unstable?*

100. In neither instance, however, should we automatically assume that Japan would move toward a realist, balance-of-power approach to international affairs. After all, West Germany went through forty years of existence faced with an existential threat in the form of the Soviet Union on its front doorstep (actually, inside the door, as it occupied one-third of Germany's national territory), and it actually became more, not less, liberal in its approach to foreign policy over time. A weak China, creating economic instability, spreading refugees, and wracked by internal power struggles and even civil wars, might also encourage Japan to seek a coordinated international effort at shoring China up.

101. For analyses of post-1945 US foreign policy that emphasize its fundamentally liberal vision, see Ikenberry, "America's Liberal Grand Strategy"; and Tony Smith, *America's Mission.*

102. "National Security Strategy of the United States," 4.

103. See, for instance, Gordon and Shapiro, *Allies at War;* and Pond, *Friendly Fire.* The roots of allied tension, however, predated the Iraq war; see Mowle, *Allies at Odds.*

104. Kim, "Anti-Americanism in Korea."

105. See, for example, Menon, "The End of Alliances"; Kupchan, *The End of the American Era;* and Prestowitz, *Rogue Nation.* For general discussions of how September 11 has changed US foreign policy in ways that challenge its traditional partnerships with the outside world, see, for instance, Daalder and Lindsay, *America Unbound;* Ikenberry, "America's Imperial Ambition"; and Fukuyama, *America at the Crossroads.*

106. According to a Nippon Television poll, 59.8 percent of those surveyed in December 2005 opposed the extension of the SDF in Iraq for another year. See Nippon Terebi Yoron Chosa. Available at http://www.ntv.co.jp/yoron/. Other polling data by a variety of organizations show similar levels of opposition.

107. In this context it is worth recalling Koizumi's willingness to travel to Pyongyang in 2002 and sign a declaration promising a new spirit of cooperation between the two nations. Even though that initiative soon floundered as a result of tensions resulting from the revelation that North Korea had kidnapped Japanese citizens in the 1970s and the discovery of a North Korean nuclear weapons program, as late as 2005 Koizumi apparently harbored some hope for restarting the diplomatic

dialogue with Japan's most troublesome neighbor. See *Yomiuri* (English-language version), July 20, 2005. Available at http://www.yomiuri.co.jp/dy/world/20050720TDY01005.htm.

108. See also Mochizuki, "Strategic Thinking Under Bush and Koizumi," for a further analysis of the gap in the strategic visions of the two nations.

109. For a different point of view, see Matthews, "Japan's New Nationalism"; and John Nathan, *Japan Unbound.*

110. In this sense, Germany provides Japan with a more natural model to emulate than does Great Britain. Like Japan, Germany has strong geopolitical as well as ideological reasons to favor multilateral institutions. But Germany, unlike Japan, is embedded in the strongly developed institutional environment of Western Europe, and therefore it has been able to adapt its foreign policy to its new geostrategic environment more readily than Japan has. As a result, Germany has already participated in joint military operations in Bosnia and Kosovo, and rather than merely supplying oil and logistic forces as part of Operation Enduring Freedom, German special forces are actively engaged in providing security on the ground in Afghanistan.

| Acronyms |

ACU	Asian currency unit
ADB	Asian Development Bank
ADIZ	Air Defense Identification Zone
AIDS	acquired immunodeficiency syndrome
AMF	Asian Monetary Fund
APEC	Asia Pacific Economic Cooperation
APT	ASEAN Plus Three
ARF	ASEAN Regional Forum
ASEAN	Association of Southeast Asian Nations
ASEM	Asia-Europe Meeting
ATSML	Anti-Terrorism Special Measures Law
BIS	Bank for International Settlements
BOJ	Bank of Japan
CGI	Consultative Group in Indonesia
CGP	Clean Government Party
CLB	Cabinet Legislation Bureau
DAC	Development Assistance Committee [of OECD]
DPJ	Democratic Party of Japan
DSP	Democratic Socialist Party
EAEC	East Asian Economic Caucus
EC	European Community
EEZ	exclusive economic zone
EU	European Union
EVSL	Early Voluntary Sectoral Liberalization
FDI	foreign direct investment
FTA	free trade agreement

G5	Group of Five
G6	Group of Six
G7	Group of Seven
G8	Group of Eight
G-10	Group of Ten
GAB	General Agreements to Borrow
GATT	General Agreement on Tariffs and Trade
GDP	gross domestic product
GNP	gross national product
GS	Government Section [of SCAP]
GSDF	Ground Self-Defense Forces
IBRD	International Bank for Reconstruction and Development
ICBM	intercontinental ballistic missile
IDA	International Development Association
IFOR	Implementation Force
IMF	International Monetary Fund
IPCHQ	International Peace Cooperation Headquarters
JBIC	Japan Bank for International Cooperation
JCP	Japan Communist Party
JDA	Japan Defense Agency
JFIR	Japan Forum on International Relations
JICA	Japan International Cooperation Agency
JSDF	Japan Self-Defense Forces
JSP	Japan Socialist Party
JVC	Japan International Volunteer Center
LCSMHRA	Law Concerning Special Measures on Humanitarian and Reconstruction Assistance
LDP	Liberal Democratic Party
LMSR	large medium-speed roll-on/roll-off
METI	Ministry of Economy, Trade, and Industry
MITI	Ministry of International Trade and Industry
MOF	Ministry of Finance
MOFA	Ministry of Foreign Affairs
MTDF	Mid-Term Defense Estimates
NAFTA	North American Free Trade Agreement
NATO	North Atlantic Treaty Organization
NDPO	National Defense Program Outline
NGO	nongovernmental organization
NLD	National League for Democracy [Burma]
NPR	National Police Reserve
NSF	National Safety Force
ODA	official development assistance
OECD	Organization for Economic Cooperation and Development

OECF	Overseas Economic Cooperation Fund
OISCA	Organization for Industrial, Spiritual, and Cultural Advancement
ONUMOZ	UN Operation in Mozambique
ONUVEH	UN Observer Group for the Verification of the Elections in Haiti
ONUVEN	UN Observation Mission for the Verification of Elections in Nicaragua
OSCE	Operation for Security Cooperation in Europe
PBEC	Pacific Basic Economic Council
PECC	Pacific Economic Cooperation Council
PKF	peacekeeping forces
PKO	peacekeeping operations
PPP	purchasing power parity
PPS	Policy Planning Staff
SCAP	supreme commander for allied powers
SDF	Self-Defense Forces
SDPJ	Social Democratic Party of Japan
SLOC	sea lines of communication
SLORC	State Law and Order Restoration Council [Burma]
UNDOF	UN Disengagement Observer Force [Golan Heights]
UNGOMAP	UN Good Offices Mission in Afghanistan and Pakistan
UNHCR	UN High Commissioner for Refugees
UNIIMOG	UN Iran-Iraq Military Observer Group
UNITAF	United Task Force
UNTAC	UN Transitional Authority in Cambodia
UNTAG	UN Transition Assistance Group [Namibia]
WHO	World Health Organization
WMD	weapons of mass destruction
WTO	World Trade Organization

| Bibliography |

Abe, Junichi. *Chūgoku Gun no Hontō no Jitsuryoku* [The Real Capability of the Chinese Military]. Tokyo: Bijinesu Sha, 2006.

Abe, Shinzō. *Utsukushii Kunie* [Toward a Beautiful Country]. Tokyo: Bungei Shunjū, 2006.

Acharya, Amitav. "Collective Identity and Conflict Management in Southeast Asia." In *Security Communities*, edited by Emmanuel Adler and Michael Barnett, 198–227. New York: Cambridge University Press, 1998.

Alagappa, Muthiah (ed.). *Asian Security Order: Instrumental and Normative Features*. Stanford, CA: Stanford University Press, 2003.

Alexander, Arthur J. *In the Shadow of the Miracle: The Japanese Economy Since the End of High-Speed Growth*. Lexington, MA: Lexington Books, 2003.

Alston, Philip. "Transplanting Foreign Norms: Human Rights and Other International Legal Norms in Japan." *European Journal of International Law* 10, no. 3 (December 1999): 625–632.

Angel, Robert S. *Explaining Economic Policy Failure: Japan in the 1969–1971 International Monetary Policy Crisis*. New York: Columbia University Press, 1991.

Arase, David. *Buying Power: The Political Economy of Japan's Foreign Aid*. Boulder, CO: Lynne Rienner, 1995.

———. "Japanese Policy Towards Democracy and Human Rights in East Asia." *Asian Survey* 33 (October 1993): 935–952.

Art, David. *The Politics of the Nazi Past in Germany and Austria*. New York: Cambridge University Press, 2006.

Asano, Atsushi. *Renritsu Seiken: Nihon no Seiji 1993* [Coalition Government: Japanese Politics Since 1993]. Tokyo: Bungeishunju, 1999.

Ashida, Hitoshi. *Shin Kempō Kaishaku* [Interpretation of New Constitution]. Tokyo: Daiamondo-sha, 1946.

Ashizawa, Kuniko P. "Japan, the United States, and Multilateral Institution-Building in the Asia-Pacific." In *Beyond Bilateralism: U.S.-Japan Relations in the New Asia-Pacific*, edited by T. J. Pempel and Ellis Krauss, 248–271. Stanford, CA: Stanford University Press, 2004.

Asia Source. "Japanese History Textbook Raises Concerns." Special report, *Asia Source,* April 9, 2001. Available at www.asiasource.org/news/at_mp_02. cfm?newid+48253 (accessed June 6, 2001).

Badgley, John H. (ed). "Reconciling Burma/Myanmar: Essays on U.S. Relations with Burma." *NBR Analysis* 15 (March 2004).

Baily, Martin, Diana Farrell, and Susan Lund. "The Color of Hot Money." *Foreign Affairs* 79, no. 2 (March/April 2000): 99–109.

Baker, James C. *The Bank for International Settlements: Evolution and Evaluation.* Westport, CT: Quorum Books, 2002.

Balassa, Bela, and Marcus Noland. *Japan in the World Economy.* Washington, DC: Institute for International Economics, 1988.

Bank for International Settlements. *Consolidated Banking Statistics.* Basel, Switzerland: Bank for International Settlements, various years.

Barkan, Elazar. *The Guilt of Nations: Restitution and Negotiating Historical Injustices.* New York: Norton, 2000.

Barnhart, Michael. *Japan Prepares for Total War: The Search for Economic Security, 1919–1941.* Ithaca, NY: Cornell University Press, 1987.

Barraclough, Geoffrey. "Watch out for Japan." *New York Review of Books* 20, no. 10 (June 1973).

Basle Committee. *International Convergence of Capital Measurement and Capital Standards: A Revised Framework—Comprehensive Version.* Basle: Basle Committee, 2006.

Basle Committee on Banking Supervision. *Overview of the Amendment to the Capital Accord to Incorporate Market Risks.* Basle: Basle Committee on Banking Supervision, 1996.

Beasley, W. G. *Japanese Imperialism 1894–1945.* Oxford: Clarendon Press, 1987.

Berger, Thomas U. *Cultures of Antimilitarism: National Security in Germany and Japan.* Baltimore, MD: Johns Hopkins University Press, 1998.

———. "Of Shrines and Hooligans: The Structure of Memory in East Asia." In *Collective Memory and Foreign Policy After 9/11,* edited by Eric Langenbacher and Yossi Schain. Forthcoming.

———. *Redefining Japan and the U.S.-Japan Alliance.* New York: Japan Society, 2004.

———. "Ripe for Rights? Problems and Prospects for Human Rights in East Asia." In *International Institutions and Governance in Asia,* edited by John Ikenberry and Takashi Inoguchi. New York: Palgrave. Forthcoming.

———. "Set for Stability? Prospects for Cooperation and Conflict in East Asia." *Review of International Studies* 26, no. 3 (Spring 2000): 408–428.

Bergsten, Fred C. *Reviving the Asian Monetary Fund.* Washington, DC: Institute for International Economics, 1998.

Bergsten, Fred C., Takatoshi Ito, and Marcus Noland. *No More Bashing: Building a New U.S.-Japanese Economic Partnership.* Washington, DC: Institute for International Economics, 2001.

Bernard, Mitchell, and John Ravenhill. "Beyond Product Cycles and Flying Geese: Regionalization, Hierarchy, and the Industrialization of East Asia." *World Politics* 47 (January 1995): 171–209.

Bhagwati, Jagdish. "The Capital Myth." *Foreign Affairs* 77, no. 3 (May/June 1998): 7–12.

Birnbaum, Pierre. *The Idea of France.* Translated by M. B. Debvoise. New York: Hill and Wang, 2001.

Bix, Herbert P. *Hirohito and the Making of Modern Japan.* New York: Harper-Collins, 2000.

Blaker, Michael. "Evaluating Japan's Diplomatic Performance." In *Japan's Foreign Policy After the Cold War: Coping with Change,* edited by Gerald Curtis, 1–43. Armonk, NY: M. E. Sharpe, 1993.

Bodnar, John. *Remaking America.* Princeton, NJ: Princeton University Press, 1992.

Boyd, J. Patrick, and Richard J. Samuels. *Nine Lives? The Politics of Constitutional Reform in Japan.* Policy Studies no. 19. Washington, DC: East-West Center, 2005.

Burma Fund. *Civil Society and Non-Governmental Organizations in Burma.* Available at http://www.burmafund.org/Pathfinders/Research_Library/civil_society_in_burma.htm.

Burma Youth Volunteer Association of Japan. Press release, April 3, 1999. Available at http://www.burmalibrary.org/reg.burma/archives/199904/msg00000.html.

Calder, Kent. *Crisis and Compensation: Public Policy and Political Stability in Japan.* Princeton, NJ: Princeton University Press, 1988.

———. "Japan as a Post-Reactive State?" *Orbis* 47, no. 4 (Fall 2003): 605–616.

———. "Japanese Foreign Economic Policy Formation: Explaining the Reactive State." *World Politics* 40, no. 4 (July 1988): 517–541.

———. *Japan's New Role in Asia.* New York: Japan Society, 1991.

Callon, Scott. *Divided Sun: MITI and the Breakdown of Japanese High-Tech Industrial Policy, 1975–1993.* Stanford, CA: Stanford University Press, 1995.

Carlile, Lonny E., and Mark C. Tilton (eds.). *Is Japan Really Changing Its Ways? Regulatory Reform and the Japanese Economy.* Washington, DC: Brookings Institution Press, 1998.

Cha, Victor D. *Alignment Despite Antagonism: The U.S.-Korea-Japan Security Triangle.* Stanford, CA: Stanford University Press, 1999.

———. "Bridging the Gap: The Strategic Context of Japan-Korea Normalization." *Korean Studies* 20 (1996): 123–160.

———. "Defensive Realism and Japan's Approach to Korean Reunification." In "Perspective of the Future of the Korean Peninsula," special issue, *NBR Analysis* (National Bureau of Asian Research) 14, no. 1 (June 2003): 5–32.

Chang, Iris. *The Rape of Nanking: The Forgotten Holocaust of World War II.* New York: Basic Books, 1997.

Chapman, J.W.M., Reinhard Drifte, and I.T.M. Gow. *Japan's Quest for Comprehensive Security.* New York: St. Martin's, 1982.

Checkel, Jeffrey T. "The Constructivist Turn in International Relations Theory." *World Politics* 50, no. 2 (January 1998): 224–248.

Chiba, Akira. *Nit-chū taiken-teki sōgo gokai* [Japan-China Mutual Misunderstanding Based on Personal Experiences]. Tokyo: Nihon Kyōhōsha, 2005.

Chiba, Akira, and Lanxin Xiang. "Traumatic Legacies in China and Japan: An Exchange." *Survival* 47, no. 2 (Summer 2005): 215–232.

Christensen, Raymond. "Electoral Reform in Japan: How It Was Enacted and Changes It May Bring." *Asian Survey* 34 (1994): 589–605.

Christensen, Thomas J. "China, the U.S.-Japan Alliance, and the Security Dilemma in East Asia." *International Security* 23, no. 4 (Spring 1999): 49–80.

———. "Fostering Stability or Creating a Monster? The Rise of China and U.S. Policy Toward East Asia." *International Security* 31, no. 1 (Summer 2006): 81–126.

Clifford, Rebecca. *Cleansing History, Cleansing Japan: Kobayashi Yoshinori's Analects of War and Japan's Revisionist Revival.* Nissan Occasional Paper Series no. 35. Oxford: Nissan Institute of Japanese Studies, 2004.

Cohen, Michael D., James G. Marsh, and Johan P. Olsen. "A Garbage Can Model of

Organizational Choice." *Administrative Science Quarterly* 17, no. 1 (March 1972): 1–25.

Congressional Budget Office. *Moving U.S. Forces.* Washington, DC: Congressional Budget Office, 1997.

Cooke, Peter. "International Convergence of Capital Adequacy Measurement and Standards." In *The Future of Financial Systems and Services: Essays in Honour of Jack Revel*, edited by Edward P.M. Gardener. London: Macmillan Press, 1990.

Cooper, Andrew F. *Niche Diplomacy: Middle Powers After the Cold War.* New York: St. Martin's Press, 1997.

Cossa, Ralph A., and Brad Glasserman. *Has Japan Become the Great Britain of Asia?* Issues and Insights 5, no. 3. Honolulu: CSIS Pacific Forum, 2005. Available at http://www.csis.org/pacfor/issues/v05n03_pdf.pdf. (accessed July 7, 2005).

Council on Security and Defense Capabilities. *Japan's Vision for Future Security and Defense Capabilities.* Tokyo: Prime Minister's Office, 2004.

Cowhey, Peter. "Domestic Institutions and the Credibility of International Commitments: Japan and the United States." *International Organization* 47 (1993): 299–326.

Crampton, Thomas. "Japanese Grant Rewards Burmese Talks." *International Herald Tribune,* April 25, 2001. Available at http://www.burmaproject.org/042501japanese_grants)reward_burmese.html.

Crichton, Michael. *Rising Sun: A Novel.* New York: Knopf, 1992.

Crone, Donald. "Does Hegemony Matter? The Reorganization of the Pacific Economy." *World Politics* 45, no. 4 (July 1993): 501–525.

Cronin, Patrick J., Paul S. Giarra, and Michael J. Green. "The Alliance Implications of Theater Missile Defense." In *The U.S.-Japan Alliance: Past, Present, and Future*, edited by Patrick J. Cronin and Michael J. Green, 170–188. New York: Council on Foreign Relations, 1999.

Cronin, Patrick J., and Michael J. Green (eds.). *The U.S.-Japanese Alliance: Past, Present, and Future.* New York: Council on Foreign Relations, 1999.

Crowley, James B. *Japan's Quest for Autonomy.* Princeton, NJ: Princeton University Press, 1966.

Curtis, Gerald L. *The Japanese Way of Democracy.* New York: Columbia University Press, 1988.

———. *The Logic of Japanese Politics: Leaders, Institutions, and the Limits of Change.* New York: Columbia University Press, 1999.

——— (ed.). *Policymaking in Japan: Defining the Role of Politicians.* Tokyo: Japan Center for International Exchange, 2002.

Daalder, Ivo H., and James M. Lindsay. *America Unbound: The Bush Revolution in Foreign Policy.* Washington, DC: Brookings Institution, 2003.

Dalpino, Catharin, and David Steinberg. "Southeast Asia Looks North: New Dynamics with China." In *Georgetown Southeast Asia Survey 2002–2003*, edited by Catharin Dalpino and David Steinberg, 43–52. Washington, DC: Georgetown University, 2003.

Dombrowski, Peter. *Policy Responses to the Globalization of American Banking.* Pittsburgh, PA: University of Pittsburgh Press, 1996.

Dore, Ronald. *Japan: Internationalism and the UN.* London: Routledge, 1997.

Dower, John W. "The Bombed: Hiroshima and Nagasaki in Japanese Memory." In *Hiroshima in History and Memory*, edited by Michael J. Hogan. Cambridge: Cambridge University Press, 1996.

———. *Embracing Defeat: Japan in the Wake of World War II.* New York: W. W. Norton, 1999.

———. *Empire and Aftermath: Yoshida Shigeru and the Japanese Experience, 1878–1954.* Cambridge, MA: Harvard University Press, 1979.

Doyle, Michael. "Kant, Liberal Legacies, and Foreign Affairs." *Philosophy and Public Affairs* 12 (1983): 205–235 (Part I) and 323–353 (Part II).

———. *Ways of War and Peace: Realism, Liberalism, and Socialism.* New York: Norton, 1997.

Doyle, Michael W., Ian Johnstone, and Robert C. Orr (eds.). *Keeping the Peace: Multidimensional UN Operations in Cambodia and El Salvador.* New York: Cambridge University Press, 1997.

Drifte, Reinhard. *Japan's Foreign Policy for the Twenty-first Century: From Economic Power to What Power.* London: Macmillan, 1996.

———. "Japan's Quest for a Permanent Seat on the Security Council." *Asia-Pacific Review* 5, no. 2 (1998): 87–110.

———. *Japan's Quest for a Permanent Security Council Seat: A Matter of Pride or Justice?* London: Macmillan, 2000.

———. *Japan's Security Relations with China Since 1989: From Balancing to Bandwagoning?* London: Routledge Curzon, 2003.

Durch, William J. *The Evolution of UN Peacekeeping: Case Studies and Comparative Analysis.* New York: Henry Stimson Center, 1993.

Economic Planning Agency. *Tsūka Kinyū Kiki no Kokufuku to 21 Seiki no Keizai Anteika ni Mukete* [Toward a Revival from Financial Crisis and Economic Stabilization in the 21st Century]. Tokyo: Ōkurashō Insatsukyoku, 1999.

Encarnation, Dennis. *Rivals Beyond Trade: America Versus Japan in Global Competition.* Ithaca, NY: Cornell University Press, 1992.

Etō, Jun. *1946 Kempō—sono kōsoku* [The 1946 Constitution—Its Constraint]. Tokyo: Bungei Shunjū, 1980.

Etzold, Thomas, and John L. Gaddis. *Containment: Documents on American Policy and Strategy, 1945–1950.* New York: Columbia University Press, 1978.

Fallows, James. *Looking at the Sun: The Rise of the New East Asian Economic and Political System.* New York: Pantheon, 1994.

Finn, Richard. *Winners in Peace: MacArthur, Yoshida, and Postwar Japan.* Berkeley: University of California Press, 1992.

Finnemore, Martha. *National Interests in International Society.* Ithaca, NY: Cornell University Press, 1996.

Finnemore, Martha, and Kathryn Sikkink. "International Norm Dynamics and Political Change." In *Exploration and Contestation in the Study of World Politics,* edited by Peter J. Katzenstein, Robert O. Keohane, and Stephen D. Krasner, 247–277. Cambridge, MA: MIT Press, 1999.

Foreign Ministry. *Diplomatic Bluebook 1991.* Tokyo: Ministry of Foreign Affairs, 1991.

Friedberg, Aaron. "Ripe for Rivalry: Prospects for Peace in a Multipolar Asia." *International Security* 18, no. 3 (Winter 1993/94): 5–33.

Frieden, Jeffry A. *Banking on the World: Politics of American International Finance.* New York: Harper and Row, 1987.

Friedman, George, and Meredith LeBard. *The Coming War with Japan.* New York: St. Martin's Press, 1991.

Fujioka, Nobukatsu. *Kyōkasho ga oshienai Rekishi* [The History That Textbooks Don't Teach You]. Tokyo: Sankei Shuppan, 1996.

———. *Ojoku no Kingendaishi* [The Shame of Modern History]. Tokyo: Tokuma Shoten, 1996.

Fujioka, Nobukatsu, and Nishio Kanji (eds). *Kokumin no Yūdan: Reikishi Kyōkasho ga Abunai* [To Neglect the People: History Textbooks Imperiled]. Tokyo: PHP Kenkyūjō, 1996.

Fujita, Naotaka. *Japan in the War on Terrorism: The Transformation in Security Policymaking.* U.S.-Japan Relations Program Occasional Paper. Cambridge, MA: Harvard University, 2005.

Fukushima, Akiko. *Japanese Foreign Policy: The Emerging Logic of Multilateralism.* New York: St. Martin's Press, 1999.

———. "Official Development Assistance (ODA) as a Japanese Foreign Policy Tool." In *Japanese Foreign Policy Today*, edited by Takashi Inoguchi and Purnendra Jain, 152–174. New York: Palgrave, 2000.

Fukuyama, Francis. *America at the Crossroads: Democracy, Power, and the Neoconservative Legacy.* New Haven, CT: Yale University Press, 2006.

Fulbrook, Mary. *German National Identity After the Holocaust.* Cambridge: Blackwell, 1999.

———. *Historical Theory: Ways of Imagining the Past.* London: Routledge, 2002.

Funabashi, Yoichi. *Asia Pacific Fusion.* Washington, DC: Institute for International Economics, 1995.

Gao, Bai. *Economic Ideology and Japanese Industrial Policy: Developmentalism from 1931 to 1965.* Cambridge: Cambridge University Press, 1997.

Gardener, Edward P.M. (ed.). *The Future of Financial Systems and Services: Essays in Honour of Jack Revell.* London: Macmillan Press, 1990.

Garon, Sheldon. *Molding Japanese Minds: The State in Everyday Life.* Princeton, NJ: Princeton University Press, 1997.

Garrett, Banning, and Bonnie Glaser. "Chinese Apprehensions About the Revitalization of the U.S.-Japan Alliance." *Asian Survey* 37, no. 4 (April 1997): 385–402.

Garrett, Geoffrey, and Peter Lange. "Internationalization, Institutions, and Political Change." In *Internationalization and Domestic Politics,* edited by Robert Keohane and Helen Milner. New York: Cambridge University Press, 1996.

Garten, Jeffrey. *A Cold Peace: America, Japan, Germany, and the Struggle for Supremacy.* New York: Times Books, 1992.

Gerlach, Michael. *Alliance Capitalism: The Social Organization of Japanese Business.* Berkeley: University of California Press, 1992.

Gerschenkron, Alexander. *Economic Backwardness in Historical Perspective.* Cambridge, MA: Belknap Press, 1962.

Goldstein, Morris. *The Asian Financial Crisis: Causes, Cures, and Systemic Implications.* Washington, DC: Institute for International Economics, 1998.

Gong, Gerrit W. (ed.). *Memory and History in East and Southeast Asia.* Washington, DC: Center for International and Strategic Studies Press, 2001.

Gordon, Philip, and Jeremy Shapiro. *Allies at War: America, Europe, and the Crisis over Iraq.* New York: McGraw Hill, 2004.

Gotoda, Masaharu. *Sei to Kan* [Politicians and Bureacrats]. Tokyo: Kodansha, 1994.

Green, Michael. *Japan's Reluctant Realism: Foreign Policy Changes in an Era of Uncertain Power.* New York: St. Martin's Press, 2001.

Green, Michael, and Benjamin L. Self. "Japan's Changing China Policy: From Commercial Liberalism to Reluctant Realism." *Survival* 38, no. 2 (Summer 1996): 35–58.

Gries, Peter. *China's New Nationalism: Pride, Politics, and Diplomacy.* Berkeley: University of California Press, 2005.

Grimes, William W. *Unmaking the Japanese Miracle.* Ithaca, NY: Cornell University Press, 2001.

Gruber, Lloyd. *Ruling the World: Power Politics and the Rise of Supranational Institutions*. Princeton, NJ: Princeton University Press, 2000.

Guitian, Manuel. *Conditionality: Past, Present, and Future*. Washington, DC: International Monetary Fund, 1995.

Hacking, Ian. *Rewriting the Soul: Multiple Personality and the Science of Memory*. Princeton, NJ: Princeton University Press, 1998.

Haggard, Stephen. *The Political Economy of the Asian Financial Crisis*. Washington, DC: Institute for International Economics, 2000.

Halbwachs, Maurice. *On Collective Memory*. Edited and translated by Lewis A. Coser. 1952. Reprint, Chicago: University of Chicago Press, 1992.

Harrison, Selig. *Japan's Nuclear Future: The Plutonium Debate and East Asian Security*. Washington, DC: Carnegie Endowment for International Peace, 1996.

Harrison, Selig S., and Clyde V. Prestowitz Jr. (eds.). *Asia After the Miracle: Redefining U.S. Economic and Security Priorities*. Washington, DC: Economic Strategy Institute, 1998.

Harwit, Eric. "Japanese Investment in China: Strategies in the Electronics and Automobile Sectors." *Asian Survey* 36, no. 10 (October 1996): 978–994.

Hashimoto, Ryūtarō. "Seeking a New Foreign Policy Toward China." Speech, Tokyo, August 28, 1997. Available at http://www.mofa.go.jp/region/asia-paci/china/seeking.html.

———. *Vision of Japan*. Tokyo: K K Besuto Serazu, 1993.

Hata, Ikuhiko. *Ianfu to Senjō no sei* [Comfort Women and Sex on the Battlefield]. Tokyo: Shinchōsha, 1999.

Hatch, Walter. *Asia in Japan's Embrace: Building a Regional Production Alliance*. New York: Cambridge University Press, 1996.

Hatoyama, Yukio. "Jieitai o Guntai to mitomeyo [Accept the SDF as the Military]." *Bungei Shunjū* 77, no. 10 (October 1989): 262–273.

Havens, Thomas. *The Fire Across the Sea: The Vietnam War and Japan 1965–1975*. Princeton, NJ: Princeton University Press, 1987.

He, Yinan. "National Mythmaking and the Problems of History in Sino-Japanese Relations." Paper delivered at the Conference on Memory and War, January 24–25, 2003, MIT.

Heginbotham, Eric, and Richard J. Samuels. "Japan." In *Strategic Asia 2002–2003: Asian After Shocks,* edited by Richard Ellings and Aaron Friedberg, 95–130. Seattle, WA: National Bureau of Asian Research, 2002.

———. "Mercantile Realism and Japanese Foreign Policy." *International Security* 22, no. 4 (Spring 1998): 171–203.

Heinrich, L. William, Jr., Akiho Shibata, and Yoshihide Soeya. *United Nations Peace-keeping Operations: A Guide to Japanese Policies*. New York: United Nations Press, 1999.

Hellmann, Donald. "The Confrontation with *Realpolitik*." In *Forecast for Japan: Security in the 1970s,* edited by James Morley. Princeton, NJ: Princeton University Press, 1972.

———. "Japanese Politics and Foreign Policy: Elitist Democracy Within an American Green House." In *The Political Economy of Japan*. Vol. 2: *The Changing International Context*, edited by Takashi Inoguchi and Daniel I. Okimoto, 345–380. Stanford, CA: Stanford University Press, 1988.

Herring, Richard J., and Robert E. Litan. *Financial Regulation in the Global Economy*. Washington, DC: Brookings Institution Press, 1995.

Herz, John. "Idealist Internationalism and the Security Dilemma." *World Politics* 2 (January 1950): 157–180.

Hicks, George. *Comfort Women: Japan's Brutal Regime of Enforced Prostitution During World War II*. New York: W. W. Norton, 1997.

———. *Japan's War Memories: Amnesia or Concealment?* Aldershot, England: Ashgate, 1997.

Higashitani, Akira. *BIS kisei no Uso* [False Reality of BIS Regulation]. Tokyo: Nikkan Kōgyō Shimbun, 1999.

Himino, Ryozō. *Kenshō BIS kisei to Nihon* [Examination: BIS Regulation and Japan]. Tokyo: Kinyūzaiseijijō Kenkyūkai, 2003.

Hirata, Keiko. "Japan as a Reactive State? Analyzing Japan's Relations with the Socialist Republic of Vietnam." *Japanese Studies* 18 (1998): 135–152.

Honda, Katsukichi. *Chūgoku no Nihongun* [The Japanese Army in China]. Tokyo: Sōjusha, 1972.

———. *Chūgoku no Tabi* [A Journey to China]. Tokyo: Asahi Shimbunsha, 1972.

Hook, Glenn. *Militarization and Demilitarization in Contemporary Japan*. London: Routledge, 1995.

Hook, Glenn D., Julie Gilson, Christopher W. Hughes, and Hugo Dobson. *Japan's International Relations: Politics, Economics, and Security*. London: Routledge, 2001.

Hook, Glenn D., and Gavan McCormack. *Japan's Contested Constitution: Documents and Analysis*. London: Routledge, 2001.

Hook, Glenn D., and Michael A. Weiner (eds.). *The Internationalization of Japan*. New York: Routledge, 1992.

Hoshi, Takeo. "The Convoy System for Insolvent Banks: How It Originally Worked and Why It Failed in the 1990s." *Japan and the World Economy* 14 (2002):155–180.

Hosoya, Chihiro, et al. *Nichibei Kankei Shiryōshu* [Data of US-Japan Relations]. Tokyo: Tokyo Daigaku Shuppankai, 1999.

Howell, William Lee. "The Inheritance of War: Japan's Domestic Political Politics and the Domestic Political Ambitions." In *Remembering and Forgetting: The Legacy of War and Peace in East Asia*, edited by Gerrit W. Gong, 82–102. Washington, DC: Center for Strategic and International Studies, 1996.

Hrebenar, Ronald J. *Japan's New Party System*. Boulder, CO: Westview Press, 2000.

Hughes, Christopher W. "Japanese Military Modernization: In Search of a 'Normal' Security Role." In *Strategic Asia 2005–06: Military Modernization in an Era of Uncertainty*, edited by Ashley J. Tellis and Michael Wills, 105–134. Seattle, WA: National Bureau of Asian Research, 2005.

———. *Japan's Re-emergence as a "Normal" Military Power*. Adelphi Paper No. 368-369. London: International Institute for Strategic Studies, 2004.

———. *Japan's Security Agenda: Military, Economic, and Environmental Dimensions*. Boulder, CO: Lynne Rienner Publishers, 2004.

Hughes, Christopher W., and Akiko Fukushima. "U.S.-Japan Security Relations— Toward Bilateralism Plus?" In *Beyond Bilateralism: U.S.-Japan Relations in the New Asia-Pacific*, edited by Ellis S. Krauss and T. J. Pempel, 55–86. Stanford, CA: Stanford University Press, 2004.

Hunt, David. "War Crimes and the Vietnamese People: American Representations and Silences." In *Citizenship and Memory in Japan, Germany, and the United States*, edited by Laura Hein and Mark Selden, 173–200. Armonk, NY: M. E. Sharpe, 2000.

Huntington, Samuel P. "Why International Primacy Matters." *International Security* 17, no. 4 (Spring 1993): 68–83.

Hutton, Patrick H. *History as an Art of Memory*. Hanover: University Press of Vermont, 1993.

Ienaga, Saburō. *The Pacific War, 1931–1945: A Critical Perspective on Japan's Role in World War II*. Translated by Frank Baldwin. New York: Pantheon Books, 1978.

———. *Taiheiyō Sensō* [The Pacific War]. Expanded version. Tokyo: Iwanami Shoten, 1986.

Ijiri, Hidenori. "Sino-Japanese Controversy Since the 1972 Diplomatic Normalization." In *China and Japan: History, Trends, and Prospects*, edited by Christopher Howe, 60–82. Oxford: Clarendon Press, 1996.

Ikeda, Tadashi. "'Ajia shugi' de wa nai Ajia gaikō [An Asian Diplomacy That Is Not 'Asianism']." *Gaikō Forum* no. 65 (February 1994).

Ikenberry, G. John. "America's Imperial Ambition." *Foreign Affairs* 81, no. 5 (September/October 2002): 44–60.

———. "America's Liberal Grand Strategy." In *American Foreign Policy: Theoretical Essays*, 4th ed., edited by G. John Ikenberry, 268–289. New York: Longman, 2001.

Immerman, Robert M. "Japan in the United Nations." In *Japan: A New Kind of Superpower?* edited by Craig C. Garby and Mary Brown Bullock. Baltimore, MD: Johns Hopkins University Press, 1994.

Inada, Juichi. "Evolution of International Development Assistance Regime: Harmonization of Aid Policies Among Major Donors and Its Structure." In *Trends in Regionalism and Future Foreign Policy Approaches for Japan (JIIA Report FY2003)*, 66–88. Tokyo: Japan Institute of International Affairs, 2004.

———. "Japan's ODA: Its Impacts on China's Industrialization and Sino-Japanese Relations." In *Japan and China: Cooperation, Competition, and Conflict*, edited by Hanns Günther Hilpert and René Haak, 121–139. London: Palgrave, 2002.

———. "ODA Seisaku ni Miru Sengo Nihon Gaikō no Kihan: Azia to Naisei Fukanshou [The Norms in Japanese Post-war ODA Diplomacy: Asia and Noninterference]." In *Nihon Gaikō no Identity* [The Identity of Japanese Diplomacy], edited by Hasegawa Yuichi. Tokyo: Nansou-sha, 2004.

Inada, Juichi, and Yasutami Shimomura (eds.). *Ajia Kinyū Kiki no Seiji-keizai-gaku* [The Political Economy of the Asian Financial Crisis]. Tokyo: Japan Institute of International Affairs, 2001.

Inoguchi, Takashi. *Tadanori to Ikkoku Haneishugi o Koete: Tenkanki no Sekai to Nihon* [Beyond Free-Riding and One-Country Prosperity: World in Transition and Japan]. Tokyo: Tōyō Keizai Shinpōsha, 1987.

Inoguchi, Takashi, and Purnendra Jain. "Beyond Karaoke Diplomacy?" In *Japanese Foreign Policy Today*, edited by Inoguchi Takashi and Purnendra Jain, xi–xix. New York: Palgrave, 2000.

Institute for International Education. *Open Doors*. New York: Institute for International Education, various years.

Institute for National Strategic Studies. *The US and Japan: Advancing Towards a Mature Partnership*. INSS Special Report. Washington, DC: National Defense University Press, 2000.

International Institute for Strategic Studies. *The Military Balance 2007*. Abingdon, UK: Routledge, 2007.

International Monetary Fund. *IMF-Supported Programs in Indonesia, Korea, and Thailand: A Preliminary Assessment*. Washington, DC: International Monetary Fund, 1999.

Inukai, Ichiro. "Why Aid and Why Not? Japan and Sub-Saharan Africa." In *Japan's Foreign Aid: Power and Policy in a New Era*, edited by Bruce M. Koppel and Robert M. Orr Jr., 252–274. Boulder, CO: Westview Press, 1993.

Iokibe, Makoto. "Nihon no Anzenhoshōkan wa Ikani Suii Shitaka [How Japanese View on Security Shifted]." *Gaikō Forum*, no. 94 (1996).

Iriye, Akira. *Japan and the Wider World: From the Mid-Nineteenth Century to the Present.* London: Longman, 1997.

Ishibashi, Masashi. *Zōho Hibusō Churitsuron* [On Unarmed Neutrality]. Tokyo: Nihon Shakaitō, 1983.

Ishihara, Shintaro. *The Japan That Can Say "No."* New York: Simon and Schuster, 1992.

Ishikawa, Shigeru. "Shijō Keiza Hatten Sokushin Apurōchi [Approach to Promote the Development of a Market Economy]." *Kaihatsu Enjo Kenkyū* [Development Aid Study], 4, no.1 (1997).

Ishikawa, Shigeru, and Yōnosuke Hara (eds.). *Vietnam no Shijō Keizaika* [Transition to a Market Economy of Vietnam]. Tokyo: Tōyō Keizai Shinpōsha, 1999.

Islam, Shafiqul (ed.). *Yen for Development.* New York: Council on Foreign Relations, 1991.

Itō, Takatoshi. "Ajia Tsūka Kiki to America no Taiō [Asian Financial Crisis and the American Response]." *Kokusai Mondai*, no. 472 (February 1999).

Itoh, Mayumi. *Globalization of Japan: Japanese Sakoku Mentality and U.S. Efforts to Open Japan.* New York: St. Martin's Press, 1998.

———. "Japanese Constitutional Revision: A Neo-liberal Proposal for Article 9 in Comprehensive Perspective." *Asian Survey* 41, no. 2 (March/April 2001): 310–327.

———. *Japan's Neo-Nationalism: The Role of the Hinomaru and Kimigayo Legislation.* JPRI Working Paper No. 79. Encinitas, CA: Japan Policy Research Institute, 2001.

Iwanaga, Kazuyuki. "The UN in Japan's Foreign Policy: An Emerging Assertive UN Centrism." In *The United Nations, Japan, and Sweden: Achievements and Challenges*, edited by Bert Edstrom. Stockholm: Swedish Institute, 1998.

Jackson, Karl D. (ed.). *Asian Contagion: The Causes and Consequences of a Financial Crisis.* Boulder, CO: Westview Press, 1999.

Jackson, Patricia, et al. *Capital Requirements and Bank Behavior: The Impact of the Basle Accord.* Basle, Switzerland: BIS, 1999.

Japan Defense Agency. *Defense of Japan, 1999, 2001, 2002, and 2006.* Tokyo: Japan Defense Agency, 1999, 2001, 2002, and 2006.

Japan International Cooperation Agency. *Report of the Fourth Country Assistance Study on Indonesia.* Tokyo: JICA, 2000.

Jervis, Robert. "Cooperation Under the Security Dilemma." *World Politics* 30, no. 2 (1978): 167–214.

———. "Realism, Neoliberalism, and Cooperation: Understanding the Debate." *International Security* 24, no. 1 (Summer 1999): 42–63.

Jiji Tsūshinsha. *Jiji Seron Chōsa Tokuhō* [Jiji Public Opinion Survey Special Reports]. Various issues.

Johnson, Chalmers A. *Japan: Who Governs?* New York: W. W. Norton, 1995.

———. *MITI and Japanese Miracle: The Growth of Industrial Policy, 1925–1975.* Stanford, CA: Stanford University Press, 1982.

———. "La Serenissima of the East." In Chalmers A. Johnson, *Japan: Who Governs?* 21–37, New York: W. W. Norton, 1995.

———. "Trade, Revisionism, and the Future of Japanese-American Relations." In

Japan's Economic Structure: Should It Change, edited by Kozo Yamamura. Seattle, WA: Society for Japanese Studies, 1990.

Kades, Charles. "Discussion of Professor Theodore McNelly's Paper, 'General Douglas MacArthur and the Constitutional Disarmament of Japan.'" *Transactions of the Asiatic Society of Japan*, 3rd ser., 17 (1982): 35–52.

Kagan, Robert. *Of Paradise and Power*. New York: Random House, 2003.

Kaikōsha. *Nankin Senshi* [Soldiers of Nanjing]. 2 vols. Tokyo: Kaikōsha, 1989.

Kakizawa, Koji. "Tennō hō-Chū go no Nit-Chū kankei"\ [Japan-China Relations After the Emperor's Visit to China]." *Chūō Kōron* (December 1992): 202–210.

Kamanishi, Akio. *GNP 1% Waku: Bōeiseisaku no Kenshō* [The 1% of GNP Barrier: An Inquiry into Defense Policy]. Tokyo: Kakugawa, 1986.

Kammen, Michael J. *Mystic Chords of Memory*. New York: Vintage, 1991.

Kant, Immanuel. "Perpetual Peace: A Philosophical Essay." In *The History of International Relations*, edited by M. G. Forsyth et al., 200–244. New York: Atherton Press, 1970.

Kapstein, Ethan. *Governing the Global Economy: International Finance and the State*. Cambridge, MA: Harvard University Press, 1994.

———. "Resolving the Regulator's Dilemma: International Coordination of Banking Regulations." *International Organization* 43, no. 2 (Spring 1989): 323–347.

Katada, Saori. "Japan's Counterweight Strategy: U.S.-Japan Cooperation and Competition in International Finance." In *Beyond Bilateralism: U.S.-Japan Relations in the New Asia-Pacific*, edited by Ellis Krauss and T. J. Pempel, 176–197. Stanford, CA: Stanford University Press, 2004.

Kataoka, Tetsuya. *The Price of a Constitution: The Origin of Japan's Postwar Politics*. New York: Crane Russak, 1991.

Kato, Junko. "Reforming the Japanese Bureaucracy: Perceptions, Potential, and Pitfalls." In *Japanese Political Reform: A Work in Progress*. An Asia Program special report, no. 117, 34–37. Washington, DC: Woodrow Wilson Center, January 2004.

Katz, Richard N. *Japan: The System That Soured*. Armonk, NY: M. E. Sharpe, 1998.

———. *Japanese Phoenix: The Long Road to Economic Revival*. Armonk, NY: M. E. Sharpe, 2003.

Katzenstein, Peter J. *Cultural Norms and National Security: Police and Military in Postwar Japan*. Ithaca, NY: Cornell University Press, 1996.

——— (ed.). *The Culture of National Security: Norms and Identity in World Politics*. New York: Columbia University Press, 1996.

———. "Same War, Different Views: Germany, Japan, and the War on Terror." *International Organization* 57, no. 4 (Fall 2003): 731–760.

Katzenstein, Peter J., and Nobuo Okawara. *Japan's National Security: Structures, Norms, and Policy Responses in a Changing World*. Ithaca, NY: East Asia Program, Cornell University, 1993.

Katzenstein, Peter J., and Takashi Shiraishi (eds.). *Beyond Japan: The Dynamics of East Asian Regionalism*. Ithaca, NY: Cornell University Press, 2006.

———. *Network Power: Japan and Asia*. Ithaca, NY: Cornell University Press, 1997.

Kawabe, Ichirō. *Kokuren to Nihon* [The UN and Japan]. Tokyo: Iwanami, 1991.

Kawai, Masahiro. "Tsūka Kiki Hakyū no Mekanizumu to Kyōkun [The Mechanism of the Spread of Financial Crisis and Lessons]." *Keizai Seminar* (June 1998): 24–31.

Kelly, William W., and Merry White. "Students, Slackers, Singles, Seniors, and Strangers." In *Beyond Japan: The Dynamics of East Asian Regionalism*, edited by Peter J. Katzenstein and Takashi Shiraishi, 63–82. Ithaca, NY: Cornell University Press, 2006.

Kenward, Lloyd R. *From the Trenches: The First Year of Indonesia's Crisis of 1997/98 as Seen from the World Bank's Office in Jakarta.* Jakarta, Indonesia: Center for Strategic and International Studies, 2002.

Keohane, Robert, and Helen Milner (eds.). *Internationalization and Domestic Politics.* New York: Cambridge University Press, 1996.

Keohane, Robert O., and Joseph S. Nye. *Power and Interdependence: World Politics in Transition.* Boston: Little, Brown, 1977.

Kim, Seung-Hwan. "Anti-Americanism in Korea." *The Washington Quarterly* 26, no. 1 (Winter 2002–2003): 109–122.

Kliman, Daniel M. *Japan's Security Strategy in the Post-9/11 World: Embracing a New Realpolitik.* Westport, CT: Praeger, 2006.

Knutsen, Tjorborn. *A History of International Relations.* 2nd ed. Manchester, England: University of Manchester Press, 2002.

Kobayashi, Yōtarō. "'Sai Ajia ka' no susume [Promote Re-Asianization]." *Foresight* (April 1991): 44–46.

Kober, Stanley. "Idealpolitik." *Foreign Policy,* no. 29 (Summer 1990): 3–24.

Kohno, Masaharu. "In Search of Proactive Diplomacy: Increasing Japan's International Role in the 1990s." Brookings Institution CNAPS Working Paper, Fall 1999. Available at http://www.brookings.edu/printme.wbs?page=/fp/cnaps/papers/1999_kohno.htm.

———. *Wahei Kōsaku: Tai Cambodia Gaikō no Shōgen* [Peacemaking: A Testimony of Japan's Diplomacy Toward Cambodia]. Tokyo: Iwanami shoten, 1999.

Kohno, Masaru. "A Changing Ministry of International Trade and Industry (MITI)." In *Beyond Japan, Inc.: Reform and Transparency in Japanese Governance,* edited by Jennifer Amyx and Peter Drysdale, 96–112. New York: Routledge, 2001.

———. "Electoral Origins of Japanese Socialists' Stagnation." *Comparative Political Studies* 30 (1997): 55–77.

———. "Japanese Defense Policy Making: The FSX Selection, 1985–1987." *Asian Survey* 29 (1989): 457–479.

———. *Japan's Postwar Party Politics.* Princeton, NJ: Princeton University Press, 1997.

———. "Nihon ni okeru Heiritsu-sei Dōnyū no Kōzai [Consequences of Introducing the Parallel Electoral System in Japan]." *Aoyama Kokusai Seikei Ronshu* 48 (1999): 43–62.

Kojima, Ryō. *Hangarii Jiken to Nihon: 1956-nen Shisōshiteki Kōsatsu* [The Hungarian Uprising and Japan: An Intellectual Inquiry into 1956]. Tokyo: Chūō Kōron Shinsho, 1987.

Kojima, Tomoyuki. "Japan's China Policy." In *Japan and China: Rivalry or Cooperation in East Asia,* edited by Peter Drysdale and Doon Dong Zhang, 33–47. Canberra, Australia: Asia Pacific Press, 2000.

Kojo, Yoshiko. "Japan's Choice of Negotiating Framework in Multi-layered International Economic Relations." In *Global Governance: Germany and Japan in the International System,* edited by Saori Katada, Hans Maull, and Takashi Inoguchi. Burlington, VT: Ashgate, 2004.

———. "Shihon Idō no Zōdai to Kokusai Seiji no Henyō: Basel Gōi ni Miru Kokusai Seido Keisei [Increasing Capital Mobility and Change in International Politics: International Institutionalization in the Case of Basle Accord]." In *Kokusai Seiji Kōza* [International Politics], vol. 3, edited by Yoshiko Kojō, 39–85. Tokyo: Tokyo University Press, 2004.

Komori, Yoshihisa. *Nit-chū yūkō no maboroshi* [Japan and China: Illusion of Friendship]. Tokyo: Shōgakkan, 2002.

Kondō, Kenhiko. *Kokusai Tsūka to APEC* [International Currency and APEC]. Tokyo: Ōkurashō Insatsukyoku, 1996.

Kōsaka, Masataka. "Reisen-go no Shin-Sekai Chitsujo to Nippon no 'Kōken' [A New World Order and Japan's 'Contribution' After the Cold War]." *Kokusai Mondai* 379 (1991): 2–16.

Koseki, Shōichi. *Shin Kenpō no Tanjō* [The Birth of the New Constitution]. Tokyo: Chuokoronsha, 1985.

Kozai, Shigeru. *Kokuren no Heiwa-iji Katsudō* [The UN Peacekeeping Operations]. Tokyo: Yuhikaku, 1991.

Krauss, Ellis S. "The United States and Japan in APEC's EVSL Negotiations: Regional Multilateralism and Trade." In *Beyond Bilateralism: U.S.-Japan Relations in the New Asia-Pacific*, edited by Ellis Krauss and T. J. Pempel, 272–295. Stanford, CA: Stanford University Press, 2004.

Krauss, Ellis S., and Benjamin Nyblade. "'Presidentialization' in Japan? The Prime Minister, Media, and Elections in Japan." *British Journal of Political Science* 35, no. 2 (April 2005): 357–368.

Krauss, Ellis S., and T. J. Pempel (eds.). *Beyond Bilateralism: U.S.-Japan Relations in the New Asia-Pacific*. Stanford, CA: Stanford University Press, 2004.

Krugman, Paul (ed.). *Strategic Trade Policy and the New International Economics*. Cambridge, MA: MIT Press, 1986.

Kunimune, Kōzō (ed.). *Ajia Tsūka Kiki* [Asian Financial Crisis]. Chiba, Japan: Institute for Developing Economies–JETRO, 2000.

Kupchan, Charles. *The End of the American Era: US Foreign Policy and the Geopolitics of the Twenty-first Century*. New York: Vintage, 2003.

Kurosawa, Yoshitaka. "*BIS kisei no Paradokkusu* [Paradox of the BIS Regulation]." *Nempō Kindai Nihon Kenkyū*, no. 15 (1993): 248–269.

LaFeber, Walter. *The Clash: U.S.-Japanese Relations Throughout History*. New York: W. W. Norton, 1997.

Lane, Timothy, et al. (eds.). *IMF-Supported Programs in Indonesia, Korea, and Thailand: A Preliminary Assessment*. Washington, DC: International Monetary Fund, 1999.

Leheny, David. "Tokyo Confronts Terror." *Policy Review*, no. 110 (December 2001–January 2002): 37–47.

Lincoln, Edward J. *Arthritic Japan: The Slow Pace of Economic Reform*. Washington, DC: Brookings Institution, 2001.

———. *East Asian Economic Regionalism*. Washington, DC: Council on Foreign Relations and Brookings Institution, 2004.

———. "Japan: Using Power Narrowly." *The Washington Quarterly* 27, no. 1 (2003): 111–127.

——— (ed.). *Japan and the Middle East*. Washington, DC: Middle East Institute, 1990.

———. *Japan Facing Economic Maturity*. Washington, DC: Brookings Institution, 1988.

———. *Japan's New Global Role*. Washington, DC: Brookings Institution, 1993.

———. *Japan's Unequal Trade*. Washington, DC: Brookings Institution, 1990.

———. *Troubled Times: U.S.-Japan Trade Relations in the 1990s*. Washington, DC: Brookings Institution, 1999.

Lind, Jennifer. "Pacifism or Passing the Buck: Testing Theories of Japanese Security Policy." *International Security* 29, no. 1 (Summer 2004): 91–121.

Loewen, James. "Teaching Vietnam in High School American History." In

Citizenship and Memory in Japan, Germany, and the United States, edited by Laura Hein and Mark Selden, 150–172. Armonk, NY: M. E. Sharpe, 2000.

Lorell, Mark A. *Troubled Partnership: A History of U.S.-Japan Collaboration on the FS-X Fighter*. New Brunswick, NJ: Transaction Publishers, 1996.

Luttwak, Edward. "From Geopolitics to Geoeconomics." *The National Interest* 17, no. 20 (Summer 1990): 17–23.

MacArthur, Douglas. *Makkāsā Kaisōki* [MacArthur Memoirs], vol. 2. Tokyo: Asahi shimbunsha, 1964. (This is the Japanese translation of Douglas MacArthur, *Reminiscenses* [New York: Fawcett, 1964].)

MacIntyre, Andrew. "Japanese and American Strategies in Asia: Dealing with ASEAN." In *Beyond Bilateralism: U.S.-Japan Relations in the New Asia-Pacific*, edited by Ellis S. Krauss and T. J. Pempel. Stanford, CA: Stanford University Press, 2004.

MacIntyre, Andrew, and Barry Naughton. "The Decline of a Japan-Led Model of the East Asian Economy." In *Remapping East Asia: The Construction of a Region*, edited by T. J. Pempel, 77–100. Ithaca, NY: Cornell University Press, 2005.

Maier, Charles. *The Unmasterable Past*. Cambridge, MA: Harvard University Press, 1988.

Markovits, Andrei S., and Simon Reich. *The German Predicament: Memory and Power in the New Europe*. Ithaca, NY: Cornell University Press, 1997.

Martin, Lisa. *Democratic Commitments: Legislatures and International Cooperation*. Princeton, NJ: Princeton University Press, 2000.

Mason, Mark. *American Multinationals and Japan: The Political Economy of Capital Controls 1899–1980*. Cambridge, MA: Harvard University Press, 1992.

Matthews, Eugene. "Japan's New Nationalism." *Foreign Affairs* 82, no. 6 (November/December 2003): 74–91.

McDonald, Terence J. (ed.). *The Historic Turn in the Human Sciences*. Ann Arbor: University of Michigan Press, 1996.

McNelly, Theodore. *The Origins of Japan's Democratic Constitution*. Lanham, MD: University Press of America, 2000.

McQuillan, Lawrence J., and Peter C. Montgomery (eds.). *The International Monetary Fund: Financial Medic to the World*. Stanford, CA: Hoover Institution Press, 1999.

Mearsheimer, John J. *The Tragedy of Great Power Politics*. New York: W. W. Norton, 2003.

Medeiros, Evan S. "Strategic Hedging and the Future of Asia-Pacific Stability." *Washington Quarterly* 29, no. 1 (Winter 2005–06): 145–167.

Menon, Raja. "The End of Alliances." *World Policy Journal* 20, no. 2 (Summer 2003): 1–19.

Midford, Paul. "Japan's Leadership Role in East Asia: Security Multilateralism: The Nakayama Proposal and the Logic of Reassurance." *The Pacific Review* 13, no. 3 (2000): 367–397.

———. "Japan's Response to the War on Terror: Dispatching the SDF to the Arabian Sea." *Asian Survey* 43, no. 2 (2003): 329–351.

Mills, C. Wright. *The Power Elite*. New York: Oxford University Press, 1956.

Milner, Helen. *Interests, Institutions, and Information: Domestic Politics and International Relations*. Princeton, NJ: Princeton University Press, 1997.

Ministry for Internal Affairs and Communications, Statistics Bureau. *Japan Statistical Yearbook*. Tokyo: Government of Japan Printing Office, various years.

Ministry of Foreign Affairs. *Diplomatic Bluebook, 1957*. Tokyo: Government of Japan Printing Office, 1957.

————. "The Guidelines for Japan-U.S. Defense Cooperation," 1997. Available at http://www.mofa.go.jp/region/n-america/us/security/guideline2.html (accessed April 5, 2006).

————. *Japan and the United Nations*. Tokyo: Ministry of Foreign Affairs, 1998.

————. "Seifu Kaihatsu Enjo [Official Development Assistance]." Available at http://www.mofa.go.jp/mofaj/gaiko/oda/siryo/siryo_2/siryo_2f.html (accessed March 8, 2004).

Miyashita, Akitoshi. "Gaiatsu and Japan's Foreign Aid: Rethinking the Reactive-Proactive Debate." *International Studies Quarterly* 43 (1999): 695–732.

————. *Limits to Power: Asymmetric Dependence and Japanese Foreign Aid Policy*. Lanham, MD: Lexington Books, 2003.

Miyazawa, Kiichi, and Yasuhiro Nakasone. *Tairon Kaiken Goken* [Debate on Constitutional Amendment and Protection of Constitution]. Tokyo: Asahi Shimbun, 1997.

Mizzima News Group. "Activists Urge Total Ban on Investments in Burma," November 30, 2000. Available at http://www.rebound88.net/00/dec/01.html.

Mochizuki, Mike M. "China-Japan Relations: Downward Spiral or a New Equilibrium?" In *Power Shift: China and Asia's New Dynamics*, edited by David Shambaugh, 135–150. Berkeley: University of California Press, 2005.

————. "Japan: Between Alliance and Autonomy." In *Strategic Asia 2004–05: Confronting Terrorism in the Pursuit of Power*, edited by Ashley J. Tellis and Michael Wills, 103–137. Seattle, WA: National Bureau of Asian Research, 2004.

————. *Japan: Domestic Change and Foreign Policy*. Santa Monica, CA: RAND, 1995.

————. "A New Bargain for a Stronger Alliance." In *Toward a True Alliance: Restructuring U.S.-Japan Security Relations*, edited by Mike M. Mochizuki, 5–40. Washington, DC: Brookings Institution Press, 1997.

————. "Strategic Thinking Under Bush and Koizumi: Implications for the US-Japan Alliance." *Asia-Pacific Review* 10, no. 1 (May 2003): 82–98.

————. "Terms of Engagement: The U.S.-Japan Alliance and the Rise of China." In *Beyond Bilateralism: U.S.-Japan Relations in the New Asia-Pacific*, edited by Ellis S. Krauss and T. J. Pempel, 87–114. Stanford, CA: Stanford University Press, 2004.

————. "U.S.-Japan Relations in the Asia-Pacific Region." In *Partnership: The United States and Japan, 1951–2001*, edited by Akira Iriye and Robert A. Wampler, 13–32. New York: Kodansha International, 2001.

Mochizuki, Mike, and Michael O'Hanlon. "A Liberal Vision for the US-Japanese Alliance." *Survival* 40, no. 2 (Summer 1998): 127–134.

Moravcsik, Andrew. "Liberal International Relations Theory: A Scientific Assessment." In *Progress in International Relations Theory: Appraising the Field*, edited by Colin Elman and Miriam Fendius Elman, 159–204. Cambridge, MA: MIT Press, 2003.

Morgenthau, Hans J. *Politics Among Nations: The Struggle for War and Peace*. 5th ed. New York: Alfred Knopf, 1978.

Morimoto, Satoshi. "Nit-chū Bō-ei Kōryū no Genjō to Kadai [The Present Situation and Themes of Japan-China Defense Exchanges]." In *Ajia Taiheiyō no Takoku-kan Anzen Hoshō* [Multilateral Security of the Asia Pacific], edited by Morimoto Satoshi, 273–289. Tokyo: Nihon Kokusai Mondai Kenkyūjō, 2003.

Morris, Ivan I. *Nationalism and the Right Wing in Japan*. London: Oxford University Press, 1960.

Motoyama, Yoshihiko. *Urareru Azia* [Asia on Sale]. Tokyo: Shinshokan, 2000.

Mowle, Thomas. *Allies at Odds: The United States and the European Union*. New York: Palgrave Macmillan, 2004.

Müller, Jan-Werner (ed.). *Memory and Power in the New Europe*. New York: Cambridge University Press, 2002.

Munakata, Naoko. "Has Politics Caught Up with Markets? In Search of East Asian Economic Regionalism." In *The Dynamics of East Asian Regionalism*, edited by Peter J. Katzenstein and Takashi Shiraishi, 141–157. Ithaca, NY: Cornell University Press, 2006.

Murai, Yoshitaka. *Suharto Family no Chikuzai* [Money Seeking of Suharto Family]. Tokyo: Commons, 1999.

Murakami, Yasusuke. "The Age of New Middle Mass Politics." *Journal of Japanese Studies* 8 (1982): 29–72.

———. *Han-koten no Seiji-keizaigaku* [Anti-classical Political Economy]. Tokyo: Chūō Kōron Sha, 1992.

Muramatsu, Michio. "An Arthritic Japan? The Relationship Between Bureaucrats and Politicians." In *Japanese Political Reform: A Work in Progress,* an Asia Program special report, no. 117. Washington, DC: Woodrow Wilson Center, 2004.

Muramatsu, Michio, and Ellis Krauss. "The Conservative Policy Line and the Development of Patterned Pluralism." In *The Political Economy of Japan*. Vol. 1: *The Domestic Transformation*, edited by Kozo Yamamura and Yasukichi Yasuba, 516–554. Stanford, CA: Stanford University Press, 1987.

Murayama, Tomiichi. *Sōja-no* [Well . . . I Suppose . . .]. Tokyo: Daisan Sho-kan, 1998.

Naikaku-fu Seifu Kōhō Shitsu. *Seron chōsa gaikō* [Public Opinion Polls on Diplomacy], October 1991. Available at http://www8.cao.go.jp/survey/h03/ H03-10-03-12.html; October 2005. Available at http://www8.cao.go.jp/ survey/h17/h17-gaikou/2-7.html.

Nakagawa, Go. "Nippi Ryō Kenpō ni miru Ruien [The Similarities Between the Constitutions of Japan and Philippines]." *Chūō Kōron* (May 1987): 178–214.

Nakasone, Yasuhiro. "Waga kaiken ron [My Opinion on Constitutional Revisions]." *Shokun* (April 2000): 54–63.

Nakata, Hiroko. "China Détente Spells Yen 74 Billion in Loans." *Japan Times*, June 7, 2006.

Nathan, John. *Japan Unbound: A Volatile Nation's Quest for Price and Purpose*. New York: Houghton Mifflin, 2004.

National Institute for Defense Studies Japan. *East Asian Strategic Review 2005*. Tokyo: Japan Times, 2005.

———. *East Asian Strategic Review 2006*. Tokyo: Japan Times, 2006.

"National Security Strategy of the United States of America," September 2002. Available at http://www.whitehouse.gov/nsc/nss.pdf.

Noble, Gregory. "The Japanese Industrial Policy Debate." In *Pacific Dynamics: The International Politics of Industrial Change*, edited by Stephen Haggard and Chung-in Moon, 53–96. Boulder, CO: Westview Press, 1989.

———. "What Can Taiwan (and the United States) Expect from Japan?" *Journal of East Asian Studies* 5 (2005): 1–34.

Noble, Gregory, and John Ravenhill (eds.). *The Asian Financial Crisis and the Architecture of Global Finance*. New York: Cambridge University Press, 2000.

Noguchi, Yukio. *1940-nen Taisei* [The 1940 System]. Tokyo: Tōyō Keizai Shimpōsha, 1995.

Nozaki, Yoshiko, and Inokuchi Hiromitsu. "Japanese Education, Nationalism, and Ienaga Saburō's Textbook Lawsuits." In *Censoring History: Citizenship and Memory in Japan, Germany, and the United States*, edited by Laura Hein and Mark Selden, 96–126. Armonk, NY: M. E. Sharpe, 2000.

Oatley, Thomas, and Robert Nabors. "Redistributive Cooperation: Market Failure, Wealth Transfers, and the Basle Accord." *International Organization* 52, no. 1 (Winter 1998): 35–54.

Ochi, Yukiko. "NGOs Activities Are Effective Diplomacy." *Japan Economic Wire*, November 18, 2002. Available at http://www.globalpolicy.org/ngos/state/2002/118diplomacy.htm.

Oda, Takashi. "Maehara Right About China Threat." *Daily Yomiuri*, December 23, 2005.

Office of the United Nations High Commissioner for Refugees [UNHCR]. *2004 Global Refugee Trends*. Geneva: UNHCR, 2005.

———. *UNHCR Statistical Yearbook 2001*. Geneva: UNHCR, 2002.

Ogata, Sadako. *Normalization with China: A Comparative Study of U.S. and Japanese Processes*. Berkeley: Institute of East Asian Studies, University of California, 1988.

Ogura, Kazuo. "'Ajia no fukken' no tame ni [For the Restoration of Asia]." *Chūō Kōron* (July 1993): 60–73.

O'Hanlon, Michael. *Expanding Global Military Capacity for Humanitarian Intervention*. Washington, DC: Brookings Institution, 2003.

———. "Transforming NATO: The Role of European Forces." *Survival* 39, no. 3 (Autumn 1997): 5–15.

Ōhashi, Hideo. "Ikigai Taikoku to ASEAN: Keizai Kiki Shien Mondai wo Chushin Ni [Outside Powers and ASEAN]." *Kokusai Mondai*, no. 472 (July 1999).

Oishi, Mikio, and Fumitaka Furuoka. "Can Japanese Aid Be an Effective Tool of Influence? Case Studies of Cambodia and Burma." *Asian Survey* 43, no. 6 (November 2003): 890–907.

Okamoto, Tomochika. *The Distortion and the Revision of History in Postwar Japanese Textbooks, 1945–1998*. Available at http://member.nifty.ne.jp/Tomochika/.

Okawara, Yoshio. *To Avoid Isolation: An Ambassador's View of U.S.A.-Japanese Relations*. Columbia: University of South Carolina Press, 1989.

Okimoto, Daniel. *Between MITI and the Marketplace: Japanese Industrial Policy for High Technology*. Stanford, CA: Stanford University Press, 1988.

Olick, Jeffrey. *In the House of the Hangman: The Agonies of German Defeat, 1943–1949*. Chicago: University of Chicago Press, 2005.

Orr, James J. *The Victim as Hero: Ideologies of Peace and National Identity in Postwar Japan*. Honolulu: University of Hawai'i Press, 2001.

Orr, Robert M., Jr. *The Emergence of Japan's Foreign Aid Power*. New York: Columbia University Press, 1990.

———. "Japanese Foreign Aid: Over a Barrel in the Middle East." In *Japan's Foreign Aid: Power and Policy in a New Era*, edited by Bruce M. Koppel and Robert M. Orr Jr., 289–304. Boulder, CO: Westview Press, 1993.

Ōta, Takeshi. *Kokusai Kinyū Genba karano Shōgen: Nichigin kara Mita Gekido no Sanjū-nen* [Turbulent 30 Years of International Finance Viewed by BOJ Officer in Charge]. Tokyo: Chūō Kōron-sha, 1991.

Ōtake, Hideo. *Adenauā to Yoshida Shigeru* [Adenauer and Shigeru Yoshida]. Tokyo: Chūō Kōron sha, 1986.

———. *Nihon no Bōei to Kokunai Seiji: Detanto kara gunkaku e* [Japanese Defense and Domestic Politics: From Détente to the Arms Buildup]. Tokyo: San ichi Shobō, 1983.

———. *Nihon Seiji no Tairitsu-Jiku* [The Dividing Axis of Japanese Politics]. Tokyo: Chūō Kōron sha, 1999.

———. "Political Realignment and Policy Conflict." In *Power Shuffles and Policy Processes: Coalition Government in Japan in the 1990s*, edited by Hideo Ōtake, 125–151. Tokyo: Japan Center for International Exchange, 2000.

———. *Saigunbi to Nashonarizumu* [Rearmament and Nationalism]. Tokyo: Chūō Kōron sha, 1988.

———. *Sengonihon no Ideorogii tairitsu jiku* [Ideological Confrontation in Postwar Japan]. Tokyo: Sanichi Shobo, 1996.

Ozawa, Ichirō. *Blueprint for a New Japan: The Rethinking of a Nation.* Translated by Louisa Rubinfien. Tokyo: Kodansha International, 1994.

———. *Nihon Kaizō Keikaku* [Blueprint for a New Japan]. Tokyo: Kōdansha, 1993.

———. "Nihonkoku Kenpōkaisei Shian [A Draft Proposal of the Revised Constitution of Japan]." *Bungei Shunju* (September 1999): 94–106.

Paul, T. V., James J. Wirtz, and Michel Fortmann (eds.). *Balance of Power: Theory and Practice in the 21st Century.* Stanford, CA: Stanford University Press, 2004.

Pei, Minxin. "China's Governance Crisis." *Foreign Affairs* 81, no. 5 (September/October 2002): 96–109.

Pekkanen, Saadia M. "At Play in the Legal Realm: The WTO and the Changing Nature of U.S.-Japan Antidumping Disputes." In *Beyond Bilateralism: U.S.-Japan Relations in the New Asia-Pacific*, edited by Ellis Krauss and T. J. Pempel, 221–247. Stanford, CA: Stanford University Press, 2004.

———. "Bilateralism, Multilateralism, or Regionalism? Japan's Trade Forum Choices." *Journal of East Asian Studies* 5, no. 1 (January–April 2005): 77–103.

Pempel, T. J. "Introduction." In *Remapping East Asia: The Construction of a Region*, edited by T. J. Pempel, 1–30. Ithaca, NY: Cornell University Press, 2005.

——— (ed.). *The Politics of the Asian Economic Crisis.* Ithaca, NY: Cornell University Press, 1999.

———. *Regime Shift: The Comparative Dynamics of the Japanese Political Economy.* Ithaca, NY: Cornell University Press, 1998.

———. *Uncommon Democracies.* Ithaca, NY: Cornell University Press, 1990.

Pharr, Susan. "Japan's Defensive Foreign Policy and the Politics of Burden Sharing." In *Japan's Foreign Policy After the Cold War: Coping with Change*, edited by Gerald L. Curtis, 235–262. Armonk, NY: M. E. Sharpe, 1993.

Pharr, Susan, and Frank Schwartz. *The State of Civil Society in Japan.* New York: Cambridge University Press, 2003.

Polak, Jacque. *The Changing Nature of IMF Conditionality.* Princeton, NJ: Princeton University Press, 1991.

Pond, Elizabeth. *Friendly Fire: The Near-Death of the Transatlantic Alliance.* Washington, DC: Brookings Institution, 2003.

Porter, Tony. *States, Markets, and Regimes in Global Finance.* London: St. Martin's Press, 1993.

Prestowitz, Clyde V., Jr. *Rogue Nation: American Unilateralism and the Failure of Good Intentions.* New York: Basic Books, 2003.

———. *Trading Places: How We Are Giving Our Future to Japan and How to Reclaim It.* New York: Basic Books, 1988.

Prime Minister's Office. *Paths to International Peace: Japan's Contributions to World Peace* (Tokyo: Prime Minister's Office, 1998).

Purrington, Courtney. "Tokyo's Policy Responses During the Gulf War and the Impact of the 'Iraqi Shock' on Japan." *Pacific Affairs* 65 (1992): 161–181.

Pyle, Kenneth B. "Abe Shinzo and Japan's Change of Course." *NBR Analysis* (National Bureau of Asian Research) 17, no. 4 (October 2006): 5–31.

———. *The Japanese Question: Power and Purpose*. Washington, DC: AEI Press, 1992.

———. "Profound Forces in the Making of Modern Japan." *Journal of Japanese Studies* 32, no. 2 (2006): 393–418.

Rahman, Bayan. "Japanese Groups Win Taiwan Rail Deal." *Financial Times,* July 24, 2002.

Rapp, William E. "Paths Diverging? The Next Decade in the U.S.-Japan Security Alliance." Carlisle, PA: Strategic Studies Institute, U.S. Army War College, 2004. Available at www.carlisle.army.mil/ssi.

Reinicke, Wolfgang. *Banking, Politics, and Global Finance*. Brookfield, VT: Edward Elgar, 1995.

Richardson, Bradley. *Japanese Democracy: Power, Coordination, and Performance*. New Haven, CT: Yale University Press, 1997.

Rix, Alan. "Japan and the Region: Leading from Behind." In *Pacific Economic Relations in the 1990s: Cooperation or Conflict*, edited by Richard Higgot, Richard Leaver, and John Ravenhill, 62–82. Boulder, CO: Lynne Rienner Publishers, 1993.

Rodrik, Dani. "Getting Intervention Right: How South Korea and Taiwan Grew Rich." *Economic Policy* 20 (1995): 55–107.

Rogowski, Ronald. *Commerce and Coalitions: How Trade Affects Domestic Political Alignments*. Princeton, NJ: Princeton University Press, 1989.

Rose, Caroline. *Sino-Japanese Relations: Facing the Past, Looking to the Future?* London: Routledge Curzon, 2005.

Rosecrance, Richard. *The Rise of the Trading State*. New York: Basic Books, 1986.

Rosecrance, Richard, and Arthur Stein. *The Domestic Bases of Grand Strategy*. Ithaca, NY: Cornell University Press, 1993.

Rosenberger, Leif Roderick. "Southeast Asia's Currency Crisis: A Diagnosis and Prescription." *Contemporary Southeast Asia* 19, no. 3 (December 1997): 223–251.

Ross, Robert S. "The Geography of Peace: East Asia in the Twenty-first Century." *International Security* 23, no. 4 (Spring 1999): 81–118.

———. "Taiwan's Fading Independence Movement." *Foreign Affairs* 85, no. 2 (March/April 2006): 141–148.

Roy, Denny. "The Sources and Limits of Sino-Japanese Tensions." *Survival* 47, no. 2 (Summer 2005): 191–214.

Russett, Bruce. *Grasping the Democratic Peace: Principles for a Post–Cold War World*. Princeton, NJ: Princeton University Press, 1993.

Safier, Joshua. "Yasukuni Shrine and the Constraints on the Discourses of Nationalism in Twentieth-Century Japan." PhD diss., University of Kansas, 1996.

Saito, Shizuo. "The Evolution of Japan's United Nations Policy." *Japan Review of International Affairs* (1987).

Sakakibara, Eisuke. *Beyond Capitalism: The Japanese Model of Market Economics*. Lanham, MD: University Press of America, 1993.

————. *Kokusai Kinyū no Genba* [On the Scene of International Finance]. Tokyo: PHP Shinsho, 1998.

————. *Structural Reform in Japan: Breaking the Iron Triangle*. Washington, DC: Brookings Institution Press, 2004.

Sakaya, Taichi. *What Is Japan? Contradictions and Transformations*. New York: Kodansha International, 1993.

Sakurada, Daizō, and Itō Go (eds.). *Hikaku Gaikō Seisaku: Iraq Sensō heno Taiō Gaikō* [Comparative Foreign Policy: Responses to the U.S. Iraqi War]. Tokyo: Akashi Shoten, 2004.

Samuels, Richard J. *The Business of the Japanese State: Energy Markets in Comparative and Historical Perspective*. Ithaca, NY: Cornell University Press, 1987.

————. "Japan's Goldilocks Strategy." *The Washington Quarterly* 29, no. 4 (Autumn 2006): 111–127.

————. *"Rich Nation, Strong Army": National Security and the Technological Transformation of Japan*. Ithaca, NY: Cornell University Press, 1994.

————. *Securing Japan*. Ithaca, NY: Cornell University Press, forthcoming.

Samuels, Richard J., and Eric Heginbotham. "Japan's Dual Hedge." *Foreign Affairs* 81, no. 5 (September/October 2002): 110–121.

Sasajima, Masahiko. "Japan's Domestic Politics and China Policymaking." In *An Alliance for Engagement: Building Cooperation in Security Relations with China*, edited by Benjamin L. Self and Jeffrey W. Thompson, 79–110. Washington, DC: Henry L. Stimson Center, 2002.

Sasaki, Hitoshi, and Yuki Koga. "Trade Between Japan and China: Dramatic Expansion and Structural Changes." Economic Commentary no. 2002–2003, Bank of Japan, Research and Statistics Department, August 2003. Available at http://www.boj.or.jp/en/ronbun/03/data/rkt03e03.pdf (accessed August 1, 2005).

Sasaki, Takao. "Sengokaikaku ni okeru Makkāsā Note no yakuwari [The Roles of the MacArthur Notes in the Postwar Reform]." In *Kakuhō-ryōiki ni okeru sengokaikaku* [The Postwar Reforms in Each Law Area], edited by Sasaki Takao et al., 1–25. Tokyo: Research Institute of Aoyama Gakuin University, 1993.

————. *Sensō Hōkijōkō no Seiritsukeii* [The Formation Processes of War Renunciation Article]. Tokyo: Seibun-do, 1997.

Sase, Masamori. *Shūdanteki Jieiken* [The Right of Collective Self-Defense]. Tokyo: Bungei Shunjūsha, 2001.

Satō, Tatsuo. *Nihonkoku Kenpō Tanjoki* [The History of the Birth of the Constitution of Japan]. Tokyo: Chūō Kōron-sha, 1999.

Satō, Yuri (ed.). *Indonesia Shiryōshu* [Documents on Indonesia]. Chiba, Japan: Institute of Developing Economies, 2002.

Scharfstetter, Susanna. "The Diplomacy of Wiedergutmachung: Memory, the Cold War, and West European Victims of Nazism, 1956–1964." *Holocaust and Genocide Studies* 17, no. 3 (Winter 2003): 459–479.

Schoppa, Leonard. *Bargaining with Japan: What American Pressure Can and Cannot Do*. New York: Columbia University Press, 1997.

Schreurs, Miranda. *Environmental Politics in Japan, Germany, and the United States*. New York: Cambridge University Press, 2003.

Schultz, Kenneth. "Do Democratic Institutions Constrain or Inform? Contrasting Two Institutional Perspectives on Democracy and War." *International Organization* 52 (1999): 233–266.

————. "Domestic Opposition and Signaling in International Crises." *American Political Science Review* 92 (1998): 829–844.

Schwarz, Adam, and Jonathan Paris (eds.). *The Politics of Post-Suharto Indonesia.* New York: Council on Foreign Relations, 1999.

Schwartz, Frank J. *Advice and Consent: The Politics of Consultation in Japan.* New York: Cambridge University Press, 1998.

Scott, Hal S., and Shinsuke Iwahara. *In Search of Level Playing: The Implementation of the Basle Capital Accord in Japan and the United States.* Washington, DC: Group of Thirty, 1994.

Searight, Amy. "MITI and Multilateralism: The Evolution of Japan's Trade Policy in the GATT Regime." Paper delivered at the Stanford Graduate Conference on Japanese Politics, Stanford University, November 15, 1997.

Seekins, Donald M. *Japan's "Burma Lovers" and the Military Regime.* JPRI Working Paper 60, September 1999. Available at http://www.jpri.org/publications/workingpapers/wp60.html.

———. "The North Wind and the Sun: Japan's Response to the Political Crisis in Burma, 1988–96." *Journal of Burma Studies* 4 (1999). Available at http://111.english.dvb.no/e_docs/82j_res_polcri.htm.

Self, Benjamin. "China and Japan: A Façade of Friendship." *Washington Quarterly* 26, no. 1 (Winter 2002/2003): 77–88.

Self, Benjamin, and Jeffrey W. Thompson (eds.). *Japan's Nuclear Option: Security, Politics, and Policy in the 21st Century.* Washington, DC: Henry L. Stimson Center, 2003.

Seraphim, Franziska. *War Memory and Social Politics in Japan, 1945–2005.* Cambridge, MA: Harvard University Asia Center, 2006.

Shambaugh, David (ed.). *Is China Unstable?* Armonk, NY: M. E. Sharpe, 2000.

Shimizu, Masayoshi. "Sengo Hoshō no Kokusaihikaku [A Comparison of Post-war Compensation]." *Sekai* (February 1994): 133–143.

Shimizu, Yoshikazu. *Chūgoku wa na-ze "'Han-Nichi' ni natta ka* [Why Did China Become 'Anti-Japan'?]." Tokyo: Bungei Shunjū, 2003.

Shinoda, Tomohito. *Kantei gaikō* [Diplomacy from the Prime Minister's Office]. Tokyo: Asahi Shimbunsha, 2004.

———. "Koizumi's Top-Down Leadership in the Anti-Terrorism Legislation: The Impact of Political Institutional Changes." *SAIS Review* 23, no. 1 (Winter-Spring 2003): 19–34.

Shinyō, Takahiro (ed.). *Kokusai Heiwa Kyōryoku Nyūmon* [An Introduction to World Peace]. Tokyo: Yuhikaku, 1995.

Shiota, Ushio. *Kinyū-arijigoku: Document Nichibei Ginkō Sensō* [Bank War Between the US and Japan]. Tokyo: Nihon Keizai Shimbunsha, 1999.

Shipper, Apichai W. "Criminals or Victims? The Politics of Illegal Foreigners in Japan." *Journal of Japanese Studies* 31, no. 2 (2005): 299–327.

Shiraishi, Takashi. *Hōkai Indonesia wa Dokoeiku* [Where Is Collapsed Indonesia Going?]. Tokyo: NTT Shuppan, 1999.

Singh, Bhubhindar. "ASEAN's Perceptions of Japan: Change and Continuity." *Asian Survey* 42, no. 2 (March–April 2002): 276–296.

Smith, Sheila A. "Abe Shinzo's Diplomatic Debut." *Pac Net no. 53* (Pacific Forum CSIS), October 26, 3006. Available at http://www.csis.org/media/csis/pubs/pac0653.pdf.

Smith, Thomas C. *The Native Sources of Japanese Industrialization.* Berkeley: University of California Press, 1988.

Smith, Tony. *America's Mission: The United States and the Worldwide Struggle for Democracy.* Princeton, NJ: Princeton University Press, 1994.

Soeya, Yoshihide. "The Misconstrued Shift in Japan's Foreign Policy." *Japan Echo* 33, no. 3 (June 2006): 16–19.

———. *Nihon no "Midoru Pawā" Gaikō* [Japan's "Middle-Power" Diplomacy]. Tokyo: Chikuma Shobo, 2005.

———. "Taiwan in Japan's Security Considerations." *China Quarterly* 165 (2001): 130–146.

Spykman, Nicholas John. *America's Strategy in World Politics*. New York: Harcourt Brace, 1942.

Starr, S. Frederick (ed.). *The Legacy of History in Russia and the New States of Eurasia*. London: M. E. Sharpe, 1994.

Stubbs, Richard. "ASEAN Plus Three: Emerging East Asian Regionalism?" *Asian Survey* 42 (May/June 2002): 440–455.

Sugimoto, Nobuyuki. *Tai-chi no Hōkō* [Roar of the Earth]. Tokyo: PHP Kenkyūjō, 2006.

Suzuki, Akinori. *Nihonkoku Kenpō o Unda Misshitsu no Kokonokakan* [The Nine Days That Produced the Constitution of Japan]. Tokyo: Sogensha, 1995.

Suzuki, Akira. *Nankin "Gyakusatsu" no Maboroshi* [The Mirage of the Nanjing "Massacre"]. Tokyo: Bungei Shunjū, 1973.

Suzuki, Yoshikatsu. "Anpōri Kamei: Gaimushō no Shosō [Joining the Security Council: Foreign Ministry's Ideas]." *Bungei Shunjū* (November 1994).

Swaine, Michael, Rachel Swanger, and Takashi Kawakami. *Japan and Ballistic Missile Defense*. Santa Monica, CA: RAND Corporation, 2001.

Takahashi, Shirō. *Rekishi kyōiku wa kore de yoi no ka* [Is History Education Good as It Is?]. Tokyo: Tōyō Keizai Shimposha, 1997.

Takahashi, Takuma, Kan Shiyu, and Sano Tetsuji. *Azia Kinyū Kiki* [Asian Financial Crisis]. Tokyo: Tōyō Keizai Shinpō Sha, 1998.

Takano, Yuichi. *Shūdan Anpo to Jieiken* [Collective Security and the Right of Self-Defense]. Tokyo: Toshindo, 1999.

Takashima, Nobuyoshi. *Kyōkasho wa kō kakinaosareta!* [This Is How Textbooks Were Rewritten!]. Tokyo: Kodansha, 1994.

Takeda, Isami. "A Third Stage in Europe-Asia Relations," unpublished speech, Athens, Greece, November 1996. Available at http://www.mofa.go.jp/j_info/japan/opinion/takeda.html.

Takeda, Yasuhiro. "Overcoming Japan-US Discord in Democracy Promotion Policies," Okazaki Institute, 1996. Available at http://www.okazaki-inst.jp/okazaki-inst/alliance-pro-eng/takeda.e.html.

Takemura, Masayoshi. *Chiisaku tomo Kirari to Hikaru Kuni Nippon* [Japan, a Country That Is Small but Sparkling]. Tokyo: Kobun-sha, 1994.

Tamamoto, Masaru. "Ambiguous Japan: Japanese National Identity at Century's End." In *International Relations Theory and the Asia-Pacific*, edited by G. John Ikenberry and Michael Mastanduno, 191–212. New York: Columbia University Press, 2003.

Tamura, Kentaro. "A Regulator's Dilemma and Two-level Games: Japan in the Politics of International Banking Regulation." *Social Science Japan Journal* 6, no. 2 (2003): 312–315.

Tanaka, Akihiko. *Anzen Hoshō: Sengo 50-nen no Mosaku* [Security: 50 years of Searching After the War]. Tokyo: Yomiuri Shimbunsha, 1997.

———. "Kokuren Heiwa-katsudō to Nihon [UN Peacekeeping Operations and Japan]." In *Kokuren PKO to Nichibei-anpō* [UN Peacekeeping: Japanese and American Perspectives], edited by Masashi Nishihara and Selig Harrison. Tokyo: Aki Shobo, 1995.

———. *Nit-chu Kankei 1945–90* [Japan-China Relations, 1945–90]. Tokyo: Tokyo Daigaku Shuppankai, 1991.

Tanaka, Hitoshi. "The ASEAN+3 and East Asia Summit: A Two-Tiered Approach to Community Building." *East Asia Insights* (Japan Center for International Exchange) 1, no. 1 (January 2006).

———. "Japan and China at a Crossroads." *East Asia Insights* (Japan Center for International Exchange) 1, no. 2 (March 2006).

Taniguchi, Tomohiko. "A Cold Peace: The Changing Security Equation in Northeast Asia." *Orbis* 49, no. 3 (Summer 2005): 445–457.

Teitel, Ruti G. *Transitional Justice*. New York: Oxford University Press, 2000.

Terada, Takashi. "The Origins of Japan's APEC Policy." *The Pacific Review* 11, no. 3 (1998): 337–363.

Terashima, Jitsurō. "'Shin Bei Nyū A' no sōgō senryaku o motomete [Aspiring for a Comprehensive Strategy of 'Close to America and Entering Asia']." *Chūō Kōron* (March 1996): 20–38.

Tett, Gillian. *Saving the Sun: A Wall Street Gamble to Save Japan from Its Trillion-Dollar Meltdown*. New York: HarperBusiness, 2003.

Thayer, Nathaniel. "Japanese Foreign Policy During the Nakasone Years." In *Japanese Foreign Policy After the Cold War*, edited by Gerald Curtis, 90–104. Armonk, NY: M. E. Sharpe, 1993.

Thurow, Lester. *Head-to-Head: The Coming Economic Battle Among Japan, Europe, and America*. New York: Morrow Books, 1992.

Tilton, Mark. *Restrained Trade: Cartels in Japan's Basic Materials Industry*. Ithaca, NY: Cornell University Press, 1996.

Togo, Kazuhiko. "A Moratorium on Yasukuni Visits." *Far Eastern Economic Review* (June 2006): 5–15.

Tokuda, Hiromi. "BIS kisei wa yōkai, minaose [The BIS Regulation Is a Monster, Reconsider It]." *Tōyōkeizai*, July 4, 1992, 20–22.

Tsuchiyama, Jitsuo. "The End of the Alliance? Dilemmas in the U.S.-Japan Relations." In *United States–Japan Relations and International Institutions After the Cold War*, edited by Peter Gourevich et al., 3–35. La Jolla: Graduate School of International Relations and Pacific Studies, University of California, San Diego, 1995.

———. "From Balancing to Networking: Models of Regional Security in Asia." In *Reinventing the Alliance: U.S.-Japan Security Partnership in an Era of Change*, edited by G. John Ikenberry and Takashi Inoguchi, 43–61. New York: Palgrave-Macmillan, 2003.

———. "Why Japan Is Allied? Politics of the US-Japan Alliance." In *Global Governance: Germany and Japan in the International System*, edited by Saori Katada, Hanns W. Maull, and Takashi Inoguchi, 71–85. London: Ashgate, 2004.

Tsugami, Toshiya. *Chūgoku no Taitō* [Rise of China]. Tokyo: Nihon Keizai Shimbun Sha, 2003.

Unger, Danny. "Japan and the Gulf War: Making the World Safe for Japan-U.S. Relations." In *Friends in Need: Burden Sharing in the Persian Gulf War*, edited by Andrew Bennett, Joseph Lepgold, and Danny Unger. New York: St. Martin's Press, 1997.

United Nations, United Nations Conference on Trade and Development. *World Investment Report 2003: Promoting Linkages*. New York: United Nations, 2003.

Urayama, Kori. "China Debates Missile Defense." *Survival* 46, no. 2 (Summer 2004): 123–142.

US Congress, House of Representatives. *Hearing Before the Subcommittee on*

General Oversight and Investigations of the Committee on Banking, Finance, and Urban Affairs, 100th Congress, 1st sess., April 30, 1987. Washington, DC: US Government Printing Office, 1987.

——. *Hearing Before the Subcommittee on General Oversight and Investigations of the Committee on Banking, Finance, and Urban Affairs*, 100th Congress, 2nd sess., April 21, 1988. Washington, DC: US Government Printing Office, 1988.

Usul, Tetsuro, and Claire Debenham. *The Relationship Between Japan and Burma*. Asian Human Rights Commission, 1993. Available at http://www.ahrchk.net/hrsolid/mainfile.php/1993vol03no1/2041.

Van Evera, Steven. *The Causes of War: Power and the Roots of Conflict*. Ithaca, NY: Cornell University Press, 1999.

Van Wolferen, Karel. *The Japanese Enigma*. New York: Alfred Knopf, 1989.

Vogel, Ezra F. *Japan as Number One: Lessons for America*. Cambridge, MA: Harvard University Press, 1979.

Vogel, Steven K. *Freer Markets, More Rules: Regulatory Reform in Advanced Industrial Societies*. Ithaca, NY: Cornell University Press, 1998.

——. *Japan Remodeled: How Government and Industry Are Reforming Japanese Capitalism*. Ithaca, NY: Cornell University Press, 2006.

Volcker, Paul, and Toyoo Gyoten. *Changing Fortunes: World's Money and the Threat to American Leadership*. New York: Times Books, 1992.

Wade, Robert. "Japan, the World Bank, and the Art of Paradigm Maintenance: The East Asian Miracle in Political Perspective." *The New Left Review*, no. 217 (May/June 1996): 3–36.

Wakamiya, Yoshibumi. *The Postwar Conservative View of Asia: How the Political Right Has Delayed Japan's Coming to Terms with Its History of Aggression in Asia*. Tokyo: LTCB International Library Foundation, 1998.

Walt, Stephen M. *The Origins of Alliances*. Ithaca, NY: Cornell University Press, 1987.

Waltz, Kenneth. *Man, the State, and War*. New York: Columbia University Press, 1959.

——. *Theory of International Politics*. Reading, MA: Addison-Wesley, 1979.

Wan, Ming. *Sino-Japanese Relations: Interaction, Logic, and Transformation*. Washington, DC: Woodrow Wilson Center Press, 2006.

——. "Tensions in Sino-Japanese Relations: The Shenyang Incident of 2002." *Asian Survey* 43, no. 5 (September/ October 2003): 826–844.

Wang, Qingxin Ken. "Taiwan in Japan's Relations with China and the United States After the Cold War." *Pacific Affairs* 73, no. 3 (Autumn 2000): 353–373.

Watanabe, Shogo. "Japan's Burma Refugees: Time to Change Tokyo's Status on Refugees." *Asahi Shimbun*, November 18, 1997. Available at http://www.ahrchk.net/hrsolid/mainfile/php/1997vol07no07/2073.

Weinstein, Martin E. *Japan's Postwar Defense Policy: 1948–1968*. New York: Columbia University Press, 1971.

Weinstein, Michael. "South Korea–Japan Dokdo-Takeshima Dispute: Towards Confrontation." *Japan Focus*, May 10, 2006, 2–3. Available at http://japanfocus.org/article.asp?id=596.

Wertsch, James V. *Voices of Collective Remembering*. Cambridge: Cambridge University Press, 2002.

Wong, Diana. "Memory Suppression and Memory Production: The Japanese Occupation of Singapore." In *Perilous Memories: The Asia-Pacific War(s)*, edited by Takashi Fujitani and Lisa Yoneyama, 218–238. Durham, NC: Duke University Press, 2001.

Woo, Meredith. *The Developmental State*. Ithaca, NY: Cornell University Press, 1998.

World Bank. *The East Asian Miracle: Economic Growth and Public Policy.* Washington, DC: Oxford University Press, 1993.

———. *World Bank Development Indicators CD-ROM 03*. Washington, DC: World Bank, 2003.

Wu, Xinbo. "The End of the Silver Lining: A Chinese View of the U.S.-Japanese Alliance." *Washington Quarterly* 29, no. 1 (Winter 2005–06): 119–130.

Yahuda, Michael. "The Limits of Economic Interdependence." In *New Directions in the Study of China's Foreign Policy*, edited by Alastair Iain Johnston and Robert S. Ross, 162–185. Stanford, CA: Stanford University Press, 2006.

Yamada, Yoshinobu, and Kikuchi Tsutomu. "Japan's Approach to APEC and Regime Creation in the Asia-Pacific." In *Asia-Pacific Crossroads: Regime Creation and the Future of APEC*, edited by Vinod Aggarwal and Charles Morrison, 191–211. New York: St. Martin's Press, 1998.

Yamakage, Susumu. "Nippon no Eai ASEAN Seisaku no Henyō [The Change of Japan's Policy Toward ASEAN]." *Kokusai Mondai,* no. 490 (January 2000).

Yamamoto, Shichihei. *Watakūshi no Naka no Nihongun* [The Japanese Army Within Me]. 2 vols. Tokyo: Bungei Shunjā, 1975.

Yamasaki, Taku. *Kenpō kaisei* [Constitutional Amendment]. Tokyo: Seisansei Shuppan, 2000.

Yang, Daqing. "The Malleable and the Contested: The Nanjing Massacre in Postwar China and Japan." In *Perilous Memories: The Asia-Pacific War*, edited by Takashi Fujitani and Lisa Yoneyama, 50–86. Durham, NC: Duke University Press, 2001.

Yardley, Jim, and Keith Bradsher. "China Accuses U.S. and Japan of Interfering on Taiwan." *New York Times*, February 21, 2005, A3.

Yasutomo, Dennis. *The New Multilateralism in Japan's Foreign Policy*. New York: St. Martin's Press, 1995.

Yokota, Kisaburō. *Sensō no Hōki* [The Renunciation of War]. Tokyo: Kokuritsu Shoin, 1947.

Yomiuri Shimbun. *Minna no Kenpō 3—Sōgō Anpōseisaku Taikō no Teigen* [The Constitution for Everybody 3—The Proposal for Comprehensive Security Policy Outline]. Tokyo: Yomiuri Shimbun, 1995.

Yomiuri Shimbun Seiji-bu. *Gaikō o Kenka ni shita Otoko* [The Man Who Made Diplomacy a Quarrel]. Tokyo: Shinchō Sha, 2006.

Yoshida, Reiji. "New Yen Loans to China Are Put on Hold for Now." *Japan Times,* March 24, 2006.

Yoshida, Shigeru. *Yoshida Memoirs*. Translated by Kenichi Yoshida. Boston: Houghton Mifflin, 1962.

Yoshida, Takashi. "A Battle over History in Japan: The Nanjing Massacre in Japan." In *The Nanjing Massacre in History and Historiography*, edited by Joshua Fogel. Berkeley: University of California Press, 2000.

Yoshida, Yutaka. *Nihonjin no Sensō Kan* [How Japanese See History]. Tokyo: Iwanami Shoten, 1995.

Yoshimi, Yoshiaki. *Jūgun Ianfu* [Comfort Women]. Tokyo: Iwanami Shoten, 1995.

Yu-Jose, Lydia N. "Global Environmental Issues: Responses from Japan." *Japanese Journal of Political Science* 5, no. 1 (May 2004): 23–47.

Zhao, Suisheng. *A Nation State by Construction: Dynamics of Modern Chinese Nationalism*. Stanford, CA: Stanford University Press, 2004.

Zoellick, Robert B., and Philip D. Zelikow (eds.). *America and the East Asian Crisis: Memos to the President*. New York: W. W. Norton, 2000.

| The Contributors |

Thomas U. Berger is associate professor in the Department of International Relations at Boston University.

Catharin Dalpino is visiting associate professor in Southeast Asian Studies at Georgetown University, and a former deputy assistant secretary of state and a former fellow at the Brookings Institution.

Juichi Inada is professor of international political economy at the School of International Economics, Senshu University.

Go Ito is professor at the School of Politics and Economics, Meiji University.

Masaru Kohno is professor at the Graduate School of Political Science and Economics, Waseda University.

Yoshiko Kojo is professor of international relations in the Department of Advanced Social and International Studies, Tokyo University.

Edward J. Lincoln is a professor of economics and director of the Center for Japan-U.S. Business and Economic Studies at the Stern School of Business, New York University, and was previously a fellow at the Brookings Institution and the Council on Foreign Relations.

Mike M. Mochizuki holds the Japan-US Relations Chair in Memory of

Gaston Sigur at the Elliott School of International Affairs, George Washington University.

Michael O'Hanlon is senior fellow and holder of the Sydney Stein, Jr., Chair at the Brookings Institution and a visiting lecturer at Princeton University.

Jitsuo Tsuchiyama is professor and dean of the School of International Politics, Economics, and Communication at Aoyama Gakuin University.

| Index |

Abe Shinzō, 18, 201, 202, 210*n76*,
210*n77*
Adenauer, Konrad, 187
Afghanistan: Soviet invasion of, 233;
support for United States in, 11, 12,
14
Akashi Yasushi, 8
Akihito, 238
Amnesty International, 225
Annan, Kofi, 84
Anti-Americanism, 13
Anti-Terrorism Special Measures Law
(ATSML), 47, 61, 85
APEC. *See* Asia Pacific Economic
Cooperation (APEC)
Armitage, Richard, 84
Article 9 and constitution, 47–71, 77;
advocates of "protection" of, 63;
ambivalence over revision of, 63–66;
Ashida amendment and, 54, 55, 59;
Constitutional Research Commissions and, 67; constitution school of
thought and, 59, 60; as constraint on
remilitarization, 58; contradictions
in, 55–59; controversies over, 53–55;
fear of entrapment/abandonment
dilemma, 60, 61; future options for,
67–69; initiative for, 53–54;
Japanese shock at war renunciation
inclusion, 51; Philippine analogy for,
52–53; as product of power vacuum,
56; pros and cons of revision of,
66–67; question of self-defense and,
54–55; security school of thought
and, 59, 60; seen as constraint to foreign policy, 48; and Self-Defense
Forces participation, 58, 81; sources
for, 51, 52; support/opposition for
revisions, 48; view of, as US domination, 48
Asahi Shimbun (newspaper), 63, 64
ASEAN. *See* Association of Southeast
Asian Nations (ASEAN)
ASEAN Plus Three (APT), 19, 151,
245, 283; Economic Partnership
Agreement and, 245
Ashida Hitoshi, 54, 55, 56, 57, 188
Asia: bilateralism in, 12; broad political
spectrum in, 215; geopolitical balance and, 56; identification with, 78;
Japanese and US economic presence
in, 155–160; monetary cooperation
in, 170–171; regional integration in,
12
Asia-Europe Meeting (ASEM), 170, 222
Asian Bond Fund, 171
Asian Currency Crisis Assistance Fund,
168
Asian Development Bank, 140
Asian financial crisis, 5, 127, 133,
151–173; Asia-centered initiatives
in, 161–163; Asian Currency Crisis

Assistance Fund, 168; assistance from International Monetary Fund and World Bank, 152–153; assistance to Indonesia through, 163–167; causes of, 159–160; Comprehensive Economic Action Plan, 168; corruption and, 160; currency crisis and, 159; effect on development in East Asia, 151; Emergency Package for Economic Stabilization of Southeast Asia, 168; exchange rate and, 159, 167*fig*; inadequate risk management and, 159, 160; international financial institutions and, 152–155; International Monetary Fund initiatives, 154–155, 161–163; Japan and US interests in, 155–160; Japanese ambivalence toward international assistance programs, 153–154; as liquidity crisis, 160; major international assistance actors in, 158*fig*; offer of aid from Japan, 151; structural problems and, 159; transnational coalition-building process in, 156; urgency of responses to, 155
Asian Games (1994), 249
Asian Monetary Fund, 129, 153, 162, 245, 283
Asia Pacific Economic Cooperation (APEC), 8, 194, 283; "Asia Pacific fusion" notion, 19; disappointment in, 31; Early Voluntary Sectoral Liberalization (EVSL) initiative, 16
Asō Tarō, 245
Association of Southeast Asian Nations (ASEAN), 8, 19; Regional Forum, 194; subsidies to Japanese companies working in, 30; trade agreements with, 129
Aung San, 216, 222
Aung San Suu Kyi, 213, 220, 221, 222, 223, 224
Australia: in ASEAN Plus Three (APT), 19; and Asian financial crisis, 161; in East Asia Summit, 19; in Global Coalition Against Terror, 75
Aw Muang, 219

Baker Plan (1985), 140
"Bali Bank corruption," 165
Bank for International Settlements (BIS), 126–127, 134, 135, 138, 150*n34*, 134, 135, 136, 139
Banking, 133–148; Basle Accord (1988), 133, 134; Basle Accord II (2004), 134; Basle Committee on Banking Supervision, 134; capital requirements in, 134; crises in, 133; financial crises and, 133–148; incentives for international regulatory framework in, 138–139; international regulatory regime in, 134; international risks, 137; lack of agreement on appropriate regulations in, 135; multilateral development, 136; regulatory rules, 133; standard supervisory regulations on capital adequacy in, 136, 137
Bank of England, 138, 139
Bank of Japan (BOJ), 140, 143, 144, 150*n34*, 158
Basle Accord (1988), 15, 16, 133, 134; defining content of capital, 136; negotiation of standardization of capital requirements in, 137–139; risk-weighted categories in, 136, 137; standard ratio of capital to risk-weighted assets, 137
Basle Accord II (2004), 134
Basle Committee on Banking Supervision, 134, 135, 136, 137, 138, 143
Belgium: imposition of risk-weighted capital adequacy standards in banking in, 139
Berger, Thomas U., 17, 19, 179–205, 259–291
BIS. *See* Bank for International Settlements (BIS)
Boutros-Ghali, Boutros, 81
Brady Plan (1989), 140
Brazil: provision of soybeans to Japan, 118, 119; renunciation of war by, 50
Bridge Asia, 225
Brzezinski, Zbigniew, 233
Buddhism, 217
Buddhist Clean Government Party, 271
Burma: aid from India, 226, 227; corruption in, 218; democratization in, 18; "idealpolitik" in, 213–216; inability to reduce debt in, 218; Japanese preference for positive

engagement with, 18; Japan-Myanmar Economic Committee, 223; nongovernmental organizations, 224–226; occupation by Japan, 216–218; official development assistance to, 190; political conflict in, 218–221; political reconciliation in, 18; pro-democracy movements in, 221, 222, 223; relations with Association of Southeast Asian Nations, 222; relations with China, 226; renunciation of reparation claims by, 190; renunciation of war by, 50; role of human rights in, 213–227; special relationship with Japan, 18, 216–218; stock exchange in, 223; Thirty Comrades and, 216; views on Japanese aggression, 205n1

Burma Aid Group, 218

Burma Youth Volunteer Association, 225

Burmese Way to Socialism, 217

Burmese Women's Union, 225

Bush, George W., 12, 18, 47, 84, 92

Cambodia: electoral infrastructure in, 216; peace process in, 12; Self-Defense Forces (SDF) in, 61, 81; UN peacekeeping operations in, 61

Canada: in Global Coalition Against Terror, 75

Capital: adequacy, 135, 142; barriers, 115; charges, 134; content of, 136, 137; controls, 117, 120, 160; elements of, 136, 137; equity, 136, 137; flight, 159; flows, 115, 117, 120, 133, 160; foreign, 115; goods, 155; investment, 27; markets, 28; ratios, 136, 142; requirements, 134, 136, 137–139; risk based standards, 138; short-selling, 159; supplementary, 136, 137

Carter, Jimmy, 233

CGI. *See* Consultative Group in Indonesia (CGI)

Chang Chun-hsiung, 249

Chiang Kai-shek, 216

Chiang Mai Initiative, 129, 169, 170, 283

China: alignment with United States against Soviet Union, 190; anti-Japanese sentiment in, 194, 195, 197, 198, 199, 203; and Asian financial crisis, 161; bilateral interaction with United States, 229; commercial opportunities in, 19; concessional loans from Japan, 235, 236; considers asking for war reparations from Japan, 239; diplomatic crisis over historical views with, 179; disintegration of relations with Japan, 194–202; as economic challenger, 16; economic growth in, 19; economic relations with Japan, 243–246; effect on diplomacy in Asia, 18, 19; efforts to influence elections in Taiwan, 197; environmental pollution in, 246; expansion into by Japan, 1; hopes for strengthening of anti-American sentiments in Japan, 190; Japanese public attitudes toward, 19; Kuomintang in, 56; limiting ambitions of, 230; military exercises by, 5, 9, 247; military spending in, 97; missile crisis (Taiwan), 48, 197; openness in political climate, 194; Peace and Friendship Treaty (1978), 232, 233; postnormalization policy regime for, 231–237; post-Tiananmen relations with Japan, 237–241; receives most-favored-nation status from United States, 237; relations with Burma, 226; renunciation of reparations claims by, 190; rise of, 229–253; rise of military capabilities of, 91; security dilemma with, 230; security policy and Japan, 246–248; stance regarding regional monetary frameworks, 169, 170; tension in relations over Yasukuni Shrine, 198, 199, 200; Tiananmen massacre in, 19, 222, 237; unfavorable climate for direct investment in, 236; US openings to, 79; US spy plane incident and, 201; use of hedging strategy with, 230; view of US-Japan defense pact, 231, 232; view on Asian Monetary Fund, 162; warns of Japanese militarism, 236

Clinton, Bill, 13, 164, 174n29, 246

Cohen, William, 164

Cold War: domestic consequences of ending of, 4–7; effects of end of, 36,

37, 38; Japanese effort to seek reconciliation and end of, 194–202; and US commitment to Japan, 2
Comprehensive Economic Action Plan, 168
Constitution. *See* Article 9 and constitution
Constitutional Research Commissions, 67
Consultative Group in Indonesia (CGI), 165
Currency: appreciation, 34, 115, 119, 122, 123; basket system, 170–171; crises, 152, 159; decline, 163, 166; dollar-peg system and, 159; internationalization of, 171; overvaluation, 159; stabilization, 170; swaps, 170

Dalpino, Catharin, 18, 213–227, 274
Democratic Party of Japan (DPJ), 48, 65, 68, 240; replacement for Japan Socialist Party (JSP), 40
Democratic Socialist Party, 80, 240
Deng Xiao-ping, 233, 236
Development: assistance, 190; banks, 136; domestic, 115, 116; economic, 2, 115, 116, 190; international, 76, 116; official development assistance, 3; of regional institutions, 151
Diaoyu Islands. *See* Senkaku Islands (Diaoyu Islands)
Diplomacy: in Asia, 18, 19; checkbook, 77, 80, 228*n7*; economic, 4, 76; friendship, 240, 243; human rights, 214; karaoke, 12; low-posture, 9; regional, 17–20, 265; shuttle, 215, 216; UN-centered, 14, 75, 78, 83
Diplomatic Bluebook, 25
Dodge, Joseph, 57
Draper, William, 72*n25*

EAEC. *See* East Asian Economic Caucus (EAEC)
Early Voluntary Sectoral Liberalization (EVSL) initiative, 16
East Asian Economic Caucus (EAEC), 19
East Asia Summit, 19
East Timor, 164, 165; peacekeeping operations to, 165
Economic: change, 115–130; crisis, 16;

development, 2, 190; diplomacy, 4, 76; domination, 280; globalization, 34, 35; growth, 19, 29; issues, 15–17; liberalization, 5, 16, 218; management, 160; predation, 285; reconstruction, 2; reform, 152, 163, 164, 166, 220; regionalism, 4, 31; strategies, 2; summits, 93*n11*
Economic Partnership Agreement, 245
Economy: bubble, 60, 135, 144–146, 269; domestic political, 28, 29; regional, 29. *See also* Japan, economic issues
Emergency Package for Economic Stabilization of Southeast Asia, 168
Environmental issues, 7, 8, 246; global warming, 13; pollution, 246
European Union, 4; lack of response to Asian financial crisis, 161
Exclusive economic zone (EEZ), 245, 248

Fang Lizhi, 237
Far Eastern Commission, 55
Federation of Economic Organizations, 223
Financial System Research Council, 142
Finland: military forces in, 103
Fiscal Investment and Loan Program, 236
Fisher, Stanley, 165
France: foreign residents in, 129; in Global Coalition Against Terror, 75; imposition of risk-weighted capital adequacy standards in banking in, 139; organization of military forces, 99; renunciation of war by, 50
Free riding, 2, 60, 265
Fujioka Nobukatsu, 196
Fujio Masayuki, 193, 194, 235
Fujiyama Aiichirō, 79
Fukuda Takeo, 62, 206*n4*, 232, 233, 234
Fukuda Yasuo, 201

General Agreement on Tariffs and Trade (GATT), 31, 117, 280
Germany, 207*n13*, 207*n15*; in Global Coalition Against Terror, 75; military forces in, 103; in Operation Allied Force in Yugoslavia, 100; organiza-

tion of military forces, 99; postwar occupation of, 186, 187, 188, 189
Giscard d'Estaing, Valery, 285
Global Coalition Against Terror, 75
Globalization: economic, 34, 35; financial, 133; international competition and, 28; strain of, 28; technological, 34
Gotoda Masaharu, 6
Greater East Asia Co-Prosperity Sphere, 215, 280
Group of Five (G5), 93n11, 133, 139
Group of Seven (G7), 76, 133, 139
Group of Ten (G-10), 134, 135, 136, 139
Guidelines for US-Japan Defense Cooperation, 60, 61, 69, 70, 277
Gulf War: effect on alliance, 60; "Iraqi shock" and, 24, 25fig, 27; Japanese financial contribution to, 4, 5, 14, 24; as turning point in Japan's international activities, 48, 75, 80–83

Habibie, B. J., 164–166, 167
Hague Treaty (1907), 54
Hammarskjöld, Dag, 79
Hashimoto Ryūtarō, 13, 164, 240, 246, 249
Hatano Yoshiro, 76
Hatoyama Ichirō, 58, 187, 188, 191
Hatoyama Yukio, 65, 68
Hayashi Fusao, 192
Higashikuni Naruhiko, 50, 51
Hirohito, 195, 210n73
Hiroshima attack, 188, 205
Honda Katsuichi, 192
Hong Kong: and Asian financial crisis, 161
Hosoda Hiroyuki, 249
Hosokawa Morihiro, 61, 195, 196, 204, 242
Hsu Li-teh, 249
Hubbard, Carroll, 149n21
Hu Jintao, 201
Hun Sen, 215
Hu Yaobang, 235

Identity: national, 9, 182, 203, 273; subnational, 182
Ienaga Saburō, 193
Ikeda Hayato, 57, 187, 285

Immigration: lack of openness to, 128, 129; rural-urban, 33
Inada, Juichi, 16, 151–173, 169, 283
India: aid to Burma, 226, 227; in ASEAN Plus Three (APT), 19; in East Asia Summit, 19
Indonesia: and Asian financial crisis, 154tab, 161, 174n29; corruption issues in, 165; currency crisis in, 159; economic recovery in, 30; economic reform in, 153, 163, 164; foreign lending to, 156fig; international assistance through Asian financial crisis, 163–167; investment by Japan in, 155, 157fig; loans from Japanese banks, 155; official development assistance, 190; renunciation of reparation claims by, 190; structural reform in, 164–166; suspension of international aid to, 165; trade agreements with, 129; US investment in, 157fig; US loans to, 155; views on Japanese aggression, 205n1
Institutions: administrative, 28; alteration of, 28; building, 12, 173n2, 200; domestic, 37; effect of globalization on, 28; electoral, 6; endogenous change in, 28, 37–40; financial, 133, 139, 140; for free trade, 5; global, 133, 140; international, 8, 24, 194, 262; multilateral, 29, 116, 117, 189; political, 28, 263; reform of, 6, 37–40; regional, 151, 179, 200
International Bank for Reconstruction and Development, 158fig
International Conference of Banking Supervisors, 140
International Cooperation Initiative (1988), 79
Internationalism, 7–10; liberal, 14; security policy views, 99–102
International Lending Act (1983), 137
International Monetary Fund, 16, 117, 122, 133, 139, 140; and Asian financial crisis, 152–153, 159, 163–167, 174n15; conditionality of, 152, 153; control of, by United States, 153; economic reform requirements of, 152; General Agreements to Borrow, 139; moral hazard avoidance and, 152, 153, 162; opposition to proposal

for Asian Monetary Fund, 162; preconditions for assistance from, 152;
skepticism of operations of, 153
International Peace Cooperation Corps,
94*n33*
International Peace Cooperation
Headquarters (IPCHQ), 81, 94*n33*
International Peace Cooperation Law
(1992), 61, 76, 77
Investment: abroad, 125, 126, 127;
asymmetries, 115, 124, 125,
128–129; capital, 27; direct, 121*tab,*
122*fig*; flows, 117; foreign direct,
125, 127, 245; inward direct, 117,
125; speculative, 159
Iraq: Coalition of the Willing in, 85;
deployment of Self-Defense Forces
and, 108–110; preemptive defensive
attack on, 47; support for United
States in, 11, 12, 14
Iriye Toshirō, 55
Ishiba Shigeru, 248
Ishibashi Tanzan, 188
Ishihara Shintarō, 9, 65
Italy: in Global Coalition Against
Terror, 75; organization of military
forces, 99; renunciation of war by, 50
Ito, Go, 14, 75–93, 278
Itō Miyoji, 52

Japan: alliance with United States, 38,
83–85; and Asian financial crisis,
151–173; back/forth relations with
United States, 11; changing international role of, 1–20; commitment to
democracy of, 18; as cornerstone of
Asian security, 72*n25*; end of Cold
War and, 4–7; English-language pro-
ficiency in, 7, 117; entry into United
Nations, 78, 79; expansion into
China by, 1; experiences in education, travel, and living abroad by citizens, 124, 127–128; in Global
Coalition Against Terror, 75; as global leader of bilateral assistance, 3, 4;
identification with Asia, 78; immigration issues, 7; improvement in
relations with South Korea, 197;
latent militarism in, 100; multilateralism and, 8; nongovernmental
organizations, 224–226; occupation
by United States, 2, 50, 72*n25,* 187;
occupations by, 1, 216–218; postwar
reparations by, 3, 190; postwar settlement debates in, 32; public attitudes toward China, 19; responses to
environmental issues, 7, 8; sense of
nationalism, 7, 9, 10–13, 98, 180;
"special relationship" with Burma,
18, 216–218; student disturbances in,
9, 10; tense relations with China and
South Korea, 194–202; working with
United Nations, 8; in World War II,
1; xenophobic reactions in, 7
Japan, defense/security issues, 2, 13–15,
275–279; in Afghanistan, 84; alternative defense posture for military
forces, 102–108; in Angola, 83; Anti-
Terrorism Special Measures Law, 47,
85; Article 9 and, 47–71; in Bosnia,
82*tab,* 83; budget for, 60; burden-
sharing, 2, 265; in Cambodia, 61, 81,
82*tab*; Chinese military exercises
and, 5, 9; commitment to Korean and
Taiwanese security, 72*n26*; comprehensive security concept, 4, 265;
conditions for use of force in, 14, 15;
confined to multilateral missions,
100, 101; constitution revision,
272–273; construction of new constitution, 50–52; cooperation, 13, 14;
debates on, 60–63; debates over constitutional revision, 48–71; defense
posture for, 97–111; defensive realism, 265; dependence on United
States, 3; in East Timor, 82*tab*; in El
Salvador, 83; emphasis on peacekeeping role, 91; forces, 2; in Golan
Heights, 82*tab*; Guidelines for the
US-Japan Defense Cooperation, 60,
61, 69; Gulf War financial participation, 4, 5; in Haiti, 80; in Indian
Ocean, 84; Integrated Security
Strategy for, 90–92; International
Peace Cooperation Law (1992), 61;
in Iraq, 82*tab,* 84, 108–110; Japan
Defense Agency in, 62, 91; Law
Concerning Special Measures on
Humanitarian and Reconstruction
Assistance, 47–48; liberal interna-
tionalist view of, 99–102; Mid-Term
Defense Estimates (MTDF), 60; mil-

itary adaptation to post–Cold War era, 99; military emergency law, 47; military middle ground for, 100; military spending in, 97; models for military forces, 102–104; in Mozambique, 82*tab*; in Namibia, 80; National Defense Program Guidelines, 13, 97; National Defense Program Outline (NDPO), 60; National Police Reserve (NPR), 57, 58; National Safety Force (NSF), 57, 58; need to reassure neighbors of military efforts, 100; in Nicaragua, 80; "Nixon shocks," 72*n26*, 79; "normalization" and, 13; North Korean missile launch, 5, 9, 48; North Korean nuclear crisis and, 5, 48; nuclear possibilities, 70; pacifist constraints, 4, 5; pacts with United States, 2; in Palestine, 83; in peacekeeping operations, 14, 61, 75–93, 278; policy, 206*n4*; protection of sea lines of communication, 60; reexamination of arms export ban, 91; reform of defense industrial/technological base, 91; with regard to China, 246–248; reluctance to tolerate casualties to forces, 109; response to emergency situations, 91; restrictions on right of self-defense in, 14, 15; in Romania, 83; in Rwanda, 82*tab*; Self-Defense Forces, 13, 38, 57; Self-Defense Law (1954), 59; Senkaku Islands (Diaoyu Islands) claims, 10; in South Africa, 83; spending, 2; strengthening intelligence capabilities, 91; support for United States in Afghanistan and Iraq, 11; Taiwan and, 97; Takeshima/Dokdo Islands claims, 10; United States military presence in, 56, 57; US-Japan Security Treaty (1951), 57–59; war renunciation and, 14, 47–71; in Yugoslavia, 82*tab*. *See also* Self-Defense Forces (SDF)

Japan, economic issues, 15–17, 279–284; adaptation to global economic change and, 115–130; aid to Vietnam, 168, 169; ambivalent view of international financial assistance programs, 153–154; Asia-centered view vs. global view, 168–171; Asian financial crisis and, 5, 127, 133; assistance to Indonesia in Asian financial crisis, 163–167; banking, 133–148; Basle Accord and, 15, 16, 134, 135–137, 139–146; broadening of international economic engagement, 115, 118–125; broader openness in, 15; bubble economy, 60, 135, 144–146, 269; convoy system in banking sector, 142, 150*n37*; coordination of policies with International Monetary Fund and World Bank, 154, 155; counterweight strategy in Asian financial crisis, 173*n2*; current account surplus in, 119–122; decline in growth, 269–271; dependence on United States, 3; direct investment and, 121*tab*; economic relations with China, 243–246; exports to Asia, 155; external assets and liabilities, 121*tab*; financial stability, 133–148; "flying-geese" order in, 16, 266; global scope of, 17; impact of economic size on global developments, 119; insularity and, 115, 116–118; internationalization, 282; investment abroad, 125, 126, 127; investment in Association of Southeast Asian Nations countries, 155; late industrializing effect, 280, 281; limited access to economy, 116; limits to regional leadership by, 16; market-oriented reform and, 11; membership in international financial institutions, 139–140; need for confidence in economic system in, 123–124, 126; neomercantilist strategies, 2; official development assistance by, 3, 76; oil shock (1973) and, 118–119; outflow of capital phase, 115; ownership of foreign assets and, 120, 121; poor recent economic performance in, 116, 125–129; promotion of financial stability in Asia Pacific by, 16; protectionism, 2, 30; recovery, 2; relations with Southeast Asia, 155; responses to Asian financial crisis, 160–167; role in international finance in postwar era, 139–140; stance regarding International

Monetary Fund/World Bank, 168–171; trade tensions with United States, 4, 9; view of international regulations of capital adequacy, 135–137

Japan, foreign policy, 1–4; adaptive state model, 267, 268, 268*tab*; alliance with United States, 4, 10–13; assistance to Burma, 217, 218; attempt to detach ideology from policy, 215; business/political debate on Burma, 221–224; changing domestic context of, 269–275; with China, 229; contrasting models of, 262–268; cultural ties to Burma, 217; domestic political process and, 42*n1*; domestic politics and, 2; economic, 279–284; economic circumstances' affect on, 15; economic relations with China, 243–246; effect of diversity in social views, 274; efforts to promote political progress in Burma by, 213–227; engaging and balancing China, 241–250; Foreign Affairs Establishment Law, 80; fragmentation in, 267; history issue and, 18; as ideological battleground, 191; immobilism in, 77; "Japan, Inc.," 264; "leading from behind," 262; mercantile realism, 264; need for greater international contribution by, 5, 23–42; need to cultivate Asian policy, 17; omnidirectional, 233, 234; pacifist, 6; passivity in, 262, 263, 264; politics of memory in, 179–205; position on Taiwan, 231; postnormalization policy regime for China by, 231–237; post-Tiananmen, 237–241; pragmatic liberalism, 259–291; preferences and strategies in, 43*n16*; protectionist stance in, 264; public opinion toward China in, 239; reactive state model, 2, 3, 20, 27, 263, 264, 268*tab*; recalibration of policy toward China, 230–253; regional diplomacy and, 17–20; "reluctant realism," 230, 231; role in United Nations, 8; role of human rights in, 213–227; security policy regarding China, 246–248; shift from accommodation with China, 230, 231; special relationship with Burma, 216–218; strategic state model, 202, 268*tab*; Taiwan question, 246, 247, 249–250; use of mixed strategy of engagement and balancing with China, 230, 231; views of Vietnam War, 187, 188, 192; Yoshida Doctrine and, 1–4. *See also* Article 9 and constitution; Japan, defense/security issues

Japan, historical memories/issues, 17, 18, 179–205, 273–274; acknowledgment of Japanese atrocities, 192, 193, 194, 195; apologies for aggression, 196, 231; "apology fatigue" and, 181; apology to China for atrocities, 194, 231; avoidance of dealing with responsibility for war in, 186, 192; change in official historical narrative, 194, 195; collective avoidance of guilt and, 188; collective memory and, 18, 179–205; Committee to Examine History and, 196; concrete implications of, 185; conservative elites in, 186; diplomatic crises over, 179; effort to seek reconciliation, 194–202; evolution of debate over history during Cold War, 191–194; historical amnesia, 17; interest and policy agendas in, 185; as major impediment to institutional development in Asia, 206*n3*; Nanjing massacre in, 191, 192, 193; national security and, 187, 188; perception that Japan remains unrepentent for, 180; polarization of political environment in, 188; politics of postwar historical representation in, 185–191; in relation to China, 241–243; reluctance to confront past and, 189; representation of Japanese people as victims in, 186, 187, 188; selective view of past, 179; sociopolitical construction of collective memory and, 181–185; support for empire in, 187, 192; textbook references, 188, 242

Japan, international contribution, 5, 23–42; in Afghanistan, 84; agendas for, 76–78; in Angola, 83; benefits to United States, 26, 27; in Bosnia, 82*tab*, 83; in Cambodia, 82*tab*; con-

fusion concerning, 24–27; debate on inclusion of military-security aspects in, 25; decisionmaking process in, 78–85; discussions on, 24–27; domestic sources of, 27–29; in East Timor, 82*tab*; economic assistance to developing countries, 23, 24; in El Salvador, 83; financial stability and, 133–148; foreign policies of, 85–90; in Golan Heights, 82*tab*; in Haiti, 80; historical memory and, 180, 181; history of, 78–85; "human contributions," 83–85; in Indian Ocean, 84; initial stage, 78–79; in Iraq, 82*tab,* 84; linguistic ambiguities over, 26; membership in international organizations, 23, 117, 118; Ministry of International Trade and Industry and, 29–32; in Mozambique, 82*tab*; in Namibia, 80; in Nicaragua, 80; nondispatch principle in, 80; nonintervention tradition and, 88–90; nonparticipation in operations with mandate to conduct enforcement actions, 89; in Palestine, 83; in peacekeeping operations, 61, 75–93; in Romania, 83; in Rwanda, 82*tab*; "second image" perspective, 27, 28; "second image reversed" perspective, 28; in South Africa, 83; in United Nations peacekeeping operations, 23, 24, 75–93; unlikely dispatch of troops in Chapter 7 resolutions by Security Council, 89, 90; in Yugoslavia, 82*tab*. *See also* Japan, foreign policy
Japan, political issues: autonomy with respect to alliance with United States, 7, 10–13; Democratic Socialist Party in, 80; domestic, 5; dramatic change in, 270–272; electoral system, 2, 5, 6; internationalism vs. nationalism debate in, 6, 7–10; inward orientation in, 29; Japan Socialist Party (JSP), 6; opposition parties in, 240; organizational rigidity in, 29; promotion of democracy in, 214; shift in majority coalition and Liberal Democratic Party, 32–37. *See also individual parties*
Japan Bank for International Cooperation (JBIC), 169

Japan-Burma Association, 219
Japan-Burma Veterans Association, 217
Japan-China Joint Initiative on Environment Toward the Twenty-First Century, 246
Japan Communist Party (JCP), 54
Japan Defense Agency (JDA), 62, 91
Japanese Air Defense Identification Zone, 248
Japanese Bankers Association, 143
Japanese Teachers' Union, 206*n4*
Japan Export-Import Bank, 157, 158*fig,* 165, 168, 236
Japan International Cooperation Agency (JICA), 157, 158*fig*
Japan International Volunteer Center (JVC), 225
Japan-Myanmar Economic Committee, 223
Japan Socialist Party (JSP), 6, 40, 240; abandonment of unarmed neutrality policy, 38, 39, 44*n33*; in coalition government, 195; diminished influence of, 40; electoral successes of, 36, 37, 38; included in Democratic Party, 40; internationalism and, 32; loss of influence of, 9; political disappearance of, 40; reversal of foreign policy orientation by, 44*n33*; support for, 37*fig*
Japan Teachers' Union, 9
Japan-US Joint Declaration on Security (1996), 277
Jiang Zemin, 197, 204, 242, 248, 249
JICA. *See* Japan International Cooperation Agency (JICA)

Kades, Charles, 51, 52, 54, 55
Kaifu Toshiki, 6, 75, 80, 195, 237, 238
Kaikōsha, 193
Kajiyama Seiroku, 247
Kakizawa Kōji, 238
Kanamori Tokujirō, 55
Kant, Immanuel, 50
Katayama Tetsu Socialist Party, 56
Katokawa Kōtarō, 194
Katō Kōichi, 247
Katō Ryōzō, 11
Kawaguchi Yoriko, 250
Kaya Okinori, 187
Keidanren, 223

Kellogg-Briand Pact (1928), 50, 52, 53, 68
Kennan, George, 56, 72*n25*
Khin Nyunt, 227
Kim Dae Jung, 197, 203, 204, 242
Kishi Nobusuke, 58, 78, 186, 188, 191, 202, 206*n4*
Kobayashi Yōtarō, 17
Kohno, Masaru, 5, 23–42, 270
Koizumi Junichirō, 6, 11, 12, 18, 33, 47, 62, 63, 84, 90, 92, 108, 179, 180, 198, 201, 204, 241, 243, 245, 273
Kojo, Yoshiko, 15, 16, 284
Kōmei Party, 67, 80, 81, 240
Konoe Fumimaro, 50, 51
Kōno Yōhei, 244
Korean War: and need for US military presence in Japan, 57
Kyoto Protocol, 13

Large-Scale Retail Stores Regulation Law, 35
Law Concerning Measures to Ensure National Independence and Security in a Situation of Armed Attack (2002). *See* Peacekeeping Law
Law Concerning Special Measures on Humanitarian and Reconstruction Assistance (LCSMHRA), 47–48
League for Democracy, 222
Lee Kuan Yew, 197
Lee Teng-hui, 249
Liberal Democratic Party, 2, 5, 240, 271; coalition with Socialist Party, 82; end of dominance by, 39, 42*n7,* 61; less accommodative posture toward China by, 240; metamorphosis of, 32–37; movement away from passive international posture by, 5, 6; New Constitution Drafting Committee in, 67; as obstacle to internationalism, 32, 33; on peacekeeping operations, 80–83; postwar rule by, 187, 188; protectionist measures by, 33; shift in majority coalition and, 32–37; support for, 35*fig*; textbook purge by, 188; transformation of, 5, 6; urban voters and, 6; view on Article 9 (constitution), 48; voter disappointment in, 34
Liberalization: of agricultural policy,

34; commitment toward, 36; economic, 5, 16, 218; financial, 142, 159; of markets, 7; political, 214
Lincoln, Edward, 15, 115–130, 169, 270, 281, 282
Li Peng, 244
Li Zhaoxing, 245

Murayama Tomiichi, 82
MacArthur, Douglas, 50, 51, 52, 53, 54, 57, 72*n25*
"MacArthur Notes," 51, 52, 68, 71*n9*
Maehara Seiji, 240
Malaysia: and Asian financial crisis, 161; official development assistance, 190; renunciation of reparation claims by, 190; trade agreements with, 129
Manchuria: seizure by Japan, 1
Manila Framework, 162, 163, 171
Markets: access to, 28; capital, 28; domestic, 7; exchange, 163; financial, 134, 143; international, 28, 200; liberalization of, 7; opening, 2; risks in, 134
Matsudaira Koto, 79
Matsumoto Jōji, 51, 53
McConnell, Mitch, 228*n19*
Megawati, 165
Meiji constitution, 52, 71*n9*; revision of, 50
Memorial Museum of Chinese People's Anti-Japanese War, 243
Memory, collective, 18, 179–205; competition and, 184; contested nature of, 182, 184, 185; defining, 182; depiction of past events in, 185; as foundation for group identity, 184; historical narratives and, 182, 183, 184; international political contexts in development of, 186; legitimation of particular policies and practices by, 185; malleability of, 184; and national interests, 182; regarding present and future, 183; relationship to individual memory, 182, 183; sociopolitical construction of, 181–185
METI. *See* Ministry of Economy, Trade, and Industry (METI)
Mexico: financial crisis, 133; trade agreements with, 129

Mid-Term Defense Estimates (MTDF), 60
Miki Takeo, 208*n40*
Militarism, 100
Ministry of Economy, Trade, and Industry (METI): commitment to multilateralism, 5; outward orientation of, 5; in World Trade Organization negotiations, 32. *See also* Ministry of International Trade and Industry (MITI)
Ministry of International Trade and Industry (MITI): change to internationalist outlook, 29–32; export-import insurance and, 30; protection of domestic industry by, 29; resistance to economic liberalization by, 5; transformation in mission by, 29–32
MITI. *See* Ministry of International Trade and Industry (MITI)
Miyazawa Kiichi, 63, 64, 81, 150*n43*, 239, 283
Mizumo Kenichi, 250
Mochizuki, Mike M., 1–20, 229–253, 270, 278, 286
Multilateralism, 8, 16, 17, 32, 116
Murayama Tomiichi, 39, 44*n33*, 196, 240, 242
Myanmar. *See* Burma

Nagasaki attack, 188, 205
Nakasone Yasuhiro, 6, 7, 36, 60, 64, 65, 68, 128, 193, 194, 206*n4*, 233, 235, 236, 243, 285
Nanjing massacre, 191, 192, 193
National Defense Program Guidelines, 97
National Defense Program Outline (NDPO), 60
Nationalism, 7, 9, 10–13, 180, 200, 206*n4*, 270, 273, 274; assertiveness of, 9; emphasis on national symbols, 9; foreign interference and, 10; generational dimension of, 9, 10; increase in, 98; perceptions of North Korea and China and, 11
National Land Agency, 193
National League for Democracy (NLD), 220
National Police Reserve (NPR), 57, 58
National Safety Force (NSF), 57, 58

New Baker Plan (1987), 140
Ne Win, 216, 217, 218, 219
New Miyazawa Initiative, 140, 165, 168, 169
New Party Harbinger, 240
New Zealand: in ASEAN Plus Three (APT), 19; in East Asia Summit, 19
Nihon-Birima Kyōkai, 219
Nihon Izokukai, 187
Nishimura Kumao, 58
Nixon, Richard, 139, 232
Nonaka Hiromu, 240
Nongovernmental organizations, 18, 224–226; Amnesty International, 225; Bridge Asia, 225; Burma Youth Volunteer Association, 225; Burmese Women's Union, 225; functions, 224; human rights and, 224, 225; Japan International Volunteer Center (JVC), 225; Organization for Industrial, Spiritual, and Cultural Advancement (OISCA), 225; People's Forum on Burma, 225
North American Free Trade Agreement (NAFTA), 4
North Atlantic Treaty Organization (NATO): in Yugoslavia, 100
North Korea: abduction of Japanese citizens by, 9, 12; missile launch by, 5, 9, 48; nuclear crisis in, 5, 48; nuclear weapons development by, 91
Nosaka Sanzō, 54

Obuchi Keiz, 174*n29*, 197, 204, 242, 248, 249
ODA. *See* Official development assistance (ODA)
OECD. *See* Organization for Economic Cooperation and Development (OECD)
OECF. *See* Overseas Economic Cooperation Fund (OECF)
Official development assistance (ODA), 3, 76, 262; concessional loans, 3; decline in value of, 126, 127; focus on Asia Pacific region, 3; humanitarian assistance, 4; human rights criteria in, 214; international contribution notion and, 25; linked to Japanese national interest, 3, 4, 283; as part of postwar reparations, 3, 190; technical

assistance, 3; and vital security interests, 215; white paper on, 25
Ogata Sadako, 8, 82
Ogura Kazuo, 17
O'Hanlon, Michael, 14, 97–111, 278
Okuno Seisuke, 193, 194
Operation Desert Storm, 102
Operation Enduring Freedom, 84, 94n20, 277
Operation Infinite Justice, 84, 94n20
Operation Iraqi Freedom, 108–110
Organization for Economic Cooperation and Development (OECD), 117
Organization for Industrial, Spiritual, and Cultural Advancement (OISCA), 225
Organizations: bureaucratic, 40; counterterrorist, 23; environmental, 23; human rights, 23; international, 23, 79, 94n29; multilateral, 122; restructuring of, 40; structural reform in, 28; trade, 23
Ōtaka Hiroshi, 218
Ōtaka Yoshiko, 219
Overseas Economic Cooperation Fund (OECF), 157, 158fig
Ozawa Ichirō, 39, 42n8, 61, 64, 65, 100, 195, 240, 247

Pacific Basin Economic Council (PBEC), 280
Pacific Economic Cooperation Council (PECC), 194
Pacifism, 2, 109
Paris Club, 165, 174n29
Paris Peace Accords (1991), 86, 215, 216
Park Chung Hee, 190, 204
Peace and Friendship Treaty (1978), 232, 233
Peacekeeping Law, 62, 80, 83, 85–88, 94n29, 94n30, 94n33
People's Forum on Burma, 225
Philippines: analogy for Article 9, 52–53; official development assistance, 190; pluralist regimes in, 194; renunciation of reparation claims by, 190; renunciation of war by, 50; trade agreements with, 129
Piracy, 101
Plaza Accord (1985), 34

Policy: agricultural, 34; alliance, 58; defense, 48, 206n4; distributive, 34; initiatives, 35; mercantilist, 60; national, 40; neutrality, 38, 86; pacifist, 2; predatory, 33; security, 58, 60, 206n4; trade, 31, 266; on use of force, 94n27
Political: favors, 33, 34; instability, 166; institutions, 28, 263; liberalization, 214; pluralization, 194, 195; process, 42n1; reconciliation, 18; reform, 38, 220
Politics: domestic, 2, 5, 27, 38, 39; foreign policy and, 2; international, 3; Liberal Democratic Party in, 2; of memory, 179–205; regional, 201
Portugal: renunciation of war by, 50
Potsdam Proclamation, 231
Protectionism, 2, 30; agricultural, 16

Quasi–nongovernmental organizations ("quangos"), 225, 226

Reform: administrative, 40, 91; economic, 152, 163, 164, 166, 220; education, 206n4; electoral, 6, 38, 39, 40, 240, 241, 271–272; financial, 174n15; institutional, 6, 37–40; market-oriented, 11; political, 38, 220; structural, 28, 33, 164; United Nations, 80
Rights: human, 23, 213–227; self-defense, 65, 68, 77
Roh Moo Hyun, 198, 199, 201, 203
Roosevelt, Franklin D., 56
Russia: military spending in, 97. See also Soviet Union

Saddam Hussein, 24
Sakakibara Eisuke, 162, 173n11, 174n24
Sakaya Taichi, 3
Sasaki Soichi, 50
Satō Eisaku, 206n4
Satō-Nixon communiqué, 72n26
Satō Tatsuo, 55
Scandinavia: military forces in, 102, 103
Schumacher, Kurt, 187
SDF. See Self-Defense Forces (SDF)
Security: collective, 26, 61; comprehen-

sive, 4, 265; guidelines, 83–85; international activities of, 14; multilateral missions, 14; national, 2; pacifist policy, 2; pacts with United States, 2; policy, 13–15, 60, 206n4; regional, 40. *See also* Japan, defense/security issues

Self-Defense Forces (SDF), 13, 57, 262, 277; air forces, 106–107; alternative defense postures for, 104–108; Anti-Terrorism Special Measures Law and, 47; Article 9 and, 58, 81; cease-fire monitoring by, 80; in conflict areas, 80; counterterrorism activities, 85; debates on constitutionality of, 58; in election monitoring, 77, 80, 94n29; ground, 107–108; humanitarian relief operations and, 77, 80; in Iraq, 108–110; legitimacy of, 65; logistical support from, 85; maritime, 62, 84, 105–106; medical treatment by, 47, 85; in noncombat areas, 47; organization of, 98, 99; in peace-keeping operations, 61, 62, 75–93, 81; preventive deployment of, 86; public support for, 59; refugee assistance, 85; supply provisions and, 47; transport duties by, 47

Self-Defense Law (1954), 59

Senkaku Islands (Diaoyu Islands), 10, 197, 232, 233, 238, 248

Shidehara Kijūrō, 51, 52, 53, 54

Shigemitsu Mamoru, 187

Shiina Etsusaburō, 190

Shirasu Jirō, 51, 57

Shunji Yanai, 84

Singapore: anti-Japanese sentiment in, 197; and Asian financial crisis, 161, 163; trade agreements with, 129

Sino-Japanese War (1937), 243

SLORC. *See* State Law and Order Restoration Council (SLORC)

Social Democratic Party, 240

South Korea: anti-Japanese sentiment in, 194, 195, 199, 203; and Asian financial crisis, 154tab, 161; authoritarian regime in, 190; currency crisis in, 159; diplomatic crisis over historical views with, 179; disintegration of relations with Japan, 194–202; economic reform in, 153; foreign

lending to, 156fig; improvement in relations with Japan, 197; investment by Japan in, 155, 157fig; loans from Japanese banks, 155; official development assistance, 190; pluralist regimes in, 194; renunciation of reparation claims by, 190; tension in relations over Yasukuni Shrine, 198, 199; trade agreements with, 16, 129; US investment in, 157fig; US loans to, 155; US plans to withdraw forces from, 72n26

Soviet Union: alignment of China and United States against, 190; collapse of, 60; end of competition with United States, 11; Japanese Left views on, 188; military presence on "northern territories," 234

Spain: renunciation of war by, 50

State Law and Order Restoration Council (SLORC), 219, 220, 221

Suharto, 163, 164, 165, 166

Summers, Lawrence, 162, 164, 174n29

Suzuki Zenkō, 60, 235

Sweden: military forces in, 103

Switzerland: military forces in, 102, 103

Taiwan: Chinese efforts to influence elections in, 197; defense of, 97; Japanese position on, 231; official development assistance to, 190; pluralist regimes in, 194; renunciation of reparation claims by, 190

Taiwan Strait, 11

Takano Norimoto, 247

Takemura Masayoshi, 26

Takeshima/Dokdo Islands, 10, 198, 199

Takeshita Noboru, 61, 79, 235, 240

Tanaka Kakuei, 193, 232, 234

Tanigaki Sadakazu, 201

Tariffs, 31, 116

Tax(es): consumption, 34; indirect, 34; privileges, 34; value-added, 174n15

Technology: foreign, 117; industrial, 27; joint research on defense missiles, 91

Terrorism, 47, 48, 65, 84; Anti-Terrorism Special Measures Law (ATSML), 47, 61; international, 91, 101; rear-echelon support measures in, 61

Thailand: and Asian financial crisis,

154, 154*tab,* 161, 174*n15*; currency crisis in, 159; economic reform in, 153; foreign lending to, 156*fig*; investment by Japan in, 155, 157*fig*; loans from Japanese banks, 155; pluralist regimes in, 194; trade agreements with, 129; US investment in, 157*fig*; US loans to, 155
Than Shwe, 227
Tōgō Kazuhiko, 204
Tōjō Hideki, 186, 193
Tokyo War Crimes Tribunal, 187, 188, 192
Trade: asymmetries, 115, 124, 125, 128–129; bilateral, 31; deterioration, 159; disputes, 17; free, 16; intra-industry, 125; negotiations, 125; open, 7; organizations, 23; policy, 31, 266; tariffs, 31, 116; world, 23
Treaty of San Francisco (1951), 190
Tsuchiyama, Jitsuo, 13, 14, 47–71, 273

Ueyama Shunpei, 192
Unilateralism, 12
United Kingdom: banking crisis in, 133; Bank of England, 138, 139; debt strategy, 140; foreign residents in, 129; in Global Coalition Against Terror, 75; imposition of risk-weighted capital adequacy standards in banking in, 139; military forces in, 102; military spending in, 97; organization of military forces, 99
United Nations: Charter, 52, 53, 89, 231; Emergency Forces, 85; financial contributions to, 8; General Assembly, 93*n11*; High Commissioner for Refugees (UNHCR), 82, 122; international role for Japan in, 77; peacekeeping operations, 14, 64, 75–93; as place for nonaligned or Third World countries, 79, 93*n11*; policy on use of force, 94*n20*; reform, 80; Security Council, 8, 76, 85, 98, 100, 198, 199, 259; suggestion for standing force in, 64
United Nations Conference on Human Rights (1993), 215
United Nations Implementation Force in Bosnia (IFOR), 89

United Nations Observation Mission for the Verification of Elections in Nicaragua (ONUVEN), 80
United Nations Observer Group for the Verification of Elections in Haiti (ONUVEH), 80
United Nations Operations in Mozambique (ONUMOZ), 81
United Nations Transitional Authority in Cambodia (UNTAC), 215, 228
United Nations Transition Assistance Group in Namibia (UNTAG), 80
United Nations Unified Task Force in Somalia (UNITAF), 89
United States: alliance with Japan, 38, 83–85; antidumping policies, 17, 283; and Asian financial crisis, 153; assistance to Indonesia in Asian financial crisis, 163–167; attempts to persuade Japan to moderate stance on Yasukuni Shrine, 200; back/forth with Japan, 11; banking crisis in, 133, 137, 138; bilateral interaction with China, 229; commitment to Asian security, 60; debt strategy, 140; demise of alliance with Soviet Union, 56; end of competition with Soviet Union, 11; Federal Deposit Insurance Corporation, 149*n18*; Federal Reserve Board, 137, 138, 149*n18*; foreign residents in, 129; gives most-favored-nation status to China, 237; in Global Coalition Against Terror, 75; International Lending Act (1983), 137; investment in Association of Southeast Asian Nations countries, 155; isolationist policy of, 4; lack of response to Asian financial crisis, 161; and loss of moral authority, 13; military forces in, 102; military spending in, 97; occupation of Japan by, 2, 50, 72*n25*, 187; opposition to proposal for Asian Monetary Fund, 162; policy preferences of, 17; pressure on Japan regarding Burma, 219; reneges on Kyoto Protocol, 13; security pacts with Japan, 2; toleration of Japanese import barriers, 117; trade tensions with Japan, 4, 9; unilateralism of, 12; use of sanctions by, 214; US-Japan Security Treaty (1951), 57–59

Uruguay: renunciation of war by, 50
US-Japan Defense Cooperation, 48
US-Japan Joint Declaration on Security (1996), 83
US-Japan Mutual Security Treaty, 206n4
US-Japan Security Treaty (1951), 57–59, 78
US-Japan Structural Impediments Initiative, 35, 237

Vietnam: financial assistance from Japan, 168, 169; official development assistance, 190; renunciation of reparation claims by, 190
Vietnam War, 192, 205n2
Volcker, Paul, 137

Wahid, Adburrahman, 165, 174n29
Wehner, Herbert, 188
Whitney, Courtney, 51, 53
Williams, Justin, 54
Willoughby, Charles, 57

World Bank, 16, 117, 122, 123–124, 140; assistance in Asian financial crisis, 152–153, 163–167; conditionality of, 152; control of, by United States, 153; economic reform requirements of, 152; preconditions for assistance from, 152
World Health Organization, 122
World Trade Organization, 17
World War II, 1

Yamasaki Taku, 68
Yang Shangkun, 238
Yasukuni Shrine, 18, 179, 193, 198, 199, 201, 202, 206n4, 208n40, 210n73, 210n77, 235, 243, 245, 248, 273
Yomiuri Shimbun (newspaper), 62, 63, 65, 67
Yoshida Doctrine, 1, 2, 48, 59, 70
Yoshida Shigeru, 1, 2, 51, 56, 57, 58, 66, 187

Zhou En-lai, 231, 232, 234

| About the Book |

How have shifts in both the international environment and domestic politics affected the trajectory of Japanese foreign policy? Does it still make sense to depict Japan as passive and reactive, or have the country's leaders become strategic and proactive? *Japan in International Politics* presents a nuanced picture of Japanese foreign policy, emphasizing the ways in which slow, adaptive changes, informed by pragmatic liberalism, have served the national interest.

The authors analyze core issues in the arenas of security policy, economic relations, and regional diplomacy. The concluding chapter of the book considers the significance of Japan's current foreign policy posture for its future role in international politics.

Thomas U. Berger is associate professor of international relations at Boston University. **Mike M. Mochizuki** holds the Japan-US Relations Chair in Memory of Gaston Sigur at George Washington University's Elliott School of International Affairs. **Jitsuo Tsuchiyama** is professor and dean of the School of International Politics, Economics, and Communication at Aoyama Gakuin University, Tokyo.